OUR HIGH CALLING

Daily devotional books
from the writings of
Ellen G. White

Christ Triumphant
Conflict and Courage
The Faith I Live By
God's Amazing Grace
In Heavenly Places
Lift Him Up
Maranatha—The Lord Is Coming
My Life Today
Our High Calling
Reflecting Christ
Sons and Daughters of God
That I May Know Him
This Day With God
The Upward Look
Ye Shall Receive Power

To order, call 1-800-765-6955

Visit us at www.rhpa.org
for more information on
Review and Herald products.

OUR HIGH CALLING

The Morning Watch texts with appropriate selections compiled from the writings of Ellen G. White

God's ideal for His children is higher than the highest human thought can reach. The living God has given in His holy law a transcript of His character. The greatest Teacher the world has ever known is Jesus Christ; and what is the standard He has given for all who believe in Him?—"Be ye therefore perfect, even as your Father in heaven is perfect." Matt. 5:48. As God is perfect in His high sphere of action, so man may be perfect in his human sphere.

The ideal of Christian character is Christlikeness. There is opened before us a path of continual advancement. We have an object to reach, a standard to gain, which includes everything good and pure and noble and elevated. There should be continual striving and constant progress onward and upward toward perfection of character.—*Counsels to Parents, Teachers, and Students,* p. 365.

REVIEW AND HERALD® PUBLISHING ASSOCIATION
HAGERSTOWN, MD 21740

ISBN 0-8280-1501-5

FOREWORD

When Ellen G. White laid aside her pen after 70 busy years of ministry, she left to us a rich legacy of ever-timely instructions, inspired counsels, and earnest admonitions touching almost every phase of practical Christian experience. *Our High Calling* is made up of choice selections from this vast treasury as found in Ellen G. White articles that appeared week by week in the journals of the church, her public discourses, her manuscripts, and letters of counsel to individuals, many of them Seventh-day Adventist youth.

It is clear that Mrs. White contemplated the use of these messages in the production of books, for she indicated in a statement written in 1905 that "I am endeavoring by the help of God to write letters that will be a help, not merely to those to whom they are addressed, but to many others who need them." Although written many years ago, these counsels speak to our hearts today, to encourage, instruct, and inspire us in victorious practical everyday Christian living and witnessing, particularly in view of the imminence of our Lord's return.

To make the reading for each day complete within the limits of a single page, it has been necessary at times to make deletions in order to bring the reading to the right length. All deletions are indicated in the usual manner. Likewise, in many instances material on a page has been drawn from more than one source. Great care has been exercised to avoid any distortion of meaning, and that which appears clearly presents the intent of the author. Proper source references for each quotation are given, whether article, pamphlet, manuscript, or book.

Our High Calling, presenting a devotional reading for each day introduced by an appropriate Bible text, has been prepared as an enrichment of the Morning Watch devotional plan and appears simultaneously in several languages. That this volume, comprised of messages inspired by the Spirit of God, will be treasured as other like volumes have been in the past, and will be the means of encouraging all who read to "press toward the mark for the prize of the high calling of God in Christ Jesus" is our sincere wish.

THE TRUSTEES OF THE ELLEN G. WHITE ESTATE

OUR HIGH CALLING

"Not as though I had already attained, either were already perfect: but I follow after, if that I may apprehend that for which also I am apprehended of Christ Jesus.

"Brethren, I count not myself to have apprehended: but this one thing I do, forgetting those things which are behind, and reaching forth unto those things which are before,

"I press toward the mark for the prize of the high calling of God in Christ Jesus." Philippians 3:12-14.

HAPPY NEW YEAR!

So teach us to number our days, that we may apply our hearts unto wisdom. Ps. 90:12.

Another year of life is now in the past. A new year is opening before us. What will be its record? What will we each inscribe upon its spotless pages? The manner in which we spend each passing day will decide this question. . . .

Let us enter upon the new year with our hearts cleansed from the defilement of selfishness and pride. Let us put away every sinful indulgence, and seek to become faithful, diligent learners in the school of Christ. A new year opens its unsullied pages before us. What shall we write upon them? . . .

Seek to begin this year with right purposes and pure motives, as beings who are accountable to God. Ever bear in mind that your acts are daily passing into history by the pen of the recording angel. You must meet them again when the judgment shall sit and the books shall be opened. . . .

If we connect with God, the source of peace, and light, and truth, His Spirit will flow through us as a channel, to refresh and bless all around us. This may be the last year of life to us. Shall we not enter upon it with thoughtful consideration? Shall not sincerity, respect, benevolence, mark our deportment toward all?

Let us withhold nothing from Him who gave His precious life for us. . . . Let us all consecrate to God the property He has entrusted to us. Above all, let us give Him ourselves, a freewill offering.[1]

May the beginning of this year be a time that shall never be forgotten—a time when Christ shall come in among us, and say, "Peace be unto you." John 20:19. Brethren and sisters, I wish you, one and all, a happy new year.

"We live in deeds, not years; in thoughts, not breaths;
In feelings, not in figures on a dial.
We should count time by heart-throbs. He most lives
Who thinks most, feels the noblest, acts the best."[2]

WHICH WAY?

Enter ye in at the strait gate: for wide is the gate, and broad is the way, that leadeth to destruction, and many there be which go in thereat: because strait is the gate, and narrow is the way, which leadeth unto life, and few there be that find it. Matt. 7:13, 14.

Before you are two ways—the broad road of self-indulgence and the narrow path of self-sacrifice. Into the broad road you can take selfishness, pride, love of the world; but those who walk in the narrow way must lay aside every weight, and the sin which doth so easily beset. Which road have you chosen—the road which leads to everlasting death, or the road which leads to glory and immortality?[3]

There never was a more solemn time in the history of the world than the time in which we are now living. Our eternal interests are at stake, and we should arouse to the importance of making our calling and election sure. We dare not risk our eternal interests on mere probabilities. We must be in earnest. What we are, what we are doing, what is to be our course of action in the future, are all questions of untold moment, and we cannot afford to be listless, indifferent, unconcerned. It becomes each one of us to inquire, "What is eternity to me?" Are our feet in the path that leads to heaven, or in the broad road that leads to perdition? . . .

Those who make a success of the Christian life will count all things as loss for the excellency of the knowledge of Christ. Only those who are abiding in Christ can know what true life is. They realize the value of true religion. They have brought their talents of influence and means and ability to the altar of consecration, seeking only to know and do the will of Him who has died to redeem them. They know that the path they must travel is strait and narrow, and that they will have to meet many obstacles and temptations, as they resist the enticements of the broader road that leads to ruin; but they will discern the footsteps of Jesus, and press onward toward the mark for the prize of the high calling in their Lord and Saviour. They will choose the royal way that leads to heaven.[4]

COMPASSED WITH GOD'S MERCY

Many sorrows shall be to the wicked: but he that trusteth in the Lord, mercy shall compass him about. Ps. 32:10.

We often think that those who serve God have more trials than the unbeliever, and that the path marked out for them to travel in is rugged. . . . But does the sinner enjoy his worldly pleasure and enjoyment unalloyed? Oh, no. There are times when the sinner is fearfully troubled. He fears God but does not love Him.

Are the wicked free from disappointment, perplexity, earthly losses, poverty, and distress? Many of them suffer a lingering sickness, yet have no strong and mighty One to lean upon, no strengthening grace from a higher power to support them in their weakness. They lean upon their own strength. They obtain no consolation by looking forward to the future, but a fearful uncertainty torments them; and thus they close their eyes in death, not finding any pleasure in looking forward to the resurrection morn, for they have no cheering hope that they shall have part in the first resurrection. . . .

The Christian is subject to sickness, disappointment, poverty, reproach, and distress. Yet amid all this he loves God, he chooses to do His will, and prizes nothing so highly as His approbation. In the conflicting trials and changing scenes of this life, he knows that there is One who knows it all, One who will bend His ear low to the cry of the sorrowful and distressed, One who can sympathize with every sorrow and soothe the keen anguish of every heart. . . .

Amid all his affliction, the Christian has strong consolation. And if God permits him to suffer a lingering, distressing sickness before he closes his eyes in death, he can with cheerfulness bear it all. . . . He contemplates the future with heavenly satisfaction. A short rest in the grave, and then the Life-giver will break the fetters of the tomb, release the captive, and bring him from his dusty bed immortal, never more to know pain, sorrow, or death. Oh, what a hope is the Christian's! Let this hope of the Christian be mine. Let it be yours.[5]

BLESSINGS TO CHEER US

Oh how great is thy goodness, which thou hast laid up for them that fear thee; which thou hast wrought for them that trust in thee before the sons of men! Ps. 31:19.

God scatters blessings all along our path to brighten our journey and lead our hearts out to love and praise Him, and He wants us to draw water from the well of salvation that our hearts may be refreshed. We may sing the songs of Zion, we may cheer our own hearts, and we may cheer the hearts of others; hope may be strengthened, darkness turned to light. God has not left us in a dark world—as pilgrims and strangers seeking a better country, even an heavenly—without giving us precious promises to lighten every burden. The borders of our path are strewn with fair flowers of promise. They blossom all around, sending forth rich fragrance.[6]

How many blessings we lose because we slight and overlook the blessings we daily receive, yearning for that which we have not. Common mercies which thickly strew our pathway are forgotten and undervalued. We may learn lessons from the humble things of God in nature. The flower in dark and humble places responds to all the rays of light it can get, and puts forth its leaves. The caged bird sings in the prison cage, in the sunless tenement, as if in the lordly, sunny dwelling. God knows whether we will make a wise and saving use of His blessings; He will never give them to us to abuse. God loves the thankful heart, trusting implicitly in His words of promise, gathering comfort and hope and peace from them; and He will reveal to us still greater depths of His love.[7]

If we praised God's holy name as we should, the flame of love would be kindled in many hearts. . . . The praise of God should continually be in our hearts and on our lips. This is the very best way to resist the temptation to indulge in idle, frivolous conversation.[8]

The Lord would have us look up, and be grateful to Him that there is a heaven. . . . Let us grasp by living faith the rich promises of God, and be thankful from morning till night.[9]

PERILS TO SHUN

O Lord, I know that the way of man is not in himself: it is not in man that walketh to direct his steps. Jer. 10:23.

The road through Knight's Canyon, always perilous to the inexperienced traveler, is often impassable in the rainy season.* We were very thankful for a pilot in this part of our journey. I dared not look either to the right or left to view the scenery, but, holding the lines firmly, and guiding my horse in the narrow passage, I followed our leader. Carelessness here would have been fatal. Had our horse turned out of the right path, we should have plunged down a steep precipice, into the ravine below.

As we rode along in almost breathless silence, I could but think how forcibly this dangerous ride illustrates the Christian's experience. We are making life's journey amid the perils of the last days. We need to watch carefully every step, and to be sure that we are following our great Leader. Skepticism, infidelity, dissipation, and crime are on every hand. It would be an easy matter to let go the reins of self-control, and plunge over the precipice to sure destruction. . . .

Infinite Love has cast up a pathway upon which the ransomed of the Lord may pass from earth to heaven. That path is the Son of God. Angel guides are sent to direct our erring feet. Heaven's glorious ladder is let down in every man's path, barring his way to vice and folly. He must trample upon a crucified Redeemer ere he can pass onward to a life of sin. Our heavenly Father's voice is calling us, Come up hither. . . . The humble, trusting ones are guided and protected in the way of peace. But He who is infinite in wisdom compels none to accept Heaven's most precious gift—compels none to walk in the path which has been cast up at such a cost. Every one is permitted to choose for himself the narrow, shining steep that leads to heaven, or that broader and easier way which ends in death.[10]

---

* Account of a journey from Healdsburg to St. Helena, California, made by Mrs. White and a friend in December 1881. Friends drove ahead to guide them through a dangerous pass.

THE BRIDGE LOVE BUILT

Herein is love, not that we loved God, but that he loved us, and sent his Son to be the propitiation for our sins. 1 John 4:10.

God's love for the world was not manifest because He sent His Son, but because He loved the world He sent His Son into the world that divinity clothed with humanity might touch humanity, while divinity lays hold of divinity. Though sin had produced a gulf between man and his God, a divine benevolence provided a plan to bridge that gulf. And what material did He use? A part of Himself. The brightness of the Father's glory came to a world all seared and marred with the curse, and in His own divine character, in His own divine body, bridged the gulf. . . . The windows of heaven were opened and the showers of heavenly grace in healing streams came to our benighted world. . . .

Had God given us less we could not have been saved. But He gave to our world so abundantly that it could not be said that He could love us more. Then how foolish is the position taken that there is to be a second probation after the first is exhausted. God has exhausted His benevolence . . . in pouring out all heaven to man in one great gift. Only in comprehending the value of this offering can we comprehend infinity. O the breadth and height and depth of the love of God! Who of finite beings can comprehend it? . . .

God claims the whole of the affections of man, the whole heart, the whole soul, the whole mind, the whole strength. He lays claim to all that there is of man, because He has poured out the whole treasure of heaven by giving us His all at once, reserving nothing greater that heaven can do. . . .

When I commence writing on this subject, I go on and on, and try to get beyond the outer edge, but I fail. When we shall reach the mansions above, Jesus will Himself lead the white-robed ones, made white in the blood of the Lamb, to the Father. "Therefore are they before the throne of God, and serve him day and night in his temple: and he that sitteth on the throne shall dwell among them." Rev. 7:15.[11]

THE ONE VAST GIFT OF GOD

Thanks be unto God for his unspeakable gift. 2 Cor. 9:15.

Those who receive Christ by faith will be looked upon by Heaven as precious pearls for which the merchantman has paid an infinite price, and the human agents who find Christ will realize that they have found a heavenly treasure. They will be anxious to sell all that they have in order to buy the field which contains this treasure. As they contemplate the love of God, as the plan of salvation opens to their view, as the mystery of Christ's condescension becomes plainer to them, as they see the sacrifice that He made for them, they count nothing too dear to give up for His sake. The more they dwell upon the wonderful love of God, the vaster becomes its proportions, and the brightness of the glory of God becomes too glorious for mortal vision.

The Lord God of heaven collected all the riches of the universe, and laid them down in order to purchase the pearl of lost humanity. The Father gave all His divine resources into the hands of Christ in order that the richest blessings of heaven might be poured out upon a fallen race. God could not express greater love than He has expressed in giving the Son of His bosom to this world. This gift was given to man to convince him that God had left nothing undone that He could do, that there is nothing held in reserve, but that all heaven has been poured out in one vast gift. The present and eternal happiness of man consists in receiving God's love, and in keeping God's commandments.

Christ is our redeemer. He is the Word that became flesh and dwelt among us. He is the fountain in which we may be washed and cleansed from all impurity. He is the costly sacrifice that has been given for the reconciliation of man. The universe of heaven, the worlds unfallen, the fallen world, and the confederacy of evil cannot say that God could do more for the salvation of man than He has done. Never can His gift be surpassed, never can He display a richer depth of love. Calvary represents His crowning work. . . . The Lord would have His followers enraptured with God through the knowledge of His paternal character.[12]

CALLING ALL YOUTH!

For thou art my hope, O Lord God: thou art my trust from my youth. Ps. 71:5.

Jesus calls to every wanderer, "My son, give me thine heart." Prov. 23:26. . . . The youth cannot be happy without the love of Jesus. He is waiting with pitying tenderness to hear the confessions of the wayward, and to accept their penitence. He watches for some return of gratitude from us, as the mother watches for the smile of recognition from her beloved child. The great God teaches us to call Him Father. He would have us understand how earnestly and tenderly His heart yearns over us in all our trials and temptations. . . .

The young should be constantly growing in grace, and in a knowledge of the truth. The Creator of all things, with whom are all the treasures of wisdom, has promised to be the guide of their youth. He who has conquered in their behalf all the powers of evil asks for their homage. There can be no higher knowledge than the knowledge of Him whom to know aright is life and peace; no purer, deeper affection than the love of our Saviour. . . .

There are temptations on every hand to ensnare the feet of the unwary. Ungodly, corrupt youth exert a strong influence to lead others into forbidden paths. These are among the most successful agents of Satan. . . . The lovers of the world will often approach under a garb of friendship, and attempt to introduce its customs and practices. Let every true soldier stand ready to resist these allurements. . . .

Satan attacks us at our weak points; but we need not be overcome. The assault may be severe and protracted, but God has promised help for us, and in His strength we may conquer. . . . The precepts and promises of God's word will arm you with divine power to resist the enemy. . . . Satan will be baffled and defeated when he finds the heart preoccupied with the truth of God. We need also to be often found at the throne of grace. Earnest, persevering prayer, uniting our human weakness to Omnipotence, will give us the victory.[13]

MINE TO CHOOSE

And if it seem evil unto you to serve the Lord, choose you this day whom ye will serve; . . . but as for me and my house, we will serve the Lord. Joshua 24:15.

In our world there are two classes. One is made up of those who behold a crucified and risen Saviour. The other includes all who have chosen to look away from the cross, and to follow the leadings of satanic influences. The latter class are busily engaged in putting stumbling blocks before God's people, to cause them to fall, and turn from the path of obedience into the broad way of disobedience and death. . . .

Many choose unrighteousness because Satan presents it in such a way that it seems attractive to those who are not on guard against his wiles. And he works in a special manner through unsanctified men and women who profess to be children of God. In some way or other the enemy will seek to deceive all, even the very elect. Only as we are partakers of the divine nature can we escape the corrupting influences that are brought to bear upon us by the enemy of our souls.

As Satan seeks to break down the barriers of the soul, by tempting us to indulge in sin, we must by living faith retain our connection with God, and have confidence in His strength to enable us to overcome every besetment. We are to flee from evil, and seek righteousness, meekness, and holiness. . . .

It is time for every one of us to decide whose side we are on. The agencies of Satan will work with every mind that will allow itself to be worked by him. But there are also heavenly agencies waiting to communicate the bright rays of the glory of God to all who are willing to receive Him.[14]

It is ours to choose whether we will be numbered with the servants of Christ or the servants of Satan. Every day we show by our conduct whose service we have chosen. . . .

Dear young reader, what choice have you made? What is the record of your daily life?[15]

A SAFE GUIDE

Then spake Jesus again unto them, saying, I am the light of the world: he that followeth me shall not walk in darkness, but shall have the light of life. John 8:12.

All who are traveling the road to heaven need a safe guide. We must not walk in human wisdom. It is our privilege to listen to the voice of Christ speaking to us as we walk the journey of life, and His words are always words of wisdom. . . .

Satan is working with great diligence to compass the ruin of the souls of men. He has come down with great power, knowing that he has but a short time to work. Our only safety lies in following closely after Christ, walking in His wisdom, and practicing His truth. We cannot always readily detect the working of Satan; we do not know where he lays his traps. But Jesus understands the subtle arts of the enemy, and He can keep our feet in safe paths. . . . "I am the way, the truth, and the life" (John 14:6) Christ declares.[16]

What would be the use of a way direct and sure in its course to glory, if no light of truth shone upon that path, that travelers should desire it? What would be the use of truth shining on the way if there was no life in the persons that walked in the way, in the pilgrims' journey from the earthly to the heavenly? Having the statement of Christ, "I am the way, the truth, and the life," all who believe in Jesus, the Leader, may in confidence walk heavenward, sure that they are in the path outlined in the Word as the way.[17]

Christ, His character and work, is the center and circumference of all truth. He is the chain upon which the jewels of doctrine are linked. In Him is found the complete system of truth.[18]

Those who walk in obedience will know what truth is. . . . In order to know the truth, we must be willing to obey. Those whose affections are placed on the world are not willing to give up their plans for the plans of Christ. They walk in darkness, not knowing whither they go.

The precious light of truth flashes upon the pathway of everyone who seeks for it.[19]

January 11

CHILDREN OF THE HEAVENLY KING

Behold, what manner of love the Father hath bestowed upon us, that we should be called the sons of God: therefore the world knoweth us not, because it knew him not. 1 John 3:1.

Let no one feel that he is stepping down in becoming a child of God. It was the only begotten Son of God who stepped down. . . . Leaving His splendor, His majesty, His high command, and clothing His divinity with humanity, that humanity might touch humanity, and divinity lay hold upon divinity, He came to this earth, and in our behalf suffered the death of the cross. . . .

Christ has made an infinite sacrifice. He gave His own life for us. He took upon His divine soul the result of the transgression of God's law. Laying aside His royal crown, He condescended to step down, step by step, to the level of fallen humanity. He hung upon Calvary's cross, dying in our behalf, that we might have eternal life. . . . Does it seem a small thing that He should endure all this, that we might be called the sons of God? Does it seem a small thing to you to become members of the royal family, children of the heavenly King, partakers of an immortal inheritance?[20]

Such is the infinite goodness of God that through Jesus Christ's merits He not only spares but pardons and justifies us, and through the righteousness of Christ imputes righteousness to us, and exalts and ennobles us by making us children of His adoption. We become members of the royal family, children of the heavenly King. He lifts men and women from their degradation and exalts them in righteousness. . . . He calls them His jewels, and a peculiar treasure unto Him. They are trophies of His grace and power, and of His greatness and riches in glory. They therefore are not their own, but are bought with a price, and through the extraordinary office of the atonement of Christ have been brought into nearness and the most sacred relationship to Jesus Christ. They are called His heritage, His children, the members of Christ's body, of His flesh and of His bones; yea, they are joined to the Lord by intimate relationship with Him.[21]

17

WHOSOEVER MEANS ME

For God so loved the world, that he gave his only begotten Son, that whosoever believeth in him should not perish, but have everlasting life. John 3:16.

We should contemplate the love of Jesus, His mission and His work in reference to us as individuals. We are to say, Jesus so loved me that He gave His own life to save me. The Father loves me, "For God so loved the world, that he gave his only-begotten Son, that whosoever believeth in him should not perish, but have everlasting life." It becomes us to ascertain upon what terms Christ promises the gift of eternal life. I answer, It is upon our faith.[22]

The gift of God's dear Son makes the promises of God ours of a surety.[23]

How many can say, "He saves me"? I know that He wants that I should be saved. He looks upon me as of value in His sight, and therefore I know that my thoughts, my words, and my works, all pass in review before Him. Everything that is connected with the purchase of the blood of Christ is of value in the sight of God. By the price paid for our redemption we are under obligation to devote our entire affections to Christ. We are to give God all there is of us; and in giving to God our all, are we to consider that we sustain a great loss?—No, for in giving to Him our talents, we are doubling them. Every gift He has given to us, when returned to Him, receives His blessing, that it may have increased influence in the work of God. Wherever you may be, you are to realize that you belong to Christ.[24]

The gift of Christ to the world was beyond computation, and no power could compete with God by giving a gift that would bear any comparison to the value of heaven's best treasure. The greatness of this gift was to furnish men with a theme of thanksgiving and praise that would last through time and through eternity. Having given His all in Christ, God lays claim to the heart, mind, soul, and strength of man. Looking upon the treasure which God has provided in the full and complete gift of Christ, we can exclaim: "Herein is love!"[25]

RICH CURRENTS OF GRACE

And God is able to make all grace abound toward you; that ye, always having all sufficiency in all things, may abound to every good work. 2 Cor. 9:8.

Is it not wonderful that we can receive the rich current of grace from Deity, and work in harmony with Deity? What does Deity want with us, poor, weak, and feeble as we are? What can Deity do with us? Everything, if we are willing to surrender all. God loves every youth. He knows all about your trials. He knows that you have to battle against the powers of darkness, who strive to gain control of the human mind.[26]

God's purpose for His children is that they shall grow to the full stature of men and women in Christ. In order to do this, we must use aright every power of mind and soul and body. We cannot afford to waste any mental or physical strength. . . .

Satan has summoned the hosts of darkness to war against the saints. We cannot afford to be indifferent to his attacks. He comes in many ways, and we must have clear spiritual discernment, that we may be able to discern when he is seeking to gain possession of our minds. God calls on those on whom the light of truth is shining to take their stand in His army. He calls upon them to show their loyalty by walking in the light He has given.[27]

The Lord desires you to understand the position you occupy as sons and daughters of the Most High, children of the heavenly King. He desires you to live in close connection with Him. . . . Cut away from everything frivolous. Do not think that you must indulge in this pleasure and that pleasure. Determine that you will be on the Lord's side. . . .

Take firm hold of the arm of Divine power. . . . Harness your habits. Put on the bit and bridle. Say, "I love the Lord, and I am determined to use every particle of my intelligence in His work." . . .

If you will stand under the bloodstained banner of Prince Emmanuel, faithfully doing His service, you need never yield to temptation; for One stands by your side who is able to keep you from falling.[28]

LOOK AND LIVE

As Moses lifted up the serpent in the wilderness, even so must the Son of man be lifted up: that whosoever believeth in him should not perish, but have eternal life. John 3:14, 15.

The same lesson that Christ bade Moses to give to the children of Israel in the wilderness is for all such souls suffering under the plague spot of sin. From the billowy cloud Christ spoke to Moses and told him to make a brazen serpent and place it upon a pole, and then bid all that were bitten with the fiery serpents to look and live. What if, in the place of looking as Christ commanded them, they had said, "I do not believe it will do me the least bit of good to look. I am too great a sufferer from the sting of the poisonous serpent." Obedience was the object to be gained, implicit and blind obedience, without stopping to inquire the reason or the science of the matter. Christ's word was, "Look and live." . . .

We want clear views of what Jesus is to us. We want to have distinct views of the victories gained in our behalf. He spoiled principalities and powers and made a show of them openly. He broke the fetters of the tomb and came forth to take again His life that He laid down for us. He ascended on high, having led captivity captive and received gifts for men. All this suffering He endured for us. . . . He will be our helper and He will be our refuge in every time of need. He should be revealed in our Christian experience as all-sufficient, a present Saviour.

Only look and live. We dishonor God when we do not go forth from the dark cellar of doubts unto the upper chamber of hope and faith. When the Light shineth in all its brightness let us take hold on Jesus Christ by the mighty hand of faith. No longer cultivate your doubts by expressing them and pouring them into other minds, and thus becoming an agent of Satan to sow the seeds of doubt. Talk faith, live faith, cultivate love to God; evidence to the world all that Jesus is to you. Magnify His holy name. Tell of His goodness; talk of His mercy, and tell of His power.[29]

A HIGHER STANDARD

The thief cometh not, but for to steal, and to kill, and to destroy: I am come that they might have life, and that they might have it more abundantly. John 10:10.

What fullness is expressed in the words, "I am the light of the world." John 8:12. "I am the bread of life." John 6:35. "I am the way, the truth, and the life." John 14:6. "I am the good shepherd." John 10:14. "I am come that they might have life, and that they might have it more abundantly." John 10:10. This life is what we must have, and we must have it *more abundantly.* God will breathe this life into every soul that dies to self and lives to Christ. But entire self-renunciation is required. Unless this takes place, we carry with us the evil that destroys our happiness. But when self is crucified, Christ lives in us, and the power of the Spirit attends our efforts.

I wish we could be what God would have us—all light in the Lord. We need to reach a higher standard, but we can never do this until self is laid on the altar, until we let the Holy Spirit control us, molding and fashioning us according to the divine similitude. . . .

We must daily consecrate ourselves to God's service. We must come to God in faith. . . . We need to humble ourselves before God. It is self that we have first to do with. Criticize the heart closely. Search it to see what hinders the free access of God's Spirit. We must receive the Holy Ghost. Then we shall have power to prevail with God.

A mere assent to truth is not enough. Daily we must live the truth. We must shut ourselves in with God, surrendering all to Him. To listen to the great and grand truths of the Word is not enough. We must ask ourselves the question, Does Christ dwell in my heart by faith? He alone can show us our necessity and reveal the dignity and glory of the truth. At the altar of self-sacrifice—the appointed place of meeting between God and the soul—we receive from the hand of God the celestial torch which searches the heart, revealing its great need of an abiding Christ.[30]

STRONG IN THE LORD

The Lord is my light and my salvation; whom shall I fear? the Lord is the strength of my life; of whom shall I be afraid? . . . Though an host should encamp against me, my heart shall not fear: though war should rise against me, in this will I be confident. Ps. 27:1, 3.

We are passing through an enemy's land. Foes are upon every side to hinder our advancement. They hate God and all who follow after Him and bear His name. But those who are our enemies are the Lord's enemies, and although they are strong and artful, yet the Captain of our salvation who leadeth us can vanquish them. As the sun disperses the clouds from its path, so will the Sun of Righteousness remove the obstacles to our progress. We may cheer our souls by looking at the things unseen which will cheer and animate us in our journey. . . .

If we cling to Him by living faith, saying with Jacob, "I will not let thee go" (Gen. 32:26); if we entreat, "Cast me not away from thy presence; and take not thy Holy Spirit from me," (Ps. 51:11), the promise is to us, "I will never leave thee, nor forsake thee." . . .

We have read an account of a noble prince who carried the picture of his father always near his heart and on important occasions when there was danger of forgetting him, he would take out the likeness and view it and say, "Let me do nothing unbecoming so excellent a father." As Christians, God has claims upon us that we should never, never lose sight of for a moment; and as we are His children by adoption, how careful should we be that we retain His image and do nothing that will belittle or degrade our holy calling, for we rank among the royal family. God has made us as vessels unto honor, prepared unto every good work. "This people have I formed for myself; they shall shew forth my praise." Isa. 43:21. God's people are called a crown, a diadem. Satan would eagerly seize the Lord's treasure, but God has secured it so that Satan cannot obtain it. "Thou shalt be a crown of glory in the hand of the Lord, and a royal diadem in the hand of thy God." Isa. 62:3. We are secure, perfectly secure from the enemy's subtlety while we have unwavering trust in God.[31]

ANGELS TO GUARD US

For he shall give his angels charge over thee, to keep thee in all thy ways. Ps. 91:11.

Oh, that we could all realize the nearness of heaven to earth! When the earthborn children know it not, they have the angels of light as their companions; for the heavenly messengers are sent forth to minister to those who shall be heirs of salvation. A silent witness guards every soul that lives, seeking to win and draw him to Christ. The angels never leave the tempted one a prey to the enemy who would destroy the souls of men if permitted to do so. As long as there is hope, until they resist the Holy Spirit to their eternal ruin, men are guarded by heavenly intelligences.[32]

Oh, that all could behold our precious Saviour as He is, a Saviour. Let His hand draw aside the veil which conceals His glory from our eyes. It shows Him in His high and holy place. What do we see? Our Saviour, not in a position of silence and inactivity. He is surrounded with heavenly intelligences, cherubim, and seraphim, ten thousand times ten thousand of angels. All these heavenly beings have one object above all others, in which they are intensely interested—His church in a world of corruption. . . . They are working for Christ under His commission, to save to the uttermost all who look to Him and believe in Him.[33]

Heavenly angels are commissioned to watch the sheep of Christ's pasture. When Satan with his deceptive snares would deceive if possible the very elect, these angels set in operation influences that will save the tempted souls if they will take heed to the Word of the Lord, realize their danger, and say, "No, I will not enter into that scheme of Satan. I have an Elder Brother on the throne in heaven, who has shown that He has a tender interest in me, and I will not grieve His heart of love."[34]

Living amid these opposing forces, we may through the exercise of faith and prayer, call to our side a retinue of heavenly angels, who will guard us from every corrupting influence.[35]

PROMISES TO THOSE WHO OBEY

Now therefore, if ye will obey my voice indeed, and keep my covenant, then ye shall be a peculiar treasure unto me above all people: for all the earth is mine. Ex. 19:5.

This pledge was given not only to Israel but to all who are obedient to God's Word. Those who live amid the perils of the last days may realize that just as at the beginning of their experience the truth united them to the Saviour, so He who is the author and finisher of their faith will perfect the work He has begun for them. God is faithful, by whom we are called to fellowship with His Son. As men and women cooperate with God in doing the work He has given them, they go forward from strength to greater strength. As they exercise simple faith, believing day by day that God will not fail to establish them in Christ, God says to them as He did to ancient Israel: "Thou art an holy people unto the Lord thy God: the Lord thy God hath chosen thee to be a special people unto himself, above all people that are upon the face of the earth." Deut. 7:6.

Thus God is able and willing to lead all who will be led. He desires to teach each one a lesson of constant trust, unwavering faith, and unquestioning submission. He says to each one, I am the Lord thy God. Walk with Me, and I will fill thy path with light. . . .

But God requires obedience to all His commands. The only way in which it is possible for men to be happy is by rendering obedience to the laws of God's kingdom.

Life, with its privileges and endowments, is God's gift. Let us remember that all we have comes from God, and is to be wholly and freely consecrated to Him. Paul declares, "I count all things but loss for the excellency of Christ Jesus my Lord, for whom I have suffered the loss of all things, and do count them but dung that I may win Christ, and be found in him, not having mine own righteousness, but the righteousness which is of God by faith." Phil. 3:8. The sacrifice of our ideas, our will, is necessary if we would be one with Christ in God. All we have and are must be laid at Christ's feet.[36]

OUR ONLY SAFETY

The fear of man bringeth a snare: but whoso putteth his trust in the Lord shall be safe. Prov. 29:25.

You are safe only as you trust in God. We have a vigilant foe to contend against. . . . He [Christ] saw that it was not possible for man to overcome the powerful foe in his own strength, therefore He came in person from the courts of heaven and bore in behalf of man the test that Adam failed to endure. . . . Christ overcame Satan, making it possible for man to overcome on his own behalf in the name of Christ. But the victory can only be gained in Christ's name, through His grace. When burdened, when pressed with temptation, when the feelings and desires of the natural heart are clamoring for the victory, earnest, fervent, importunate prayer in the name of Christ brings Jesus to your side as a helper, and through His name you gain the victory and Satan is vanquished. . . .

I implore you to trust wholly in God. "Resist the devil, and he will flee from you. Draw nigh to God, and he will draw nigh to you." James 4:7, 8. The Christian life is a life of conflict, of self-denial and conquest. It is a continual battle and a march. Every act of obedience to Christ, every victory obtained over self, is a step in the march to glory and final victory. Take Christ for your Guide and He will lead you safely along. The pathway may be rough and thorny and the ascents steep, requiring toil. You may have to press on when weary, when you long for rest. You may have to fight on when faint and hope on when discouraged, but, with Christ as your Guide, you cannot lose the path of immortal life. You cannot fail to reach the exalted seat by the side of your Guide, whose own feet trod the rough path before you, evening the way for your feet. If you follow pride and selfish ambition you will find it pleasant at first, but the end is pain and sorrow. You may follow selfishness, which will promise you much but will poison and embitter your life. To follow Christ is safe. He will not suffer the powers of darkness to hurt one hair of your head. Trust in your Redeemer and you are safe.[37]

LIGHT OR SHADOW?

Woe unto them that call evil good, and good evil; that put darkness for light, and light for darkness; that put bitter for sweet, and sweet for bitter! Isa. 5:20.

God is light, and in Him is no darkness at all. If there were no light, there would be no shade. But while the shade comes by the sun, it is not created by it. It is some obstruction that causes the shadow. So darkness emanates not from God, but is the result of an intruding object between the soul and God. . . . Disregard of the light that God has given brings the sure result. It creates a shadow, a darkness that is more dark because of the light which has been sent. . . . If a man withdraws himself from light and evidence, and yields to Satan's seducing arts, he himself draws the curtain of unbelief about him, so that light cannot be distinguished from darkness. More light and evidence would only be misunderstood by him. The greater the evidence, the greater will be the indifference. This will lead the deceived soul to call darkness light and truth error.[38]

Satan is constantly working to lead men to deny the light. It is but a step from the straightforward path to a diverging one, in which Satan leads the way, and where light is all darkness, and darkness light. . . . It is a dangerous thing to open the heart to unbelief, for it drives the Spirit of God away from the heart, and Satan's suggestions come in. . . . We must . . . avoid the first admission of doubt and unbelief.[39]

"Whatsoever a man soweth, that shall he also reap." Gal. 6:7. God destroys no man. Every man who is destroyed will destroy himself. When a man stifles the admonitions of conscience, he sows the seeds of unbelief and these produce a sure harvest. . . .

"They would none of my counsel, they despised all my reproof. Therefore shall they eat of the fruit of their own way, and be filled with their own devices. For the turning away of the simple shall slay them, and the prosperity of fools shall destroy them. But whoso hearkeneth unto me shall dwell safely, and shall be quiet from fear of evil." Prov. 1:30-33.[40]

January 21

HOPE FOR THE HOPELESS

Let the wicked forsake his way, and the unrighteous man his thoughts: and let him return unto the Lord, and he will have mercy upon him; and to our God, for he will abundantly pardon. For my thoughts are not your thoughts, neither are your ways my ways, saith the Lord. Isa. 55:7, 8.

It is your thought that your mistakes and transgressions have been so grievous that the Lord will not have respect unto your prayers, and will bless and save you. . . . The closer you come to Jesus, the more faulty you will appear in your own eyes; for your vision will be clearer, and your imperfections will be seen in broad and distinct contrast to His perfect nature. But do not be discouraged. This is evidence that Satan's delusions have lost their power; that the vivifying influence of the Spirit of God is arousing you, and your indifference and unconcern are passing away.

No deep-seated love for Jesus can dwell in the heart that does not see and realize its own sinfulness. The soul that is transformed by grace will admire His divine character; but if we do not see our own moral deformity, it is unmistakable evidence that we have not had a view of the beauty and excellence of Christ. The less we see to esteem in ourselves, the more we shall see to esteem in the infinite purity and loveliness of our Saviour. A view of our own sinfulness drives us to Him who can pardon. . . .

God does not deal with us as finite men deal with one another. His thoughts are thoughts of mercy, love, and tenderest compassion. "He will abundantly pardon." He says, "I have blotted out, as a thick cloud, thy transgressions." . . .

Look up, you who are tried, tempted, and discouraged, look up. . . . It is ever safe to look up; it is fatal to look down. If you look down, the earth reels and sways beneath you; nothing is sure. But heaven above you is calm and steady, and there is divine aid for every climber. The hand of the Infinite is reaching over the battlements of heaven to grasp yours in its strong embrace. The mighty Helper is nigh to bless, lift up, and encourage the most erring, the most sinful, if they will look to Him by faith. But the sinner must look up.[41]

27

NEVER ABSENT FROM THE MIND OF GOD

Casting all your care upon him; for he careth for you. 1 Peter 5:7.

To enlarge our views of God's goodness, Christ calls upon us to behold the works of His hands. "Behold the fowls of the air," He says, "they sow not, neither do they reap, nor gather into barns; yet your heavenly Father feedeth them. Are ye not much better than they?" Matt. 6:26. . . .

Though men and women have sinned grievously, they are not forsaken. The hand that upholds the world, upholds and strengthens His weakest child. The great Master Artist, whose skill is infinitely beyond the skill of any human being, who gives to the lily of the field its delicate and beautiful tints, cares for the little sparrow. Not one falls to the ground without His notice. . . .

If the flower is given a beauty that outvies the glory of Solomon, what can be the measurement of the estimate God places on His purchased heritage? Christ points us to the care bestowed on the things that wither in a day, to show us how much love God must have for the beings created in His own image. . . . He opens before us the volume of providence, and bids us behold the names written therein. In this volume every human being has a page, on which is written the events of his life history. And from the mind of God these names are never absent for a moment. Wonderful indeed is God's love and care for the beings He has created. . . .

That He might save the souls of perishing human beings, He made a gift of such magnitude that it can never be said that God could have made His gift, His donation to the human family, greater. His gift defies computation. All this God did that man might become impregnated with the divine love and benevolence. Thus He would assure sinners that sins of the greatest magnitude can be forgiven if the transgressor seeks for pardon, surrendering himself, body, soul, and spirit, to be transformed by the grace of God and changed into His likeness.

In behalf of man God has poured out the whole treasury of heaven, and in return He expects and claims our entire affections.[42]

TO BE LIKE CHRIST

For ye are dead, and your life is hid with Christ in God. Col. 3:3.

Jesus wants you to be happy, but you cannot be happy in having your own way and following the impulses of your own heart. . . . Our notions, our peculiarities, are wholly human and must not be humored or indulged. Self is to be crucified, not now and then but daily, and the physical, mental, and spiritual must be subordinate to the will of God. The glory of God, the perfection of Christian character, is to be the aim, the purpose, of our life. Christ's followers must imitate Christ in disposition. . . . *Like Christ* is the watchword, not like your father or your mother, but like Jesus Christ—hid in Christ, clothed with Christ's righteousness, imbued with the Spirit of Christ. All the peculiarities given us as an inheritance or acquired by indulgence or through erroneous education must be thoroughly overcome, decidedly resisted. Love of esteem and pride of opinion, all must be brought to the sacrifice. . . .

Jesus is our helper; in Him and through Him we must conquer. . . . The grace of Christ is waiting your demand upon it. He will give you grace and strength as you need it if you ask Him. . . . The religion of Christ will bind and restrain every unholy passion, will stimulate to energy, to self-discipline, and industry, even in the matters of homely, everyday life, leading us to learn economy, tact, and self-denial, and to endure even privation without a murmur. The Spirit of Christ in the heart will be revealed in the character, will develop noble qualities and powers. "My grace is sufficient" (2 Cor. 12:9) says Christ.[43]

God has done so much to make it possible for us to be free in Christ, free from the slavery of wrong habits and evil inclinations. Dear young friends, will you not strive to be free in Christ? You point to this and that professed Christian, saying, We have no confidence in them. If their lives are examples of Christianity, we want none of it. Look not at those around you. Look instead at the only perfect pattern, the man Christ Jesus. Beholding Him, you will be changed into the same image.[44]

STAY CLOSE TO JESUS

Nevertheless I am continually with thee: thou hast holden me by my right hand. Thou shalt guide me with thy counsel, and afterward receive me to glory. Ps. 73:23, 24.

Before you engage in any important work, remember that Jesus is your counselor, and that it is your privilege to cast all your care upon Him. . . . Do not keep Jesus in the background and never mention His name, never call the attention of your friends to Him who is at your side to be your counselor. Would not your friends look upon you as disrespectful were they at your side, and you never spoke to them or of them? . . .

Many complain that Jesus seems a long way off. Who has placed Him a long way off? Has it not been your own course of action that has separated you from Jesus? He has not forsaken you, but you have forsaken Him for other lovers. . . . It is when you wander from His side, and are charmed with the voice of the seducer, and fasten your affections upon some trifling thing, that you are in danger of losing your peace and trust and confidence in God. . . . Then it is that Satan presents to you the thought that Jesus has forsaken you; but is it not that you have forsaken Jesus? . . . We dare not let His name languish on our lips, and His love and memory die out of our hearts.

"Well," says the cold, formal professor, "this is making Christ too much like a human being"; but the Word of God warrants us to have these very ideas. It is the want of these practical, definite views of Christ, that hinders so many from having a genuine experience in the knowledge of our Lord and Saviour Jesus Christ. This is the reason that many are fearing and doubting and mourning. Their ideas of Christ and the plan of salvation are vague, dreary, and confused. If they had, like David, set the Lord ever before them, . . . their feet would be upon solid rock. Behold Jesus crucified for you. Behold Him grieved with your sins; and when you pray, repent, and earnestly desire to see Him as your sin-pardoning Redeemer, ready to bless you, and to hear your acknowledgment of Him. Keep close to His side.[45]

THE BIBLE A LIGHT FOR MY WAY

Thy word is a lamp unto my feet, and a light unto my path.
Ps. 119:105.

> *"Most wondrous book! bright candle of the Lord!*
> *Star of eternity! the only light*
> *By which the bark of man can navigate*
> *The sea of life, and gain the coast of bliss securely."*

Why should not this book—this precious treasure—be exalted and esteemed as a valued friend? This is our chart across the stormy sea of life. It is our guide-book, showing us the way to the eternal mansions, and the character we must have to inhabit them. There is no book the perusal of which will so elevate and strengthen the mind as the study of the Bible. Here the intellect will find themes of the most elevated character to call out its powers. There is nothing that will so endow with vigor all our faculties as bringing them in contact with the stupendous truths of revelation. The effort to grasp and measure these great thoughts expands the mind. We may dig down deep into the mine of truth, and gather precious treasures with which to enrich the soul. Here we may learn the true way to live, the safe way to die.

A familiar acquaintance with the Scriptures sharpens the discerning powers, and fortifies the soul against the attacks of Satan. The Bible is the sword of the Spirit, which will never fail to vanquish the adversary. It is the only true guide in all matters of faith and practice. The reason why Satan has so great control over the minds and hearts of men is that they have not made the Word of God the man of their counsel, and all their ways have not been tried by the true test. The Bible will show us what course we must pursue to become heirs of glory.[46]

As the heart is opened to the entrance of the Word, light from the throne of God will shine into the soul. That Word, cherished in the heart, will yield to the student a treasure of knowledge that is priceless. Its ennobling principles will stamp the character with honesty and truthfulness, temperance and integrity.[47]

January 26

TRUTH IN THE HEART

I have chosen the way of truth: thy judgments have I laid before me. Ps. 119:30.

The cause of God needs men and women who will stand on the platform of truth without wavering, and who will hold the banner of truth firmly aloft, so that no man can fail to see on which side they are standing. Their position is to be clearly defined. Their hearts are to be pure and holy, free from pretense or deception.[48]

The truth must find an abiding place in the heart. Then through the power of the Holy Spirit it will exert its influence in all you do and say. Shall we try to keep the truth out of sight? No, no, not for a moment! It is to be sacredly regarded. Its principles are to be consulted in all your transactions. It is to be a counselor in all your difficulties, a guide in all your relations of life, a present help in every time of need. In public, in private, where no human eye can see, where no ear but God's can hear, there the truth should control us, directing our thoughts, prompting our words and deeds.[49]

You may show to the world that the truth which you profess sanctifies and ennobles the character and leads to industry and frugality, while it avoids avarice, overreaching, and every species of dishonesty. In your words manifest patience and forbearance, and you may every day be preaching a sermon upon the power of truth and do effectual service to the cause of God. Let no one say that the truth you profess makes you no different from the worldling. . . . Do not give the least occasion for anyone to speak ill of your faith because you are not sanctified through the truth.[50]

When the truth as it is in Jesus molds our characters, it will be seen to be truth indeed. As it is contemplated by the true believer, it will grow brighter, shining in its original beauty. As we behold it, it will increase in value, brightening in its own natural loveliness, quickening and vivifying the mind, and subduing our selfish, un-Christlike coarseness of character. It will elevate our aspirations, enabling us to reach the perfect standard of holiness.[51]

32

ENJOYMENT OF THE TRUTH

Teach me thy way, O Lord; I will walk in thy truth: unite my heart to fear thy name. Ps. 86:11.

Say with your whole heart, "I will walk in Thy truth." Every resolution expressed in the fear of God will give strength to purpose and to faith. It will tend to stimulate and to humble, to strengthen and confirm. "I will walk in thy truth." Truth deserves our confidence none the less because the world is flooded with fables. Because error and counterfeit are in circulation it only evidences the fact that there is truth, genuine truth, somewhere. . . .

It is not enough for us to hear the truth only. God requires of us obedience. "Blessed are they that hear the word of God, and keep it." Luke 11:28. "If ye know these things, happy are ye if ye do them." John 13:17.

We may walk in the enjoyment of the truth. It need not be to us a yoke of bondage, but a consolation, a message to us of glad tidings of great joy, animating our hearts and causing us to make melody in our hearts unto God. Through patience and comfort of the Scriptures we have hope. The Christian hope is not gloomy, comfortless. Oh, no, no. It does not shut us up in a prison of doubts and fears. The truth makes free those who love and are sanctified through it. They walk in the glorious liberty of the sons of God.[52]

We who claim to believe the truth should reveal its fruits in our words and character. We are to be far advanced in a knowledge of Jesus Christ, in the reception of His love for God and for our neighbor, in order to have the sunlight of heaven shining in our daily life. Truth must reach down to the deepest recesses of the soul, and cleanse away everything unlike the spirit of Christ, and the vacuum be supplied by the attributes of His character who was pure and holy and undefiled, that all the springs of the heart may be as flowers, fragrant with perfume, a sweet-smelling savor, a savor of life unto life.[53]

It is truth enshrined in the soul that makes one a man of God.[54]

TRUTH A PRECIOUS TREASURE

Buy the truth, and sell it not; also wisdom, and instruction, and understanding. Prov. 23:23.

The truth is precious; it has wrought important changes upon the life and character, exerting a masterly influence over words, deportment, thoughts, and experience.[55]

The religion of Jesus Christ never degrades the receiver. If it finds men and women earthly, common, coarse, unkindly in words, harsh in speech, selfish and self-caring, truth received in the heart commences its purifying, refining process. In words, in dress, in all our habits, there is seen reformation and those things that please God. Then all the world may see its influence in the transforming process.

Truth refines the taste and sanctifies the judgment. It elevates and ennobles, and is silently and constantly doing its leavening work till the whole being is cleansed and made a vessel unto honor, under the operation of the Holy Spirit, to make the receiver of truth fit for the society of pure and sinless angels. . . .

A salvation which was purchased for humanity at such an infinite cost should be held in the most precious vessel by every believer. That which is of such value should ever be highly regarded and not cheapened and made common by the coarseness and roughness retained by those who receive the truth.[56]

Truth as it is in Jesus is not cold and lifeless and formal. . . . Truth is full of warmth, of evidence from the presence of Jesus. . . .

We have a message to bear to the world. It involves a cross. The truths are unpleasant because they require self-denial and self-sacrifice. Then how essential that those who bear the truth, as they speak the truth faithfully, shall by every word and act show that the love of Christ moves them. Truth is . . . always lovely, and those who live the truth as it is in Jesus should study how to present the truth so that its loveliness may appear.[57]

Treasure the truth above everything; sell it not for any price.[58]

THE BIBLE WITHOUT A RIVAL

The words of the Lord are pure words: as silver tried in a furnace of earth, purified seven times. Ps. 12:6.

The Bible is second to no other book; it is without a rival. A knowledge and acceptance of its teachings will impart vigor and health of mind. A comprehension of its teachings requires the student to grasp the knowledge of God's infinite will. The Word of God teaches men and women how to become the sons and daughters of God. No other book, no other study, can equal this; the principles it instills, like the power and nature of its Author, are omnipotent. It is capable of imparting the highest education to which the mortal mind can attain.[59]

It is not safe for us to turn from the Holy Scriptures, with only a casual reading of their sacred pages. . . . Rein the mind up to the high task that has been set before it, and study with determined interest, that you may understand divine truth. Those who do this, will be surprised to find to what the mind can attain.[60]

The minds of all who make the Word of God their study will enlarge. Far more than any other study its influence is calculated to increase the powers of comprehension and endow every faculty with a new power. It brings the mind in contact with broad, ennobling principles of truth. It brings all heaven into close connection with human minds, imparting wisdom and knowledge and understanding.

In dealing with commonplace productions, and feeding on the writings of uninspired men, the mind becomes dwarfed and cheapened. . . . The understanding unconsciously accommodates itself to the comprehension of the things with which it is familiar, and in the consideration of these finite things, the understanding is weakened, its powers contracted, and after a time it becomes unable to expand. . . .

All knowledge gained in this life of probation which will help us to form characters that will fit us to be companions of the saints in light is true education. It will bring blessings to ourselves and others in this life, and will secure to us the future, immortal life with its imperishable riches.[61]

SURE REMEDY FOR THE SOUL

Who forgiveth all thine iniquities; who healeth all thy diseases.
Ps. 103:3.

Christ has given us His Word, that men and women may be thoroughly furnished with a remedy for all spiritual diseases. The Word is a test of human character. It points out the disease, and prescribes the remedy. In the Word is a prescription for every spiritual ailment. The plain commands of God will exert a healthful influence upon the mind, and upon the whole body. If taken in faith and faithfully practiced, its remedies are infallible.[62]

Before the humblest is opened the promises of the Word of God. God declares, "If any of you lack wisdom, let him ask of God, that giveth to all men liberally. . . ." James 1:5. He will never be sent away empty. And the man who lives by every word of God will improve in mental and moral capabilities. He will have a clearer understanding than he manifested before he opened his heart to the entrance of the Word of life. Connected by faith with the living Source of wisdom and knowledge, the mental powers will grow and expand. While the powers of the intellect were under the sway of Satan, the whole man was deformed. But when the power of the truth is brought into the heart, it influences the entire being.[63]

The Lord has uttered His voice in His Holy Word. Those blessed pages are full of instruction and life, harmonious with truth. They are a perfect rule of conduct. Instructions are given, principles are laid down, which apply to every circumstance in life, even though some particular case may not be stated. Nothing is left unrevealed which is essential to a complete system of faith and a correct line of practice. Every duty that God requires at our hands is made plain. . . . None will err from the right path who meekly and honestly take the Bible as their guide, making it the man of their counsel.[64]

Depend on this: If you study the Word of God with a sincere desire to get help, the Lord will fill your soul with light. Your work will be approved of God, and your influence will be a savor of life.[65]

STORING THE MIND WITH TRUTH

*That which I see not teach thou me: if I have done iniquity, I will
do no more. Job 34:32.*

Take your Bible and present yourself before your heavenly
Father, saying, "Enlighten me; teach me what is truth." The Lord will
regard your prayer, and the Holy Spirit will impress the truth upon
your soul. In searching the Scriptures for yourself, you will become
established in the faith. It is of the greatest importance that you continually search the Scriptures, storing the mind with the Word of
God, for you may be separated from the companionship of
Christians, and placed where you will not have the privilege of
meeting with the children of God. You need the treasures of God's
Word hidden in your heart, that when opposition comes upon you,
you may bring everything to the Scriptures. . . .

We are living in the last days, when error of a most deceptive
character is accepted and believed, while truth is discarded. Many
are drifting into darkness and infidelity, picking flaws with the Bible,
bringing in superstitious inventions, unscriptural theories, and spec-
ulations of vain philosophy; but it is the duty of everyone to seek a
thorough knowledge of the Scriptures.[66]

Truth is efficient only as it is carried out in practical life. If the
Word of God condemns some habit you have indulged, a feeling
you have cherished, a spirit you have manifested, turn not from the
Word of God, but turn away from the evil of your doings, and let
Jesus cleanse and sanctify your heart. Confess your faults, and for-
sake them.[67]

Do not merely assent to the truth, and fail to be a doer of the
words of Christ. The truth must be applied to self; it must bring men
and women who receive it to the Rock, that they may fall upon the
Rock and be broken. Then Jesus can mold and fashion their characters after His own divine character. If we would listen to His voice,
we must let silence reign in the heart. The clamors of self, its preten-
sions, its lusts, must be rebuked, and we must put on the robe of humility, and take our place as humble learners in the school of Christ.[68]

LET JESUS LEAD

Jesus saith unto him, I am the way, the truth, and the life: no man cometh unto the Father, but by me. John 14:6.

Oh, that we who are pilgrims and strangers in this foreign country . . . might comprehend Christ, the way, the truth, and the life. He says, "No man cometh unto the Father, but by me." The path He has marked out is so plain and distinct that the veriest sinner, loaded with guilt, need not miss his way. Not one trembling seeker need fail of finding the true path, and of walking in pure and holy light, for Jesus leads the way.

The path is so narrow, so holy, that sin cannot be tolerated therein, yet access to the path has been made for all, and not one desponding, doubting, trembling soul needs to say, "God cares nought for me." Every soul is precious in His sight. . . . When Satan was triumphing as the prince of the world, when he claimed the world as his kingdom, when we were all marred and corrupted with sin, God sent His messenger from heaven, even His only begotten Son, to proclaim to all the inhabitants of the world, "I have found a ransom. I have made a way of escape for all the perishing. I have your emancipation papers provided for you, sealed by the Lord of heaven and earth." . . .

It is not because there is any flaw in the title which has been purchased for you that you do not accept it. It is not because the mercy, the grace, the love of the Father and the Son is not ample, and has not been freely bestowed, that you do not rejoice in pardoning love. . . . If you are lost, it will be because you will not come unto Christ that you might have life.

God waits to bestow the blessing of forgiveness of sins, of pardon for iniquity, of the gift of righteousness upon all who will believe in His love, and accept of His salvation. Christ is ready to say to the repenting sinner, ". . . Behold, I have caused thine iniquity to pass from thee. . . ." Zech. 3:4-7. Christ is the connecting link between God and man. The blood of Jesus Christ is the eloquent plea that speaks in behalf of sinners.[1]

MAN MORE PRECIOUS THAN GOLD

I will make a man more precious than fine gold; even a man than the golden wedge of Ophir. Isa. 13:12.

Few appreciate the value of man, and the glory that would redound to God were he to cultivate and preserve purity, nobility, and integrity of character. . . . The short space of time allotted to men here is exceedingly valuable. Now, while probation lingers, God proposes to unite His strength with the weakness of finite man. . . . Those who truly love God will desire so to improve the talents that He has given them, that they may be a blessing to others. And by and by the gates of heaven will be thrown wide open to admit them, and from the lips of the King of glory the benediction will fall upon their ears like richest music, "Come, ye blessed of my Father, inherit the kingdom prepared for you from the foundation of the world." Matt. 25:34.

Thus the redeemed will be welcomed to the mansions that Jesus is preparing for them. There their companions will not be the vile of earth—liars, idolaters, the impure, or the unbelieving; but they will associate with those who have overcome Satan and his devices, and through divine aid have formed perfect characters. Every sinful tendency, every imperfection that afflicts them here, has been removed by the blood of Christ; and the excellence and brightness of His glory, far exceeding the brightness of the sun in its meridian splendor, is imparted to them. And the moral beauty, the perfection of His character, shines through them, in worth far exceeding this outward splendor. They are without fault around the great white throne, sharing the dignity and privileges of the angels.

"Eye hath not seen, nor ear heard, neither have entered into the heart of man, the things which God hath prepared for them that love him." 1 Cor. 2:9. In view of the glorious inheritance which may be his, "what shall a man give in exchange for his soul?" He may be poor; yet he possesses in himself a wealth and dignity that the world could never bestow. The soul redeemed and cleansed from sin, with all its noble powers dedicated to the service of God, is of surpassing worth.[2]

I AM NOT MY OWN

Ye are bought with a price; be not ye the servants of men. 1 Cor. 7:23.

How natural it is to regard ourselves as complete owners of ourselves! But the Inspired Word declares, "Ye are not your own." "Ye are bought with a price." 1 Cor. 6:19, 20. . . . In our relation to our fellow men we are owners of our entrusted mental and physical capabilities. In our relation to God, we are borrowers, stewards of His grace.

Time is to be used judiciously, earnestly, and under the sanctification of the Holy Spirit. We are to understand just what is right and what is wrong to do with property and with mental and physical capabilities. God has a positive ownership of every power He has committed to the human agent. By His own wisdom He makes the terms of man's use of every gift of God. He will bless the proper use of every power put forth for His own name's glory. The talent of speech, of memory, of property, all are to accumulate for the glory of God, to advance His kingdom. God has left us in charge of His goods in His absence. Each steward has his own special work to do in advancing God's kingdom. Not one is excused.[3]

The youth must be educated to respect themselves because they are bought with a price.[4]

Christ clothed His divinity with humanity and paid the ransom for man, and He desires that man shall estimate the life thus provided for him by the infinite price paid.[5]

It is your privilege to obey the living Word of God as a truly converted and transformed soul, to perform the highest service as a free, heaven-born spirit, to give evidence that you are worthy of the sacred trust that God has given you by sending His only begotten Son to die for you. If you believe in Christ as your personal Saviour, you receive every grace, every spiritual endowment, necessary for the perfecting of the Christian character. Show that you appreciate the sacrifice made for you, and regard it as too great to allow you to make a mock of your religious profession by being molded and fashioned after the world's criterion.[6]

PURCHASE OF CHRIST'S BLOOD

Forasmuch as ye know that ye were not redeemed with corruptible things, as silver and gold, from your vain conversation received by tradition from your fathers; but with the precious blood of Christ, as of a lamb without blemish and without spot. 1 Peter 1:18, 19.

You must consider that you are not at your own disposal to do that which you please for your own self. You are the Lord's property. Christ has purchased you with the price of His own blood. Your body is to be sanctified unto the Lord as a vessel unto honor. It is Christ's purchased possession. Then preserve every power, every organ, as an instrument unto righteousness. Satan desires to have your brain power, and your will, but they belong to Jesus. Consider always, "I am not my own. I must carefully and holily cherish every part of Christ's purchased possession." . . .

Satan may try to bind you to his car [chariot] as a helpless soul. But shout in victory that Christ has made you a free man. Do not dishonor God by one expression of inefficiency and inability to overcome fully, entirely, and gloriously through Jesus Christ, who has died to redeem you, and make you a free man. Conquer, yes, conquer. Put your will every moment on the side of God's will. Think hopefully and courageously. In faith cry out against Satan, and looking unto Jesus who is the author and finisher of your faith, say, "Jesus, my Redeemer, I am weak. I cannot do anything without Thy special help. I hang my helpless soul on Thee." Then let your imagination dwell on the thought that you are in the presence of Jesus, walking with God, your life hid with Christ in God. . . . Then you will not glorify Satan by imagining yourself weak and helpless. You will keep yourself uplifted into a pure and holy atmosphere. You will receive the Holy Spirit as a comforter, as a sanctifier. . . . You will have a calm, restful spirit in God. You will say, "Jesus lives, and because He lives I will live also. He has conquered Satan in my behalf, and I will not be conquered by the devil once. I will not disgrace my Lord and Leader; but I will triumph in His holy name, and come off more than conqueror."[7]

GOD WANTS HIS OWN PROPERTY

But now thus saith the Lord that created thee, O Jacob, and he that formed thee, O Israel, Fear not: for I have redeemed thee, I have called thee by thy name; thou art mine. Isa. 43:1.

Every man and woman has had the ransom money paid by Jesus Christ. "Ye are not your own. For ye are bought with a price" even the precious blood of the Son of God.[8]

Whether we give ourselves to the Lord or not, we are His. Ye are not your own; ye are bought with a price. We are the Lord's by creation, and we are His by redemption. Therefore we have no right to think that we can do as we please. All we handle is the Lord's. We have no right of ourselves to anything, not even to an existence. All our money, time, and talents belong to God, and are lent us by Him that we may accomplish the work He has given us to do. He has given us the charge, "Occupy till I come." Luke 19:13.[9]

Do not make it a business to serve yourselves and become indifferent in regard to the claims of God upon you. You are His property. . . . Jesus has bought you at an infinite cost. Your thoughts should be kept pure; they are the Lord's. Give them to Him. We can merit nothing from God. We can give Him nothing which is not His own. Will we keep back from God what is His own? Do not rob God and pawn His time, His talents, and His strength with the world. He asks your affections; give them to Him. They are His own. He asks your time, moment by moment; give it to Him. It is His own. He asks your intellect; give it to Him. It is His own. . . .

The Lord wants His own property. When we have given to God soul, body, and spirit; when we have kept appetite under the control of enlightened conscience, and wrestled against every lust, showing that we consider each organ as God's property, intended for His service; when all our affections move in harmony with the Lord's mind, fastening on objects "which are above, where Christ sitteth on the right hand of God"—then we have given the Lord His own. O God, "all things come of thee, and of thine own have we given thee." 1 Chron. 29:14.[10]

TAKE CARE OF GOD'S PROPERTY

Who gave himself for our sins, that he might deliver us from this present evil world, according to the will of God and our Father. Gal. 1:4.

You have cost much. "Glorify God in your body, and in your spirit, which are God's." 1 Cor. 6:20. That which you may regard as your own is God's. Take care of His property. He has bought you with an infinite price. Your mind is His. What right has any person to abuse a body that belongs not to himself, but to the Lord Jesus Christ? What satisfaction can anyone take in gradually lessening the powers of body and mind by selfish indulgence of any form?

God has given to every human being a brain. He desires that it shall be used to His glory. By it, man is enabled to cooperate with God in efforts to save perishing fellow mortals. We have none too much brain power or reasoning faculties. We are to educate and train every power of mind and body—the human mechanism that Christ has bought—in order that we may put it to the best possible use. We are to do all we can to strengthen these powers; for God is pleased to have us become more and still more efficient colaborers with Him. . . .

In Exodus we read that at the time the Lord directed the Israelites to build a tabernacle in the wilderness, He gave certain men special ability, talent, and skill in devising, and then He appointed them to the work. He will deal with us in the same way. . . . And although we may have to begin in a very small way, He will bless us and multiply our talents as a reward for faithfulness.[11]

Christ has died for you, and you are to live as unto God. Let your reasoning powers, refined, purified, sanctified, be brought to God. The Lord requires the sanctification of the whole being. The mind, as well as the whole body, is to be elevated and ennobled. God has claims upon mind, soul, and body.[12]

It is not in the power of those who have named the name of Jesus to give Him more than is His own. He has bought every human agent with an infinite price, and we are His property for both time and eternity.[13]

TAKE GOD INTO YOUR COUNSEL

Who his own self bare our sins in his own body on the tree, that we, being dead to sins, should live unto righteousness: by whose stripes ye were healed. 1 Peter 2:24.

Christ bore our sins in His own body on the tree. . . . What must sin be, if no finite being could make atonement? What must its curse be if Deity alone could exhaust it? The cross of Christ testifies to every man that the penalty of sin is death. . . . Oh, must there be some strong bewitching power which holds the moral senses, steeling them against the impressions of the Spirit of God? I entreat of you, as Christ's ambassador, . . . to be diligent in securing the grace of God. You need it every day, that you make no mistake in your life. . . .

You may feel that you are competent to manage yourself, to lay plans and execute them in your own judgment. This is unsafe for you or for any one to do. I speak of the things I know. Take God into your counsel. Seek Him for guidance. He will not be sought of in vain. . . . I entreat of you not to let these precious hours of probation pass without spiritual advancement. In no case allow your moral powers to become dwarfed. . . .

Heaven with its attractions is before you, an eternal weight of glory, which you may lose or gain. Which shall it be? Your life and your character will testify the choice you have made. I feel the more anxious because I see so many indifferent upon the subjects of infinite importance. They are always busy here and there about matters of minor importance, and the one great subject is put out of their thoughts. They have no time to pray, no time to watch, no time to search the Scriptures. They are altogether too busy to make the necessary preparation for the future life. They cannot devote time to perfect Christian characters and in diligence to secure a title to heaven.

If you have life eternal, you must be earnest and work to the point. . . . Glorify God by choosing His way, His will. He will be your wise counselor and your fast, unchanging friend.[14]

THE CORD LET DOWN FROM HEAVEN

And being found in fashion as a man, he humbled himself, and became obedient unto death, even the death of the cross. Phil. 2:8.

Measure the cord, if you can, that has been let down from heaven to lift man up. The only estimate we can give you of the length of that chain is to point you to Calvary.[15]

Fallen men could not have a home in the paradise of God without the Lamb slain from the foundation of the world. Shall we not then exalt the cross of Christ? . . .

Angelic perfection failed in heaven. Human perfection failed in Eden, the paradise of bliss. All who wish for security in earth or heaven must look to the Lamb of God. The plan of salvation, making manifest the justice and love of God, provides an eternal safeguard against defection in unfallen worlds, as well as among those who shall be redeemed by the blood of the Lamb. Our only hope is perfect trust in the blood of Him who can save to the uttermost all that come unto God by Him. The death of Christ on the cross of Calvary is our only hope in this world, and it will be our theme in the world to come. Oh, we do not comprehend the value of the atonement! If we did, we would talk more about it. The gift of God in His beloved Son was the expression of an incomprehensible love. It was the utmost that God could do to preserve the honor of His law, and still save the transgressor.[16]

Jesus placed the cross in line with the light coming from heaven, for it is there that it shall catch the eye of man. The cross is in direct line with the shining of the divine countenances, so that by beholding the cross men may see and know God and Jesus Christ, whom He hath sent. In beholding God we behold the One who poured out His soul unto death. In beholding the cross the view is extended to God, and His hatred of sin is discerned. But while we behold in the cross God's hatred of sin, we also behold His love for sinners, which is stronger than death. To the world the cross is the incontrovertible argument that God is truth and light and love.[17]

THE CENTER OF MY HOPE

But God forbid that I should glory, save in the cross of our Lord Jesus Christ, by whom the world is crucified unto me, and I unto the world. Gal. 6:14.

Remove the cross from the Christian and it is like blotting out the sun which illumines the day, and dropping the moon and the stars out of the firmament of the heavens at night. The cross of Christ brings us nigh to God, reconciling man to God, and God to man. The Father looks upon the cross, upon the suffering He has given His Son to endure in order to save the race from hopeless misery and to draw man to Himself. He looks upon it with the relenting compassion of a Father's love. The cross has been almost lost sight of, but without the cross there is no connection with the Father, no unity with the Lamb in the midst of the throne in heaven, no welcome reception of the wandering who would return to the forsaken path of righteousness and truth, no hope for the transgressor in the day of judgment. Without the cross there is no means provided for overcoming the power of our strong foe. Every hope of the race hangs upon the cross.[18]

When the sinner reaches the cross, and looks up to the One who died to save him, he may rejoice with fullness of joy; for his sins are pardoned. Kneeling at the cross, he has reached the highest place to which man can attain. The light of the knowledge of the glory of God is revealed in the face of Jesus Christ; and the words of pardon are spoken: Live, O ye guilty sinners, live. Your repentance is accepted; for I have found a ransom.

Through the cross we learn that our heavenly Father loves us with an infinite and everlasting love, and draws us to Him with more than a mother's yearning sympathy for a wayward child. Can we wonder that Paul exclaimed, "God forbid that I should glory, save in the cross of our Lord Jesus Christ"? It is our privilege also to glory in the cross of Calvary, our privilege to give ourselves wholly to Him who gave Himself for us. Then with the light of love that shines from His face on ours, we shall go forth to reflect it to those in darkness.[19]

EFFICACY OF CHRIST'S BLOOD

It is the blood that maketh an atonement for the soul. Lev. 17:11.

Christ was the Lamb slain from the foundation of the world. To many it has been a mystery why so many sacrificial offerings were required in the old dispensation, why so many bleeding victims were led to the altar. But the great truth that was to be kept before men, and imprinted upon mind and heart, was this, "Without shedding of blood is no remission." Heb. 9:22. In every bleeding sacrifice was typified "the Lamb of God, which taketh away the sin of the world." John 1:29.

Christ Himself was the originator of the Jewish system of worship, in which, by types and symbols, were shadowed forth spiritual and heavenly things. . . . Today we are living when type has met antitype in the offering of Christ for the sins of the world; we are living in the day of increased light, and yet how few are benefited with the grand and all-important truth that Christ has made an ample sacrifice for all! What justice required, Christ had rendered in the offering of Himself, and "how shall we escape if we neglect so great salvation?" Heb. 2:3. Those who reject the gift of life will be without excuse.[20]

Thank God that He who spilled His blood for us, lives to plead it, lives to make intercession for every soul who receives Him. "If we confess our sins, he is faithful and just to forgive us our sins, and to cleanse us from all unrighteousness." 1 John 1:9. The blood of Jesus Christ cleanses us from all sin. It speaketh better things than the blood of Abel, for Christ ever liveth to make intercession for us. We need to keep ever before us the efficacy of the blood of Jesus. That life-cleansing, life-sustaining blood, appropriated by living faith, is our hope. We need to grow in appreciation of its inestimable value, for it speaks for us only as we by faith claim its virtue, keeping the conscience clean and at peace with God.

This is represented as the pardoning blood, inseparably connected with the resurrection and life of our Redeemer, illustrated by the everflowing stream that proceeds from the throne of God, the water of the river of life.[21]

CHRIST'S HUMANITY A GOLDEN CHAIN

For we have not an high priest which cannot be touched with the feeling of our infirmities; but was in all points tempted like as we are, yet without sin. Heb. 4:15.

Christ's overcoming and obedience is that of a true human being. In our conclusions, we make many mistakes because of our erroneous views of the human nature of our Lord. When we give to His human nature a power that it is not possible for man to have in his conflicts with Satan, we destroy the completeness of His humanity. His imputed grace and power He gives to all who receive Him by faith.

The obedience of Christ to His Father was the same obedience that is required of man. Man cannot overcome Satan's temptations without divine power to combine with his instrumentality. So with Jesus Christ; He could lay hold of divine power. He came not to our world to give the obedience of a lesser God to a greater, but as a man to obey God's Holy Law, and in this way He is our example. The Lord Jesus came to our world, not to reveal what a God could do, but what a man could do, through faith in God's power to help in every emergency. Man is, through faith, to be a partaker in the divine nature, and to overcome every temptation wherewith he is beset.

The Lord now demands that every son and daughter of Adam, through faith in Jesus Christ, serve Him in human nature which we now have. The Lord Jesus has bridged the gulf that sin has made. He has connected earth with heaven, and finite man with the infinite God. Jesus, the world's Redeemer, could only keep the commandments of God in the same way that humanity can keep them.[22]

We are not to serve God as if we were not human, but we are to serve Him in the nature we have, that has been redeemed by the Son of God; through the righteousness of Christ we shall stand before God pardoned, and as though we had never sinned.[23]

The humanity of the Son of God is everything to us. It is the golden chain that binds our souls to Christ, and through Christ to God.[24]

AN ADVOCATE WITH THE FATHER

My little children, these things write I unto you, that ye sin not. And if any man sin, we have an advocate with the Father, Jesus Christ the righteous. 1 John 2:1.

How careful is the Lord Jesus to give no occasion for a soul to despair. How He fences about the soul from Satan's fierce attacks. If through manifold temptations we are surprised or deceived into sin, He does not turn from us and leave us to perish. No, no, that is not our Saviour. . . . He was tempted in all points like as we are; and having been tempted, He knows how to succor those who are tempted. Our crucified Lord is pleading for us in the presence of the Father at the throne of grace. His atoning sacrifice we may plead for our pardon, our justification, and our sanctification. The Lamb slain is our only hope. Our faith looks up to Him, grasps Him as the One who can save to the uttermost, and the fragrance of the all-sufficient offering is accepted of the Father.[25]

If you make failures and are betrayed into sin, do not feel then you cannot pray . . . but seek the Lord more earnestly.[26]

The blood of Jesus is pleading with power and efficacy for those who are backslidden, for those who are rebellious, for those who sin against great light and love. Satan stands at our right hand to accuse us, and our Advocate stands at God's right hand to plead for us. He has never lost a case that has been committed to Him. We may trust in our Advocate; for He pleads His own merits in our behalf. . . . He is making intercession for the most lowly, the most oppressed and suffering, for the most tried and tempted ones. With upraised hands He pleads, "I have graven thee upon the palms of my hands." Isa. 49:16.[27]

I would I might sound the glad note to earth's remotest bounds. "If any man sin, we have an Advocate with the Father, Jesus Christ the righteous." Oh, precious redemption! How broad this great truth is—that God for Christ's dear sake, forgives us the moment we ask Him in living faith, believing that He is fully able![28]

CONNECTING LINK BETWEEN GOD AND MAN

Wherefore he is able also to save them to the uttermost that come unto God by him, seeing he ever liveth to make intercession for them. Heb. 7:25.

Christ is the connecting link between God and man. He has promised His personal intercession by employing His name. He places the whole virtue of His righteousness on the side of the suppliant. Christ pleads for man, and man, in need of divine help, pleads for himself in the presence of God, using the power of the influence of the One who gave His life for the world. As we acknowledge before God our appreciation of Christ's merits, fragrance is given to our intercessions. Oh, who can value this great mercy and love! As we approach God through the virtue of Christ's merits, we are clothed with His priestly vestments. He places us close by His side, encircling us with His human arm, while with His divine arm He grasps the throne of the Infinite. He puts His merits, as sweet incense, in a censer in our hands, in order to encourage our petitions. He promises to hear and answer our supplications.[29]

Everyone who will break from the slavery and service of Satan, and will stand under the blood-stained banner of Prince Immanuel will be kept by Christ's intercessions. Christ, as our Mediator, at the right hand of the Father, ever keeps us in view, for it is as necessary that He should keep us by His intercessions as that He should redeem us with His blood. If He lets go His hold of us for one moment, Satan stands ready to destroy.[30]

As the prayers of the sincere and contrite ones ascend to heaven Christ says to the Father, "I will take their sins. Let them stand before You innocent." As He takes their sins from them, He fills their hearts with the glorious light of truth and love.[31]

Our need of Christ's intercession is constant. Day by day, morning and evening, the humble heart needs to offer up prayers to which will be returned answers of grace and peace and joy. "By him therefore let us offer the sacrifice of praise to God continually." Heb. 13:15.[32]

FAULTLESS IN CHRIST'S PERFECTION

For he hath made him to be sin for us, who knew no sin; that we might be made the righteousness of God in him. 2 Cor. 5:21.

Pardon and justification are one and the same thing. Through faith, the believer passes from the position of a rebel, a child of sin and Satan, to the position of a loyal subject of Christ Jesus, not because of an inherent goodness, but because Christ receives him as His child by adoption. The sinner receives the forgiveness of his sins, because these sins are borne by his Substitute and Surety. The Lord speaks to His heavenly Father, saying: "This is My child. I reprieve him from the condemnation of death, giving him My life insurance policy—eternal life—because I have taken his place and have suffered for his sins. He is even My beloved son." Thus man, pardoned, and clothed with the beautiful garments of Christ's righteousness, stands faultless before God. . . .

It is the Father's prerogative to forgive our transgressions and sins, because Christ has taken upon Himself our guilt and reprieved us, imputing to us His own righteousness. His sacrifice satisfies fully the demands of justice.[33]

Many feel that their faults of character make it impossible for them to meet the standard that Christ has erected; but all that such ones have to do is to humble themselves at every step under the mighty hand of God; Christ does not estimate the man by the amount of work he does, but by the spirit in which the work is performed.

When He sees men lifting the burdens, trying to carry them in lowliness of mind, with distrust of self and with reliance upon Him, He adds to their work His perfection and sufficiency, and it is accepted of the Father. We are accepted in the beloved. The sinner's defects are covered by the perfection and fullness of the Lord our righteousness. Those who with sincere will, with contrite heart, are putting forth humble efforts to live up to the requirements of God, are looked upon by the Father with pitying, tender love; He regards such as obedient children, and the righteousness of Christ is imputed unto them.[34]

THE FAITH THAT JUSTIFIES

Therefore being justified by faith, we have peace with God through our Lord Jesus Christ. Rom. 5:1.

Justification by faith is to many a mystery. A sinner is justified by God when he repents of his sins. He sees Jesus upon the cross of Calvary. . . . He looks to the atoning Sacrifice as his only hope, through repentance toward God—because the laws of His government have been broken—and faith toward our Lord Jesus Christ as the One who can save and cleanse the sinner from every transgression.

The mediatorial work of Christ commenced with the commencement of human guilt and suffering and misery, as soon as man became a transgressor. The law was not abolished to save man and bring him into union with God. But Christ assumed the office of his surety and deliverer in becoming *sin for man,* that man might become the righteousness of God in and through Him who was one with the Father. Sinners can be justified by God only when He pardons their sins, remits the punishment they deserve, and treats them as though they were really just and had not sinned, receiving them into divine favor and treating them as if they were righteous. They are justified alone through the imputed righteousness of Christ. The Father accepts the Son, and through the atoning sacrifice of His Son accepts the sinner. . . .

There are thousands who believe in the gospel and in Jesus Christ as the world's Redeemer, but they are not saved by that faith. . . . They do not repent and have that faith that lays hold upon Christ as their sin-pardoning Saviour; their belief is not unto repentance. . . .

The faith that justifies always produces first true repentance, and then good works, which are the fruit of that faith. There is no saving faith that does not produce good fruit. God gave Christ to our world to become the sinner's substitute. The moment true faith in the merits of the costly atoning sacrifice is exercised, claiming Christ as a personal Saviour, that moment the sinner is justified before God, because he is pardoned.[35]

ACCEPTED IN THE BELOVED

To the praise of the glory of his grace, wherein he hath made us accepted in the beloved. Eph. 1:6.

The Father gave all honor to His Son, seating Him at His right hand, far above all principalities and powers. He expressed His great joy and delight in receiving the Crucified One, and crowning Him with glory and honor. And all the favors He has shown to His Son in His acceptance of the great atonement, are shown to His people. Those who have united their interests in love with Christ are accepted in the Beloved. They suffered with Christ in His deepest humiliation, and His glorification is of great interest to them, because they are accepted in Him. God loves them as He loves His Son. Christ, Emmanuel, stands between God and the believer, revealing the glory of God to His chosen ones, and covering their defects and transgressions with the garments of His own spotless righteousness.[36]

"The Lord taketh pleasure in them that fear him, in them that hope in his mercy." Ps. 147:11. But it is only through the value of the sacrifice made for us that we are of value in the Lord's sight. It is because of the imputed righteousness of Christ that we are counted precious by God. For Christ's sake He pardons them that fear Him. He does not see in them the vileness of the sinner; He recognizes in them the likeness of His Son, in whom they believe. In this way only can God take pleasure in any of us. "As many as received him, to them gave he power to become the sons of God, even to them that believe on his name." John 1:12.

The more perfectly the Lord sees the character of His beloved Son revealed in His people, the greater is His satisfaction and delight in them. God Himself and the heavenly universe rejoice over them with singing, because Christ has not died for them in vain. The believing sinner is pronounced innocent, while the guilt is placed on Jesus Christ. The righteousness of Christ is placed on the debtor's account, and against his name on the balance sheet is written, Pardoned. Eternal Life.[37]

OUR REDEEMER A TRIED STONE

Therefore thus saith the Lord God, Behold, I lay in Zion for a foundation a stone, a tried stone, a precious corner stone, a sure foundation: he that believeth shall not make haste. Isa. 28:16.

Our Redeemer is a "Tried Stone." The experiment has been made, the great test has been applied, and with perfect success. In Him is fulfilled all the purpose of God for the saving of a lost world. Never was a foundation subject to so severe a trial and test as this "Tried Stone." The Lord Jehovah knew what this foundation stone could sustain. The sins of the whole world could be piled upon it. The Lord's chosen were to be revealed, heaven's gates to be thrown open to all who would believe; its untold glories were to be given to the overcomers.

"A Tried Stone" is Christ, tried by the perversity of man. Thou, O our Saviour, hast taken the burden; Thou hast given peace and rest; Thou hast been tried, proved by believers who have taken their trials to Thy sympathy, their sorrows to Thy love, their wounds to Thy healing, their weakness to Thy strength, their emptiness to Thy fullness; and never, never has one soul been disappointed. Jesus, my Tried Stone, to Thee will I come, moment by moment. In Thy presence I am lifted above pain. "When my heart is overwhelmed, lead me to the Rock that is higher than I." Ps. 61:2.

It is our privilege to enjoy sweet communion with God. Precious to the believer is His atoning blood, precious is His justifying righteousness. "Unto you therefore which believe he is precious." 1 Peter 2:7.

When I meditate upon this fountain of living power from which we may draw, I mourn that so many are losing the delight they might have had in considering His goodness. We are to be sons and daughters of God, growing into a holy temple in the Lord. "No more strangers and foreigners, but fellowcitizens with the saints, and of the household of God. . . . Built upon the foundation of the apostles and prophets, Jesus Christ himself being the chief corner stone." Eph. 2:19, 20. This is our privilege.[38]

JESUS OUR BEST FRIEND

A man that hath friends must shew himself friendly: and there is a friend that sticketh closer than a brother. Prov. 18:24.

How few are constantly beholding the unseen Guest, realizing that He is at their right hand! How many ignore His presence! Did we treat others as we treat Jesus, what discourtesy it would be thought!

Suppose a friend were with us, and we should meet an acquaintance on the way and direct our whole attention to our new-found acquaintance, ignoring the presence of our friend, what opinion would men have of our loyalty to our friend, of our degree of respect to him? And yet this is the way we treat Jesus. We forget that He is our companion. We engage in conversation, and never mention His name. . . . We talk of worldly business matters, and where it does not bruise the soul, where it is essential, we do not dishonor Jesus, but we do dishonor Him when we fail to mention Him in our intercourse with our friends and associates. He is our best friend, and we should seek for opportunities to speak of Him. . . . We should ever keep Him in view. Our conversation should be of a character that would be of no offense to God.[39]

I know that in many hearts the inquiry arises, "Where shall I find Jesus?" There are many who want His presence, want His love and His light; but they know not where to look for Him for whom their hearts yearn. And yet Jesus does not hide Himself away; no one need search for Him in vain. "Behold," He says, "I stand at the door, and knock: if any man hear my voice, and open the door, I will come in to him, and will sup with him, and he with me." Rev. 3:20. Jesus invites us to accept His presence; we are to open the door of the heart, and let Him in. But He will not share a divided heart. If it be given to the service of mammon, if selfishness and pride fill its chambers, there will be no room for the heavenly Guest; He will not take up His abode with us until the soul-temple has been emptied and cleansed. Yet there is no need of making a failure in the Christian life. Jesus is waiting to do a great work for us, and all heaven is interested in our salvation.[40]

JESUS IS ALWAYS NEAR

But straightway Jesus spake unto them, saying, Be of good cheer; it is I; be not afraid. Matt. 14:27.

I think of the disciples in that sore tempest; the boat labored with strong winds and heavy gales. They have given up their efforts as hopeless, and while the hungry waves talk with death, amid the storm a light form is seen walking upon the foam-capped billows. . . . A voice is heard amid the roar of the tempest, "Be of good cheer; it is I; be not afraid."

Oh, how many in this time of peril, are making a hard pull against a head sea! The moon and stars seem to be hidden by storm clouds, and in despondency and despair, many of us say, "It is no use; our efforts are as nothing. We shall perish. We have toiled at the oars, but without any success." . . . Jesus is just as near to us amid scenes of tempest and trial as He was to His followers who were tossed on the Sea of Galilee. We must have calm, steady, firm, unwavering trust in God. . . . We must now have an individual experience in holding fast unto God. Christ is on board the vessel. Believe that Christ is our Captain, that He will take care, not only of us, but of the ship. . . .

That night in that boat was to the disciples a school where they were to receive their education for the great work which was to be done afterwards. The dark hours of trial are to come to every one as a part of his education for higher work, for more devoted, consecrated effort. The storm was not sent upon the disciples to shipwreck them, but to test and prove them, individually. . . .

The time of our educating will soon be over. We have no time to lose in walking through clouds of doubt and uncertainty. . . . We may stand close to the side of Jesus. Let none . . . shirk one hard lesson or lose the blessing of one hard discipline. . . .

Whatever be our condition in life, our business, we have a sure Guide. Whatever be our condition, He is our counselor. Whatever be our loneliness, He is our friend in whom we may ever trust.[41]

OUR GREAT EXEMPLAR

Wherefore, holy brethren, partakers of the heavenly calling, consider the Apostle and High Priest of our profession, Christ Jesus. Heb. 3:1.

I present before you the great Exemplar. . . . As really did He meet and resist the temptations of Satan as any of the children of humanity. In this sense alone could He be a perfect example for man. He subjected Himself to humanity to become acquainted with all the temptations wherewith man is beset. He took upon Him the infirmities and bore the sorrows of the sons of Adam.

He was "made like unto his brethren." Heb. 2:17. He felt both joy and grief as they feel. His body was susceptible to weariness, as yours. His mind, like yours, could be harassed and perplexed. If you have hardships, so did He. Satan could tempt Him. His enemies could annoy Him. The ruling powers could torture His body; the soldiers could crucify Him; and they can do no more to us. Jesus was exposed to hardships, to conflict and temptation, as a man. He became the Captain of our Salvation through suffering. He could bear His burden better than we, for He bore it without complaint, without impatience, without unbelief, without repining; but this is no evidence He felt it less than any of the suffering sons of Adam. . . .

The period of His childhood and youth was one of comparative obscurity, but of the highest importance. He was in this obscurity laying the foundation of a sound constitution and vigorous mind. He "grew, and waxed strong in spirit." Luke 1:80. It is not as a man bending under the pressure of age that Jesus is revealed to us traversing the hills of Judea. He was in the strength of His manhood. Jesus once stood in age just where you now stand.* Your circumstances, your cogitations at this period of your life, Jesus has had. He cannot overlook you at this critical period. He sees your dangers. He is acquainted with your temptations. He invites you to follow His example.[42]

---

*This extract is from a letter to a young man.

REFLECTING CHRIST'S IMAGE

But we all, with open face beholding as in a glass the glory of the Lord, are changed into the same image from glory to glory even as by the Spirit of the Lord. 2 Cor. 3:18.

Looking unto Jesus, dwelling upon His virtues, mercies, and purity will create in the soul an utter abhorrence for that which is sinful, and an intense longing and thirsting for righteousness. The more closely we discern Jesus, the more will we see our own defects of character: then confess these things to Jesus and with true contrition of soul cooperate with the divine power, the Holy Spirit, to put these things away.[43]

It is the Holy Spirit, the Comforter, which Jesus said He would send into the world, that changes our character into the image of Christ; and when this is accomplished, we reflect, as in a mirror, the glory of the Lord. That is, the character of the one who thus beholds Christ is so like His, that one looking at him sees Christ's own character shining out as from a mirror. Imperceptibly to ourselves we are changed day by day from our own ways and will into the ways and will of Christ, into the loveliness of His character. Thus we grow up into Christ, and unconsciously reflect His image.[44]

It is not by looking away from Him that we imitate the life of Jesus, but by talking of Him, by dwelling upon His perfections, by seeking to refine the taste and elevate the character, by trying, through faith and love, and by earnest, persevering effort, to approach the perfect Pattern. By having a knowledge of Christ—His words, His habits, and His lessons of instruction—we borrow the virtues of the character we have so closely studied, and become imbued with the spirit we have so much admired. Jesus becomes to us "the chiefest among ten thousand," the One "altogether lovely."[45]

When the soul is brought into close relationship with the great Author of light and truth, impressions are made upon it revealing its true position before God. Then self will die, pride will be laid low, and Christ will draw His own image in deeper lines upon the soul.[46]

IN LOVE WITH CHRIST

For such an high priest became us, who is holy, harmless, undefiled, separate from sinners, and made higher than the heavens. Heb. 7:26.

The character of Christ was one of unexampled excellence, embracing everything pure, true, lovely, and of good report. We have no knowledge of His ever visiting a party of pleasure or a dance hall, and yet He was the perfection of grace and courtly bearing. Christ was no novice; He was distinguished for the high intellectual powers He possessed even in the morning of His life. His youth was not wasted in indolence, neither was it wasted in sensual pleasure, self-indulgence, or frittered away in things of no profit. Not one of His hours from childhood to manhood was misspent, none were misappropriated. . . .

Jesus was sinless and had no dread of the consequences of sin. With this exception His condition was as yours. You have not a difficulty that did not press with equal weight upon Him, not a sorrow that His heart has not experienced. His feelings could be hurt with neglect, with indifference of professed friends, as easily as yours. Is your path thorny? Christ's was so in a tenfold sense. Are you distressed? So was He. How well fitted was Christ to be an example! . . .

The Inspired Record says of Him: "Jesus increased in wisdom and stature, and in favour with God and man." Luke 2:52. As He grew in years He grew in knowledge. He lived temperately; His precious hours were not wasted in dissipating pleasures. He had a truly healthy body and true powers of mind. The physical and mental powers could be expanded and developed as yours or any other youth's. The Word of God was His study, as it should be yours.

Take Jesus as your standard. Imitate His life. Fall in love with His character. Walk as Christ walked. A new spring will be given to your intellectual faculties, a larger scope to your thoughts, when you bring your powers into vigorous contact with eternal things which are intrinsically grand and great.[47]

TO GOD BE THE GLORY

Simon Peter, a servant and an apostle of Jesus Christ, to them that have obtained like precious faith with us through the righteousness of God and our Saviour Jesus Christ. 2 Peter 1:1.

What a grand theme this is for contemplation—the righteousness of God and our Saviour Jesus Christ! Contemplating Christ and His righteousness leaves no room for self-righteousness, for the glorifying of self. In this chapter there is no standstill. There is continual advancement in every stage in the knowledge of Christ. . . .

In God we are to glory. The prophet says, "Thus saith the Lord, Let not the wise man glory in his wisdom, neither let the mighty man glory in his might, let not the rich man glory in his riches: but let him that glorieth glory in this, that he understandeth and knoweth me, that I am the Lord which exercise lovingkindness, judgment, and righteousness, in the earth." Jer. 9:23, 24. . . .

We have been called to the knowledge of Christ, and that is to the knowledge of glory and virtue. It is a knowledge of the perfection of the divine character, manifested to us in Jesus Christ, that opens up to us communion with God. . . . Scarcely can the human mind comprehend what is the breadth and depth and height of the spiritual attainments that can be reached by becoming partakers of the divine nature.[48]

I long to address the young men and women who are so willing to reach only cheap standards. O that the Lord might influence their minds to see what perfection of character is! O that they might know the faith that works by love, and purifies the soul! We are living in days of peril. Christ alone can help us and give us the victory. Christ must be all in all to us; He must dwell in the heart; His life must circulate through us, as the blood circulates through the veins. His Spirit must be a vitalizing power that will cause us to influence others to become Christlike and holy.[49]

If our youth would take heed to the rules laid down in this chapter, and practice them, what an influence they would exert on the side of right![50]

February 24

THE HIGHEST EXERCISE OF OUR POWERS

And this is life eternal, that they might know thee the only true God, and Jesus Christ, whom thou hast sent. John 17:3.

To comprehend and enjoy God is the highest exercise of the powers of man. This may be attained only when our affections are sanctified and ennobled by the grace of Christ. . . . In Christ was the brightness of His Father's glory, the express image of His person. Said our Saviour, "He that hath seen me, hath seen the Father." John 14:9. In Christ is the life of the soul. In the outgoings of our hearts to Him, in our earnest, affectionate yearnings for His excellence, in our eager searching into His glory, we find life. In communion with Him we eat the bread of life.

When we allow objects of minor importance to absorb our attention, to the forgetfulness of Christ, turning away from Him to accept other companionship, we set our feet in a path which leads away from God and from heaven. Christ must be the central object of our affections, and then we shall live in Him, then we shall have His spirit. . . .

What constitutes the brightness of heaven? In what will consist the happiness of the redeemed? Christ is all in all. They will gaze with rapture unutterable upon the Lamb of God. They will pour out their songs of grateful praise and adoration to Him whom they loved and worshiped here. That song they learned and began to sing on earth. They learned to put their trust in Jesus while they were forming characters for heaven. Their hearts were attuned to His will here. Their joy in Christ will be proportioned to the love and trust which they learned to repose in Him here.[51]

God must be ever in our thoughts. We must hold converse with Him while we walk by the way, and while our hands are engaged in labor. In all the purposes and pursuits of life we must inquire, What will the Lord have me to do? How shall I please Him who has given His life a ransom for me? Thus may we walk with God, as did Enoch of old; and ours may be the testimony which he received, that he pleased God.[52]

61

FOLLOW ON TO KNOW THE LORD

Then shall we know, if we follow on to know the Lord: his going forth is prepared as the morning; and he shall come unto us as the rain, as the latter and former rain unto the earth. Hosea 6:3.

We may think we understand something about the truth and the Bible, but the revelation of truth is much beyond anything that our finite vision can comprehend. Christ leads us. When we are caught up to meet Him, and enter through the pearly gates into the city of God, He leads us by the living waters, and all the time He is educating and talking with us about things that He would have opened to our understanding upon the earth if we could have borne it. But we do not walk fast enough. We take too many back steps. We do not advance heavenward; therefore the light that would have come in glorious rays, could not come to us because we were not prepared for it. We take a step back into the world, to the gratifications of earth, and then we take a step toward heaven, and then we take a step back, and then we take a step toward heaven.

If you follow on to know the Lord, you shall know that His goings forth are prepared as the morning. You know the morning light first breaks upon us in a very dim light, and then increases and increases in brightness until the king of the day marches in the heavens in all his glory, in all his beauty. . . . Now if God's glory were to shine first upon us as He wants to let it shine, we could not endure it. . . . That is just why Christ came in humanity. We could not have borne Him if He had come in all His glory. . . .

Now if we will follow on, and if we will not backslide a step or two every now and then, and have to gather up our forces and go on—it is better to gather up our forces than to remain in a backslidden condition and keep on backsliding, but I wish that we did not lose so much time and so much strength—we may know more of God and more of heaven, and become better acquainted with the precious truth and the rich blessings that God has for us if we will only comprehend them. He has prepared wonderful things for us.[53]

THE GIRDLE OF GLADNESS

Thou hast turned for me my mourning into dancing: thou hast put off my sackcloth, and girded me with gladness. Ps. 30:11.

Many who are seeking for happiness will be disappointed in their hopes, because they seek it amiss. True happiness is not to be found in selfish gratification, but in the path of duty. God desires man to be happy, and for this reason He gave him the precepts of His law, that in obeying these he might have joy at home and abroad. While he stands in his moral integrity, true to principle, having the control of all his powers, he cannot be miserable. With its tendrils entwined about God, the soul will flourish amid unbelief and depravity. But many who are constantly looking forward for happiness fail to receive it, because, by neglecting to discharge the little duties and observe the little courtesies of life, they violate the principles upon which happiness depends.[54]

The currents of spiritual life must not become stagnant. The water of the living fountain should be in us, a well of water springing up into everlasting life, and sweeping away the selfishness of the natural heart. . . . Many build up barriers between themselves and Jesus so that His love cannot flow into their hearts, and then they complain that they do not see the Sun of Righteousness. Let them forget self and live for Jesus, and the light of Heaven will bring gladness to their souls. . . .

The fact that Jesus died to bring happiness and heaven within our reach should be a theme for constant gratitude. The beauty spread before us in God's created works, as an expression of His love, should bring gladness to our hearts. We open to ourselves the floodgates of woe or joy. If we permit our thoughts to be engrossed with the troubles and trifles of earth, our hearts will be filled with unbelief, gloom, and foreboding. If we set our affections on things above, the voice of Jesus will speak peace to our souls; murmurings will cease; vexing thoughts will be lost in praise to our Redeemer. Those who dwell upon God's great mercies, and are not unmindful of His lesser gifts, will put on the girdle of gladness, and make melody in their hearts to the Lord.[55]

LIFE WITH A PURPOSE

Happy is he that hath the God of Jacob for his help, whose hope is in the Lord his God. Ps. 146:5.

Your only safety and happiness are in making Christ your constant counselor. You can be happy in Him if you had not another friend in the wide world. Your feelings of unrest and homesickness or loneliness may be for your good. Your heavenly Father means to teach you to find in Him the friendship and love and consolation that will satisfy your most earnest hopes and desires. . . .

Do not be overanxious about anything. Go quietly about your duty which the day brings you. Do the best you can; ask God to be your helper. . . . Feel every day, "I am doing my work for God. I am not living for myself, to glorify myself, but to glorify God." Oh, trust in Jesus and not in your own heart! Cast your burden and yourself upon Him. If you feel no joy, no consolation, do not be discouraged. Hope and believe. You may have a precious experience in the things of God. Wrestle with your discouragements and doubts until you gain the victory over them in Jesus' name. Do not encourage grief, despondency, and darkness. . . . Repose in the broad, sure promises of God. Rest in these promises, without a doubt.[56]

I have seen that those who live for a purpose, seeking to benefit and bless their fellow men and to honor and glorify their Redeemer, are the truly happy ones on the earth, while the man who is restless, discontented, and seeking this and testing that, hoping to find happiness, is always complaining of disappointment. He is always in want, never satisfied, because he lives for himself alone. Let it be your aim to do good, to act your part in life faithfully.[57]

Find time to comfort some other heart, to bless with a kind, cheering word someone who is battling with temptation and maybe with affliction. In thus blessing another with cheering, hopeful words, pointing him to the Burden Bearer, you may unexpectedly find peace, happiness, and consolation yourself.[58]

JOY UNSPEAKABLE AND FULL OF GLORY

Whom having not seen, ye love; in whom, though now ye see him not, yet believing, ye rejoice with joy unspeakable and full of glory. 1 Peter 1:8.

Christ has said: "If any man thirst, let him come unto me, and drink." John 7:37. Have you exhausted the fountain?—No; for it is inexhaustible. Just as soon as you feel your need, you may drink, and drink again. The fountain is always full. And when you have once drunk of that fountain, you will not be seeking to quench your thirst from the broken cisterns of this world; you will not be studying how you can find the most pleasure, amusement, fun, and frolic. No; because you have been drinking from the stream which makes glad the city of God. Then your joy will be full.[59]

Why should not the religion of Christ be represented as it really is, as full of attractiveness and power? Why should we not present before the world the loveliness of Christ? Why do we not show that we have a living Saviour, one who can walk with us in the darkness as well as in the light, and that we can trust in Him? . . .

We have seen clouds interpose between us and the sun, but we did not mourn and clothe ourselves in sackcloth for fear that we should never see the sun again. We manifested no anxiety about it, but waited as cheerfully as possible until the cloud passed away and revealed the sun. Just so in our trials and temptations. Clouds may seem to shut from us the bright beams of the Sun of Righteousness; but we know that the face of our Redeemer is not forever hidden. He is looking upon us with love and tender compassion. Let us not cast away our confidence, which hath great recompense of reward, but when clouds hang over the soul, let us keep our eyes fixed where we can see the Sun of Righteousness, and rejoice that we have a living Saviour. Think how beautiful was the light which we enjoyed, keep the mind stayed on Jesus, and the light will again shine upon us, and dismal thoughts will flee. We shall have joy in Christ, and shall go singing on our way to Mount Zion.[60]

CHRIST, THE LADDER TO HEAVEN

And he dreamed, and behold a ladder set up on the earth, and the top of it reached to heaven: and behold the angels of God ascending and descending on it. Gen. 28:12.

Let us consider this ladder which was presented to Jacob. . . . The sin of Adam cut off all intercourse between heaven and earth. Up to the moment of man's transgression of God's law there had been free communion between earth and heaven. They were connected by a path which Deity could traverse. But the transgression of God's law broke up this path and man was separated from God. . . .

Every link which bound earth to heaven and man to the infinite God seemed broken. Man might look to heaven, but how could he attain it? But joy to the world! The Son of God, the Sinless One, the One perfect in obedience, becomes the channel through which the lost communion may be renewed, the way through which the lost paradise may be regained. Through Christ, man's substitute and surety, man may keep the commandments of God. He may return to his allegiance and God will accept him. Christ is the ladder. "By me if any man enter in, he shall be saved, and shall go in and out and find pasture." John 10:9. . . .

The ladder is the medium of communication between God and man. Through the mystic ladder the gospel was preached to Jacob. As the ladder stretched from earth, reaching to the highest heavens, and the glory of God was seen above the ladder, so Christ in His divine nature reached immensity and was one with the Father. As the ladder, though its top penetrated into heaven, had its base upon the earth, so Christ, though God, clothed His divinity with humanity and was in the world "found in fashion as a man" (Phil. 2:8). The ladder would be useless if it rested not on the earth or if it reached not to the heavens.

God appeared in glory above the ladder, looking down with compassion on erring, sinful Jacob. . . . It is through Christ that the Father beholds sinful man. . . . The broken links have been repaired. A highway has been thrown up along which the weary and heavy laden may pass. They may enter heaven and find rest.[1]

THE PRECIOUS TREASURE OF FAITH

Grace and peace be multiplied unto you through the knowledge of God, and of Jesus our Lord, according as his divine power hath given unto us all things that pertain unto life and godliness, through the knowledge of him that hath called us to glory and virtue. 2 Peter 1:2, 3.

"Simon Peter, a servant and an apostle of Jesus Christ, to them that have obtained like precious faith with us through the righteousness of God and our Saviour Jesus Christ: . . . Whereby are given unto us exceeding great and precious promises: that by these ye might be partakers of the divine nature, having escaped the corruption that is in the world through lust." 2 Peter 1:1-4.

"Like precious faith" . . . is a genuine faith. It is not a fruitless faith. True, saving faith is a precious treasure of inestimable value. It is not superficial. The just lives by faith a truly spiritual, Christlike life. It is through faith that the steps are taken one at a time up the ladder of progress. Faith must be cultivated. It unites the human with the divine nature.

The life of obedience to all of God's commandments is a life of progression, a life of constant advancement. As the elect, precious, have increased understanding of the mediatorial work of Jesus Christ, they see and grasp the rich promises that come through the righteousness of Christ. The more they receive of the divine grace the more they work on the plan of addition.

"Grace and peace" will be multiplied "through the knowledge of God and of Jesus our Lord." Here is the Source of all spiritual power, and faith must be in constant exercise, for all spiritual life is from Christ. Knowledge of God inspires faith in Him as the only channel to convey heaven's blessing to the soul, elevating, ennobling, refining the soul, as—through the knowledge of God—it is brought up to the high attainment of glory and virtue. "According as his divine power hath given unto us all things that pertain unto life and godliness, through the knowledge of him that hath called us to glory and virtue." [2]

VIRTUE AND KNOWLEDGE

And beside this, giving all diligence, add to your faith virtue; and to virtue knowledge. 2 Peter 1:5.

"*Add* to your faith virtue." There is no promise given to the one who is retrograding. The apostle, in his testimony, is aiming to excite the believers to advancement in grace and holiness. They already profess to be living the truth, they have a knowledge of the precious faith, they have been made partakers of the divine nature. But if they stop here they will lose the grace they have received. . . .

Without giving "all diligence" to make step after step upward to God above the ladder, there is no gaining ground in peace and grace and the work of holiness. "Strive," said Jesus, "to enter in at the strait gate." Luke 13:24. The way of the believer is marked out by God above the ladder. All his endeavors will be in vain if he has not virtue of character, a practical knowledge of Christ through obedience to all His requirements. Those who have faith must be careful to show their faith by their works. . . .

"Add to your faith virtue; and to virtue knowledge"—knowledge of the truth as it is in Jesus, knowledge of the great plan of salvation. To be ignorant of God's commandments and laws will not excuse a soul. He will not dare to plead around the throne of God, "I did not know the truth. I was ignorant." The Lord has given His Word to be our guide, our instructor, and with this heavenly enlightening there is no excuse for ignorance. . . .

Truth is an active, working principle, molding heart and life so that there is a constant upward movement. . . . In every step of climbing, the will is obtaining a new spring of action. The moral tone is becoming more like the mind and character of Christ. The progressive Christian has grace and love which passes knowledge, for divine insight into the character of Christ takes a deep hold upon his affections. The glory of God revealed above the ladder can only be appreciated by the progressive climber, who is ever attracted higher, to nobler aims which Christ reveals. All the faculties of mind and body must be enlisted.[3]

"AND TO KNOWLEDGE TEMPERANCE"

And to knowledge temperance; and to temperance patience; and to patience godliness. 2 Peter 1:6.

To knowledge must be added temperance. "Know ye not that they which run in a race run all, but one receiveth the prize? So run, that ye may obtain. And every man that striveth for the mastery is temperate in all things. Now they do it to obtain a corruptible crown; but we an incorruptible. I therefore so run, not as uncertainly; so fight I, not as one that beateth the air: but I keep under my body, and bring it into subjection." 1 Cor. 9:24-27.

Athletes cheerfully comply with the conditions in order to be trained for the highest taxation of their physical strength. They do not indulge appetite, but put a constant restraint upon themselves, refraining from food which would weaken or lessen the full power of any of their organs. Yet they fight "as one that beateth the air," while Christians are in a real contest. Combatants in the games seek for mere perishable laurels. Christians have before them a glorious crown of immortality, incorruptible. And in this heavenly race there is plenty of room for all to obtain the prize. Not one will fail if he runs well, if he does according to the light which shines upon him, exercising his abilities which, to the best of his knowledge, he has kept in a healthful condition. . . .

Any habit or practice which will weaken the nerve and brain power or the physical strength disqualifies for the exercise of the next grace which comes in after temperance—patience. . . .

A man who is intemperate, who uses stimulating indulgences—beer, wine, strong drinks, tea and coffee, opium, tobacco, or any of these substances that are deleterious to health—cannot be a patient man. So temperance is a round of the ladder upon which we must plant our feet before we can add the grace of patience. In food, in raiment, in work, in regular hours, in healthful exercise, we must be regulated by the knowledge which it is our duty to obtain that we may, through earnest endeavor, place ourselves in right relation to life and health.[4]

THE PERFECT WORK OF PATIENCE

Knowing this, that the trying of your faith worketh patience. But let patience have her perfect work, that ye may be perfect and entire, wanting nothing. James 1:3, 4.

The apostle says we succeed in the grace of temperance that we may add patience. Patience under trials will keep us from saying and doing those things which will injure our own souls and injure those with whom we associate. Let your trials be what they will, nothing can seriously injure you if you exercise patience, if you are calm and unexcited when in trying positions. . . .

We can see the wisdom of Peter in placing temperance to be added to knowledge before patience. This is one strong reason for overcoming the appetite for all stimulants, for as the nerves become excited under the influence of these irritating substances, how many and grievous are the evils that are done! . . .

There is necessity for the Christian adding patience to temperance. There will need to be firm principle and fixedness of purpose not to offend in word or action either our own conscience or the feelings of others. There must be a rising above the customs of the world in order to bear reproach, disappointment, losses and crosses without one murmur, but with uncomplaining dignity. . . . A petulant, ill-natured man or woman really knows not what it is to be happy. Every cup which he puts to his lips seems to be bitter as wormwood and his path seems strewn with rough stones, with briars and thorns; but he must add to temperance patience and he will not see or feel slights.

Patience must have its perfect work or we cannot be perfect and entire, wanting nothing. Troubles and afflictions are appointed unto us, and shall we bear them all patiently or shall we make everything bitter by our complaining? The gold is put into the furnace that the dross may be removed. Shall we, then, not be patient under the eye of the refiner? We must refuse to sink into a sad and disconsolate state of mind, but show calm trust in God, counting it all joy when we are permitted to endure trials for Christ's sake.[5]

"TO PATIENCE GODLINESS"

For bodily exercise profiteth little: but godliness is profitable unto all things, having promise of the life that now is, and of that which is to come. 1 Tim. 4:8.

Having added patience to temperance, we are then to ascend the ladder of progress and add to patience godliness. This is the very outgrowth of patience. Said the apostle Paul, "We glory in tribulations also: knowing that tribulation worketh patience; and patience, experience; and experience, hope." . . . Rom. 5:3, 4.

Here, then, is an advance grace, godliness, which is to have the spirit and the likeness of the character of Jesus Christ. To raise us to His divine ideal is the one end of all the dealings of God with us, and of the whole plan of salvation. . . . The corruption of the world is seeking to steal our senses, all the unholy influences on every side are working to hold us to a low, earthly level—blinding our sensibilities, degrading our desires, enfeebling our conscience and crippling our religious faculties by urging us to give sway to the lower nature. . . .

To draw us away from all this is the precious ladder. The eye is attracted to God above the ladder. The invitation comes from the glory above it, Come up higher. The heart is attracted. Steps are taken in advance, one after another. Higher and still higher we ascend. At every step the attraction becomes greater. Higher, holier ambitions take possession of the soul. The guilt of the past life is left behind. We dare not look down the ladder at those things which long poisoned the springs of true happiness and kindled remorse, weakened and depraved the will, and repressed every better impulse. . . .

The aim of God's Word is to inspire hope, to lead us to . . . climb step by step heavenward, with ever-increasing vigor. . . . We attain a likeness of character to God by the imparting of His own grace. . . . As wax takes the counterpart of the seal, so the soul receives and retains the moral image of God. We become filled and transfigured by His brightness, as the cloud—dark in itself—when filled with the light is turned to stainless whiteness.[6]

THE VIRTUE OF BROTHERLY KINDNESS

And to godliness brotherly kindness; and to brotherly kindness charity. 2 Peter 1:7.

The Word of God enjoins upon every one of His children: "Be ye all of one mind, having compassion one of another, love as brethren, be pitiful, be courteous." 1 Peter 3:8. Now unless godliness was added to patience man would not show that brotherly kindness. In His mission to our world, Christ has shown man the graces of the Spirit of God which, when accepted, fashion and mold the entire man, externally as well as internally, by abasing his pride and leading him not to esteem himself highly but to esteem his brother as precious in the sight of God because Christ paid an infinite price for his soul. When man is valued as God's property then we will be kind, amiable, and condescending toward him.

The religion of Jesus Christ is a system of the true heavenly politeness and leads to a practical exhibition of habitual tenderness of feeling, kindness of deportment. He who possesses godliness will also add this grace, taking a step higher on the ladder. The higher he mounts the ladder, the more of the grace of God is revealed in his life, his sentiments, his principles. He is learning, ever learning the terms of his acceptance with God, and the only way to obtain an inheritance in the heavens is to become like Christ in character. The whole scheme of mercy is to soften down what is harsh in temper, and refine whatever is rugged in the deportment. The internal change reveals itself in the external actions. The graces of the Spirit of God work with hidden power in the transformation of character. The religion of Christ never will reveal a sour, coarse, and uncourteous action. Courtesy is a Bible virtue. The virtue of this grace of brotherly kindness characterized the life of Christ. Never was such courtesy exhibited upon the earth as Christ revealed, and we cannot overestimate its value. . . .

Growing in grace is an earnest working out of what God works in. It is an earnest of future glory, the working out here upon the earth of the spirit that is cherished in heaven.[7]

CHARITY THE TOPMOST ROUND

And above all these things put on charity, which is the bond of perfectness. Col. 3:14.

The next step in the ladder is charity. Add "to brotherly kindness charity," which is love. Love to God and love to our neighbor constitute the whole duty of man. Without brotherly kindness we cannot exhibit the grace of love to God or to our fellow men.

This last step in the ladder gives to the will a new spring of action. Christ offers a love that passeth knowledge. This love is not something kept apart from our life, but it takes hold of the entire being. The heaven to which the Christian is climbing will be attained only by those who have this crowning grace. This is the new affection which pervades the soul. The old is left behind. Love is the great controlling power. When love leads, all the faculties of mind and spirit are enlisted. Love to God and love to man will give the clear title to heaven.

No one can love God supremely and transgress one of His commandments. The heart softened and subdued with the beauty of Christ's character and bridled by the pure and lofty rules which He has given us will put into practice what it has learned of love, and will follow Jesus forthwith in humble obedience. The living power of faith will reveal itself in loving acts.

What evidence have we that we have the pure love, without alloy? God has erected a standard—His commandments. "He that hath my commandments, and keepeth them, he it is that loveth me." John 14:21. The words of God must have an abiding place in our hearts.

We are to love our brethren as Christ has loved us. We are to be patient and kind, and yet there is something lacking—we must love. Christ tells us that we must forgive the erring even seventy times seven. . . . When there is much forgiven, the heart loves much. Love is a tender plant. It needs to be constantly cultured or it will wither and die.

All these graces we must have. We must climb the whole length of the ladder.[8]

MAKE YOUR CALLING
AND ELECTION SURE

For if these things be in you, and abound, they make you that ye shall neither be barren nor unfruitful in the knowledge of our Lord Jesus Christ. 2 Peter 1:8.

The only safety for the Christian is to be unwearied in his efforts to live on the plan of addition. The apostle shows the advantages to be gained in thus doing. For those who add grace to grace, God will work on the plan of multiplication, so that the graces will be in and abound in the religious life and he will not "be barren nor unfruitful. . . ." Those abounding in the Christian graces will be zealous, lively, vigorous in all practical Christianity, and will practice righteousness—just as the branch abiding in the vine will produce the same fruit that the vine bears. . . .

He who does not climb the ladder of progress and add grace to grace "is blind, and cannot see afar off." He fails to discern that without taking these successive steps in ascending the ladder round after round, in growing in grace and the knowledge of our Lord Jesus Christ, he is not placing himself in a position where the light of God above the ladder is reflected upon him. As he does not add grace to grace, he has forgotten the claims of God upon him, and that he was to receive the forgiveness of sins through obedience to the requirements of God. . . .

"Wherefore the rather, brethren, give diligence to make your calling and election sure." 2 Peter 1:10. We need not have a supposed hope, but an assurance. To make our calling and election sure is to follow the Bible plan to closely examine ourselves, to make strict inquiry whether we are indeed converted, whether our minds are drawn out after God and heavenly things, our wills renewed, our whole souls changed. To make our calling and election sure requires far greater diligence than many are giving to this important matter. "For if ye do these things"—live on the plan of addition, growing in grace and the knowledge of our Lord Jesus Christ—ye shall mount up, step by step, the ladder Jacob saw, and "ye shall never fall."[9]

HOLDING FAST TO CHRIST, THE LADDER

For so an entrance shall be ministered unto you abundantly into the everlasting kingdom of our Lord and Saviour Jesus Christ. 2 Peter 1:11.

We ascend to heaven by climbing the ladder—the whole height of Christ's work—step by step. There must be a holding fast to Christ, a climbing up by the merits of Christ. To let go is to cease to climb, is to fall, to perish. We are to mount by the Mediator and all the while to keep hold on the Mediator, ascending by successive steps, round above round, stretching the hand from one round to the next above. . . . There is fearful peril in relaxing our efforts in spiritual diligence for a moment, for we are hanging, as it were, between heaven and earth.

We must keep the eye directed upward to God above the ladder. The question with men and women gazing heavenward is, How can I obtain the mansions for the blessed? It is by being a partaker of the divine nature. It is by escaping the "corruption that is in the world through lust." It is by entering into the holiest by the blood of Jesus, laying hold of the hope set before you in the gospel. It is by fastening yourself to Christ and straining every nerve to leave the world behind. . . . It is by being in Christ and yet led by Christ; by believing and working, . . . holding onto Christ and constantly mounting upward toward God. . . .

We point you to the mansions Christ is preparing for all those who love Him. We point you to that city that hath foundations, whose builder and maker is God. We show you its massive walls, with the twelve foundations, and tell you that these walls must be scaled. You look discouraged at the magnitude of the work before you. We point you to the ladder set up on earth, reaching to the city of God. Plant your feet on the ladder. Forsake your sins. Climb step by step and you will reach God above the ladder, and the Holy City of God. . . .

When the successive steps have all been mounted, when the graces have been added one after another, the crowning grace is the perfect love of God—supreme love to God and love to our fellow men. And then the abundant entrance into the kingdom of God.[10]

THE PRIVILEGE OF ASSURANCE

And hereby we know that we are of the truth, and shall assure our hearts before him. 1 John 3:19.

I would impress upon our young men and young women the necessity of making their calling and election sure. I would beseech you to do no haphazard or uncertain work where your eternal interests are involved. By so doing you lose happiness, peace, comfort, and hope in this life, and you lose also your immortal inheritance.

My young friends, you are judgment bound, and through the grace of Christ you may render obedience to the commands of God, and daily gain fortitude and strength of character, so that you need not fail or be discouraged. Divine grace has been abundantly provided for every soul, so that each one may engage in the conflict and come off victorious. Do not become sluggish; do not flatter yourselves that you may be saved in walking in accordance with the natural traits of your character—that you may drift with the current of the world, and indulge and please self, and yet be able to withstand the forces of evil in a time of crisis, and come off victorious when the battle waxes hot. . . . You must learn every day to obey the orders of the Captain of the Lord's host.

My young friends, do you pray? Are you educating yourselves to offer petitions for pure thoughts, for holy aspirations, for a pure heart and clean hands? Are you educating your lips to sing the praises of God, and are you seeking to do the will of God? This is the kind of education that will be of the greatest value to you; for it will aid you in the formation of Christlike character.[11]

Do not settle down in Satan's easy chair, and say that there is no use, you cannot cease to sin, that there is no power in you to overcome. There is no power in you apart from Christ, but it is your privilege to have Christ abiding in your heart by faith, and He can overcome sin in you, when you cooperate with His efforts. . . . You may be living epistles, known and read of all men. You are not to be a dead letter, but a living one, testifying to the world that Jesus is able to save.[12]

CHOSEN OF GOD

Thou whom I have taken from the ends of the earth, and called thee from the chief men thereof, and said unto thee, Thou art my servant; I have chosen thee, and not cast thee away. Isa. 41:9.

Many have confused ideas as to what constitutes faith, and they live altogether below their privileges. They confuse feeling and faith, and are continually distressed and perplexed in mind; for Satan takes all possible advantage of their ignorance and inexperience. . . . We are to accept of Christ as our personal Saviour, or we shall fail in our attempt to be overcomers. It will not answer for us to hold ourselves aloof from Him, to believe that our friend or our neighbor may have Him for a personal Saviour, but that we may not experience His pardoning love. We are to believe that we are chosen of God, to be saved by the exercise of faith, through the grace of Christ and the work of the Holy Spirit; and we are to praise and glorify God for such a marvelous manifestation of His unmerited favor. It is the love of God that draws the soul to Christ, to be graciously received, and presented to the Father. Through the work of the Spirit the divine relationship between God and the sinner is renewed. The Father says: "I will be to them a God, and they shall be to me a people. I will exercise forgiving love toward them, and bestow upon them my joy. They shall be to me a peculiar treasure; for this people whom I have formed for myself shall show forth my praise."

The Father sets His love upon His elect people who live in the midst of men. These are the people whom Christ has redeemed by the price of His own blood; and because they respond to the drawing of Christ, through the sovereign mercy of God, they are elected to be saved as His obedient children. Upon them is manifested the free grace of God, the love wherewith He hath loved them. Everyone who will humble himself as a little child, who will receive and obey the word of God with a child's simplicity, will be among the elect of God.[13]

You can prove yourself elected of Christ by being faithful, you can prove yourself the chosen of Christ by abiding in the vine.[14]

FULLNESS OF CHRIST'S RANSOM

According as he hath chosen us in him before the foundation of the world, that we should be holy and without blame before him in love: having predestinated us unto the adoption of children by Jesus Christ to himself, according to the good pleasure of his will. Eph. 1:4, 5.

In the council of heaven, provision was made that men, though transgressors, should not perish in their disobedience, but, through faith in Christ as their substitute and surety, might become the elect of God. . . . God wills that all men should be saved; for ample provision has been made, in giving His only begotten Son to pay man's ransom. Those who perish will perish because they refuse to be adopted as children of God through Christ Jesus. The pride of man hinders him from accepting the provisions of salvation. But human merit will not admit a soul into the presence of God. That which will make a man acceptable to God is the imparted grace of Christ through faith in His name. No dependence can be placed in works or in happy flights of feelings as evidence that men are chosen of God; for the elect are chosen through Christ.

Jesus says, "Him that cometh unto me I will in no wise cast out." John 6:37. When the repenting sinner comes to Christ, conscious of his guilt and unworthiness, realizing that he is deserving of punishment, but relying on the mercy and love of Christ, he will not be turned away. The pardoning love of God is appropriated, and joyful gratitude springs up in his heart for the infinite compassion and love of his Saviour. That provision was made for him in the councils of heaven before the foundation of the world, that Christ should take upon Himself the penalty of man's transgression and impute to him His righteousness, overwhelms him with amazement.[15]

The Father laid our sins where none but His own eyes could discern them. And as He hid His face from the innocence of Christ, so He will hide His eyes from the guilt of the believing sinner, because of the righteousness imputed to him. The righteousness of Christ laid upon us will draw upon us the most precious blessings in this life, and will bestow upon us everlasting life in the kingdom of God.[16]

GOD CALLS FOR OUR BEST AFFECTIONS

No man can serve two masters: for either he will hate the one, and love the other; or else he will hold to the one, and despise the other. Ye cannot serve God and mammon. Matt. 6:24.

Many are on the enchanted ground of the enemy. Things of the least importance—foolish social parties, singing, jesting, joking—engross their minds and they serve God with a divided heart. . . . The declaration of Christ, "No man can serve two masters," is unheeded.[17]

One of the most marked features of the earth's inhabitants in the days of Noah was their intense worldliness. They made eating and drinking, buying and selling, marrying and giving in marriage, the supreme objects of life. It is not sinful, but the fulfillment of a duty, to eat and drink, if that which is lawful is not carried to excess. . . . God Himself instituted marriage when He gave Eve to Adam. All God's laws are marvelously adapted to meet the nature of man. The sin of the antediluvians was in perverting that which in itself was lawful. They corrupted God's gifts by using them to minister to their selfish desires. . . .

Excessive love and devotion to that which in itself is lawful, proves the ruination of thousands upon thousands of souls. To matters of minor importance is often given the strength of intellect that should be wholly devoted to God. We need always to be guarded against carrying to excess that which, rightly used, is lawful. Many, many souls are lost by engaging in those things which, properly managed, are harmless, but which, perverted and misapplied, become sinful and demoralizing.[18]

If we are constantly thinking of and struggling for the things that pertain to this life, we cannot keep our thoughts fixed on the things of heaven. Satan is seeking to lead our minds away from God, and to center them on the fashions, the customs, and the demands of the world, which bring disease and death. . . .

In this world we are to obtain a fitness for the higher world. God has left a trust with us, and He expects us to use all our faculties in helping and blessing our fellow men. He calls for our best affections, our highest powers.[19]

WHICH CAPTAIN?

For this God is our God for ever and ever; he will be our guide even unto death. Ps. 48:14.

We are all under one or the other of two great captains. One, the Creator of man and of the world, is the greatest of all. All owe Him the allegiance of their whole being, the devotion of their entire affection. If the mind is given to His control, and if God has the molding and developing of the powers of the mind, new moral power will be received daily from the Source of all wisdom and all strength. Moral blessings and divine beauties will reward the efforts of everyone whose mind is heaven bent. We may grasp revelations—heavenly beauties—that lie beyond the short vision of the worldling, that outshine the imagination of the greatest mind. . . .

Satan is the leader of the worldly. . . . His highest aim is to gather under his banner the majority of the world, that numbers may stand against the power of righteousness and eternal truth. Talent and ability given of God to be devoted to His service, are laid at the feet of the great rebel of God's government. . . .

While the worldly wise is skimming along the surface, grasping the things of sight and sense, the one who fears and reveres God is reaching into eternity, penetrating the deepest recesses and gathering the knowledge and riches that are as enduring as eternity. Justice, honor, love, and truth are the attributes of God's throne. They are the principles of His government. . . . These are jewels to be sought after and cherished for time and for eternity. . . .

To walk the world a pure man of untarnished morals, bearing the sacred principles of truth in your heart, its influence seen in the acts of your life; to live uncorrupted by the baseness, falsity, and dishonesty of a world which must soon be purified of its moral corruption by the fires of God's retributive justice, is to be a man whose record is immortalized in heaven, honored among the pure angels who weigh and appreciate moral worth. This is what it is to be a man of God.[20]

THE CAUSE OF ALL OUR WOES

But exhort one another daily, while it is called To day; lest any of you be hardened through the deceitfulness of sin. Heb. 3:13.

Mark the words "deceitfulness of sin." Satan always presents his temptations under the guise of goodness. Beware that you yield not to them. One violation of straightforward truthfulness prepares the way for the second violation, and wrongs are repeated, until the heart of unbelief becomes hardened, and the conscience loses its sensitiveness.[21]

Let none flatter themselves that the sins of their youth can easily be given up by and by. This is not so. Every sin cherished weakens the character and strengthens the habit; and physical, mental, and moral depravity result. You may repent of the wrong you have done, and set your feet in right paths; but the mold of your mind and your familiarity with evil will make it difficult for you to distinguish between right and wrong. Through the wrong habits you have formed Satan will assail you again and again.[22]

Many . . . look upon sin as a little thing. . . . Many take counsel of their own wishes and desires and follow their inclinations and finally conclude that sin is not so very offensive, not so terrible and dreadful in the sight of God. Sin that may appear little, that may be termed little by the blunted conscience, is so grievous a thing in the sight of God that nothing but the blood of God's own Son could wash it away. This fact places the true estimate upon sin. God will never tarnish His glory to come to our ideas and views. We shall certainly have to come to His. Just in proportion to the excellence of God is the heinous character of sin. . . .

God seeks our real happiness. If anything lies in the way of this, He sees it must first be removed. He will thwart our purposes and disappoint our expectations and bring us through disappointments and trials to reveal to us ourselves as we are. . . . Sin is the cause of all our woes. If we would have true peace and happiness of mind, sin must be removed.[23]

IN SELF-DISTRUST WE CRY TO GOD

I acknowledged my sin unto thee, and mine iniquity have I not hid. I said, I will confess my transgressions unto the Lord; and thou forgavest the iniquity of my sin. Ps. 32:5.

David often triumphed in God, and yet he dwelt much upon his own unworthiness and sinfulness. His conscience was not asleep or dead. "My sin," he cried, "is ever before me." Ps. 51:3. He did not flatter himself that sin was a matter with which he had nothing to do, and that should not concern him. As he saw the depths of deceit in his heart, he . . . prayed that God would . . . cleanse him from secret faults.

It is not safe for us to close our eyes and harden our consciences, that we shall not see or realize our sins.[24]

The humble heart will not think confession beneath him. He will not feel it a disgrace to confess if he has in any way, even in thought, hurt his brother or hindered God's work through him.[25]

Sins not repented of are sins not forgiven. Those who think themselves forgiven for sins of which they have never felt the sinfulness and over which they have never felt contrition of soul, only deceive themselves. . . . Our strength lies in our conscious weakness. . . . In self-distrust we cry to God for help, and work out our salvation with fear and trembling. Casting away all confidence in the arm of flesh, we cling with firm grasp to Jesus. . . .

Heaven will never be reached by an easy-going people merely professing to be Christians. God calls for thorough work on the part of every one of His followers. . . .

By resolute self-denial,
By constant watchfulness,
By earnest prayer,
By the diligent use of every means of grace,
And by the help of Jesus Christ our Redeemer,
  We shall come off victorious.
The rest in heaven is for the weary,
The crown for the brows of the warriors.[26]

FULL PROVISION FOR PARDON

The Lord is nigh unto them that are of a broken heart; and saveth such as be of a contrite spirit. Ps. 34:18.

Do not think that because you have made mistakes you must always be under condemnation, for this is not necessary. . . .

Shall we look at our sins, and begin to mourn, and say, I have done wrong, and I cannot come to God with any degree of confidence? Does not the Bible say, "If we confess our sins, he is faithful and just to forgive us our sins, and to cleanse us from all unrighteousness"? 1 John 1:9. It is a proper thing for us to have a realization of the terrible character of sin. It was sin that caused Christ to suffer ignominious death on Calvary. But while we should understand that sin is a terrible thing, yet we should not listen to the voice of our adversary, who says, "You have sinned, and you have no right to claim the promises of God." You should say to the adversary, "It is written, 'If any man sin, we have an advocate with the Father, Jesus Christ the righteous' (1 John 2:1)." . . .

The psalmist says, "I acknowledged my sin unto thee, and mine iniquity have I not hid. I said, I will confess my transgressions unto the Lord; and thou forgavest the iniquity of my sin." Ps. 32:5. . . . This is the kind of experience that we should have.[27]

David was pardoned of his transgression because he humbled his heart before God in repentance and contrition of soul, and believed that God's promise to forgive would be fulfilled. He confessed his sin, repented, and was reconverted. In the rapture of the assurance of forgiveness, he exclaimed, "Blessed is he whose transgression is forgiven, whose sin is covered. Blessed is the man unto whom the Lord imputeth not iniquity, and in whose spirit there is no guile." Ps. 32:1, 2. The blessing comes because of pardon; pardon comes through faith that the sin, confessed and repented of, is borne by the great Sin Bearer. Thus from Christ cometh all our blessings. His death is an atoning sacrifice for our sins. He is the great Medium through whom we receive the mercy and favor of God.[28]

BUILDING FOR ETERNITY

Therefore whosoever heareth these sayings of mine, and doeth them, I will liken him unto a wise man, which built his house upon a rock: and the rain descended, and the floods came, and the winds blew, and beat upon that house; and it fell not: for it was founded upon a rock. Matt. 7:24, 25.

The formation of character is the work of a lifetime, and it is for eternity. If all could realize this, if they would awake to the thought that we are individually deciding our own destiny for eternal life or eternal ruin, what a change would take place! How differently would this probationary time be occupied! . . .

In character building it is of the greatest importance that we dig deep, removing all the rubbish and building on the immovable, solid Rock, Christ Jesus. The foundation firmly laid, we need wisdom to know how to build. . . . In His law God has given us a pattern, and it is after this pattern that we are to build. The law is the great standard of righteousness. It represents the character of God, and is the test of our loyalty to His government.

Thoroughness is necessary to success in character building. There must be an earnest desire to carry out the plans of the Master Builder. The timbers used must be solid; no careless, unreliable work can be accepted; it would ruin the building. The whole being is to be put into this work. It demands strength and energy; there is no reserve to be wasted in unimportant matters. There must be determined human force put into the work, in cooperation with the divine Worker. There must be earnest, persevering effort to break away from the customs and maxims and associations of the world. Deep thought, earnest purpose, steadfast integrity, are essential. There must be no idleness. Life is a sacred trust; and every moment should be wisely improved. . . .

Remember that you are building for eternity. See that your foundation is sure; then build firmly, and with persistent effort, but in gentleness, meekness, and love. So shall your house stand unshaken, not only when the storms of temptation come but when the overwhelming flood of God's wrath shall sweep over the world.[29]

GIVE NO PLACE TO TEMPTATION

In the fear of the Lord is strong confidence: and his children shall have a place of refuge. Prov. 14:26.

God requires that we confess our sins and humble our hearts before Him; but at the same time we should have confidence in Him as a tender Father, who will not forsake those who put their trust in Him. We do not realize how many of us walk by sight and not by faith. We believe the things that are seen, but do not appreciate the precious promises given us in His Word. And yet we cannot dishonor God more decidedly than by showing that we distrust what He says.[30]

Do not for a moment acknowledge Satan's temptations as being in harmony with your own mind. Turn from them as you would from the adversary himself. Satan's work is to discourage the soul. Christ's work is to inspire the heart with faith and hope. Satan seeks to unsettle our confidence. He tells us that our hopes are built upon false premises, rather than upon the sure, immutable word of Him who cannot lie.[31]

When he [Satan] suggests doubts as to whether we are really the people whom God is leading, whom by tests and provings He is preparing to stand in the great day, be ready to meet his insinuations by presenting the clear evidence from the Word of God that this is the remnant people who are keeping the commandments of God and the faith of Jesus.[32]

Let us trust fully, humbly, unselfishly, in God. We are His little children, and thus He deals with us. When we draw near to Him, He mercifully preserves us from the assaults of the enemy. Never will He betray one who trusts in Him as a child trusts in its parents. He sees the humble, trusting souls drawing near to Him, and in pity and love He draws near to them, and lifts up for them a standard against the enemy. "Touch them not," He says, "for they are mine. I have graven them upon the palms of my hands." He teaches them to exercise unquestioning faith in His power to work in their behalf. With assurance they say, "This is the victory that overcometh the world, even our faith." 1 John 5:4.[33]

ABOVE THE FOG OF DOUBT

Be of good courage, and he shall strengthen your heart, all ye that hope in the Lord. Ps. 31:24.

Even Christians of long experience are often assaulted with the most terrible doubts and waverings. . . . You must not consider that for these temptations your case is hopeless. . . . Hope in God, trust in Him and rest in His promises.[34]

When the devil comes with his doubts and unbeliefs, shut the door of your heart. Shut your eyes so that you will not dwell upon his hellish shadow. Lift them up where they can behold the things which are eternal, and you will have strength every hour. The trial of your faith is much more precious than gold. . . . It makes you valiant to fight the battle of the Lord. . . .

Satan connects with everyone that will connect with him. If he can get those that have had an experience in religion, they are his most effectual agents to reach just such men and compass their souls with unbelief. You cannot afford to let any doubts come into your mind. Do not please the devil enough to tell about the terrible burdens you are carrying. Every time you do it, Satan laughs that his soul can control you and that you have lost sight of Jesus Christ your Redeemer. . . .

We are to show forth Him who hath called us out of darkness into His marvelous light. It is by living faith that we rest in that light. It is by living faith that we rejoice in that light every day. We are not to talk our doubts and trials, because they grow bigger every time we talk them. Every time we talk them, Satan has gained the victory; but when we say, "I will commit the keeping of my soul unto Him, as unto a faithful witness," then we testify that we have given ourselves to Jesus Christ without any reservation, and then God gives us light and we rejoice in Him.[35]

The soul that loves God, rises above the fog of doubt; he gains a bright, broad, deep, living experience, and becomes meek and Christlike. His soul is committed to God, hid with Christ in God.[36]

PROGRESSIVE CONQUEST OF EVIL

Blessed is the man that endureth temptation: for when he is tried, he shall receive the crown of life, which the Lord hath promised to them that love him. James 1:12.

It is not the order and will of God to shield His people from temptation. . . . When truth takes possession of the heart, the Christian will be brought into conflict. . . . There are opposing elements in his own household, even in his own heart, and nothing but the free Spirit of God can ensure for him the victory.[37]

The beginning of yielding to temptation is in the sin of permitting the mind to waver, to be inconsistent in your trust in God. The wicked one is ever watching for a chance to misrepresent God, and to attract the mind to that which is forbidden. If he can, he will fasten the mind upon the things of the world. He will endeavor to excite the emotions, to arouse the passions, to fasten the affections on that which is not for your good; but it is for you to hold every emotion and passion under control, in calm subjection to reason and conscience. Then Satan loses his power to control the mind. The work to which Christ calls us is to the work of progressive conquest over spiritual evil in our characters. Natural tendencies are to be overcome. . . . Appetite and passion must be conquered, and the will must be placed wholly on the side of Christ.[38]

We pray to our heavenly Father, "Lead us not into temptation," and then, too often, we fail to guard our feet against leading us into temptation. We are to keep away from the temptations by which we are easily overcome. Our success is wrought out by ourselves through the grace of Christ. We are to roll out of the way the stone of stumbling that has caused us and others so much sadness.[39]

Temptation and trial will come to us all, but we need never be worsted by the enemy. Our Saviour has conquered in our behalf. Satan is not invincible. . . . Christ was tempted that He might know how to help every soul that should afterward be tempted. Temptation is not sin; the sin lies in yielding. To the soul who trusts in Jesus, temptation means victory and greater strength.[40]

March 23

BEWARE OF SATAN'S DEVICES

Lest Satan should get an advantage of us: for we are not ignorant of his devices. 2 Cor. 2:11.

Satan's plans and devices are soliciting us on every hand. We should ever remember that he comes to us in disguise, covering his motives and the character of his temptations. He comes in garments of light, clad apparently in pure angel robes, that we may not discern that it is he. We need to use great caution, to closely investigate his devices, lest we be deceived.[41]

Satan has his evil angels around us; and though they cannot read men's thoughts, they closely watch their words and actions. Satan takes advantage of the weaknesses and defects of character that are thus revealed, and presses his temptations where there is the least power of resistance. He makes evil suggestions, and inspires worldly thoughts, knowing that he can thus bring the soul into condemnation and bondage. To those who are selfish, worldly, avaricious, proud, faultfinding, or given to detraction—to all who are cherishing errors and defects of character—Satan presents the indulgence of self, and leads the soul off upon a track that the Bible condemns. . . .

For every class of temptations there is a remedy. We are not left to ourselves to fight the battle against self and our sinful natures in our own finite strength. Jesus is a mighty helper, a never-failing support. . . . None need fail or become discouraged, when such ample provision has been made for us.

The mind must be restrained, and not allowed to wander. It should be trained to dwell upon the Scriptures, and upon noble, elevating themes. Portions of Scripture, even whole chapters, may be committed to memory, to be repeated when Satan comes in with his temptations. The fifty-eighth chapter of Isaiah is a profitable one for this purpose. Wall the soul in with the restrictions and instructions given by inspiration of the Spirit of God. When Satan would lead the mind to dwell upon earthly and sensual things, he is most effectually resisted with "It is written."[42]

HOW SATAN'S POWER IS BROKEN

Stand fast therefore in the liberty wherewith Christ hath made us free, and be not entangled again with the yoke of bondage. Gal. 5:1.

The repentance of one soul sends inexpressible joy through all the host of heaven. Melody is called forth from every harp and every voice in glorious anthems because another name is registered in the book of life, another light is kindled to shine amid the moral darkness of this corrupt world. The very same event spreads consternation among the fallen angels and humiliates the great leader in the rebellion against God's holy law. The prince of darkness, seeing a soul whom he has counted his own escaping from under his control as a bird out of the snare of the fowler, and making Christ his refuge, works with hellish intensity to again entrap the one escaped.[43]

We must dwell more on the results of genuine conversion. Not only is the sinner forgiven when he repents and confesses his iniquity; he becomes a child of God. . . . an heir of God and a joint heir with Christ to an immortal inheritance. . . . The power of Satan is broken. Man is brought into sacred unity with Christ.[44]

There is not a soul won to Christ . . . without defeat to the tempter, and bruising of the head of the serpent. This will arouse the malice of the adversary to greater activity. . . . Alarmed because he is losing his prey, Satan will first seek to deceive, next to oppress and persecute. Evil men, rebuked by the precept and example of those who come to the light of Bible truth, will become agents of the great adversary of souls and will leave no means untried to draw them away from their allegiance to God and induce them to leave the narrow path of holiness.

But none need to be alarmed and afraid. God's word is pledged that if they are true to principle, if they believe and obey all God's requirements, they are members of the royal family, children of the heavenly King. They are certain to have enlisted in their behalf the agencies of heaven and to come off victorious through the merits of Christ—more than conquerors through Him that loved them.[45]

NOT SAVED BY PROXY

Let every man prove his own work, and then shall he have rejoicing in himself alone, and not in another. Gal. 6:4.

No one can serve God by proxy. There are so many who seem to think that there is someone in this world stronger than Christ, upon whom they can lean. And instead of coming right to Christ, just as they are, giving themselves unreservedly to Him, they reach out for human help. God wants us to have an individual experience. . . . I cannot work out a character for you, and you cannot work out a character for me.[46]

The gospel deals with individuals. Every human being has a soul to save or to lose. Each has an individuality separate and distinct from all others. Each must be convicted for himself, converted for himself. He must receive the truth, repent, believe, and obey for himself. He must exercise his will for himself. . . . Each must surrender to God by his own act.[47]

The Lord does not desire that our individuality shall be destroyed; it is not His purpose that any two persons shall be exactly alike in tastes and dispositions. All have characteristics peculiar to themselves, and these are not to be destroyed, but to be trained, molded, fashioned, after the similitude of Christ. The Lord turns the natural aptitudes and capabilities into profitable channels. In the improvement of the faculties God has given, talent and ability are developed if the human agent will recognize the fact that all his powers are an endowment from God, to be used, not for selfish purposes, . . . but for the glory of God and the good of our fellow men.[48]

To every man God—not man—has given his work. This is an individual work—the formation of a character after the divine similitude. The lily is not to strive to be like the rose. There are distinctions in the formation of the flowers and in the fruits, but all derive their peculiar variance from God. . . . So it is God's design that even the best of men shall not all be of the same character. A life consecrated to the service of God will be developed and beautified in its individuality.[49]

GOD'S PART AND MINE

Wherefore, my beloved, as ye have always obeyed, not as in my presence only, but now much more in my absence, work out your own salvation with fear and trembling. For it is God which worketh in you both to will and to do of his good pleasure. Phil. 2:12, 13.

"Work out your own salvation with fear and trembling." What does this mean? It means that every day you are to distrust your own human efforts and wisdom. You are to fear to speak at random, fear to follow your own impulses, fear that pride of heart and love of the world and lust of the flesh shall exclude the precious grace the Lord Jesus is longing to bestow upon you.[50]

Man's working, as brought out in the text, is not an independent work he performs without God. His whole dependence is upon the power and grace of the Divine Worker. Many miss the mark here, and claim that man must work his own individual self, free from divine power. This is not in accordance with the text. Another argues that man is free from all obligation, because God does it all, *both* the *willing* and the *doing*. The text means that the salvation of the human soul requires the will power to be subjective to the divine will power. . . . And it is the very hardest, sternest conflict which comes with the purpose and hour of great resolve and decision of the human to incline the will and way to God's will and God's way.[51]

Man is allotted a part in this great struggle for everlasting life; he must respond to the working of the Holy Spirit. It will require a struggle to break through the powers of darkness, but the Spirit that works in him can and will accomplish this. But man is no passive instrument to be saved in indolence. He is called upon to strain every muscle in the struggle for immortality, yet it is God that supplies the efficiency.[52]

Here are man's works, and here are God's works. . . . With these two combined powers, man will be victorious, and receive a crown of life at last. . . . He puts to the stretch every spiritual nerve and muscle that he may be a successful overcomer in this work, and that he may obtain the precious boon of eternal life.[53]

THE STRUGGLE OF UNSEEN FORCES

For we wrestle not against flesh and blood, but against principalities, against powers, against the rulers of the darkness of this world, against spiritual wickedness in high places. Eph. 6:12.

The Lord would have our minds aroused regarding the influence of evil angels. Christ does not tell us of the danger threatening us from the attacks of the apostate foe without furnishing us with power to resist every attack. . . . Angelic agencies, both good and evil, are striving for the mastery, and every influence that is now exerted is to be closely investigated.[54]

Satan is ever on the alert to deceive and mislead. He is using every enchantment to allure men into the broad road of disobedience. He is working to confuse the senses with erroneous sentiments, and remove the landmarks by placing his false inscription on the signposts which God has established to point the right way. It is because these evil agencies are striving to eclipse every ray of light from the soul that heavenly beings are appointed to do their work of ministry, to guide, guard, and control those who shall be heirs of salvation. None need despair because of the inherited tendencies to evil, but when the Spirit of God convicts of sin, the wrongdoer must repent and confess and forsake the evil. Faithful sentinels are on guard to direct souls in right paths.[55]

Either the evil angels or the angels of God are controlling the minds of men. Our minds are given to the control of God, or to the control of the powers of darkness; and it will be well for us to inquire where we are standing today—whether under the blood-stained banner of Prince Emmanuel, or under the black banner of the powers of darkness.[56]

So long as the people of God preserve their fidelity to Him, so long as they cling by living faith to Jesus, they are under the protection of heavenly angels, and Satan will not be permitted to exercise his hellish arts upon them to their destruction.[57]

It is the greatest joy of the angels of heaven to spread the shield of their tender love over souls who turn to God.[58]

CHRIST'S EXAMPLE IN OVERCOMING

Keep back thy servant also from presumptuous sins; let them not have dominion over me: then shall I be upright, and I shall be innocent from the great transgression. Ps. 19:13.

The great leading temptations wherewith man would be beset, Christ met and overcame in the wilderness. His coming off victor over appetite, presumption, and the world shows how we may overcome. Satan has overcome his millions in tempting the appetite and leading men to give up to presumptuous sins. There are many who profess to be followers of Christ, . . . who, with hardly a thought, plunge into scenes of temptation that would require a miracle to bring them forth unsullied. Meditation and prayer would have preserved them and led them to shun the dangerous positions in which they have placed themselves and which give Satan the advantage over them.

The promises of God are not for us to claim rashly, to protect us while we rush on recklessly into danger, violating the laws of nature, or disregarding prudence and the judgment God has given us to use. This would not be genuine faith but presumption. . . . Satan comes to us with worldly honor, wealth, and the pleasures of life. These temptations are varied to meet men of every rank and degree, tempting them away from God to serve themselves more than their Creator. "All these things will I give thee," said Satan to Christ. "All these things will I give thee," says Satan to man. "All this money, this land, all this power, and honor, and riches, will I give thee"; and man is charmed, deceived, and treacherously allured on to his ruin. If we give ourselves up to worldliness of heart and of life, Satan is satisfied.

The Saviour overcame the wily foe, showing us how we may overcome. He has left us His example, to repel Satan with Scripture. He might have had recourse to His own divine power, . . . but His example would not then have been as useful to us. Christ used only Scripture. How important that the Word of God be thoroughly studied and followed, that in case of emergency we may be "throughly furnished unto all good works" and especially fortified to meet the wily foe.[59]

HOW TO MAINTAIN YOUR INTEGRITY!

Likewise reckon ye also yourselves to be dead indeed unto sin, but alive unto God through Jesus Christ our Lord. Let not sin therefore reign in your mortal body, that ye should obey it in the lusts thereof. Rom. 6:11, 12.

Some regard sin as altogether so light a matter that they have no defense against its indulgence or its consequence. . . .

If you suppose for a moment that God will treat sin lightly, or make provisions or exemptions so that you can go on in committing sin, and the soul suffer no penalty from so doing, you are under a terrible delusion of Satan. Any willful violation of the righteous law of Jehovah exposes your soul to the full assaults of Satan.

When you lose your conscious integrity, your soul becomes a battlefield for Satan; you have doubts and fears enough to paralyze your energies and drive you to discouragement. . . .

Remember that temptation is not sin. Remember that however trying the circumstances in which a man may be placed, nothing can really weaken his soul so long as he does not yield to temptation but maintains his own integrity. The interests most vital to you individually are in your own keeping. No one can damage them without your consent. All the satanic legions cannot injure you unless you open your soul to the arts and arrows of Satan. Your ruin can never take place until your will consents. If there is not pollution of mind in yourself, all the surrounding pollution cannot taint or defile you.

Eternal life is worth everything to us or it is worth nothing. Those only who put forth persevering effort and untiring zeal with intense desire proportionate to the value of the object they are in pursuit of, will gain that life which measures with the life of God. . . .

We have the example of Adam and Eve before us, and the result of their transgression should lead every soul of us to avoid sin, to abhor sin as the hateful thing it is, and to feel, in view of the sufferings which sin is sure to inflict, that it is better to suffer loss of all things than to depart from the least of God's commandments.[60]

SUCCESS IN RESISTANCE

Submit yourselves therefore to God. Resist the devil, and he will flee from you. James 4:7.

There are those who recklessly place themselves in scenes of danger and peril, and expose themselves to temptations, out of which it would require a miracle of God to bring them unharmed and untainted. These are presumptuous acts, with which God is not pleased. Satan's temptation to the Saviour of the world to cast Himself from the pinnacle of the temple, was firmly met and resisted. The archenemy quoted a promise of God as security, that Christ might with safety do this on the strength of the promise. Jesus met this temptation with Scripture: "It is written, Thou shalt not tempt the Lord thy God." In the same way Satan urges men into places where God does not require them to go, presenting Scripture to justify his suggestions.

The precious promises of God are not given to strengthen man in a presumptuous course, or for him to rely upon when he rushes needlessly into danger. . . . We are required, as children of God, to maintain the consistency of our Christian character. We should exercise prudence, caution, and humility, and walk circumspectly toward them that are without. Yet we are not in any case to surrender principle.

Our only safety is in giving no place to the devil; for his suggestions and purposes are ever to injure us, and hinder us from relying upon God. He transforms himself into an angel of purity, that he may, through his specious temptations, introduce his devices in such a manner that we may not discern his wiles. The more we yield, the more powerful will be his deceptions over us. It is unsafe to controvert or to parley with him. For every advantage we give the enemy, he will claim more. Our only safety is to reject firmly the first insinuation to presumption. God has given us grace through the merits of Christ sufficient to withstand Satan, and be more than conquerors. Resistance is success. "Resist the devil, and he will flee from you." Resistance must be firm and steadfast. We lose all we gain if we resist today only to yield tomorrow.[61]

THE CLOSER, THE SAFER

Draw nigh to God, and he will draw nigh to you. Cleanse your hands, ye sinners; and purify your hearts, ye double minded. James 4:8.

"Draw nigh to God." How? By secret, earnest examination of your own heart, by childlike, heartfelt, humble dependence upon God, making known all your weakness to Jesus, and by confessing your sins.[62]

We cannot draw nigh to God and behold His loveliness and compassion without realizing our defects and being filled with a desire to rise higher. "And he will draw nigh to you." The Lord will draw nigh to him who confesses to his brethren the wrongs he has done them, and then comes to God in humility and contrition.

He who feels his own danger is on the watch lest he shall grieve the Holy Spirit and then draw away from God because he knows that He is not pleased with his course of action. How much better and safer it is to draw nigh to God, that the pure light shining from His Word may heal the wounds that sin has made in the soul. The closer we are to God, the safer we are, for Satan hates and fears the presence of God.[63]

Draw nigh to Him by prayer, by contemplation, by reading His Word. When He draws nigh to you, He lifts up for you a standard against the enemy. Let us take courage; for the enemy cannot pass this standard.[64]

If we draw nigh to God, individually, then don't you see what the result will be? Can't you see that we will draw nigh to one another? We cannot draw nigh to God, and come to the same cross, without our hearts being blended together in perfect unity, answering the prayer of Christ that they may be one as He is with the Father. And therefore we should seek in spirit, in understanding, in faith, that we may be one, that God may be glorified in us as He is glorified in the Son; and that God shall love us as He loves the Son.[65]

The soul that loves God, loves to draw strength from Him by constant communion with Him. When it becomes the habit of the soul to converse with God, the power of the evil one is broken; for Satan cannot abide near the soul that draws nigh unto God.[66]

"COME UNTO ME"

Come unto me, all ye that labour and are heavy laden, and I will give you rest. Matt. 11:28.

Many who hear this invitation, while sighing for rest, yet press on the rugged path, hugging their burdens close to their heart. Jesus loves them, and longs to bear their burdens and themselves also in His strong arms. He would remove the fears and uncertainties that rob them of peace and rest; but they must first come to Him, and tell Him the secret woes of their heart. . . .

Sometimes we pour our troubles into human ears, and tell our afflictions to those who cannot help us, and neglect to confide all to Jesus, who is able to change the sorrowful way to paths of joy and peace. . . .

He proposes to be our friend, to walk with us through all the rough pathways of life. He says to us, I am the Lord thy God; walk with me, and I will fill thy path with light. Jesus, the Majesty of Heaven, proposes to elevate to companionship with Himself those who come to Him with their burdens, their weaknesses, and their cares. . . .

His invitation to us is a call to a pure, holy, and happy life—a life of peace and rest, of liberty and love—and to a rich inheritance in the future, immortal life. . . . It is our privilege to have daily a calm, close, happy walk with Jesus.[1]

Rest is found when all self-justification, all reasoning from a self-ish standpoint, is put away. Entire self-surrender, an acceptance of His ways, is the secret of perfect rest in His love. . . . Do just what He has told you to do, and be assured that God will do all that He has said He would do. . . . Have you come to Him, renouncing all your makeshifts, all your unbelief, all your self-righteousness? Come just as you are, weak, helpless, and ready to die.

What is the "rest" promised?—It is the consciousness that God is true, that He never disappoints the one who comes to Him. His pardon is full and free, and His acceptance means rest to the soul, rest in His love.[2]

REST FOR THE RESTLESS

For thus saith the Lord God, the Holy One of Israel; In returning and rest shall ye be saved; in quietness and in confidence shall be your strength. Isa. 30:15.

Jesus invites the restless, the murmuring, the oppressed and sorrowing, to come to Him.[3]

Jesus loves you and He wants your love. He would have you remember that He gave His precious life that you should not perish; and He will be unto you a present help in every time of need. Only look to Jesus and tell Him every perplexity and trial. . . . Ask Him to help and strengthen and bless you, and believe that He hears your prayers. . . .

All heaven is looking upon you with deep interest. One soul for whom Christ has died is worth more than the whole world. I wish every young man and woman could appreciate the value of the human soul. If they would give themselves to Jesus just as they are, though sinful and polluted, He will accept them the very moment that they give themselves to Him, and Jesus will put His Spirit in the humble seeker's heart. Whosoever cometh unto Him, He will in no wise cast out. You may love Jesus with your whole heart, and He will never disappoint that love and confidence. His words are life, comfort, and hope. Satan knows that all you have to do is to look to Jesus, an uplifted Saviour. The wounded, bruised, stricken soul will find in Jesus a balm for his wounds. . . .

There will be peace, constant peace, flowing into the soul, for the rest is found in perfect submission to Jesus Christ. Obedience to God's will finds the rest. The disciple that treads in the meek and lowly steps of the Redeemer finds rest which the world cannot give, and the world cannot take away. "Thou wilt keep him in perfect peace whose mind is stayed on thee: because he trusteth in thee." Isa. 26:3.[4]

Lowliness and meekness of mind, which ever characterized the life of the divine Son of God, possessed by His true followers, bring contentment, peace, and happiness, that elevate them above the slavery of artificial life.[5]

April 3

"LEARN OF ME"

Take my yoke upon you, and learn of me; for I am meek and lowly in heart: and ye shall find rest unto your souls. Matt. 11:29.

"Learn of me," said the Divine Teacher, "for I am meek and lowly in heart. . . ." We must learn self-denial, we must learn courage, patience, fortitude, and forgiving love. . . . If we have faith in Jesus as our helper, if our eyes of faith are directed to Him constantly, we shall become like Jesus in character. He will abide in our hearts and we will abide in Christ. Being clothed with the righteousness of Christ, our lives are hid with Christ in God. He will be our counselor. If we ask Him in faith, He will enlighten our understanding. . . . The lessons which Christ has given us will be practiced.[6]

As Christ the Pattern is constantly kept before the mind's eye, new habits will be formed, powerful hereditary and cultivated tendencies will be subdued and overcome, self-esteem will be laid in the dust, old habits of thought will be constantly resisted, love for the supremacy will be seen in its real, despicable character, and will be overcome.[7]

Christ must be blended with all our thoughts, our feelings, our affections. He must be exemplified in the minutest details of everyday service in the work that He has given us to do. When, in the place of leaning upon human understanding or conforming to worldly maxims, we sit at the feet of Jesus, eagerly drinking in His words, learning of Him, and saying, "Lord, what wilt Thou have me to do?" our natural independence, our self-confidence, our strong self-will, will be exchanged for a childlike, submissive, teachable spirit. When we are in right relation to God, we shall recognize Christ's authority to direct us, and His claim to our unquestioning obedience.[8]

We will have such exalted views of Jesus Christ that self will be abased. Our affections will center in Jesus, our thoughts will be strongly drawn heavenward. Christ will increase, *I will decrease. . . .* We will cultivate the virtues that dwell in Jesus, that we may reflect to others a representation of His character.[9]

WEARING CHRIST'S YOKE

For my yoke is easy, and my burden is light. Matt. 11:30.

Wearing the yoke with Christ, means to work in His lines, to be a copartner with Him in His sufferings and toils for lost humanity.[10]

In accepting Christ's yoke of restraint and obedience, you will find that it is of the greatest help to you. Wearing this yoke keeps you near the side of Christ, and He bears the heaviest part of the load.[11]

The yoke and the cross are symbols representing the same thing—the giving up of the will to God. Wearing the yoke unites finite man in companionship with the dearly beloved Son of God. Lifting the cross cuts away self from the soul, and places man where he learns how to bear Christ's burdens. We cannot follow Christ without wearing His yoke, without lifting the cross and bearing it after Him. If our will is not in accord with the divine requirements, we are to deny our inclinations, give up our darling desires, and step in Christ's footsteps. . . .

Men frame for their own necks yokes that seem light and pleasant to wear, but they prove galling in the extreme. Christ sees this, and He says, "Take My yoke upon you. The yoke you would place upon your own neck, thinking it a precise fit, will not fit at all. Take My yoke upon you, and learn of Me the lessons essential for you to learn." [12]

Your work is not to gather up burdens of your own. . . . We often think we are having a hard time in bearing burdens, and it is too often the case, because God has not made any provision for us to carry these burdens; but when we bear His yoke and carry His burdens, we can testify that the yoke of Christ is easy and His burdens are light, because He has made provision for these.[13]

Yet that yoke will not give us a life of ease and freedom and selfish indulgence. The life of Christ was one of self-sacrifice and self-denial at every step; and with consistent, Christlike tenderness and love, His true follower will walk in the footsteps of the Master; and as he advances in this life, he will become more and more inspired with the spirit and life of Christ.[14]

LEARNING IN CHRIST'S SCHOOL

What man is he that feareth the Lord? him shall he teach in the way that he shall choose. Ps. 25:12.

Jesus has opened a school for the education and training of His chosen ones, and they are ever to be learning to practice the lessons that He gives them, in order that they may know Him fully.

Those who think they are very nearly good enough, and do not work diligently for the perfection of Christian character, will set up idols in their hearts, and will continue to practice sinful habits until sin will no longer appear sinful. . . .

Jesus offers Himself to every sin-sick soul, to every soul who is struggling to overcome. The Holy Spirit is making intercession for every sincere wrestler, and Christ will make His words to be spirit and life, the power of God unto salvation to every one that believeth. But you will certainly fail if you permit the devil to control your mind, to guide your imaginings. . . . God will not be trifled with; He will not accept a divided heart. He claims entire, wholehearted service. He has paid the ransom money of His own life for every son and daughter of Adam. . . .

Christ has a claim upon every soul; but many choose a life of sin. Some will not come unto Jesus that He may give them life. Some say, "I go, sir," to His invitation; but they do not go; they do not make an entire surrender to abide in Jesus alone, which is life and peace and joy unspeakable, and full of glory. . . . Will you not rise to be wise and to make diligent work for eternity? Seek the grace of Christ with the whole heart, might, mind, and strength. . . .

God has given you a right to take hold of Him through the prayer of faith. Believing prayer is the very essence of pure religion, the secret of power with every Christian. . . .

Take time to pray, to search the Scriptures, to put self under discipline to Jesus Christ. Live in contact with the living Christ, and as soon as you do this, He will take hold of you and hold you firmly by a strong hand that will never let go.[15]

April 6

PREPARING FOR THE HIGHER SCHOOL

Lead me in thy truth, and teach me: for thou art the God of my salvation; on thee do I wait all the day. Ps. 25:5.

Those who in this earth become sons of God sit together with Christ in the preparatory school, getting ready to be received into the higher school. Day by day we are to make an individual preparation; for in the courts above no one will be represented by proxy. Each one must heed for himself the call, "Come unto me, . . . and I will give you rest. . . ."

The Lord Jesus has paid your tuition fees. All that you have to do is to learn of Him. The Christlike politeness practiced in the higher school is to be practiced in this lower school, by both old and young believers. All who learn in Christ's school are under the training of heavenly agencies; and they are never to forget that they are a spectacle to the world, to angels, and to men.

They are to represent Christ. They are to help one another to become worthy of admission into the higher school. They are to help one another to be pure and noble, and to cherish a true idea of what it means to be a child of God. They are to speak encouraging words. They are to lift up the feeble hands and strengthen the feeble knees. Upon every heart there is to be inscribed the words, as with the point of a diamond, "There is nothing that I fear, save that I shall not know my duty, or shall fail to do it." . . .

A self-controlled spirit, words of love and tenderness, honor the Saviour. Those who speak kind, loving words, words that make for peace, will be richly rewarded. . . . We are to let His spirit shine forth in the meekness and lowliness learned of Him.[16]

Jesus is the great Teacher. . . . He is so willing, so ready to take you into a closer fellowship with Himself. He is willing to teach you how to pray with the believing confidence and assurance of a little child. . . . Enroll your name anew as a student in His school. Learn to pray in faith. Receive the knowledge of Jesus. . . .

Will you not sit at the feet of Jesus and learn of Him?[17]

THE TRUE FORCE OF THE WILL

For if there be first a willing mind, it is accepted according to that a man hath, and not according to that he hath not. 2 Cor. 8:12.

Pure religion has to do with the will. The will is the governing power in the nature of man, bringing all the other faculties under its sway. The will is not the taste or the inclination, but it is the deciding power which works in the children of men unto obedience to God or unto disobedience. . . .

You desire to make your life such as will fit you for heaven at last. You are often discouraged at finding yourself weak in moral power, in slavery to doubt, and controlled by the habits and customs of your old life in sin. . . . Your promises are like ropes of sand. . . .

You will be in constant peril until you understand the true force of the will. You may believe and promise all things, but your promises or your faith are of no value until you put your will on the side of faith and action. If you fight the fight of faith with all your will power, you will conquer. Your feelings, your impressions, your emotions, are not to be trusted, for they are not reliable. . . .

But you need not despair. . . . It is for you to yield up your will to the will of Jesus Christ; and as you do this, God will immediately take possession and work in you to will and to do of His good pleasure. Your whole nature will then be brought under the control of the Spirit of Christ, and even your thoughts will be subject to Him. You cannot control your impulses, your emotions, as you may desire; but you can control the will, and you can make an entire change in your life. By yielding up your will to Christ, your life will be hid with Christ in God and allied to the power which is above all principalities and powers. You will have strength from God that will hold you fast to His strength; and a new light, even the light of living faith, will be possible to you. But your will must cooperate with God's will. . . .

Will you not say, "I will give my will to Jesus, and I will do it now," and from this moment be wholly on the Lord's side?[18]

WHEN MY WILL IS SAFE

But now being made free from sin, and become servants to God, ye have your fruit unto holiness, and the end everlasting life. Rom. 6:22.

The Spirit of God does not create new faculties in the converted man, but works a decided change in the employment of those faculties. When mind and heart and soul are changed, man is not given a new conscience, but his will is submitted to a conscience renewed, a conscience whose dormant sensibilities are aroused by the working of the Holy Spirit.[19]

Through yielding to sin, man placed his will under the control of Satan. He became a helpless captive in the tempter's power. God sent His Son into our world to break the power of Satan, and to emancipate the will of man. He sent Him to proclaim liberty to the captives, to undo the heavy burdens, and to let the oppressed go free. By pouring the whole treasury of heaven into this world, by giving us in Christ all heaven, God has purchased the will, the affections, the mind, the soul, of every human being. When man places himself under the control of God, the will becomes firm and strong to do right, the heart is cleansed from selfishness, and filled with Christlike love. The mind yields to the authority of the law of love, and every thought is brought into captivity to the obedience of Christ.[20]

When the will is placed on the Lord's side, the Holy Spirit takes that will and makes it one with the divine will.

The Lord loves man. He has given evidence of this love by giving His only begotten Son to die for man, that through His grace He might redeem him from hostility to God, and bring him back to his loyalty. If man will cooperate with God, the Lord will bring his will into connection with Himself, and will vitalize it by His own Spirit. . . . The gospel must be received in order to regenerate the heart, and the reception of truth will mean the surrender of mind and will to the will of divine power.[21]

The will of man is only safe when united with the will of God.[22]

April 9

A SUBMISSIVE WILL

If any man will do his will, he shall know of the doctrine, whether it be of God, or whether I speak of myself. John 7:17.

Those who have yielded their will to God are trained in Christ's school. . . . They are disciplined to habits of obedience, to do service to God. We are not creatures devoid of moral nature. The gospel does not address the understanding alone. If it did, we might approach it as we approach the study of a book dealing with mathematical formulas, which relate to the intellect alone. . . . Its aim is the heart. It addresses our moral nature, and takes possession of the will. It casts down imaginations, and every high thing that exalts itself against the knowledge of God, and brings into captivity every thought to the obedience of Christ.

It is the wayward heart that has dragged down the faculties of the soul. All who would learn the science of salvation must be submissive students in the school of Christ, that the soul temple may be the abiding place of the most High. If we would learn of Christ, the soul must be emptied of all its proud possessions, that Christ may imprint His image on the soul. . . .

Then we shall have such a view of Christ's infinite sacrifice in our behalf that the soul will be softened and humbled and made full of thanksgiving to God. An intense desire will be begotten by the Holy Spirit for a favorable opportunity to witness for Christ and to express gratitude and devotion to Him who has redeemed us. Loyalty and love will be seen in all the service. A burning desire to be like Christ will keep the soul tender, leading it to give vent to grateful emotion, and in the sight of heaven to offer thanks to God for His goodness, His love, and His compassion. Such have a grace that cannot be repressed into a tame, everyday evenness of assenting to truth, while the heart is not affected.

Oh, how much more safe it is to agonize to enter into the strait gate! It is only at the altar of God that human beings can receive the celestial torch.[23]

A p r i l   1 0

CULTIVATING GOD'S GARDEN

And be not conformed to this world: but be ye transformed by the renewing of your mind, that ye may prove what is that good, and acceptable, and perfect, will of God. Rom. 12:2.

Man, fallen man, may be transformed by the renewing of the mind, so that he can "prove what is that good, and acceptable, and perfect, will of God." How does he prove this? By the Holy Spirit taking possession of his mind, spirit, heart, and character.[24]

The rubbish of questionable principles and practices is to be swept away. The Lord desires the mind to be renovated, and the heart filled with the treasures of truth.[25]

Truth has a power to elevate the receiver. It has a sanctifying influence upon mind and character. . . . Only by a continual improvement of the intellectual as well as the moral powers can we hope to answer the purpose of our Creator. . . .

A Christian should possess more intelligence and keener discernment than the worldling. The study of God's Word is continually expanding the mind and strengthening the intellect. There is nothing that will so refine and elevate the character, and give vigor to every faculty, as the continual exercise of the mind to grasp and comprehend weighty and important truths.

The human mind becomes dwarfed and enfeebled when dealing with commonplace matters only, never rising above the level of time and sense to grasp the mysteries of the unseen. The understanding is gradually brought to the level of the things with which it is constantly familiar. . . . Man need not cease to grow intellectually and spiritually during his lifetime.[26]

We are to cultivate the talents given us by God. They are His gifts, and are to be used in their right relation to each other, so as to make a perfect whole. God gives the talents, the powers of the mind; man makes the character. The mind is the Lord's garden, and man must cultivate it earnestly in order to form a character after the divine similitude.[27]

IN UNISON WITH GOD

Jesus saith unto them, My meat is to do the will of him that sent me, and to finish his work. John 4:34.

Christ declared, "I came . . . not to do my own will, but the will of him that sent me." John 6:38. His will was put into active exercise to save the souls of men. His human will was nourished by the divine. His servants today would do well to ask themselves, "What kind of will am I individually cultivating? Have I been gratifying my own desires, confirming myself in selfishness and obstinacy?" If we are doing this, we are in great peril, for Satan will always rule the will that is not under the control of the Spirit of God. When we place our will in unison with the will of God, the holy obedience that was exemplified in the life of Christ will be seen in our lives. . . .

Paul declares, "I am crucified with Christ." Gal. 2:20. There is nothing so hard as the crucifixion of the will. Christ was tempted in all points like as we are; but His will was ever kept on the side of God's will. In His humanity He had the same free will that Adam had in Eden. He could have yielded to temptation as Adam yielded. And Adam, by believing God and being a doer of His word, could have resisted temptation as Christ resisted it. Had Christ so willed it, He could have commanded the stones to be made bread. He might have cast Himself down from the pinnacle of the Temple. He might have yielded to Satan's temptation to fall down and worship him, the usurper of the world. But at every point He met the tempter with, "It is written." His will was in perfect obedience to the will of God, and the will of God was revealed throughout His entire life. . . .

Christ's obedience to His Father's commandments is to be the measure of our obedience. Those who follow Christ, if they would become complete in Him, must keep their will surrendered to the will of God. Abundant provision has been made that those who will seek God with the whole heart may find Him a present help in every time of trouble. Help has been laid on One that is mighty. Christ has promised, I will be your helper.[28]

"LET THIS MIND BE IN YOU"

Let this mind be in you, which was also in Christ Jesus. Phil. 2:5.

The prayer that Christ has given us, that the will of God shall be done in earth as it is in heaven, is to be answered. Wonderful is this prayer, which we are to offer to God, and then fulfill in the daily life! The science of holiness, the ethics that the gospel inculcates, acknowledge no standard but the perfection of God's mind, God's will. It is the character and mind of Christ which, by conversion and transformation, men are to receive. Through His Son, God has revealed the excellency to which man is capable of attaining. And before the world God is developing us as living witnesses of what man may become through the grace of Christ. Oh, why do so many grieve the heart of infinite love? . . .

God permits every person to exercise his individuality. No human mind should be submerged in another human mind. But the invitation has been given, "Let *this mind* be in you, which was also in Christ Jesus." Each person is to stand before God with an individual faith, an individual experience, knowing for himself that Christ is formed within, the hope of glory. For us to imitate the example of any man—even a person who in our human judgment we might regard as nearly perfect in character—would be to put our trust in an imperfect, defective human being, who is unable to impart one jot or tittle of perfection to any other human being.

As our pattern we have One who is all and in all, the chiefest among ten thousand, One whose excellency is beyond comparison. What saith the Divine Teacher?—"Be ye therefore perfect, even as your Father which is in heaven is perfect." Matt. 5:48. Would Christ tantalize us by requiring of us an impossibility?—Never, never! What an honor He confers upon us, in urging us to be holy in our sphere, as the Father is holy in His sphere. And through His power we are able to do this; for He declares, "*All* power is given unto me in heaven and in earth." Matt. 28:18. This unlimited power it is your privilege and mine to claim.[29]

THE INFLUENCE OF MIND ON MIND

For God hath not given us the spirit of fear; but of power, and of love, and of a sound mind. 2 Tim. 1:7.

The influence of mind on mind, so strong a power for good when sanctified, is equally strong for evil in the hands of those opposed to God. This power Satan used in his work of instilling evil into the minds of the angels, and he made it appear that he was seeking the good of the universe. . . . Cast out of heaven, Satan set up his kingdom in this world, and ever since, he has been untiringly striving to seduce human beings from their allegiance to God. He uses the same power that he used in heaven—the influence of mind on mind. Men become tempters of their fellow men. The strong, corrupting sentiments of Satan are cherished, and they exert a masterly, compelling power.[30]

Clear spiritual eyesight is needed to distinguish between the chaff and the wheat, between the science of Satan and the science of the Word of truth. Christ, the Great Physician, came to our world to give health and peace and perfection of character to all who will receive Him. His gospel does not consist of outward methods and performances through which the science of an evil work may be introduced as a great blessing, afterward to prove a great curse. In the second chapter of Philippians is found a presentation of true godliness. "Let this mind be in you, which was also in Christ Jesus." Phil. 2:5. . . .

To advocate the science of mind cure is opening a door through which Satan will enter to take possession of mind and heart. Satan controls both the mind that is given up to be controlled by another, and the mind that controls. May God help us to understand the true science of building on Christ, our Saviour and Redeemer.

Christ is the greatest of all physicians. He is a physician of the soul as well as of the body. Had He not come to this world to redeem us from Satan's hellish power, we would have had no hope of gaining eternal life. . . . Let us not point minds to erring human beings. Let us say, "Behold the Lamb of God, which taketh away the sin of the world." John 1:29.[31]

ENTANGLED MINDS

Beware lest any man spoil you through philosophy and vain deceit, after the tradition of men, after the rudiments of the world, and not after Christ. Col. 2:8.

Satan often finds a powerful agency for evil in the power which one human mind is capable of exerting on another human mind. This influence is so seductive that the person who is being molded by it is often unconscious of its power. God has bidden me speak warning against this evil, that His servants may not come under the deceptive power of Satan. The enemy is a master worker, and if God's people are not constantly led by the Spirit of God, they will be snared and taken. For thousands of years Satan has been experimenting upon the properties of the human mind, and he has learned to know it well. By his subtle workings in these last days, he is linking the human mind with his own, imbuing it with his thoughts; and he is doing this work in so deceptive a manner that those who accept his guidance know not that they are being led by him at his will. The great deceiver hopes so to confuse the minds of men and women, that none but his voice will be heard.[32]

The gospel of Christ is to be wrought into our everyday experience. The mind must be in a state to appreciate the divine claims of the gospel. It must be girded about, and disciplined to habits of self-control and obedience. . . .

The teachings of the living oracles cast down imaginations, and every high thing that exalteth itself against the knowledge of God, and bring into captivity every thought to the obedience of Christ. Satan has great power over the soul, to drag it down to a low level. Those who really want to learn of Christ will have to empty the soul of all its proud imaginings, that there may be room to enthrone Him there.[33]

The controversy between Christ and Satan is not yet ended. The latter is constantly seeking to establish his own power and authority. If he can entangle minds, he will do it. . . . The deceptions of Satan are manifold, but the Lord will be our helper if we seek Him earnestly.[34]

April 15

PREOCCUPYING THE MIND

A good man out of the good treasure of his heart bringeth forth that which is good; and an evil man out of the evil treasure of his heart bringeth forth that which is evil: for of the abundance of the heart his mouth speaketh. Luke 6:45.

The mind is so constituted that it must be occupied with either good or evil. If it takes a low level, it is generally because it is left to deal with commonplace subjects. . . . Man has the power to regulate and control the workings of the mind, and give direction to the current of his thoughts. But this requires greater effort than we can make in our own strength. We must stay our minds on God, if we would have right thoughts, and proper subjects for meditation.

Few realize that it is a duty to exercise control over their thoughts and imaginations. It is difficult to keep the undisciplined mind fixed upon profitable subjects. But if the thoughts are not properly employed, religion cannot flourish in the soul. The mind must be preoccupied with sacred and eternal things, or it will cherish trifling and superficial thoughts. Both the intellectual and the moral powers must be disciplined, and they will strengthen and improve by exercise.

To understand this matter aright, we must remember that our hearts are naturally depraved, and we are unable, of ourselves, to pursue a right course. It is only by the grace of God, combined with the most earnest efforts on our part, that we can gain the victory.

There are, in the Christian faith, subjects upon which every one should accustom his mind to dwell. The love of Jesus, which passeth knowledge, His sufferings for the fallen race, His work of mediation in our behalf, and His exalted glory—these are the mysteries into which angels desired to look. Heavenly beings find in these themes enough to attract and engage their deepest thoughts; and shall we, who are so intimately concerned, manifest less interest than the angels, in the wonders of redeeming love?

The intellect, as well as the heart, must be consecrated to the service of God. He has claims upon all there is of us.[35]

111

TRAINING THE THOUGHTS

Wherefore gird up the loins of your mind, be sober, and hope to the end for the grace that is to be brought unto you at the revelation of Jesus Christ. 1 Peter 1:13.

Many need to make a decided change in the tenor of their thoughts and actions, if they would please Jesus.[36]

The thoughts must be trained. Gird up the loins of the mind that it shall work in the right direction, and after the order of well-formed plans; then every step is one in advance, and no effort or time is lost in following vague ideas and random plans. We must consider the aim and object of life, and ever keep worthy purposes in view. Every day the thoughts should be trained and kept to the point as the compass to the pole. Every one should have his aims and purposes, and then make every thought and action of that character to accomplish that which he purposes. The thoughts must be controlled. There must be a fixedness of purpose to carry out that which you shall undertake. . . .

No one but yourself can control your thoughts. In the struggle to reach the highest standard, success or failure will depend much upon the character, and the manner in which the thoughts are disciplined. If the thoughts are well girded, as God directs they shall be each day, they will be upon those subjects that will help us to greater devotion. If the thoughts are right, then as a result the words will be right; the actions will be of that character to bring gladness and comfort and rest to souls. . . .

Those who move without thoughtful consideration move unwisely. They make fitful efforts, strike out here and there, catch at this and that, but it amounts to nothing. They resemble the vine; its tendrils untrained and left to struggle out in every direction will fasten upon any rubbish within their reach; but before the vine can be of any use these tendrils must be broken off from the things they have grasped, and trained to entwine about those things which will make them graceful and well formed.[37]

April 17

HOW TO DISCIPLINE THE MIND

Let the words of my mouth, and the meditation of my heart, be acceptable in thy sight, O Lord, my strength, and my redeemer. Ps. 19:14.

The thoughts must be pure, the meditations of the heart must be clean, if the words of the mouth are to be words acceptable to Heaven, and helpful to your associates.[38]

The natural, selfish mind, if left to follow out its own evil desires, will act without high motives, without reference to the glory of God or the benefit of mankind. The thoughts will be evil, and only evil, continually. . . . The Spirit of God produces a new life in the soul, bringing the thoughts and desires into obedience to the will of Christ. . . .

The youth should begin early to cultivate correct habits of thought. We should discipline the mind to think in a healthful channel, and not permit it to dwell upon things that are evil. . . . As God works upon the heart by His Holy Spirit, man must cooperate with Him. . . .

We should meditate upon the Scriptures, thinking soberly and candidly upon the things that pertain to our eternal salvation. The infinite mercy and love of Jesus, the sacrifice made in our behalf, call for most serious and solemn reflection. We should dwell upon the character of our dear Redeemer and Intercessor. We should seek to comprehend the meaning of the plan of salvation. We should meditate upon the mission of Him who came to save His people from their sins. By constantly contemplating heavenly themes, our faith and love will grow stronger. Our prayers will be more and more acceptable to God, because they will be more and more mixed with faith and love. They will be more intelligent and fervent. There will be more constant confidence in Jesus, and you will have a daily, living experience in the willingness and power of Christ to save unto the uttermost all that come unto God by Him. . . .

There will be a hungering and thirsting of soul to be made like Him whom we adore. The more our thoughts are upon Christ, the more we shall speak of Him to others, and represent Him to the world.[39]

PROPER LEVEL OF THE HUMAN MIND

Humble yourselves in the sight of the Lord, and he shall lift you up. James 4:10.

What gives the proper level to the human mind? It is the cross of Calvary. By looking unto Jesus, who is the Author and Finisher of our faith, all the desire for self-glorification is laid in the dust. There comes, as we see aright, a spirit of self-abasement that promotes lowliness and humbleness of mind. As we contemplate the cross, we are enabled to see the wonderful provision it has brought to every believer. God in Christ . . . if seen aright, will level human exaltation and pride. There will be no self-exaltation, but there will be true humility.[40]

The light reflected from the cross of Calvary will humble every proud thought. Those who seek God with all the heart, and accept the great salvation offered them, will open the door of the heart to Jesus. They will cease to ascribe glory to themselves. They will not pride themselves on their acquirements, or take credit to themselves for their capabilities, but will regard all their talents as God's gifts, to be used to His glory. Every intellectual ability they will regard as precious only as it can be used in the service of Christ.[41]

Christ's humiliation in clothing His divinity with humanity is worthy of our consideration. Had this subject been studied as carefully as it should have been, there would be far less of "I" heard and far more of Christ. It is self-esteem that stands between the human agent and his God and impedes the vital current that flows from Christ to enrich every human being. When we follow Jesus in the path of self-denial and the cross, we shall find that we do not have to strive for humility. As we walk in Christ's footsteps, we shall learn His meekness and lowliness of heart. Very few thoughts should be devoted to self; for we can never make ourselves great. It is Christ's gentleness that makes us great.[42]

God's faithful, humble, believing people will cut the idolatry of self out of their hearts, and Christ will become all and in all.[43]

THE BRIGHTEST SUBJECT
OF OUR THOUGHTS

*My meditation of him shall be sweet: I will be glad in the Lord.
Ps. 104:34.*

Why not keep your minds fixed on the unsearchable riches of
Christ, that you may present to others the gems of truth? In the Word
of God there are rich mines of truth that we may spend our whole
lifetime in exploring, and yet we shall find that we have only begun
to view their precious stores. Sink the shaft deep, and bring up the
hidden treasures. But it is impossible to do this while we indulge an
idle, restless spirit, seeking constantly for something that will merely
gratify the senses, something to amuse, and cause a foolish laugh.
. . . Minds that are occupied with frivolous reading, with exciting stories, or with seeking after amusement, do not dwell upon Christ, and
cannot rejoice in the fullness of His love. The mind that finds pleasure in foolish thoughts and trifling conversation, is as destitute of the
joy of Christ as were the hills of Gilboa of dew or rain.

Does not your own experience testify to this? How much peace of
mind do you have at the close of a day spent in frivolity, in light and trifling conversation? Can you retire to rest at night, saying, "It is well, it is
well with my soul"? . . . How often when you come into the house of
God, into the solemn assembly, your thoughts are turned to that foolish
remark which someone has made, to that idle story, or that comical
thing which you read or saw. And the thought will come at just such a
time as to eclipse a bright ray of the glory of Christ, and you lose the
benefit of the heaven-sent light which you ought to receive. . . .

We need to be constantly filling the mind with Christ, and emp-
tying it of selfishness and sin. . . . just as surely as you empty your
mind of vanity and frivolity, the vacuum will be supplied with that
which God is waiting to give you—His Holy Spirit. Then out of the
good treasure of the heart you will bring forth good things, rich gems
of thought, and others will catch the words. . . . Your thoughts and
affections will dwell upon Christ, and you will reflect upon others
that which has shone upon you from the Sun of Righteousness.[44]

April 20

TIME FOR MEDITATION

But his delight is in the law of the Lord; and in his law doth he meditate day and night. Ps. 1:2.

Your last thought at night, your first thought in the morning, should be of Him in whom is centered your hope of eternal life.[45]

Many seem to begrudge moments spent in meditation, and the searching of the Scriptures, and prayer, as though the time thus occupied was lost. I wish you could all view these things in the light God would have you; for you would then make the kingdom of heaven of the first importance. . . . As exercise increases the appetite, and gives strength and healthy vigor to the body, so will devotional exercises bring an increase of grace and spiritual vigor.

The affections should center upon God. Contemplate His greatness, His mercy and excellences. Let His goodness and love and perfection of character captivate your heart. Converse upon His divine charms, and the heavenly mansions He is preparing for the faithful. He whose conversation is in heaven, is the most profitable Christian to all around him. His words are useful and refreshing. They have a transforming power upon those who hear them.[46]

There is constant need of private communion with God. We must take in the spirit of Christ if we would impart it to others. We cannot meet satanic and human agencies combined unless we spend much time in intercourse with the Source of all strength. There are times when we should get away from the sounds of earthly toil and human voices, and in retired places listen to the voice of Jesus. Thus we may taste of His love and imbibe His spirit. Thus we shall learn to crucify self. This course of action may seem impossible to the human mind. "I have not time," you may say. But when you consider the matter as it really is, you lose no time; for when you secure the power and grace that come alone from God, *you* do not accomplish the work. It is Jesus who is the real worker. "Without me," says Christ, "ye can do nothing." John 15:5. . . . Reflection and earnest prayer will inspire to holy endeavor.[47]

WHAT IS FAITH?

Now faith is the substance of things hoped for, the evidence of things not seen. Heb. 11:1.

Faith in Christ is not the work of nature, but the work of God on human minds, wrought in the very soul by the Holy Spirit, who reveals Christ, as Christ revealed the Father. Faith is the substance of things hoped for, the evidence of things not seen. With its justifying, sanctifying power, it is above what men call science. It is the science of eternal realities. Human science is often deceptive and misleading, but this heavenly science never misleads. It is so simple that a child can understand it, and yet the most learned men cannot explain it. It is inexplainable and immeasurable, beyond all human expression.[48]

The acceptance of Christ's atonement is the groundwork of true faith. . . . Those who will look long enough into the divine mirror to see and despise their sins, their unlikeness to the meek and lowly Jesus, will have strength to overcome. All who truly believe will confess and forsake their sins. They will cooperate with Christ in the work of bringing their hereditary and cultivated tendencies to wrong under the control of the divine will, so that sin shall not have dominion over them. Looking to Jesus, the author and finisher of their faith, they will be changed into His likeness. They will grow up into the full stature of men and women in Christ Jesus. . . . Those who truly believe, who confess and forsake their sins, will grow more and more like Christ, until of them it can in heaven be said, "Ye are complete in him." Col. 2:10.[49]

"Ask, and it shall be given you" (Matt. 7:7) is the promise. Our part is to rest on the Word with unwavering faith, believing that God will do according to His promise. Let faith cut its way through the shadow of the enemy. When a questioning doubt arises, go to Christ and let the soul be encouraged by communion with Him. The redemption He has purchased for us is complete. The offering He made was plenteous and without stint. Heaven has a never-failing supply of help for all who are needy.[50]

April 22

SAVED BY GOD'S GRACE

For by grace are ye saved through faith; and that not of yourselves: it is the gift of God: not of works, lest any man should boast. Eph. 2:8, 9.

The divine favor, the grace of God bestowed upon us through Jesus Christ, is too precious to be given in exchange for any supposed meritorious work on the part of finite, erring man. Man has nothing in himself. The most exalted talent does not originate from man, but is the endowment of his Creator, and can purchase nothing from God. Gold and silver cannot buy the favor of God; for the wealth of the world is the entrusted talent of the Lord. Let no one think that costly offerings to benevolent enterprises will elevate him in the sight of God, or purchase for him the favor of Heaven, or procure for him a place in the mansions which Jesus has gone to prepare for those who love Him. The precious blood of Christ is wholly efficacious. . . .

The resurrection of Christ from the dead was the Father's seal to the mission of Christ. It was a public expression of His entire satisfaction in the atoning work. He accepted the sacrifice that Jesus had made on our behalf. It was everything that God required, perfect and complete. No human being by any work of his own could piece out the work of Christ. When on the cross Jesus uttered the cry, "It is finished!" glory and joy thrilled heaven, and discomfiture fell upon the confederacy of evil. After that triumphant cry, the world's Redeemer bowed His head and died, . . . but by His death He was a conqueror, and He has opened the gates of eternal glory so that all who believe in Him may not perish, but have everlasting life.

The sinner's only hope is to rely wholly upon Jesus Christ. . . . Our acceptance with God is sure only through His beloved Son, and good works are but the result of the working of His sin-pardoning love. They are no credit to us, and we have nothing accorded to us for our good works by which we may claim a part in the salvation of our souls. Salvation is God's free gift to the believer, given to him for Christ's sake alone. The troubled soul may find peace through faith in Christ. . . . He cannot present his good works as a plea for the salvation of his soul.[51]

118

FEELING NOT A SAFE GUIDE

The just shall live by his faith. Hab. 2:4.

Many pass long years in darkness and doubt because they do not feel as they desire. But feeling has nothing to do with faith. That faith which works by love and purifies the soul is not a matter of impulse. It ventures out upon the promises of God, firmly believing that what He has said, He is able also to perform. Our souls may be trained to believe, taught to rely upon the Word of God. That Word declares that "the just shall live by faith" (Rom. 1:17), not by feeling.[52]

Let us put away everything like distrust and want of faith in Jesus. Let us commence a life of simple, childlike trust, not relying upon feeling, but upon faith. Do not dishonor Jesus by doubting His precious promises. He wants us to believe in Him with unwavering faith.

There is a class who say, "I believe, I believe," and lay claim to all the promises which are given on condition of obedience; but they do not the works of Christ. God is not honored by any such faith. It is spurious. Another class are trying to keep all the commandments of God, but many of them do not come up to their exalted privilege in claiming the promises that were given for them. God's promises are for those who keep His commandments, and do those things that are pleasing in His sight.

I find that I have to fight the good fight of faith every day. I have to exercise all my faith, and not rely upon feeling; I have to act as though I knew the Lord heard me, and would answer me and bless me. Faith is not a happy flight of feeling; it is simply taking God at His word—believing that He will fulfill His promises because He said He would.[53]

Hope in God, trust in Him, and rest in His promises, whether you feel happy or not. A good emotion is no evidence that you are a child of God, neither are disturbed, troubled, perplexing feelings an evidence that you are not a child of God. Come to the Scriptures and intelligently take God at His word. Comply with the conditions and believe He will accept you as His child. Be not faithless, but believing.[54]

FEELING AND FAITH DISTINCT

For we walk by faith, not by sight. 2 Cor. 5:7.

When we comply with the Written Word then we are to walk by faith. We dishonor God when we fail to trust Him after He has given such wonderful evidence of His compassionate love in the gift of His Son. We are to keep looking to Jesus, offering up our prayers in faith, taking hold of His strength. If we would give more expression to our faith, rejoice more in the blessings that we know we have, we would daily have great cheerfulness and strength.

Feeling and faith are as distinct from each other as the east is from the west. Faith is not dependent on feeling. Daily we should dedicate ourselves to God, and believe that Christ understands and accepts the sacrifice, without examining ourselves to see if we have that degree of feeling that we think should correspond with our faith. Have we not the assurance that our heavenly Father is more willing to give the Holy Spirit to them that ask Him in faith than parents are to give good gifts to their children? We should go forward as if to every prayer that we send to the throne of God we heard the response from the One whose promises never fail. Even when depressed by sadness it is our privilege to make melody in our hearts to God. When we do this the mists and clouds will be rolled back and we will pass from the shadow and darkness into the clear sunshine of His presence.

If we educated our souls to have more faith, more love, greater patience, a more perfect trust in our heavenly Father, we would have more peace and happiness as we pass through the conflicts of this life. The Lord is not pleased to have us fret and worry ourselves out of the arms of Jesus. He is the only source of every grace, the fulfillment of every promise, the realization of every blessing. . . . Our pilgrimage would indeed be lonely were it not for Jesus. "I will not leave you comfortless," (John 14:18) He says to us. Let us cherish His words, believe His promises, repeat them by day and meditate upon them in the night season, and be happy.[55]

April 25

FAITH THAT WORKS AND PURIFIES

Who gave himself for us, that he might redeem us from all iniquity, and purify unto himself a peculiar people, zealous of good works. Titus 2:14.

When you look to Calvary it is not to quiet your soul in the non-performance of duty, not to compose yourself to sleep, but to create faith in Jesus, faith that will work, purifying the soul from the slime of selfishness. When we lay hold of Christ by faith, our work has just begun. Every man has corrupt and sinful habits that must be overcome by vigorous warfare. Every soul is required to fight the fight of faith. If one is a follower of Christ, he cannot be sharp in deal, he cannot be hardhearted, devoid of sympathy. He cannot be coarse in his speech. He cannot be full of pomposity and self-esteem. He cannot be overbearing, nor can he use harsh words, and censure and condemn.

The labor of love springs from the work of faith. Bible religion means constant work. . . . We are to be zealous of good works; be careful to maintain good works. And the true Witness says, "I know thy works." While it is true that our busy activities will not in themselves ensure salvation, it is also true that faith which unites us to Christ will stir the soul to activity.[56]

The true Christian abounds in good works; he brings forth much fruit. He feeds the hungry, clothes the naked, visits the sick, and ministers to the afflicted. Christians take a heartfelt interest in the children that are about them, who, through the subtle temptations of the enemy, are ready to perish. Fathers and mothers, if you have guarded your own children from the wiles of the foe, look about you to save the souls of the children who have not such care. . . . There are youth all around us to whom the members of the church owe a duty; for Christ has died for them. . . . They are precious in the sight of God, and He desires their eternal happiness. . . . Christ calls for voluntary cooperation on the part of His agents in doing earnest, consistent work for the salvation of souls.[57]

A religion which shines out in good works emits a clear, sure, safe light.[58]

121

THE PLACE OF GOOD WORKS

For we are his workmanship, created in Christ Jesus unto good works, which God hath before ordained that we should walk in them. Eph. 2:10.

Let no one take the limited, narrow position that any of the works of man can help in the least possible way to liquidate the debt of his transgression. This is a fatal deception. If you would understand it, you must . . . with humble hearts survey the atonement. This matter is so dimly comprehended that thousands upon thousands claiming to be sons of God are children of the wicked one, because they will depend on their own works. God always demanded good works, the law demands it, but because man placed himself in sin where his good works were valueless, Jesus' righteousness alone can avail.[59]

But are good works of no real value? Is the sinner who commits sin every day with impunity, regarded of God with the same favor as the one who through faith in Christ tries to work in his integrity? The Scripture answers, "We are his workmanship, created in Christ Jesus unto good works, which God hath before ordained that we should walk in them." In His divine arrangement, through His unmerited favor, the Lord has ordained that good works shall be rewarded. We are accepted through Christ's merit alone; and the acts of mercy, the deeds of charity, which we perform, are the fruits of faith; and they become a blessing to us; for men are to be rewarded according to their works. It is the fragrance of the merit of Christ that makes our good works acceptable to God, and it is grace that enables us to do the works for which He rewards us. Our works in and of themselves have no merit. . . . We deserve no thanks from God. We have only done what it was our duty to do, and our works could not have been performed in the strength of our own sinful natures.[60]

Christ is able to save to the uttermost. All that man can possibly do toward his own salvation is to accept the invitation, "Whosoever will, let him take the water of life freely." Rev. 22:17. No sin can be committed by man for which satisfaction has not been met on Calvary.[61]

DON'T BE A PRETENDER

Verily, verily, I say unto you, He that believeth on me, the works that I do shall he do also; and greater works than these shall he do; because I go unto my Father. John 14:12.

Christians are to be indeed the representatives of Jesus Christ; they are not to be pretenders. Shall the world form its conceptions of God by the course of those who only take the name of Christ, and do not His works? Shall they point to those who claim to be believers, but who are not believers at heart, who betray sacred trusts, and work the works of the enemy, and say, "O these are Christians, and they will cheat and lie, and they cannot be trusted"? These are not the ones who truly represent God. But God will not leave the world to be deceived. The Lord has a peculiar people on the earth, and He is not ashamed to call them brethren; for they do the works of Christ. They make it manifest that they love God, because they keep His commandments. They bear the divine image. They are a spectacle unto the world, to angels, and to men.[62]

The reward, the glories of heaven, bestowed upon the overcomers, will be proportionate to the degree in which they have represented the character of Christ to the world. "He which soweth sparingly shall reap also sparingly." 2 Cor. 9:6. Thank God that it is our privilege to sow on earth the seed that will be harvested in eternity. The crown of life will be bright or dim, will glitter with many stars, or be lighted by few gems, in accordance with our own course of action. Day by day we may be laying up a good foundation against the time to come. By self-denial, by the exercise of the missionary spirit, by crowding all the good works possible into our life, by seeking so to represent Christ in character that we shall win many souls to the truth, we shall have respect unto the recompense of reward.

It rests with us to walk in the light, to make the most of every opportunity and privilege, to grow in grace and in the knowledge of our Lord Jesus Christ, and so we shall work the works of Christ, and insure for ourselves treasure in the heavens.[63]

HOLD YOUR POSITION HOUR BY HOUR

Let us hold fast the profession of our faith without wavering; (for he is faithful that promised). Heb. 10:23.

It is our privilege, as children of God, to hold fast the profession of our faith without wavering. At times the masterly power of temptation seems to tax our will power to the uttermost, and to exercise faith seems utterly contrary to all the evidences of sense or emotion; but our will must be kept on God's side. We must believe that in Jesus Christ is everlasting strength and efficiency. . . . Hour by hour we must hold our position triumphantly in God, strong in His strength. . . .

All things are possible to them that believe. Since God is working in you, you can safely set your face as a flint to do His will, and you may trust the Lord perfectly. . . .

You must make a daily, personal consecration of all to God. You must daily renew your covenant to be His wholly and forever. Place no dependence upon changeable feelings, but plant your feet upon the sure platform of the promises of God: Thou hast said it; I believe the promise. This is an intelligent faith.

Your feelings will be troubled as you see some pursuing a course contrary to the principles of Christ; trials and tests of faith will come to you; but I entreat you to look only to Jesus, and allow none of these things to harden your heart, or to cause darkness or unbelief. Let nothing cause your faith to fail. Live as in the sight of God. Talk with Jesus as you would speak with a friend. He is ready to help you in the sorest trial; He is with you in the gravest perplexity. . . .

A feeling of assurance is not to be despised; we should praise God for it; but when your feelings are depressed, do not think that God has changed. Praise Him just as much, because you trust in His word, and not in feelings. You have covenanted to walk by faith, not to be controlled by feelings. Feelings vary with circumstances. . . .

Walk before God by faith, and rest fully upon His promises. Jesus says, "Lo, I am with you alway, even unto the end of the world." Matt. 28:20.[64]

STRENGTH FOR TODAY

As thy days, so shall thy strength be. Deut. 33:25.

I thank the Lord for the assurance of His grace, that is for His people now, today. . . . The promise is not that we will have strength today for a future emergency, that anticipated future trouble will be provided for beforehand, before it comes to us. We may, if we walk by faith, expect strength and provision for us as fast as our circumstances demand it. We live by faith, not by sight. The Lord's arrangement is for us to ask Him for the very things that we need. The grace of tomorrow will not be given today. Men's necessity is God's opportunity. . . . The grace of God is never given to be squandered, to be misapplied or perverted, or to be left to rust with disuse. . . .

While you are bearing daily responsibilities in the love and fear of God, as obedient children walking in all humility of mind, strength and wisdom from God will be given to meet every trying circumstance.

We will not be able to meet the trials of this time without God. We are not to have the courage and fortitude of martyrs of old until brought into the position they were in. . . . We are to receive daily supplies of grace for each daily emergency. Thus we grow in grace and in the knowledge of our Lord Jesus Christ, and if persecution comes upon us, if we must be enclosed in prison walls for the faith of Jesus and the keeping of God's holy law, "As thy days, so shall thy strength be." Should there be a return of persecution there would be grace given to arouse every energy of the soul to show a true heroism. . . .

We are to keep close to the Source of our strength day by day, and when the enemy comes in like a flood the Spirit of the Lord lifts up a standard for us against the enemy. The promise of God is sure, that strength shall be proportioned to our day. We may be confident for the future only in the strength that is given for the present necessities. The experience in God is daily becoming more precious. . . . Do not borrow anxiety for the future. It is today that we are in need. . . . The Lord is our helper, our God, and our strength in every time of need.[65]

VICTORY AFTER VICTORY

For whatsoever is born of God overcometh the world: and this is the victory that overcometh the world, even our faith. 1 John 5:4.

When clouds come between your soul and God, when all around you is dark and forbidding, when the enemy stands ready to rob the soul of its integrity to God and the truth, and when error stands out plausible and attractive, then it is time to pray and exercise faith in God. . . . Cherishing faith, the soul is enabled to rise beyond itself, and penetrate the hellish shadow which the enemy casts athwart the pathway of every soul that is striving for an immortal crown. . . .

Jesus said, "Watch ye and pray, lest ye enter into temptation." Mark 14:38. We are to watch and pray just as long as Satan brings up clouds of unbelief, composed of every evil thing that he can devise to lead the human mind to yield to temptation. But this cloud that lies between God and the human agent cannot envelop man and penetrate his soul unless he opens his mind and heart to its dark beams. The angels of God will guard from the poisonous malaria of temptations of the wicked one every man who will rise beyond self and circumstances and surroundings, looking unto Jesus through every mist and fog and cloud, and penetrating by faith the darkest temptations. . . .

United with Christ, all the power you require will be given you. Abiding in Him, you can fight manfully. The more you believe and trust as a child in the Lord Jesus, the greater will be your capacity for believing. By faith you stand. Only by exercising faith can you conquer self. . . . Self is the ground where Satan always meets and manages those whom he wishes to deceive and conquer. But if the righteousness of Christ is revealed in you, you become strong. Looking beyond yourself to a crucified Saviour, a risen and ascended Lord, who is, as your Advocate, making intercession for you, taking hold of Christ's power and efficiency, you can conquer.[66]

No victories ever won can compare in any wise with the victories of faith. Never let go your hold upon faith. It may triumph amid discouragement, gaining victory after victory.[67]

PRAYER, THE CHANNEL OF ALL BLESSINGS

And all things, whatsoever ye shall ask in prayer, believing, ye shall receive. Matt. 21:22.

Prayer is the breath of the soul, the channel of all blessings. As, with a realization of the needs of humanity, with a feeling of self-loathing, the repentant soul offers its prayer, God sees its struggles, watches its conflicts, and marks its sincerity. He has His finger upon its pulse, and He takes note of every throb. Not a feeling thrills it, not an emotion agitates it, not a sorrow shades it, not a sin stains it, not a thought or purpose moves it, of which He is not cognizant. That soul was purchased at an infinite cost, and is loved with a devotion that is unalterable. . . .

Christ our Saviour . . . had bodily wants to be supplied, bodily weariness to be relieved. It was by prayer to His Father that He was braced for duty and for trial. Day by day He followed His round of duty, seeking to save souls. His heart went out in tender sympathy for the weary and heavy laden. And He spent whole nights in prayer in behalf of the tempted ones. . . .

The Christian is given the invitation to carry his burdens to God in prayer, and to fasten himself closely to Christ by the cords of living faith. The Lord authorizes us to pray, declaring that He will hear the prayers of those who trust in His infinite power. He will be honored by those who draw nigh to Him, who faithfully do His service. "Thou wilt keep him in perfect peace, whose mind is stayed on thee: because he trusteth in thee." Isa. 26:3. The arm of Omnipotence is outstretched to guide us and lead us onward and still onward. Go forward, the Lord says; I understand the case, and I will send you help. Continue to pray. Have faith in Me. It is for My name's glory that you ask, and you shall receive. I will be honored before those who are watching critically for your failure. They shall see the truth triumph gloriously. "All things, whatsoever ye ask in prayer, believing, ye shall receive.". . .

True faith, true prayer—how strong they are![1]

AN OPEN DOOR TO GOD'S THRONE

Behold, I have set before thee an open door, and no man can shut it. Rev. 3:8.

The true Witness declares: "Behold, I have set before thee an open door." Let us thank God with heart and soul and voice; and let us learn to approach unto Him as through an open door, believing that we may come freely with our petitions, and that He will hear and answer. It is by a living faith in His power to help, that we shall receive strength to fight the battles of the Lord with the confident assurance of victory.[2]

Those who are seeking to be faithful to God may be denied many of the privileges of the world; their way may be hedged up and their work hindered by the enemies of truth; but there is no power that can close the door of communication between God and their souls. The Christian himself may close this door by indulgence in sin, or by rejection of heaven's light. He may turn away his ears from hearing the message of truth, and in this way sever the connection between God and his soul. . . . Every day we have the precious privilege of connecting ourselves with Christ, who has set before us an open door. All heaven is at our command. If we are obedient children of God, we may draw daily supplies of grace. Whatever temptations, trials, or persecutions may come upon us, we need not be discouraged. Neither man nor Satan can close the door which Christ has opened for us.[3]

Whenever tempted, we have this open door to behold. No power can hide from us the light of the glory which shines from the threshold of heaven along the whole length of the ladder we are to climb; for the Lord has given us strength in His strength, courage in His courage, light in His light. When the powers of darkness are overcome, when the light of the glory of God floods the world, we shall see and understand more clearly than we do today. If we only realized that the glory of God is round about us, that heaven is nearer earth than we suppose, we should have a heaven in our homes while preparing for the heaven above.[4]

BLESSINGS FOR THOSE WHO ASK

Ye have not, because ye ask not. James 4:2.

The grace of Christ we cannot do without. We must have help from above if we resist the manifold temptations of Satan, and escape his devices. Amid the prevailing darkness, we must have light from God to reveal the traps and gins of error, or we shall be ensnared. We should improve the opportunity for prayer, both in secret and around the family altar. Many need to learn how to pray. . . . When we in humility tell the Lord our wants, the Spirit itself makes intercession for us; as our sense of need causes us to lay bare our souls before the all-searching eye of Omnipotence, our earnest, fervent prayers enter within the vail, our faith claims the promises of God, and help comes to us. . . .

Prayer is both a duty and a privilege. We must have help which God alone can give, and that help will not come unasked. If we are too self-righteous to feel our need of help from God, we shall not have His help when we need it most. If we are too independent and self-sufficient to throw ourselves daily by earnest prayer upon the merits of a crucified and risen Saviour, we shall be left subject to Satan's temptations. . . . Earnest, sincere . . . prayer would bring strength and grace to resist the powers of darkness. God wants to bless. He is more willing to give the Holy Spirit to them that ask Him than are parents to give good gifts to their children. But many do not feel their need. They do not realize that they can do nothing without the help of Jesus. . . .

I have been shown angels of God all ready to impart grace and power to those who feel their need of divine strength. But these heavenly messengers will not bestow blessings unless solicited. They have waited for the cry from souls hungering and thirsting for the blessing of God; often have they waited in vain. There were, indeed, casual prayers, but not the earnest supplication from humble, contrite hearts. . . .

Those who would receive the blessing of the Lord, must themselves prepare the way, by confession of sin, by humiliation before God, with true penitence, and with faith in the merits of the blood of Christ.[5]

M a y   4

LEARN HOW TO PRAY

Lord, teach us to pray. Luke 11:1.

Christ did not give this prayer [the Lord's Prayer, Luke 11:2-4] for men to repeat as a form. He gave it as an illustration of what our prayers should be—simple, earnest, and comprehensive.[6]

Many prayers are offered without faith. A set form of words is used, but there is no real importunity. These prayers are doubtful, hesitating; they bring no relief to those who offer them, and no comfort or hope to others. The form of prayer is used, but the spirit is wanting, showing that the petitioner does not feel his need. . . .

Learn to pray short and right to the point, asking for just what you need. Learn to pray aloud where only God can hear you. Do not offer make-believe prayers, but earnest, feeling petitions, expressing the hunger of the soul for the Bread of Life. If we prayed more in secret, we should be able to pray more intelligently in public. These doubtful, hesitating prayers would cease. And when we engaged with our brethren in public worship, we could add to the interest of the meeting; for we should bring with us some of the atmosphere of heaven, and our worship would be a reality, and not a mere form. . . . If the soul is not drawn out in prayer in the closet and while engaged in the business of the day, it will be manifest in the prayer meeting. . . .

The life of the soul depends upon habitual communion with God. Its wants are made known, and the heart is open to receive fresh blessings. Gratitude flows from unfeigned lips; and the refreshing that is received from Jesus is manifested in words, in deeds of active benevolence, and in public devotion. There is love to Jesus in the heart; and where love exists, it will not be repressed, but will express itself. Secret prayer sustains this inner life. The heart that loves God will desire to commune with Him, and will lean on Him in holy confidence.

Let us learn to pray intelligently, expressing our requests with clearness and precision. Let us . . . pray as though we meant it. "The effectual fervent prayer of a righteous man availeth much." James 5:16.[7]

SEEK GOD WITH ALL THE HEART

Turn you to the strong hold, ye prisoners of hope: even to day do I declare that I will render double unto thee. Zech. 9:12.

We need to educate the soul to lay hold, and hold fast the rich promises of Christ. The Lord Jesus knows that it is not possible for us to resist the many temptations of Satan, only as we shall have divine power given us from God. He well knows that in our own human strength we should surely fail. Therefore every provision has been made, that in every emergency and trial we shall flee to the Stronghold. . . . We have the word of promise from lips that will not lie. . . . We must individually cherish the faith that we receive of Him the things He hath promised.

God will be to us everything we will let Him be. Our languid, halfhearted prayers will not bring us returns from heaven. Oh, we need to press our petitions! Ask in faith, wait in faith, receive in faith, rejoice in hope, for everyone that seeketh findeth. Be in earnest in the matter. Seek God with all the heart. People put soul and earnestness into everything they undertake in temporal things, until their efforts are crowned with success. With intense earnestness learn the trade of seeking the rich blessings that God has promised, and with persevering, determined effort you shall have His light and His truth and His rich grace.[8]

In sincerity, in soul hunger, cry after God. Wrestle with the heavenly agencies until you have the victory. Put your whole being into the Lord's hands, soul, body, and spirit, and resolve to be His loving, consecrated agency, moved by His will, controlled by His mind, infused by His Spirit.[9]

Tell Jesus your wants in the sincerity of your soul. You are not required to hold a long controversy with, or preach a sermon to, God, but with a heart of sorrow for your sins, say, "Save me, Lord, or I perish." There is hope for such souls. They will seek, they will ask, they will knock, and they will find. When Jesus has taken away the burden of sin that is crushing the soul, you will experience the blessedness of the peace of Christ.[10]

VICTORY THROUGH WATCHFULNESS

Watch ye and pray, lest ye enter into temptation. Mark 14:38.

Temptations may be all around you, yet you are safe as long as you do not enter into them. Many of us are overcome by Satan because we walk right into temptation. . . . It is your business to keep aloof from everyone and everything which will have a tendency to lead you away from duty and divert your mind from God. . . . If compelled to be in the society of those who are evil, you are not compelled to enter into or engage in their evil. You can, by prayer and watching, remain unsullied by the evil manifested about you.[11]

"Watch and pray" is an injunction often repeated in the Scriptures. In the lives of those who obey this injunction there will be an undercurrent of happiness that will bless all with whom they are brought in contact. Those who are sour and cross in disposition will become sweet and gentle; those who are proud will become meek and lowly.[12]

A man cannot be a happy Christian unless he is a watchful Christian. He who overcomes must watch; for with worldly entanglements, error, and superstition, Satan strives to win Christ's followers from Him, and to keep their minds employed with his devices. It is not enough that we avoid glaring dangers and perilous, inconsistent moves. We are to keep close to the side of Christ, walking in the path of self-denial and self-sacrifice. We are not to allow our spiritual perceptions to be blinded, as they often are, by a strong, determined will. And in order to detect the artifices of Satan and to withstand his unexpected attacks, we must have the grace of Christ and the impartation of His Spirit. . . .

God's Word warns us that we have manifold enemies, not open and avowed, but enemies who come with smooth words and fair speeches, and who would deceive if possible the very elect. Thus Satan comes. And again, when it suits his purpose, he goes about as a roaring lion, seeking whom he may devour. Man's will, unless kept in subjection to the will of God, is as often on the enemy's side as on the Lord's side. Therefore watch unto prayer; watch and pray always.[13]

HUMBLE, PERSEVERING PRAYER

Elias was a man subject to like passions as we are, and he prayed earnestly that it might not rain: and it rained not on the earth by the space of three years and six months. And he prayed again, and the heaven gave rain, and the earth brought forth her fruit. James 5:17, 18.

Important lessons are presented to us in the experience of Elijah. When upon Mount Carmel he offered the prayer for rain, his faith was tested, but he persevered in making known his request unto God.[14]

The servant watched while Elijah prayed. Six times he returned from the watch, saying, There is nothing, no cloud, no sign of rain. But the prophet did not give up in discouragement. He kept reviewing his life, to see where he had failed to honor God. . . . As he searched his heart, he seemed to be less and less, both in his own estimation and in the sight of God. It seemed to him that he was nothing, and that God was everything; and when he reached the point of renouncing self, while he clung to the Saviour as his only strength and righteousness, the answer came. The servant appeared, and said, "Behold, there ariseth a little cloud out of the sea, like a man's hand." 1 Kings 18:34.[15]

We have a God whose ear is not closed to our petitions; and if we prove His word, He will honor our faith. He wants us to have all our interests interwoven with His interests, and then He can safely bless us; for we shall not then take glory to self when the blessing is ours, but shall render all the praise to God. God does not always answer our prayers the first time we call upon Him; for should He do this, we might take it for granted that we had a right to all the blessings and favors He bestowed upon us. Instead of searching our hearts to see if any evil was entertained by us, any sin indulged, we should become careless, and fail to realize our dependence upon Him. . . .

Elijah humbled himself until he was in a condition where he would not take the glory to himself. This is the condition upon which the Lord hears prayer, for then we shall give the praise to Him. . . . God alone is worthy to be glorified.[16]

WAIT FOR GOD'S ANSWER

It is good that a man should both hope and quietly wait for the salvation of the Lord. Lam. 3:26.

There are precious promises in the Scriptures to those who wait upon the Lord. We all desire an immediate answer to our prayers, and we are tempted to become discouraged if our prayer is not immediately answered. Now my experience has taught me that this is a great mistake. The delay is for our special benefit. Our faith has a chance to be tested to see whether it is true, sincere, or changeable like the waves of the sea. We must bind ourselves upon the altar with the strong cords of faith and love, and let patience have her perfect work. Faith strengthens through continual exercise.[17]

We must pray more and in faith. We must not pray and then run away as though afraid we should receive an answer. God will not mock us. He will answer if we watch unto prayer, if we believe we receive the things we ask for, and keep believing and never lose patience in believing. This is watching unto prayer. We guard the prayer of faith with expectancy and hope. We must wall it in with assurance and be not faithless, but believing. The fervent prayer of the righteous is never lost. The answer may not come according as we expected, but it will come, because God's word is pledged.[18]

We need a calm waiting upon God. The need of this is imperious. It is not the noise and bustle we make in the world which proves our usefulness. See how silently God works! . . . Those who desire to labor with God have need of His Spirit every day; they need to walk and labor in meekness and humility of spirit, without seeking to accomplish extraordinary things, satisfied to do the work before them and doing it faithfully. Men may not see or appreciate their efforts, but the names of these faithful children of God are written in heaven among His noblest workers, as scattering His seed in view of a glorious harvest.[19]

Wait for the Lord, not in fretful anxiety, but in undaunted faith and unshaken trust.[20]

MEMENTOS IN MEMORY'S HALLS

Then Samuel took a stone, and set it between Mizpeh and Shen, and called the name of it Ebenezer, saying, Hitherto hath the Lord helped us. 1 Sam. 7:12.

There is more encouragement to us in the least blessing which we receive ourselves than in reading biographical works relating to the faith and experience of noted men of God. The things we ourselves have experienced of the blessings of God through His gracious promises we may hang in memory's halls, and whether rich or poor, learned or illiterate, we may look and may consider these tokens of God's love. Every token of God's care and goodness and mercy should be hung as imperishable mementos in memory's halls. God would have His love, His promises, written upon the tablets of the mind. Guard the precious revealings of God that not a letter shall become obliterated or dimmed.

When Israel obtained special victories after leaving Egypt, memorials were preserved of these victories. Moses and Joshua were commanded of God to do this, to build up remembrances. When the Israelites had won a special victory over the Philistines, Samuel set up a commemorative stone and called it Ebenezer, saying, "Hitherto hath the Lord helped us." . . .

Can we not, in view of the past, look on new trials and increased perplexities—even afflictions, privations, and bereavements—and not be dismayed, but look upon the past and say, "'Hitherto hath the Lord helped us.' I will commit the keeping of my soul unto Him as unto a faithful Creator. He will keep that which I have committed to His trust against that day." [21]

Let us look to the monumental pillars, reminders of what the Lord has done to comfort us and to save us from the hand of the destroyer. Let us keep fresh in our memory all the tender mercies that God has shown us—the tears He has wiped away, the pains He has soothed, the anxieties removed, the fears dispelled, the wants supplied, the blessings bestowed—thus strengthening ourselves for all that is before us through the remainder of our pilgrimage. [22]

ON THE MOUNT BEFORE GOD

*And he said, Go forth, and stand upon the mount before the Lord.
1 Kings 19:11.*

This command comes to every one of us who is looking to his discouragements and mourning over his frailties and giving to the world an example of distrust of God, refusing to look and live. . . . You please the enemy of God and of man by keeping in the cave of darkness where there is not a ray of the Light of life. . . .

I want to lift up my voice for Jesus and say, Whosoever believeth in Him shall not perish, but have eternal life. Go forth from the cave by faith. Look to Jesus, your helper. Behold the Lamb of God who taketh away the sins of the world. Look to your atoning Sacrifice lifted up upon the cross, the Innocent dying for the guilty. . . .

His offering of Himself was full and ample. Nothing was wanting. It was indeed a whole and ample atonement that was made. Then why . . . indicate by words and example that Christ has died for you in vain? After the exhibitions of love that was without a parallel, you say by your words of doubt and mournful discouragement, "He does not love me. He will not forgive me. My sins are of too hard a character to be cured by the blood of Jesus. The offering is not of sufficient value to pay the debt I owe for the rescue of my soul."

If men and women could only see and realize how their unbelief and mournful murmurings exalt Satan and give him honor, while they rob Jesus Christ of His glory in the work of saving them, wholly and entirely, from all sin! . . . Let us come out of the cavern of darkness. Let us educate our intellects to discern what Jesus is to us. Let us train our minds to stand on the mount before God in faith, strong in God under any and every temptation. . . .

In the mount we shall have correct views of Jesus. Satan will not have power to cast his hellish shadow between our souls and Jesus, eclipse our view of Jesus, falsify Him, and encourage our hearts in cruel unbelief of His goodness, His mercy, and His love wherewith He hath loved us.[23]

GOD'S LAW A WALL OF PROTECTION

Blessed are the undefiled in the way, who walk in the law of the Lord. Ps. 119:1.

God, the great governor of the universe, has put everything under law. The tiny flower and the towering oak, the grain of sand and the mighty ocean, sunshine and shower, wind and rain, all obey nature's laws. But man has been placed under a higher law. He has been given an intellect to see, and a conscience to feel, the powerful claims of God's great moral law, the expression of what He desires His children to be.

God has made known His will so plainly that none need err. He desires all to have a correct understanding of His law, to feel the power of its principles; for their eternal interests are here involved. He who has an understanding of the far-reaching claims of God's law can understand something of the heinousness of sin. And the more exalted his ideas of God's requirements, the greater will be his gratitude for the pardon granted him. . . .

In his own strength the sinner cannot meet the demands of God. He must go for help to the One who paid the ransom for him. . . .

Christ is our hope. Those who trust in Him are cleansed. The grace of Christ and the government of God walk together in perfect harmony. When Jesus became man's substitute, mercy and truth met together, and righteousness and peace kissed each other. The cross of Calvary bears witness to the high claims of God's law.[24]

The law of ten commandments is not to be looked upon as much from the prohibitory side, as from the mercy side. Its prohibitions are the sure guarantee of happiness in obedience. As received in Christ, it works in us the purity of character that will bring joy to us through eternal ages. To the obedient it is a wall of protection. We behold in it the goodness of God, who by revealing to men the immutable principles of righteousness, seeks to shield them from the evils that result from transgression.[25]

A COMPLETE RULE OF LIFE

*And the temple of God was opened in heaven, and there was seen
in his temple the ark of his testament. Rev. 11:19.*

Our Redeemer testifies: "Behold, I have set before thee an open
door, and no man can shut it." Rev. 3:8. Through this open door into
the temple of God, we see the royal law, deposited in the ark of the
testament. Through this open door, light shines from that holy, just,
and good law, presenting to man the true standard of righteousness,
that he may make no mistake in the formation of a character that will
meet the requirements of God. Sin is condemned by that law; we
must put it away. Pride and selfishness can find no place in the character without crowding out Him who was meek and lowly of heart.

The law of God is the standard by which character is to be
tested; if we erect a standard to suit ourselves, and attempt to follow
a criterion of our own devising, we shall utterly fail to secure heaven
at last. . . .

The mind must yield obedience to the royal law of liberty, the
law which the Spirit of God impresses upon the heart, and makes
plain to the understanding. The expulsion of sin must be the act of
the soul itself, in calling into exercise its noblest powers. The only
freedom a finite will can enjoy, consists in coming into harmony
with the will of God, complying with the conditions that make man
a partaker of the divine nature.[26]

The law of God given from Sinai is a copy of the mind and will
of the Infinite God. It is sacredly revered by the holy angels.
Obedience to its requirements will perfect Christian character, and
restore man, through Christ, to his condition before the Fall. The sins
forbidden in the law could never find place in heaven.

It was the love of God to man that prompted Him to express His
will in the ten precepts of the Decalogue. . . . God has given man a
complete rule of life in His law. Obeyed, he shall live by it, through
the merits of Christ. Transgressed, it has power to condemn. The law
sends men to Christ, and Christ points them back to the law.[27]

WEIGHING IN FOR HEAVEN

Let me be weighed in an even balance, that God may know mine integrity. Job 31:6.

True measure is everything. It is the very law of God. He puts His law into the least of men's acts and dealings, that learning and living it they may be elevated, ennobled, and sanctified in heart and affection—faithful in the least.[28]

God weighs motives, purposes, character. All men are weighed in the balances of the sanctuary, and God would have all realize this fact. Hannah said, "The Lord is a God of knowledge, and by him actions are weighed." 1 Sam. 2:3. David hath said, "Men of low degree are vanity, and men of high degree are a lie: to be laid in the balance, they are altogether lighter than vanity." Ps. 62:9. Isaiah says: "Thou, most upright, dost weigh the path of the just." Isa. 26:7. . . .

The God of heaven is true. There is not a motive in the depths of the heart, not a secret within us, not a design that God does not fully comprehend. But what is the standard of justice? God's law. God's law is placed in one scale, His holy immutable law whose claims are specified, taking, in the first four commandments, supreme love to God, and in the last six, love to our neighbor. "Thou shalt love the Lord thy God with all thy heart, . . . and thy neighbour as thyself." Luke 10:27. From this standard we will not subtract one atom. God requires all the heart, mind, soul, and strength, and "love thy neighbour as thyself." This is placed in one scale, while every individual character has to pass the weighing test by being placed in the opposite scale. And by its just comparison every man's doom is irretrievably fixed. . . .

Shall there be written, "Weighed in the balance, and found wanting"? If found wanting in the day of God it will be a terrible thing, therefore we want to be closely examining our own motives and actions by the holy law of God, to repent of every act of transgression, and as sinners lay hold of the merits of Christ to supply the deficiency. The blood of Christ alone will do this.[29]

HEART ALLEGIANCE

Not with eyeservice, as menpleasers; but as the servants of Christ, doing the will of God from the heart. Eph. 6:6.

The law of Jehovah is exceedingly broad. Jesus . . . plainly declared to His disciples that this holy law of God may be violated in even the thoughts and feelings and desires, as well as in the word and deed. The heart that loves God supremely will not in any way be inclined to narrow down His precepts to the very smallest possible claims, but the obedient, loyal soul will cheerfully tender full spiritual obedience when the law is seen in its spiritual power. Then will the commandments come home to the soul in their real force. Sin will appear exceedingly sinful. . . . There is no longer self-righteousness, self-esteem, self-honor. Self-security is gone. Deep conviction of sin and self-loathing is the result, and the soul in its desperate sense of peril lays hold on the blood of the Lamb of God as his only remedy. . . .

Many are deceiving their own souls today. They restrict the injunctions of God to condemn outward acts alone, and do not consider it sin to dishonor God in thoughts and affections. They flatter themselves that they are keeping the law of Jehovah while their life and character as daguerreotyped [photographed] in the books of heaven reveal them as venturing to see how far they can go in the direction of wrongdoing without being branded as transgressors of God's law. . . .

Every soul who desires to depart from all iniquity . . . will be ever laboring to be on the Lord's side in thought, in word, and in character, obedient to all His requirements. In the place of seeking opportunities to evade the law of God, he will give the largest interpretation to His far-reaching commandments and will strive most earnestly to bring the will, the affections, and all the heart to exemplify the great principles of His holy commandments. . . . The work must begin at the heart. . . . If the heart is right with God, then the whole life will be purified, refined, ennobled, sanctified. If the eye is single the whole body is filled with light. Religion is not a matter of externalities. . . . Religion is a thing of the heart.[30]

BLENDING THE LAW AND GOSPEL

Do we then make void the law of God through faith? God forbid: yea, we establish the law. Rom. 3:31.

We hear so many who are deceived by the enemy constantly claiming, "I am saved"; but . . . they show such contempt of God's rule of righteousness that we know that they . . . know nothing of saving grace. The heart is not in harmony with the law of God, but is at enmity with that law. Thus was the great rebel in heaven. Will the Lord take men and women to heaven who have no respect for the law of His universe? . . .

What is to bring the sinner to the knowledge of his sins unless he knows what sin is? The only definition of sin in the Word of God is given us in 1 John 3:4. "Sin is the transgression of the law." The sinner must be made to feel that he is a transgressor. Christ dying upon the cross of Calvary is drawing his attention. Why did Christ die? Because it was the only means for man to be saved. . . . He took upon Himself our sins that He might impute His righteousness to all who believe in Him. . . . The goodness and the love of God lead the sinner to repentance toward God and faith toward our Lord Jesus Christ. The awakened sinner . . . is pointed to the law he has transgressed. It calls to him to repent, yet there is no saving quality in law to pardon the transgression of law, and his case seems hopeless. But the law draws him to Christ. However deep are his sins of transgression, the blood of Jesus Christ can cleanse him from all sin. . . .

The law and the gospel go hand in hand. The one is the complement of the other. The law without faith in the gospel of Christ cannot save the transgressor of law. The gospel without the law is inefficient and powerless. The law and the gospel are a perfect whole. The Lord Jesus laid the foundation of the building, and He lays "the headstone thereof with shoutings, crying, Grace, grace unto it." Zech. 4:7. He is the author and finisher of our faith, the Alpha and Omega, the beginning and the end, the first and the last. The two blended—the gospel of Christ and the law of God—produce the love and faith unfeigned.[31]

PATHWAY TO PURITY

And every man that hath this hope in him purifieth himself, even as he is pure. 1 John 3:3.

Does this text mean that the human agent can remove one stain of sin from his soul? No. Then what does it mean to purify himself? It means to look upon the Lord's great moral standard of righteousness, the holy law of God, and see that he is a sinner in the light of that law. "Whosoever committeth sin transgresseth also the law: for sin is the transgression of the law. And ye know that he was manifested to take away our sins; and in him is no sin." 1 John 3:4, 5. It is through faith in Jesus Christ that . . . the human agent is purified and cleansed. . . . "Whosoever abideth in him sinneth not." Verse 6. God has power to keep the soul that is in Christ. . . . A mere profession of godliness is worthless. It is he that abideth in Christ that is a Christian. . . .

In every clime, in every nation, our youth should cooperate with God. The only way a person can be pure is to become like-minded with God. How can we know God? By studying His Word. . . .

Unless the mind of God becomes the mind of man, every effort to purify himself will be useless; for it is impossible to elevate man except through a knowledge of God. The outward gloss may be put on, and men may be as were the Pharisees whom Jesus describes as "whited sepulchres," full of corruption and dead men's bones. But all the deformity of the soul is open to Him who judgeth righteously, and unless the truth is planted in the heart, it cannot control the life. Cleansing the outside of the cup will never make the vessel pure within. A nominal acceptance of truth is good as far as it goes, and the ability to give a reason for our faith is a good accomplishment, but if the truth does not go deeper than this, the soul will never be saved. The heart must be purified from all moral defilement. "I know also my God, that thou triest the heart, and hast pleasure in uprightness." 1 Chron. 29:17. "Search me, O God, and know my heart: try me, and know my thoughts: and see if there be any wicked way in me, and lead me in the way everlasting." Ps. 139:23, 24.[32]

AN ENLIGHTENED CONSCIENCE

And herein do I exercise myself, to have always a conscience void of offence toward God, and toward men. Acts 24:16.

In the Word of God we read that there are good and bad consciences. . . . Take your conscience to the Word of God, and see if your life and character are in accordance with the standard of righteousness which God has there revealed. You can then determine whether or not you have an intelligent faith, and what manner of conscience is yours. The conscience of man cannot be trusted unless it is under the influence of divine grace. Satan takes advantage of an unenlightened conscience, and thereby leads men into all manner of delusions.[33]

It is not enough for a man to think himself safe in following the dictates of his conscience. . . . The question to be settled is, Is the conscience in harmony with the Word of God? If not, it cannot safely be followed, for it will deceive. The conscience must be enlightened by God. Time must be given to a study of the Scriptures and to prayer. Thus the mind will be stablished, strengthened, and settled.[34]

It is the privilege of everyone to so live that God will approve and bless him. You may be hourly in communion with Heaven; it is not the will of your heavenly Father that you should ever be under condemnation and darkness. It is not pleasing to God that you should demerit yourself. You should cultivate self-respect by living so that you will be approved by your own conscience, and before men and angels. . . . It is your privilege to go to Jesus and be cleansed, and to stand before the law without shame and remorse. "There is therefore now no condemnation to them which are in Christ Jesus, who walk not after the flesh, but after the Spirit." Rom. 8:1. While we should not think of ourselves more highly than we ought, the Word of God does not condemn a proper self-respect. As sons and daughters of God, we should have a conscious dignity of character, in which pride and self-importance have no part.[35]

A conscience void of offense toward God and man is a wonderful acquirement.[36]

FRUIT-BEARING BRANCHES

I am the true vine, and my Father is the husbandman. Every branch in me that beareth not fruit he taketh away: and every branch that beareth fruit, he purgeth it, that it may bring forth more fruit. John 15:1, 2.

The Saviour . . . points out the sign of discipleship: "Herein is my Father glorified, that ye bear much fruit; so shall ye be my disciples." By faith we are to lay hold on a living God, and maintain an experience that shall breathe love, tenderness, kindness, compassion, and affection. These traits of character are the fruit that the Lord Jesus desires us to produce, and to present before the world as a witness that we have a Saviour who can uplift and who can satisfy. . . . We need not be on the losing side, for in everything He is our sufficiency.

What we need is the presence of Jesus Christ. We want His truth shining in our hearts, pervading all our life actions. This will determine whether or not we are branches of the True Vine. If we are fruit-bearing branches we may expect that the Great Husbandman will prune us, that we may bring forth more fruit. All that is useless, all that would hinder our growth in the Christian life, must be removed.[37]

When the purging comes, we frequently feel that the Lord is against us. Instead of this we should look to ourselves and see if there is not something we have left undone or something we need to take away from our lives before we can stand in right relation to God. . . .

We must be living branches of the True Vine, daily laying hold of our Redeemer that we may bear the fruits of a Christian character. . . . When we are willing to practice self-denial and self-sacrifice, as Christ practiced it in His life, we shall bear fruit to God's glory.[38]

It is the Saviour's delight to see His followers colaborers with God, receiving bountifully all the means of fruit bearing, and giving bountifully, as workers under Him. Christ glorified His Father by the fruit He bore, and the lives of His true followers will produce the same result. Receiving and imparting, His workers will produce much fruit.[39]

ABIDING IN CHRIST

Abide in me, and I in you. As the branch cannot bear fruit of itself, except it abide in the vine; no more can ye, except ye abide in me. John 15:4.

As the severed branch, leafless, and apparently lifeless, is ingrafted into the living stock, and, fiber by fiber, and vein by vein, drinks in the life and strength of the vine until it buds and blossoms and bears fruit, even so may the sinner, by repentance and faith, connect himself with Christ, become a partaker of the divine nature, and bring forth in words and deeds the fruit of a holy life.

Jesus "has life in himself," and this life He offers to impart freely, to souls that are dead in trespasses and sins. Yea, He shares with them His purity, His honor, and exaltation. . . . The sapless branch, ingrafted into the living vine, becomes a part of the vine. It lives while united to the vine. So the Christian lives by virtue of his union with Christ. The sinful and human is linked to the holy and divine. The believing soul abides in Christ, and becomes one with Him. When persons are closely united in the relations of this life, their tastes become similar, they come to love the same things. So those who abide in Christ will love the things which He loves. They will sacredly cherish and obey His commandments. . . .

The vine-branch, nourished from the parent stock, becomes flourishing and fruitful. Its rich and fragrant clusters attest its union with the living vine. So the Christian, abiding in Jesus, will bring forth fruit. In character and life will be manifested, like the teeming cluster of the vine, the precious graces of the Spirit—love, joy, peace, longsuffering, gentleness, goodness, faith, meekness, temperance. . . .

Resolve that you will be fruit-bearing members of the living Vine. The scion can flourish only as it receives life and strength from the parent stock. Improve, then, every opportunity to connect yourselves more closely with Christ. It is by believing Him, loving Him, copying Him, and depending wholly upon Him, that you are to become one with Him; and through you His life and character will be revealed to the world.[40]

THE SOURCE OF MY STRENGTH

I am the vine, ye are the branches: He that abideth in me, and I in him, the same bringeth forth much fruit: for without me ye can do nothing. John 15:5.

We are finite, but a wonderful arrangement has been made that we may have close connection with the Infinite. . . . Finite beings at their best can do but little, but Christ working through humanity may accomplish wonderful results.

It is a painful thought to me that I can do so little. The limited sphere of human capabilities leads me to feel indeed the words of Christ, "Without *Me* ye can do *nothing.*" Many are endowed with superior talents and do not use them, because they have no living connection with God. . . . My own scanty knowledge and feeble energies drive me to Jesus, and the language of my heart is, "Oh God, I can do nothing. I hang my helpless soul on Thee, Jesus Christ my Saviour. Put Thy grace into my heart. Attract my mind from my weakness to Thy almighty strength, from my ignorance to Thy eternal wisdom, from my frailty to Thy enduring might. Give me correct views of the great plan of redemption. Let me see and understand what Christ is to me, and that my heart, soul, mind, and strength are bought with a price. Christ has imparted to me that I may impart to others. Lift up my soul; strengthen and enlighten my mind that I may comprehend more clearly the character of God as revealed in Jesus Christ, that I may know that it is my privilege to be a partaker of the divine nature."

The great and eternal power of God fills my mind with awe, and sometimes even terror. . . . May I indeed look upon Jesus, full of goodness and compassion and love, and behold the Lord God, and call Him by the endearing name of Father.

The deep struggles of my own soul against temptations, the earnest longings of my mind and heart to know God and Jesus Christ as my personal Saviour, and to have assurance, peace, and rest in their love, lead me to desire every day to be where the beams of the Sun of Righteousness can shine upon me.[41]

REJOICING IN ASSURANCE

If ye abide in me, and my words abide in you, ye shall ask what ye will, and it shall be done unto you. John 15:7.

Precious are the privileges accorded him who abides in Christ. . . . The mind of Christ dwells in His faithful followers; their desires are in accordance with His will; their petitions are indited by His Spirit. They obtain answers to their prayers; for they ask for such blessings as He delights to bestow.

. But there are thousands of prayers daily offered that God does not answer. There are faithless prayers. "He that cometh to God must believe that he is, and that he is a rewarder of them that diligently seek him." Heb. 11:6. There are selfish prayers, proceeding from a heart that is cherishing idols. . . . There are petulant, fretful prayers, murmuring because of the burdens and cares of life, instead of humbly seeking grace to lighten them. Those who offer such petitions are not abiding in Christ. They have not submitted their will to the will of God. They do not comply with the condition of the promise, and it is not fulfilled to them.

They that are abiding in Jesus have the assurance that God will hear them, because they love to do His will. They offer no formal, wordy prayer, but come to God in earnest, humble confidence as a child to a tender father, and pour out the story of their grief and fears and sins, and in the name of Jesus present their wants; they depart from His presence rejoicing in the assurance of pardoning love and sustaining grace.[42]

With a sense that Jesus is by your side, you will have cheerfulness, hope, courage, and joy. . . . Never, never separate from Jesus. He never separates from us. By the cross of Calvary He has given evidence of His deep love for us. He does not leave us to fight the battle in our own finite strength. He says, "I will never leave thee nor forsake thee." Heb. 13:5. . . . Jesus does not cast us off, even when we grieve Him; He clings to us still. Let your heart be animated by the love of Jesus to ardent activity for His glory.[43]

MOST HAPPY PEOPLE ON EARTH

These things have I spoken unto you, that my joy might remain in you, and that your joy might be full. John 15:11.

We, as Christians, are not required to go about with long faces, sighing as though we had no Saviour and no hope. This will not glorify God. He desires us to be cheerful. He desires us to be filled with praises to His name. He desires us to carry light in our countenances, and joy in our hearts. We have a hope that is far above any pleasures that the world can give, and this fact should be made manifest.

Why should not our joy be full—full, lacking nothing? We have an assurance that Jesus is our Saviour, and that we may draw freely from Him. We may partake freely of the rich provision that He has made for us in His Word. We may take Him at His word, believe on Him, and know that He will give us grace and power to do just as He bids us. . . . We may constantly seek the joy of His presence. We need not be all the time upon our knees in prayer, but we may be constantly asking for His grace, even when we are walking on the streets, or when we are engaged in our ordinary daily duties. We may constantly keep the mind ascending to Christ, and He will freely impart to us of His grace. . . .

The joy of Christ is a pure, unalloyed cheerfulness. It is not a cheap gaiety, that leads to vanity of words or lightness of conduct. No, we are to have *His* joy, and His greatest joy was to see men obeying the truth. . . . Plead with God, saying, "I make an entire surrender. I give myself away to Thee." Then be joyful. The Word is in you, purifying and cleansing your character. God does not want His children to go about with anxiety and sorrow expressed in their faces. He wants the lovely expression of His countenance to be revealed in every one of us who are partakers of the divine nature; for we have power to escape the corruptions of the world. . . .

We are not, because Christ died, left a company of orphans. . . . It is possible for us to obtain victory after victory, and be the most happy people on the face of the earth.[44]

FRIENDSHIP WITH JESUS

Ye are my friends, if ye do whatsoever I command you. John 15:14.

The character and course of the Christian is in marked contrast to that of worldlings. The Christian cannot find pleasure in the amusements and in the varied scenes of gaiety of the world. Higher and holier attractions engage the affections. Christians will show that they are the friends of God by their obedience. "Ye are my friends," says Christ, "if ye do whatsoever I command you. . . . If ye were of the world, the world would love his own: but because ye are not of the world, but I have chosen you out of the world, therefore the world hateth you."

Christ is your rock and your fortress. Unto His name the righteous runneth and are safe. . . . The righteousness and excellency of His requirements are not comprehended by the world, who look upon the religion of Christ as a yoke of bondage, a surrender of their liberty. Each of God's requirements is an order to become wise, rich, and noble by uniting our weak strength with the power of the Infinite. While following the footsteps of Christ we need never blush, for our conscience will never reproach us. His service is always reasonable. His work is always honorable and glorious. Our friends who desire us to choose the pleasures of the world and to conform to the customs of the world, who look upon us as obstinate, can have no claims upon us that bear any comparison with the claims of Christ. . . .

The value of man as God estimates him is through his union with Christ; for God is the only One able to raise man in the scale of moral worth through the righteousness of Christ. Worldly honor and worldly greatness are of just that value that the Creator of man places upon them. Their wisdom is foolishness, their strength weakness.

Let us value what God esteems. True elevation of character is found alone through Christ. Our Saviour imputes His righteousness to the man who yields to Him his heart's best and holiest affections. Our value is in proportion to our alliance to God.[45]

JESUS' CROWNING GIFT

Nevertheless I tell you the truth; It is expedient for you that I go away: for if I go not away, the Comforter will not come unto you; but if I depart, I will send him unto you. John 16:7.

Christ declared that after His ascension, He would send to His church, as His crowning gift, the Comforter, who was to take His place. This Comforter is the Holy Spirit—the soul of His life, the efficacy of His church, the light and life of the world. . . .

In the gift of the Spirit, Jesus gave to man the highest good that heaven could bestow. . . . It is the Spirit that makes effectual what has been wrought out by the world's Redeemer. It is by the Spirit that the heart is made pure. Through the Spirit the believer becomes a partaker of the divine nature. Christ has given His Spirit as a divine power to overcome all hereditary and cultivated tendencies to evil, and to impress His own character upon the church. . . . It is the privilege of every son and daughter of God to have the indwelling of the Spirit.[46]

Let every church member kneel before God, and pray earnestly for the impartation of the Spirit. Cry, "Lord, increase my faith. Make me to understand thy word; for the entrance of thy word giveth light. Refresh me by thy presence. Fill my heart with thy Spirit." . . .

When a man is filled with the Spirit, the more severely he is tested and tried, the more clearly he proves that he is a representative of Christ. The peace that dwells in the soul is seen on the countenance. The words and actions express the love of the Saviour. . . . Self is renounced. The name of Jesus is written on all that is said and done.

We may talk of the blessings of the Holy Spirit, but unless we prepare ourselves for its reception, of what avail are our works? Are we striving with all our power to attain to the stature of men and women in Christ? Are we seeking for His fullness, ever pressing toward the mark set before us—the perfection of His character? When the Lord's people reach this mark, they will be sealed in their foreheads. Filled with the Spirit, they will be complete in Christ, and the recording angel will declare, "It is finished."[47]

May 25

SPIRIT GIVEN ON CONDITION

If ye then, being evil, know how to give good gifts unto your children: how much more shall your heavenly Father give the Holy Spirit to them that ask him? Luke 11:13.

Christ has promised the gift of the Spirit to His church, and the promise belongs to us as much as to the first disciples. But like every other promise, it is given on conditions. There are many who believe, and profess to claim the Lord's promise; they talk about Christ and about the Holy Spirit, yet receive no benefit. They do not surrender the soul to be guided and controlled by the divine agencies. We cannot use the Holy Spirit. The Spirit is to use us. Through the Spirit, God works in His people "to will and to do of his good pleasure." Phil. 2:13. But many will not submit to this. They want to manage themselves. This is why they do not receive the heavenly gift. Only to those who wait humbly upon God, who watch for His guidance and grace, is the Spirit given. . . .

There is no limit to the usefulness of one who, putting aside self, makes room for the working of the Holy Spirit upon his heart, and lives a life wholly consecrated to God. . . . If His people will remove the obstructions, He will pour forth the waters of salvation in abundant streams through human channels. . . .

The Spirit furnishes the strength that sustains striving, wrestling souls in every emergency, amid the unfriendliness of relatives, the hatred of the world, and the realization of their own imperfections and mistakes. A union of divine and human endeavor, a close connection first, last, and ever, with God, the source of all strength—this is absolutely necessary.[48]

To Jesus, who emptied Himself for the salvation of lost humanity, the Holy Spirit was given without measure. So it will be given to every follower of Christ when the whole heart is surrendered for His indwelling. Our Lord Himself has given the command, "Be filled with the Spirit," and this command is also a promise of its fulfillment. It was the good pleasure of the Father that in Christ should "all the fulness" dwell; and "in him ye are made full" (Col. 2:9, 10, R.V.).[49]

CHRIST'S REPRESENTATIVE

And when he is come, he will reprove the world of sin, and of righteousness, and of judgment. John 16:8.

As the Comforter shall come, and reprove you of sin, of righteousness, and of judgment, be careful lest you resist the Spirit of God. . . . Be willing to discern what it shall reveal to you. Yield up your self-will, the long idolized habits peculiar to yourself, that you may receive the principles of truth.[50]

At the cost of infinite sacrifice and suffering, Christ has provided for us every essential to success in the Christian warfare. The Holy Spirit brings power that enables man to overcome. It is through the agency of the Spirit that the government of Satan is to be subdued. It is the Spirit that convinces of sin, and, with the consent of the human being, expels sin from the heart. The mind is then brought under a new law—the royal law of liberty.[51]

The Lord Jesus acts through the Holy Spirit; for it is His representative. Through it He infuses spiritual life into the soul, quickening its energies for good, cleansing from moral defilement, and giving it a fitness for His kingdom. Jesus has large blessings to bestow, rich gifts to distribute among men. He is the wonderful Counselor, infinite in wisdom and strength; and if we will acknowledge the power of His Spirit, and submit to be molded by it, we shall stand complete in Him. What a thought is this! In Christ "dwelleth all the fulness of the Godhead bodily. And ye are complete in him." Col. 2:9, 10.

Never will the human heart know happiness until it is submitted to be molded by the Spirit of God. The Spirit conforms the renewed soul to the model, Jesus Christ. Through its influence, enmity against God is changed into faith and love, and pride into humility. The soul perceives the beauty of truth, and Christ is honored in excellence and perfection of character. As these changes are effected, angels break out in rapturous song, and God and Christ rejoice over souls fashioned after the divine similitude.[52]

YIELDING TO THE SPIRIT'S CONTROL

For if ye live after the flesh, ye shall die: but if ye through the Spirit do mortify the deeds of the body, ye shall live. For as many as are led by the Spirit of God, they are the sons of God. Rom. 8:13, 14.

The will of man is aggressive, and is constantly striving to bend all things to its purposes. If it is enlisted on the side of God and right, the fruits of the Spirit will appear in the life; and God has appointed glory, honor, and peace to every man that worketh good.

When Satan is permitted to mold the will, he uses it to accomplish his ends. . . . He stirs up the evil propensities, awakening unholy passions and ambitions. He says, "All this power, these honors, and riches, and sinful pleasures, will I give thee"; but his conditions are that integrity shall be yielded, conscience blunted. Thus he degrades the human faculties, and brings them into captivity to sin.[53]

But God is ever seeking to impress our hearts by His Holy Spirit, that we shall be convinced of sin, of righteousness, and of judgment to come. We may place our will on the side of God's will, and in His strength and grace resist the temptations of the enemy. As we yield to the influence of the Spirit of God, our conscience becomes tender and sensitive, and sin that we have passed by with little thought, becomes exceeding sinful.[54]

God calls upon men to oppose the powers of evil. He says: "Let not sin therefore reign in your mortal body, that ye should obey it in the lusts thereof. Neither yield ye your members as instruments of unrighteousness unto sin; but yield yourselves unto God, as those that are alive from the dead, and your members as instruments of righteousness unto God." Rom. 6:13, 14. . . .

In this conflict of righteousness against unrighteousness, we can be successful only by divine aid. Our finite will must be brought into submission to the will of the Infinite; the human will must be blended with the divine. This will bring the Holy Spirit to our aid; and every conquest will tend to the recovery of God's purchased possession, to the restoration of His image in the soul.[55]

REVEALER OF CHRIST'S GRACE

Howbeit when he, the Spirit of truth, is come, he will guide you into all truth: for he shall not speak of himself; but whatsoever he shall hear, that he shall speak: and he will shew you things to come. John 16:13.

Of the Comforter it is written, "He will guide you into all truth. . . ." Through the Holy Spirit, Christ will open more clearly to those who believe on Him that which He has inspired holy men to write concerning the truth.[56]

Christ said of the Spirit, "He shall glorify me." John 16:14. As Christ glorified the Father by the demonstration of His love, so the Spirit was to glorify Christ by revealing to the world the riches of His grace. The very image of God is to be reproduced in humanity. The honor of God, the honor of Christ, is involved in the perfection of the character of His people. . . .

The Spirit works in us by bringing to mind, vividly and often, the precious truths of the plan of redemption. We should forget these truths, and for us God's rich promises would lose their efficiency, were it not for the Spirit, who takes of the things of God, and shows them to us. . . . The Spirit illumines our darkness, informs our ignorance, and helps us in our manifold necessities. But the mind must be constantly going out after God. If worldliness is allowed to come in, if we have no desire to pray, no desire to commune with Him who is the source of strength and wisdom, the Spirit will not abide with us. Those who are unbelieving do not receive the rich endowment of grace that would make them wise unto salvation, patient, forbearing, quick to perceive and appreciate heavenly ministrations, quick to discern Satan's devices, and strong to resist sin.[57]

The religion of Christ means more than the forgiveness of sin; it means that sin is taken away, and that the vacuum is filled with the Spirit. It means that the mind is divinely illumined, that the heart is emptied of self, and filled with the presence of Christ. When this work is done for church members, the church will be a living, working church.[58]

THE TIME OF THE SPIRIT'S POWER

But ye shall receive power, after that the Holy Ghost is come upon you: and ye shall be witnesses unto me both in Jerusalem, and in all Judaea, and in Samaria, and unto the uttermost part of the earth. Acts 1:8.

We should pray as earnestly for the descent of the Holy Spirit as the disciples prayed on the day of Pentecost. If they needed it at that time, we need it more today. All manner of false doctrines, heresies, and deceptions are misleading the minds of men; and without the Spirit's aid, our efforts to present divine truth will be in vain.

We are living in the time of the Holy Spirit's power. It is seeking to diffuse itself through the agency of humanity, thus increasing its influence in the world. For if any man drinks of the water of life, it will be in him "a well of water springing up into everlasting life" (John 4:14); and the blessing will not be confined to himself, but will be shared by others. . . .

To reject the Holy Spirit, through whose power we conquer the forces of evil, is the sin that surpasses all others; for it cuts us off from the source of our power—from Christ and communion with Him. . . .

The warfare between good and evil has not grown less fierce than it was in the days of the Saviour. The path to heaven is no smoother now than it was then. All our sins must be put away. Every darling indulgence that hinders our religious life must be cut off. The right eye or the right hand must be sacrificed, if it causes us to offend. Are we willing to renounce our own wisdom, and to receive the kingdom of heaven as a little child? Are we willing to part with our self-righteousness? Are we willing to sacrifice the approbation of men? The prize of eternal life is of infinite value. Are we willing to welcome the Holy Spirit's aid, and cooperate with it, putting forth efforts and making sacrifices proportionate to the value of the object to be obtained?[59]

The heart of man may be the abode of the Holy Spirit. The peace of Christ, which passeth understanding, may rest in your soul; and the transforming power of His grace may work in your life, and fit you for the courts of glory.[60]

PLEDGE OF OUR ACCEPTANCE

And Jesus, when he was baptized, went up straightway out of the water: and, lo, the heavens were opened unto him, and he saw the spirit of God descending like a dove, and lighting upon him: and lo a voice from heaven, saying, This is my beloved Son, in whom I am well pleased. Matt. 3:16, 17.

What does this scene mean to us? How thoughtlessly we have read the account of the baptism of our Lord, not realizing that its significance was of the greatest importance to us, and that Christ was accepted of the Father in man's behalf. As Jesus bowed on the banks of Jordan and offered up His petition, humanity was presented to the Father by Him who had clothed His divinity with humanity. Jesus offered Himself to the Father in man's behalf, that those who had been separated from God through sin, might be brought back to God through the merits of the divine Petitioner. . . .

The prayer of Christ in behalf of lost humanity cleaved its way through every shadow that Satan had cast between man and God, and left a clear channel of communication to the very throne of glory. . . .

The voice of God was heard in answer to the petition of Christ, and this tells the sinner that his prayer will find a lodgment at the throne of the Father. The Holy Spirit will be given to those who seek for its power and grace, and will help our infirmities when we would have audience with God. Heaven is open to our petitions, and we are invited to come "boldly unto the throne of grace, that we may obtain mercy, and find grace to help in time of need." Heb. 4:16.[61]

With all our sins and weaknesses we are not cast aside as worthless. "He hath made us accepted in the beloved." Eph. 1:6. The glory that rested upon Christ is a pledge of the love of God for us. It tells of the power of prayer—how the human voice may reach the ear of God, and our petitions find acceptance in the courts of heaven. The light that fell from the open portals upon the head of our Saviour, will fall upon us as we pray for help to resist temptation. The voice that spoke to Jesus says to every believing soul, "This is my beloved child, in whom I am well pleased."[62]

THREE MIGHTY HELPERS

Therefore we are buried with him by baptism into death: that like as Christ was raised up from the dead by the glory of the Father, even so we also should walk in newness of life. Rom. 6:4.

Jesus was our example in all things that pertain to life and godliness. He was baptized in Jordan, just as those who come to Him must be baptized.[63]

Christ made baptism the entrance to His spiritual kingdom. . . . Those who receive the ordinance of baptism thereby make a public declaration that they have renounced the world, and have become members of the royal family. . . . Those who do this are to make all worldly considerations secondary to their new relations. Publicly they have declared that they will no longer live in pride and self-indulgence. . . . They are bound by a solemn covenant to live to the Lord. They are to use for Him all their entrusted capabilities.[64]

When we submit to the solemn rite of baptism, we testify to angels and to men that we are purged from our old sins, and that henceforth, having died to the world, we will "seek those things which are above. . . ." (Col. 3:1). Let us not forget our baptismal vow. In the presence of the three highest powers of heaven—the Father, the Son, and the Holy Spirit—we have pledged ourselves to do the will of Him who . . . declared, "I am the resurrection, and the life." John 11:25. Christ forgives every penitent sinner, and as the forgiven one, at the time of baptism, rises from the watery grave, he is declared a new creature, whose life is hid with Christ in God. Let us ever remember that it is our high privilege to be purged from our old sins.[65]

When the Christian takes his baptismal vow, divine help is pledged to him. The Father, the Son, and the Holy Spirit stand ready to work in his behalf. God places at his command the resources of heaven, that he may be an overcomer. His own power is small; but God is omnipotent, and God is his helper. Daily he is to make known his wants at the throne of grace. By faith and trust, by availing himself of the resources provided, he can be more than a conqueror.[66]

SUMMERTIME WITH GOD

For, lo, the winter is past, the rain is over and gone; the flowers appear on the earth; the time of the singing of birds is come, and the voice of the turtle is heard in our land. S. of Sol. 2:11, 12.

This lovely morning all nature appears fresh and beautiful. Earth has put on her summer robes of green and is smiling in almost Edenic loveliness.

I think our enjoyment of the summertime is heightened by the memory of the long, cold months of winter; and on the other hand, the hope of summer helps us to endure more cheerfully the winter's reign. If we were to permit our minds to dwell upon the barrenness and desolation with which the ice king surrounds us, we might be very unhappy; but, being wiser than this, we look forward in anticipation to the coming springtime, which is to bring back the birds, awaken the sleeping flowers, clothe the earth in her robes of green, and fill the air with light and fragrance and song.

The Christian's sojourn in this world may be fitly compared to the long, cold winter. Here we experience trials, sorrows, and disappointments, but we should not permit our minds to dwell upon these. Let us rather look forward with hope and faith to the coming summer when we shall be welcomed to our Eden home, where all is light and joy, where all is peace and love.

Had the Christian never experienced the storms of affliction in this world, had his heart never been chilled by disappointment or oppressed by fear, he would scarcely know how to appreciate heaven. We will not be despondent, though often weary, sad, and heartsick; the winter will not always last. The summer of peace, joy, and eternal gladness soon will come. Then Christ will dwell with us and will lead us to fountains of living waters, and will wipe all tears from our eyes.[1]

Let nothing . . . hinder you from making thorough work for eternity. . . . There will be no chilling winds, no wintry colds, but an eternal summer. There is light for the intellect, love that is abiding, sincere. There will be health and immortality, vigor for every faculty. There will be shut out forever every sorrow and every grief.[2]

THE SIGN OF THE NEW HEART

A new heart also will I give you, and a new spirit will I put within you: and I will take away the stony heart out of your flesh, and I will give you an heart of flesh. Eze. 36:26.

One of the most earnest prayers recorded in the Word of God is that of David when he pleaded, "Create in me a clean heart, O God." Ps. 51:10. God's response to such a prayer is, A new heart will I give you. This is a work that no finite man can do. Men and women are to begin at the beginning, seeking God most earnestly for a true Christian experience. They are to feel the creative power of the Holy Spirit. They are to receive the new heart, that is kept soft and tender by the grace of heaven. The selfish spirit is to be cleansed from the soul. They are to labor earnestly and with humility of heart, each one looking to Jesus for guidance and encouragement. Then the building, fitly framed together, will grow into a holy temple in the Lord.[3]

The youth especially stumble over this phrase, "a new heart." They do not know what it means. They look for a special change to take place in their feelings. This they term conversion. Over this error thousands have stumbled to ruin, not understanding the expression, "Ye must be born again." John 3:7.

Satan leads people to think that because they have felt a rapture of feeling, they are converted. But their experience does not change. Their actions are the same as before. Their lives show no good fruit. They pray often and long, and are constantly referring to the feelings they had at such and such a time. But they do not live the new life. They are deceived. Their experience goes no deeper than feeling. They build upon the sand, and when adverse winds come, their house is swept away. . . .

When Jesus speaks of the new heart, He means the mind, the life, the whole being. To have a change of heart is to withdraw the affections from the world, and fasten them upon Christ. To have a new heart is to have a new mind, new purposes, new motives. What is the sign of a new heart?—A changed life.[4]

BEWARE OF THE HARD HEART

For he is our God; and we are the people of his pasture, and the
sheep of his hand. To day if ye will hear his voice, harden not your
heart, as in the provocation, and as in the day of temptation in the
wilderness. Ps. 95:7, 8.

No man can even once devote his God-given powers to the service of worldliness or pride without placing himself on the enemy's
ground. . . . Every repetition of the sin weakens his power of resistance, blinds his eyes, and stifles conviction. . . .

The Lord sends us warning, counsel, and reproof, that we may
have opportunity to correct our errors before they become second
nature. But if we refuse to be corrected, God does not interfere to
counteract the tendencies of our own course of action. He works no
miracle that the seed sown may not spring up and bear fruit. That
man who manifests an infidel hardihood or a stolid indifference to
divine truth, is but reaping the harvest which he has himself sown.
Such has been the experience of many. They listen with stoical indifference to the truths which once stirred their very souls. They
sowed neglect, indifference, and resistance to the truth; and such is
the harvest which they reap. The coldness of ice, the hardness of
iron, the impenetrable, unimpressible nature of rock—all these find
a counterpart in the character of many a professed Christian. It was
thus that the Lord hardened the heart of Pharaoh. God spoke to the
Egyptian king by the mouth of Moses, giving him the most striking
evidences of divine power; but the monarch stubbornly refused the
light which would have brought him to repentance. God did not
send a supernatural power to harden the heart of the rebellious
king, but as Pharaoh resisted the truth, the Holy Spirit was withdrawn, and he was left to the darkness and unbelief which he had
chosen. By persistent rejection of the Spirit's influence, men cut
themselves off from God. He has in reserve no more potent agency
to enlighten their minds. No revelation of His will can reach them in
their unbelief.[5]

Unbending principle will mark the course of those who sit at the
feet of Jesus and learn of Him.[6]

THE WORK OF HEART-KEEPING

*Keep thy heart with all diligence; for out of it are the issues of life.
Prov. 4:23.*

Diligent heart-keeping is essential to a healthy growth in grace.
The heart in its natural state is a habitation for unholy thoughts and
sinful passions. When brought into subjection to Christ, it must be
cleansed by the Spirit from all defilement. This can not be done
without the consent of the individual.

When the soul has been cleansed, it is the duty of the Christian
to keep it undefiled. Many seem to think that the religion of Christ
does not call for the abandonment of daily sins, the breaking loose
from habits which have held the soul in bondage. They renounce
some things condemned by the conscience, but they fail to represent Christ in the daily life. They do not bring Christlikeness into the
home. They do not show a thoughtful care in their choice of words.
Too often, fretful, impatient words are spoken, words which stir the
worst passions of the human heart. Such ones need the abiding
presence of Christ in the soul. Only in His strength can they keep
guard over the words and actions.

In the work of heart-keeping we must be instant in prayer, unwearied in petitioning the throne of grace for assistance. Those who
take the name of Christian should come to God in earnestness and humility, pleading for help. . . . The Christian cannot always be in the position of prayer, but his thoughts and desires can always be upward.[7]

To keep your heart in heaven will give vigor to all your graces
and put life into all your duties. To discipline the mind to dwell
upon heavenly things will put life and earnestness into all our endeavors. Our efforts are languid, and we run the Christian race
slowly, and manifest indolence and sloth, because we so little value
the heavenly prize. We are dwarfs in spiritual attainments. It is the
privilege and duty of the Christian to be increasing in the knowledge
of the Son of God, "unto a perfect man."[8]

June 5

WHO HAS CONTROL OF MY LIFE?

Search me, O God, and know my heart: try me, and know my thoughts: and see if there be any wicked way in me, and lead me in the way everlasting. Ps. 139:23, 24.

God leads His people on, step by step. He brings them into positions which are calculated to reveal the motives of the heart. Some endure at one point, but fall off at the next. At every advance step the heart is tested, and tried a little closer. If any find their hearts opposed to the straight work of God, it should convince them that they have a work to do in overcoming, or they will be finally rejected of the Lord.

This world is the place in which to prepare to appear in God's presence. Individuals will here show what power affects their hearts, and controls their actions. . . . If they prize anything higher than the truth, their hearts are not prepared to receive Jesus, and He is consequently shut out. If individuals, when tested, refuse to sacrifice their idols, . . . the Spirit of God will leave them with their sinful traits unsubdued, to the control of evil angels.

Many who profess to be Christ's followers are unwilling to closely examine their own hearts, to see whether they have passed from death unto life. Some lean upon an old experience, seeming to think a mere profession of the truth will save them; but God's Word reveals the terrible fact that all such are cherishing a false hope. . . .

Young and old, God is now testing you. You are now deciding your own eternal destiny. Pride, fashion, empty conversation, and selfishness are evils which, if fostered, will increase, and choke the good seed sown in your hearts.[9]

Let us, as Christ's followers, search our hearts as with a lighted candle to see what manner of spirit we are of. For our present and eternal good, let us criticize our actions, to see how they stand in the light of the law of God.[10]

We need those who will follow Christ fully, whose head, hands, ears, and every faculty and power are consecrated to Jesus. It is not purse power or brain power, but heart power we need.[11]

June 6

SOLDIERS ON LIFE'S BATTLEFIELD

Fight the good fight of faith, lay hold on eternal life, whereunto thou art also called, and hast professed a good profession before many witnesses. 1 Tim. 6:12.

When souls are converted, their salvation is not yet accomplished. They then have the race to run; the arduous struggle is before them to "fight the good fight of faith." . . . The battle is lifelong, and must be carried forward with determined energy proportionate to the value of the object you are in pursuit of, which is eternal life. . . .

Satan is ever seeking to destroy; he is casting his hellish shadow between our souls and the light of the Sun of Righteousness. When you talk doubts, and distrust your heavenly Father's love, Satan comes in and deepens the impression, and that which is shadowed is made the blackness of despair. Now, your only hope is to cease talking darkness. In dwelling on the dark side, you cast away your confidence in God, and this is just what Satan wants you to do. He wants to sift you as wheat; but Jesus is making intercession for you; His love is broad and deep. Perhaps you will say, "How do you know He loves me?" I look where you may look, to the cross of Calvary. That blood shed upon the cross cleanseth from all sin. . . .

We are daily working out our destiny. We have a crown of eternal life to win, a hell to shun. We certainly cannot save ourselves, and we know that Christ wants us to be saved. He gave His own life that He might pay the ransom for our souls. When He has made this infinite sacrifice, He does not regard us with indifference. . . .

We want to cling to the Way, the Truth, and the Life. . . . We have a living Saviour, a living Intercessor, one who will help us in every time of need. When tempted to go into the dark cave of doubt and despair, sing,

> *"Arise, my soul, arise! Shake off thy guilty fears;*
> *The bleeding Sacrifice in thy behalf appears;*
> *Before the throne my Surety stands;*
> *My name is written in His hands."*[12]

THE COURT OF HOLY LIFE

But ye are a chosen generation, a royal priesthood, an holy nation, a peculiar people; that ye should shew forth the praises of him who hath called you out of darkness into his marvellous light. 1 Peter 2:9.

The church of Christ on earth is amid the moral darkness of a disloyal world, which is trampling upon the law of Jehovah. But their Redeemer, who has purchased their ransom with the price of His own precious blood, has made every provision that His church shall be a transformed body, illumined with the Light of the world, possessing the glory of Emmanuel. The bright beams of the Sun of Righteousness, shining through His church, will gather into His fold every lost, straying sheep who will come unto Him and find refuge in Him. They will find peace and light and joy in Him who is peace and righteousness forever.[13]

The members of the church should individually keep the light of God's love burning brightly in their own souls, that it may also shine forth to others. We have too much at stake to allow spiritual lethargy to creep over us. Let us beware of indulging a disrelish for religious services and religious duties. Let us resolutely battle against that sluggishness of soul which is so fatal to the growth and even the life of the Christian. That church will be healthy and prosperous whose members are putting forth active, personal effort to do good to others, to save souls. This will be a constant incentive to every good work. Such Christians will labor with greater earnestness to secure their own salvation. The dormant energies will be aroused, the whole soul inspired with an unconquerable determination to win the Saviour's plaudit of "Well done," and to wear the victor's crown.[14]

Christ makes His church a beautiful temple for God. "Where two or three are gathered together in my name," He declared, "there am I in the midst of them." Matt. 18:20. His church is the court of holy life, filled with varied gifts, and endowed with the Holy Spirit. Appropriate duties are assigned by Heaven to each member of the church on earth, and all are to find their happiness in the happiness of those whom they help and bless.[15]

IN THE WORKSHOP OF GOD

Ye also, as lively stones, are built up a spiritual house, an holy priesthood, to offer up spiritual sacrifices, acceptable to God by Jesus Christ. 1 Peter 2:5.

The Jewish temple was built of hewn stones quarried out of the mountains; and every stone was fitted for its place in the Temple, hewn, polished, and tested, before it was brought to Jerusalem. And when all were brought to the ground, the building went together without the sound of ax or hammer. This building represents God's spiritual temple, which is composed of material gathered out of every nation, and tongue, and people, of all grades, high and low, rich and poor, learned and unlearned. These are not dead substances, to be fitted by hammer and chisel. They are living stones, quarried out from the world by the truth; and the great Master Builder, the Lord of the temple, is now hewing and polishing them, and fitting them for their respective places in the spiritual temple. When completed, this temple will be perfect in all its parts, the admiration of angels and of men; for its Builder and Maker is God.[16]

The care shown in the building of the temple is a lesson to us regarding the care that we are to show in our character building. No cheap material was to be used. No haphazard work was to be done in matching the different parts. Piece must fit piece perfectly. Just as God's temple was, so must His church be. Into their character building His people are to bring no worthless timbers, no careless, indifferent work.[17]

Now we are in the workshop of God, and the process is going on in these hours of probation to fit us for the glorious temple. We cannot now be indifferent, and negligent, and careless, and refuse to depart from sin, . . . and expect to become pure and holy and fashioned in character after the similitude of a palace. . . . Now is the day of preparation; now is the time when we can have our defects removed.[18]

A stone that does not shine is worthless. That which constitutes the value of our churches is not dead, lusterless stones, but living stones, stones that catch the bright beams from the Chief Cornerstone, even the Sun of Righteousness.[19]

THE BLESSINGS
OF CHRISTIAN FELLOWSHIP

Not forsaking the assembling of ourselves together, as the manner of some is; but exhorting one another: and so much the more, as ye see the day approaching. Heb. 10:25.

Those who are of the household of faith should never neglect the assembling of themselves together; for this is God's appointed means of leading His children into unity, in order that in Christian love and fellowship they may help, strengthen, and encourage one another. . . .

As brethren of our Lord, we are called with a holy calling to a holy, happy life. Having entered the narrow path of obedience, let us refresh our minds by communion with one another and with God. As we see the day of God approaching, let us meet often to study His Word and to exhort one another to be faithful unto the end. These earthly assemblies are God's appointed means by which we have opportunity to speak with one another and to gather all the help possible to prepare, in the right way, to receive in the heavenly assemblies the fulfillment of the pledges of our inheritance.

Remember that in every assembly you meet with Christ, the Master of assemblies. Encourage a personal interest in one another; for it is not enough simply to know men. We must know men *in Christ Jesus.* We are enjoined to "consider one another." This is the keynote of the gospel. The keynote of the world is self.[20]

I would encourage those who assemble in little companies to worship God. Brethren and sisters, be not disheartened because you are so few in number. The tree that stands alone upon the plain, strikes its roots deeper into the earth, spreads out its branches farther on every side, and grows stronger and more symmetrical while wrestling singly with the tempest or rejoicing in the sunshine. So the Christian, cut off from earthly dependence, may learn to rely wholly upon God, and may gain strength and courage from every conflict.

May the Lord bless the scattered and lonely ones, and make them efficient workers for Him.[21]

ONE WITH THE CHURCH ABOVE

For this cause I bow my knees unto the Father of our Lord Jesus Christ, of whom the whole family in heaven and earth is named. Eph. 3:14, 15.

The church of God upon the earth is one with the church of God above. Believers on the earth, and those who have never fallen in heaven, are one church. Every heavenly intelligence is interested in the assemblies of the saints, who on earth meet to worship God in spirit and truth, and in the beauty of holiness. In the inner court of heaven they listen to the testimonies of the witnesses for Christ in the outer court on earth, and the praise and thanksgiving that comes from the church below, is taken up in the heavenly anthem, and praise and rejoicing resounds through the heavenly court because Christ has not died in vain for the fallen sons of Adam. While angels drink from the fountainhead, the saints on earth drink of the pure streams flowing from the throne of God, making glad the city of God. . . .

In every assembly of the saints below, are the angels of God listening to the thanksgiving, the praise, the supplication, that is offered by the people of God in testimonies, songs, and prayers. Let them remember that their praises are supplemented by the choirs of the angelic host above. . . .

The company of believers may be few in number, but they have been taken by the cleaver of truth as rough stones from the quarry of the world . . . to be fitted up by test and trial for a place in God's heavenly temple, and they are very precious in the sight of the Lord. . . . Even in the rough they are precious in the sight of God. The ax and the hammer and the chisel of trial and test are in the hands of One who is skillful, and are used not to destroy, not to bring to nothingness, but to work out the perfections of every soul. . . .

The Lord will no more cast off the humblest, lowliest believer in Jesus, than He will demolish His throne. We are accepted in the Beloved. We are members of the royal family, children of the heavenly King, heirs of God, and joint heirs with Jesus Christ.[22]

MOST PRECIOUS OF ALL MEETINGS

Then they that feared the Lord spake often one to another: and the Lord hearkened, and heard it, and a book of remembrance was written before him for them that feared the Lord, and that thought upon his name. Mal. 3:16.

What a hope-inspiring picture is this, where the Lord is represented as bending down and hearkening to the testimonies borne by His witnesses! . . .

The words to which God and the angels listen with delight are words of appreciation for the great gift that has been made to the world in the only-begotten Son of God. Every word of praise for the blessing of the light of truth . . . is written in the heavenly records. Every word that acknowledges the merciful kindness of our heavenly Father in giving Jesus to take away our sins, and to impute to us His righteousness, is recorded in the book of His remembrance. Testimonies of this kind "shew forth the praises of him who hath called us out of darkness into his marvellous light." 1 Peter 2:9. . . .

The time and season are very precious. The assembled believers are in the audience chamber of the universe of heaven. They are to witness for God and the Lord Jesus Christ who gave His life for the world. . . . What deep and grave importance is attached to these little assemblies! Jesus Christ has paid the ransom money of His own blood for their souls, and He is in the midst of them when they meet to worship God. The Majesty of heaven identifies His interests with those of the believers, however humble may be their circumstances. And wherever they are privileged to meet together, it is appropriate that they speak often one to another, giving utterance to the gratitude and love that results from thinking upon the name of the Lord. Thus shall God be glorified as He hearkens and hears, and the testimony meeting will be considered the most precious of all meetings. . . .

Let all remember that . . . angels are recording in the book of remembrance every word that vindicates the character and mission of Christ. Of those who testify of the love of God, the Lord says, "They shall be mine, . . . in that day when I make up my jewels." Mal. 3:17.[23]

UNITY IN DIVERSITY

There is one body, and one Spirit, even as ye are called in one hope of your calling; . . . one God and Father of all, who is above all, and through all, and in you all. But unto every one of us is given grace according to the measure of the gift of Christ. Eph. 4:4-7.

Unity in diversity is God's plan. Among the followers of Christ there is to be the blending of diverse elements, one adapted to the other, and each to do its special work for God. Every individual has his place in the filling up of one great plan bearing the stamp of Christ's image. . . . One is fitted to do a certain work, another has a different work for which he is adapted, another has a still different line; but each is to be the complement of the others. . . . The Spirit of God, working in and through the diverse elements, will produce harmony of action. . . . There is to be only one master spirit—the Spirit of Him who is infinite in wisdom, and in whom all the diverse elements meet in beautiful, matchless unity. . . .

Differences of character exist by nature, but our unity depends upon the degree in which we yield to the transforming influence of the Spirit of God. Through the grace of Christ, some persons possess precious traits of character, a kindly and genial disposition; their very rebukes are imbued with tenderness, for the Spirit of Christ seems manifest in them. . . . The power of His grace will mold and fashion character according to the divine Model, renewing it in softness and beauty, in conformity to His own blessed image. . . .

How great the diversity manifested in the natural world! Every object has its peculiar sphere of action; yet all are found to be linked together in the great whole. Christ Jesus is in union with the Father, and from the great center this wonderful unity is to extend . . . through all classes and diversities of talents. We are all to respect one another's talent; we are to harmonize in goodness, in unselfish thoughts and actions, because the Spirit of Christ, as the living, working agency, is circulating through the whole. . . . It is not striking actions that produce unity; it is the mold of the Holy Spirit upon the character.[24]

169

UNITED IN CHRIST

That they all may be one; as thou, Father, art in me, and I in thee, that they also may be one in us: that the world may believe that thou hast sent me. John 17:21.

The solemn, earnest prayer of Christ . . . reaches down along the line to our time. What a position is this for fallen man to attain through obedience—oneness with God through Jesus Christ! To what heights we are permitted to rise if we will have respect unto the recompense of the reward! We are to receive power from God that human nature, under the divine working, may not always be perverted and not always be under the depraving, corrupting influence of sin. Human nature, through Jesus Christ, becomes allied to angels—yes, even to the great God.[25]

Those who are truly connected with God will not be at variance with one another. . . . His Spirit ruling in their hearts will create harmony, love, and unity. The opposite of this works in the children of Satan; there is with them a continual contradiction. Strife and envy and jealousy are the ruling elements. The characteristic of the Christian is the meekness of Christ. Benevolence, kindness, mercy, and love originate from Infinite Wisdom, while the opposite is the unholy fruit of a heart that is not in harmony with Jesus Christ. . . . In union there is strength. In division there is weakness and defeat.[26]

The most convincing argument we can give to the world of Christ's mission is to be found in perfect unity. . . . In proportion to our unity with Christ will be our power to save souls.[27]

If we reach the standard of perfection, our peculiar traits of disposition must be molded in harmony with Christ's will. Then we shall sit together in heavenly places in Christ. Brethren will work together, without a thought of collision. Little differences, dwelt upon, lead to actions that destroy Christian fellowship. . . . Let us keep drawing near to God, and He will draw near to us. Then, as one, we shall reach upward to Him. The churches will be as gardens of the Lord, under His cultivation. God's people will be trees of righteousness, planted by the Lord, and watered with the river of life.[28]

ONE GREAT BROTHERHOOD

Now I beseech you, brethren, by the name of our Lord Jesus Christ, that ye all speak the same thing, and that there be no divisions among you; but that ye be perfectly joined together in the same mind and in the same judgment. 1 Cor. 1:10.

We have one Lord, one faith, one baptism. The gospel of Christ is to reach all classes, all nations, all tongues and people. The influence of the gospel is to unite in one great brotherhood. We have only one Model that we are to imitate in character building, and then we all shall have Christ's mold; we shall be in perfect harmony; nationalities will blend in Jesus Christ, having the same mind, and the same judgment, speaking the same things, and with one mouth glorifying God. This is the work the world's Redeemer is to do for us. If we accept the truth as it is in Jesus, national prejudices and jealousies will be broken down, and the Spirit of truth will blend hearts in one. We will love as brethren; we will esteem others better than ourselves; we will be kind and courteous, meek and lowly, easy to be entreated; full of mercy and good fruits. . . .

God knows just how to meet the peculiarities of different nationalities. . . . The third angel's message . . . is to unite the people to do a special work, preparing them with perfection of character to unite in one great family in the mansions Christ has gone to prepare for those who love Him. . . .

The truth is all powerful and far reaching. It will unite nationalities in one great brotherhood. . . . Christ in men unites them on one grand platform, preparing for the uniting in one family in heaven. It is the truth that makes men one and removes national prejudice. . . .

The truth will have the same molding influence upon hearts whatever the nationalities. Every human heart that accepts the truth will bow to the majesty of its sway, and when Christ is abiding in the heart by faith they will be of one mind, for Christ is not divided. They will be strong in His strength, happy and united in His peace. The truth is the same in its subduing power upon all hearts. It will refine and ennoble the heart of the receiver.[29]

VICTORY OVER EVERY FOE

By the word of truth, by the power of God, by the armour of righteousness on the right hand and on the left. 2 Cor. 6:7.

Through the ages of moral darkness, through centuries of strife and persecution, the church of Christ has been as a city set on a hill. From age to age, through successive generations to the present time, the pure doctrines of the Bible have been unfolding within her borders. The church of Christ, enfeebled and defective though she may appear, is the one object on earth on which He bestows in a special sense His love and regard. The church is the theater of His grace, in which He delights to make experiments of mercy on human hearts.

The church is God's fortress, His city of refuge, which He holds in a revolted world. Any betrayal of her sacred trust is treachery to Him who has bought her with the precious blood of His only begotten Son. All down through the history of the world, faithful souls have constituted the church on earth. . . .

Today, as in the past, all heaven is watching to see the church develop in the true science of salvation. . . . Christ calls upon us to enter the narrow pathway, where every step means a denial of self. He calls upon us to stand upon the platform of eternal truth, and contend, yes, contend earnestly, for the faith once delivered to the saints. . . .

As we near the time . . . when Satan's deceptive power will be so great that, if it were possible, he would deceive the very elect, our discernment must be sharpened by divine enlightenment, that we may not be ignorant of Satan's devices. The whole treasury of heaven is at our command in the work of preparing the way of the Lord.[30]

It is God's design that His church shall ever advance in purity and knowledge, from light to light, from glory to glory.[31]

Our hope is not in man, but in the living God. With full assurance of faith, we may expect that He will unite His omnipotence with the efforts of human instrumentalities, for the glory of His name. Clad with the armor of His righteousness, we may gain the victory over every foe.[32]

THE GOLDEN CHAIN OF LOVE

A new commandment I give unto you, That ye love one another; as I have loved you, that ye also love one another. By this shall all men know that ye are my disciples, if ye have love one to another. John 13:34, 35.

The love of Christ is a golden chain that binds finite, human beings who believe in Jesus Christ to the Infinite God. The love that the Lord has for His children passeth knowledge. No science can define or explain it. No human wisdom can fathom it.[33]

Selfishness and pride hinder the pure love that unites us in spirit with Jesus Christ. If this love is truly cultivated, finite will blend with finite, and all will center in the Infinite. Humanity will unite with humanity, and all will be bound up with the heart of Infinite Love. Sanctified love for one another is sacred. In this great work Christian love for one another—far higher, more constant, more courteous, more unselfish, than has been seen—preserves Christian tenderness, Christian benevolence, and politeness, and enfolds the human brotherhood in the embrace of God, acknowledging the dignity with which God has invested the rights of man.[34]

The golden chain of love, binding the hearts of the believers in unity, in bonds of fellowship and love, and in oneness with Christ and the Father, makes the connection perfect and bears to the world a testimony of the power of Christianity that cannot be controverted. . . . Then will selfishness be uprooted and unfaithfulness will not exist. There will not be strife and divisions. There will not be stubbornness in anyone who is bound up with Christ. Not one will act out the stubborn independence of the wayward, impulsive child who drops the hand that is leading him and chooses to stumble on alone and walk in his own ways.[35]

Love is a tender plant, and it must be cultivated and cherished, and the roots of bitterness all have to be plucked up around it in order for it to have room to circulate, and then it will bring in under its influence all the powers of the mind, all the heart, so that we shall love God supremely, and our neighbor as ourselves.[36]

UNDER THE YOKE OF CHRIST

He that loveth his brother abideth in the light, and there is none occasion of stumbling in him. 1 John 2:10.

Satan is seeking by his temptations to obtain advantage over souls. Let nothing that you may do or say prove a temptation or discouragement to any soul. Remember he is the purchase of the blood of Christ. Every soul is precious. Only as you look to the cross of Calvary can you place a right estimate upon the soul. How sad a thing it would be to have anything you may do or say balance a soul in the wrong direction. You are bound by cords of obligation to God and to your fellow man; you cannot break these cords and free yourself from these obligations.[37]

Do not be troubled by what other people think or say, . . . but cling to the Lord; He will never fail you. . . . We must ever bear in mind that Satan is working hard to secure every soul. We must work on the Lord's side, not giving the least occasion which anyone can take advantage of. . . . If words are spoken and charges made to provoke you, the very best reproof you can give is to remain silent, as though you heard not. . . . We are all to remember that we are under the yoke of Christ, and we must not disgrace our Saviour or the yoke He has invited us to wear. We will just as surely rule our spirit as we wear the yoke.[38]

What others may do, what others may say, what others may think of you, will not change God's thoughts toward you. He that doeth righteousness is righteous, and the opinion of man will not change his character. . . . Jesus loves you; and He takes no man's measurement of your character. You are to behold Jesus and reflect His image. Keep His love in your thoughts. Invite the heavenly Guest to abide with you. . . .

Let your spirit be cleansed from all earthliness, all unholy, uncharitable thoughts. Let your words be clean, sanctified, vivifying and refreshing all with whom you associate. Be not easily provoked. Let the praise of God be in your hearts and upon your lips, that no evil thing may truthfully be said of you.[39]

THE OUTFLOW OF LOVE

Beloved, let us love one another: for love is of God; and every one that loveth is born of God, and knoweth God. 1 John 4:7.

When the heavenly principle of eternal love fills the heart, it will flow out to others, not merely because favors are received of them, but because love is the principle of action, and modifies the character, governs the impulses, controls the passions, subdues enmity, and elevates the affections. This love is not contracted, so as merely to include "me and mine," but is as broad as the world and as high as heaven. It is in harmony with that of the angel workers. This love, cherished in the soul, sweetens the entire life, and sheds a refining influence on all around. Possessing it, we cannot but be happy, let fortune smile or frown. And if we love God with all the heart, we must love His children also. This love is the spirit of God. It is the heavenly adorning that gives true nobility and dignity to the soul.[40]

A soul filled with the love of Jesus lends to the words, the manners, the looks, hope, courage, and serenity. . . . It awakens a desire for a better life; souls ready to faint are strengthened; those struggling against temptation will be fortified and comforted. The words, the expression, the manners, throw out a bright ray of sunshine, and leave behind them a clear path toward heaven. . . . Every one of us has opportunities of helping others. We are constantly making impressions upon the youth about us. The expression of the countenance is itself a mirror of the life within. Jesus desires that we shall become like Himself, filled with tender sympathy, exerting a ministry of love in the small duties of life. . . .

Our duty is to live in the atmosphere of Christ's love, to breathe His love deeply, and to reflect its warmth around us. Oh, what a sphere of influence is open before us! How carefully we should cultivate the garden of the soul, so that it may bring forth only pure, sweet, fragrant flowers! Words of love, tenderness, and charity sanctify our influence over others.[41]

THE SILKEN CORD THAT BINDS HEARTS

By love serve one another. Gal. 5:13.

Love is the silken cord that binds hearts together. We are not to feel that we must set up ourselves as a pattern. As long as we think of ourselves and what is due to us from others it will be impossible for us to do our work of saving souls. When Christ takes possession of our hearts we shall no longer make the narrow circle of self the center of our thoughts and of our attentions.

What a wonderful reverence for human life Jesus expressed in His life mission! He stood not among the people as a king, demanding attention, reverence, service, but as one who wished to serve, to uplift humanity. He said He had not come to be ministered unto but to minister. . . . Wherever Christ saw a human being, He saw one who needed human sympathy. Many of us are willing to serve particular ones—those whom we honor—but the very ones to whom Christ would make us a blessing if we were not so cold-hearted, so unkind and selfish, we pass by as unworthy of our notice. . . .

The great lesson of forgiveness must be more perfectly learned by all of us. . . . The greatest wrong we can do to others is to be unforgiving if we think they injure us in any way. This is a most dangerous position for a professed Christian, because just in the manner in which he treats his brethren so will the Lord of heaven treat him.

We need to have higher and more distinct views of the character of Christ. . . . We are not to think of God only as a judge and to forget Him as a loving Father. Nothing can do our souls greater harm than this, for our whole spiritual life is molded from our conceptions of God's character. We have lessons to learn of Jesus' love.[42]

"Be ye therefore followers of God, as dear children; and walk in love, as Christ also hath loved us, and hath given himself for us an offering and a sacrifice to God for a sweetsmelling savour." Eph. 5:1, 2. This is the height of the love we are required to reach. And the texture of this love is not tainted with selfishness.[43]

June 20

HELP FOR THE ERRING ONE

Brethren, if a man be overtaken in a fault, ye which are spiritual, restore such an one in the spirit of meekness; considering thyself, lest thou also be tempted. Gal. 6:1.

Here is a special direction to deal tenderly with those overtaken in a fault. "Overtaken" must have its full significance. . . . To be led into sin unawares—not intending to sin, but to sin through want of watchfulness and prayer, not discerning the temptation of Satan and so falling into his snare—is very different from the one who plans and deliberately enters into temptation and plans out a course of sin. . . .

More effective measures are needed to check the premeditated sin, but the apostle directs the treatment to be given to those who are overtaken or surprised or overcome by temptation. . . . Restore him in meekness, "considering thyself, lest thou also be tempted." Faith and reproofs will be needed, and kindly counsel and supplications to God, to bring them to see their danger and sin. The original word is, set in joint, as a dislocated bone; therefore the efforts should be made to set them in joint, and bring them to themselves by convincing them of their sin and error. . . . There should be no triumphing in a brother's fall. But in meekness, in the fear of God, in love for their soul's sake, seek to save them from sin.[44]

When men have to swim against the stream, there is a weight of waves driving them back. Let a hand then be held out, as was the Elder Brother's hand to a sinking Peter. . . . Let the one who is supposed to have moved wrongly be given no occasion by his brother to become discouraged, but let him feel the strong clasp of a sympathizing hand; let him hear the whisper, "Let us pray." The Holy Spirit will give a rich experience to both. It is prayer that unites hearts. It is prayer to the Great Physician to heal the soul that will bring the blessing of God. Prayer unites us with one another and with God. Prayer brings Jesus to our side, and gives new strength and fresh grace to the fainting, perplexed soul to overcome the world, the flesh, and the devil. Prayer turns aside the attacks of Satan.[45]

177

ONE TO A HUNDRED

Then came Peter to him, and said, Lord, how oft shall my brother sin against me, and I forgive him? till seven times? Jesus saith unto him, I say not unto thee, Until seven times: but, Until seventy times seven. Matt. 18:21, 22.

There is a great work before us. There are men and women straying from the fold of Christ, and as they become cold and indifferent, and lose all disposition to return, they will not run after you. You must take them where they are. . . . When you find a wandering sheep, call him to the fold; and leave him not until you see him safely enfolded there. . . . Go out for the lost sheep of the house of Israel.

If there is any point on which you have committed one wrong, although he may have committed one hundred, take that which you have done out of the way and open the way for him to come back again. Perhaps that was the very thing that was keeping a soul away. In your humility, confess your one wrong, and perhaps it may touch him and lead him with weeping to confess his hundred wrongs, and to take them out of the way. Thus a soul for whom Christ died will be saved. . . .

You may say, I have tried to save this one and that one, and they have only wounded me, and I am not going to try to help them any more. But do not become discouraged if they do not *at once* return to the fold. Reach out still for your fellow mortals around you. You shall reap if you faint not.[46]

Press together. Do not make little wedges of slight differences of opinion, and drive them in to separate heart from heart, but see how you can love one another even as Christ has loved you. See how you can forgive those who trespass against you, even as you want your Father in heaven to forgive your trespasses. Then you can be definite in your requests; you can be bold in Christ; for Christ presents your requests to God with the heavenly credentials which are His own righteousness, and you can believe that Christ does hear, believe that He does bless, and say, "I am His, and He is mine."[47]

ALL HONOR TO THE PEACEMAKERS!

Blessed are the peacemakers: for they shall be called the children of God. Matt. 5:9.

Peacemakers! What a treasure is a peacemaker in the family; what a blessing in the church! Peacemakers may be tempted, but their life is hid with Christ in God. They look unto Jesus, copying His pattern. . . . They receive the peace which Christ gives. . . .

The true nature of our religion is not found in the position we occupy, but in the gentle spirit, the kindness, the peace which we manifest. Our religion is made manifest in the home circle by the atmosphere surrounding the soul that brings happiness to the family. . . .

True Christians will not . . . speak in a cheap or fretting way. In the familiar circle of the home they will do services of love and Christian courtesy. These services may seem very commonplace, but the universe of heaven will be interested in the consistent walk of those who seek to benefit others. . . .

It is not only our privilege but our duty to cultivate gentleness, to have the peace of Christ in the heart and as peacemakers and followers of Christ to sow precious seed that will produce a harvest unto eternal life. Professed followers of Christ may possess many good and useful qualities; but their characters are greatly marred by an unkind, fretful, faultfinding, harshly judging temper. The husband or the wife who cherishes suspicion and distrust creates dissension and strife in the home. Neither of them should keep his gentle words and smiles for strangers alone, and manifest irritability in the home, thus driving out peace and contentment. . . .

It is practical Christlikeness alone that can make one a peacemaker in the home, in the church, in the neighborhood, and in the world. Home religion is practical sanctification. . . . The true quality of religion is gauged by the manner in which each member in the family does his duty to his associates. . . . Learn the precious lesson of being peacemakers in your home life.[48]

June 23

NO CASTE WITH GOD

My brethren, have not the faith of our Lord Jesus Christ, the Lord of glory, with respect of persons. James 2:1.

The wrongs existing in the society of the world should never, never find sanction among Christians. . . . God demands that you open your hand wide to the needy, and have the tenderest compassion for those who are afflicted, or who are suffering from want. . . .

If you have the spirit of Christ, you will love as brethren; you will honor the humble disciple in his poor home, because God loves him as much as He loves you, and it may be more. He recognizes no caste. He places His own signet upon men, not by their rank, not by their wealth, not by intellectual greatness, but by their oneness with Christ. It is purity of heart, singleness of purpose, that constitutes the true value of human beings. . . . All who are living in daily communion with Christ, will place His estimate upon men. They will reverence the good and pure, although these are poor in this world's goods. . . . Avarice, selfishness, and covetousness are idolatry, and are dishonoring to God. . . . Tenderness, compassion, and benevolence are enjoined upon Christians.[49]

We should study to copy the Pattern, that the Spirit that dwelt in Christ may dwell in us. The Saviour was not found among the exalted and honorable of the world. He did not spend His time among those who were seeking their ease and pleasure. He went about doing good. His work was to help those who needed help, to save the lost and perishing, to lift up the bowed down, to break the yoke of oppression from those who were in bondage, to heal the afflicted, and to speak words of sympathy and consolation to the distressed and sorrowing. We are required to copy this pattern. Let us be up and doing, seeking to bless the needy and comfort the distressed. The more we partake of the spirit of Christ, the more we shall see to do for our fellow men. We shall be filled with a love for perishing souls, and shall find our delight in following the footsteps of the Majesty of heaven.[50]

June 24

ROOT OUT THE POISONOUS PLANTS

Above all things have fervent charity among yourselves: for charity shall cover the multitude of sins. 1 Peter 4:8.

How close and tender should be the tie that binds us together! How careful we should be to have our words and actions in harmony with the sacred truths that God has committed to us! . . .

Let your conversation be of such a nature that you will have no need to repent of it. . . . If a word is dropped that is detrimental to the character of a friend or brother, never encourage this evilspeaking; for it is the work of the enemy. Remind the speaker that God's Word forbids this kind of conversation. . . . The Redeemer has told us how we may reveal Him to the world. If we cherish His spirit, if we manifest His love toward others, if we guard one another's interests, if we are kind, patient, forbearing, the fruits we bear will give evidence to the world that we are God's children. . . . To build up one another in the most holy faith is a blessed work; to tear down is a work full of bitterness and sorrow. . . .

We should seek to lighten one another's burdens by manifesting the love of Jesus to those around us. If our conversation were upon heaven and heavenly things, evilspeaking would soon cease to have any attraction for us. We would not then be placing our feet upon dangerous ground; nor would we enter into temptation, falling under the power of the evil one.

Instead of finding fault with others, let us be critical with ourselves. Every one should inquire, Is my heart right before God? Am I glorifying my heavenly Father? If you have cherished a wrong spirit, banish it from the soul. Eradicate from your heart everything that is of a defiling nature. Pluck up every root of bitterness, lest others be contaminated by the baleful influence. Do not allow one poisonous plant to remain in the soil of your heart. Root it out this very hour, and cultivate in its stead the plant of love. Let Jesus be enshrined in the soul-temple. . . . "If we love one another, God dwelleth in us, and his love is perfected in us." 1 John 4:12.[51]

HELPING ONE ANOTHER

As we have therefore opportunity, let us do good unto all men, especially unto them who are of the household of faith. Gal. 6:10.

In the Lord's plan human beings have been made necessary to one another. If all would do their utmost to help those who need their help, their unselfish sympathy and love, what a blessed work might be done. To every one God has entrusted talents. These talents we are to use to help one another to walk in the narrow path. In this work each one is connected with the other, and all are united with Christ. It is by unselfish service that we improve and increase our talents.

The members of the church of God on this earth are as the different parts of a machine, all closely related to one another, and all closely related to and dependent on one great center. There is to be unity in diversity. No member of the Lord's firm can work successfully in independence, detached from the others. . . . All are to use their entrusted capabilities in His service, that each may minister to the perfection of the whole. Each is to work under the supervision of God.

By Christ's wonderful union of divinity with humanity, we are assured that even in this world we may be partakers of the divine nature. . . . Christ has pledged Himself to cooperate with those to whom He has entrusted talents. He has pledged Himself to train us to be His colaborers. He will help us to follow His example, doing good and refusing to do evil. We are to be consecrated channels through whom the love of Christ flows to those in need of help. . . .

Christ sends His light to those who keep the windows of the soul open heavenward. Under the Holy Spirit's influence, they work the works of God. He who approaches nearest to obedience to the divine law will be of the most service to God. He who follows Christ, reaching out after His goodness, His compassion, His love for the human family, will be accepted by God as a worker together with Him. Such a one will not be content to remain on a low level of spirituality. He will constantly reach higher and higher.[52]

THE GRACE OF SYMPATHY

We then that are strong ought to bear the infirmities of the weak, and not to please ourselves. Rom. 15:1.

What we all need is a more pure, Christlike sympathy; not sympathy for those who are perfect—they do not need it—but sympathy for poor, suffering, struggling souls who are often overtaken in fault, sinning and repenting, tempted and discouraged. The effect of grace is to soften and subdue the soul. Then all this cold unapproachableness is melted, subdued, and Christ appears.

The love of God alone can open and expand the heart, and give to love and sympathy a breadth and height that is without measure. Those who love Jesus will love all the children of God. The sense of personal infirmities and imperfections will lead the human agent to look away from self to Christ; and the Saviour's love will break down every cold, Pharisaical barrier, it will banish all harshness and selfishness, and there will be a blending of soul with soul, even with those who are opposite in temperament.

The goodness and forbearance of God, His self-sacrificing love to sinful men, must lead all who discern His grace to manifest the same, to give sympathy liberally to others. The wonderful example of the life of Christ, the matchless tenderness with which He entered into the feelings of the oppressed soul, weeping with those that wept, rejoicing with all that rejoiced in His love, must have a deep influence upon the character of all who love God and keep His commandments.

They will give sympathy, not grudgingly but liberally; by kindly words and acts they will try to make the path just as easy for weary feet as they desire the path to be made for their feet. As we receive daily and hourly the blessing of God, we can do no less to show our gratitude than to have a kindly, unselfish interest in those for whom Christ has died. Have we blessings? Yes, we have. Well, Christ says, Pass them along to others, not to a favored few, but to all with whom we come in contact. We must give grace for grace.[53]

June 27

"WHO IS MY NEIGHBOUR?"

Be kindly affectioned one to another with brotherly love; in honour preferring one another. Rom. 12:10.

A Christian life will be revealed by Christian thoughts, Christian words, and Christian deportment. In Christ there is a divine completeness of character. In Christ we will work the works of Christ. We shall in Christ sense our binding, far-reaching obligations to God and to our fellow man. . . . There are many cords which unite us to our fellow men, to humanity, and to God, and this relationship is solemn with its weight of responsibility.[54]

As long as we are in this world, we must be linked one with another. Humanity is interlaced and interwoven with humanity. As Christians we are members one of another. . . . The Lord designs us as His sons and daughters, whom He calls His friends, to help one another. This is to be a part of our practical Christian work.

"Who is my neighbour?" . . . He is the very one who needs help the most. Thy brother, sick in spirit, needs you as you needed him. He needs the experience of one who has been as weak as himself, who can sympathize with and help him. The very knowledge of his own weakness helps that one to help another in his weakness.

Let it not be that the sympathetic cords, which should be quick to vibrate at the least touch, shall be cold as steel, frozen, as it were, and unable to help where help is needed.[55]

Seek to help, to strengthen, to bless those with whom you are associated. The Lord will be merciful to those who are merciful. The Lord will be tender and pitiful to those who exercise tenderness and compassion and pity for others. We must realize that we are in Christ's school, not to learn how we may esteem ourselves, how we shall conduct ourselves so as to receive honor of men, but how we may cherish the meekness of Christ. Self and selfishness will be ever striving for the mastery. It is a fight we must have with ourselves, that self shall not have the victory. Through Christ you may triumph; through Christ you may conquer.[56]

June 28

IN THE FOOTSTEPS OF JESUS

Wherefore lift up the hands which hang down, and the feeble knees; and make straight paths for your feet, lest that which is lame be turned out of the way; but let it rather be healed. Heb. 12:12, 13.

The efficiency of Satan's kingdom is found in the blending together of satanic forces to extend the contagion of evil; but the Lord Jesus has devised a plan whereby He may work counter to the work of Satan. He designs to imbue His human agents, the subjects of His kingdom, with the principles of love and unity. With sanctified heart they are to build one another up and strengthen and extend that which is good. Reciprocating Christ's love, they are to deal in the goods of heaven. His church is to bear His superscription, and thus testify to the world that God has sent His Son to be the Saviour of the world. . . . Love is to be interwoven as threads of gold in all their actions.

Every Christian who is happy in the Lord will work zealously to bring the same happiness into the heart and life of one who is in need and affliction. Followers of Christ will produce their own happiness in the hearts of others by performing Christlike works. They will diffuse an atmosphere which is pure, peaceful, and Christlike. They will act out heavenly attributes, and will produce fruit after the heavenly kind and quality. That which they sow they shall also reap.

It is essential that every soul that names the name of Christ should make straight paths for his feet. Why? Lest the lame be turned out of the way. It is a terrible, terrible thing to give a soul a wrong example, and to lead him in a crooked course by the way in which you may walk. . . . Whatever you may see others doing that your judgment convicts you as being unseemly for a Christian, see to it that you never do the same things yourself. . . . Just as long as you will follow in the footsteps of Jesus, you will walk securely. . . .

We must look on the faults of others not to condemn, but to restore and heal. Watch unto prayer, go forward and upward, catching more and more of the spirit of Jesus, and sowing the same beside all waters.[57]

JOY IN HUMBLE SERVICE

Lord, what wilt thou have me to do? Acts 9:6.

It matters not what our position may be or how limited our ca-
pacities, we have a work to do for the Master. Our graces are developed and matured by exercise. With the truth of God burning in
the soul we cannot be idle. The happiness we shall experience in
doing will compensate even in this life for every effort. Those only
who have experienced happiness resulting from self-denying effort
in the service of Christ can speak of the matter understandingly. It is
indeed joy so pure, so deep, that language cannot express it.

"... Through life's transient day
There is a special work marked out for you;
It may be of the lowliest kind, it may
Be such as shall the loftiest powers display.
But none besides yourself your work can do.
'What wilt Thou have me do?' With single eye
To your Redeemer's glory, work for Him;
Illumined every moment from on high,
Strive in each action God to glorify,
Nor let one thought of self life's radiance dim." ...

We may have Christ with us while engaged in our daily avoca-
tions. Wherever we are, in whatever we are engaged, we may be indeed elevated because we are united to Christ. We may take up our
humble life duties ennobled by and sanctified through the assurance
of the love of God. Working from principle in the humblest calling
invests it with dignity. The consciousness that we are indeed the servants of Christ will give a higher tone of character to our everyday
duties—ever cheerful, patient, forbearing, and gentle. ...

If you are seen to be firm in principle, fearless in duty, zealous
in seeking to exemplify Christ in your daily work, yet humble, lowly,
gentle and tender, patient and forgiving, ready to suffer and to forgive injuries, you will be a living epistle known and read of all men.[58]

June 30

THE PRECIOUS TREASURE OF TIME

The night is far spent, the day is at hand: let us therefore cast off the works of darkness, and let us put on the armour of light. Rom. 13:12.

If we would at last share the reward of the righteous, we must wisely improve the time of our probation. Moments are more precious than gold. . . .

The coming of the Lord draweth nigh. We have but a little time in which to make ready. If precious opportunities are slighted, it will result in eternal loss. We need a close connection with God. We are not safe a moment unless guided and controlled by the Holy Spirit. . . .

The months . . . are swiftly passing. Soon this year, with its burden of records, will be numbered with the past. Let the precious months remaining be devoted to earnest soul labor for our Master. Could we behold a faithful record of the manner in which we have spent the months already past, would the view be satisfactory? Deduct every action which would benefit no one, . . . and how little remains of willing service, performed for the glory of God! Is not the record alarming? How many precious hours have been squandered in selfish gratification! How often, to please ourselves, have we neglected opportunities to work for Christ! . . .

Life, with its marvelous privileges and opportunities, will soon be ended. The time for improvement in character will be past. Unless our sins are now repented of, and blotted out by the blood of the Lamb, they will stand in the ledger of heaven to confront us in the coming day. . . .

Life is short. The things of the world must perish with the using. Let us be wise, and build for eternity. We cannot afford to idle away our precious moments, or engage in busy activities that will bring forth no fruit for eternity. Let the time hitherto devoted to idleness, frivolity, worldliness, be spent in gaining a knowledge of the Scriptures, in beautifying our life, and blessing and ennobling the life and character of others. This work will meet the approval of God, and win for us the heavenly benediction of "Well done." [59]

July 1

MORE, MORE, MORE!

Riches and honour are with me; yea, durable riches and righteousness. My fruit is better than gold, yea, than fine gold; and my revenue than choice silver. Prov. 8:18, 19.

The covetous man becomes more covetous as he draws near his death. The man who all through his life is accumulating earthly treasure, cannot readily withdraw himself from his accustomed pursuits. Shall not he who is seeking a heavenly treasure become more earnest, more zealous, and more intensely interested in seeking the treasure which is above? Shall he not covet the best and most enduring substance? Shall he not seek the crown of glory that is imperishable, the riches which moth and rust doth not corrupt, nor thieves break through and steal? The more ardent his hopes, the more strenuous are his efforts and the more determined he is not to fail of the immortal treasure. . . . His business on the earth is to secure eternal riches. He cannot, will not, consent, after tasting of the heavenly gifts of God, to be a pauper, left in destitution for eternity. The soul passion is more, more. This is the real want of the soul. We want more of the divine grace, more enlightenment, more faith. . . .

Oh, if all the misdirected energies were devoted to the one great object—the rich provisions of the grace of God in this life—what testimonials we could hang in memory's halls, recounting the mercies and favors of God! . . . Then the habit would be carried with us as an abiding principle to accumulate spiritual treasures as earnestly and perseveringly as the worldly aspirants labor for the earthly and temporal things. You may well be dissatisfied with the present supply when the Lord has a heaven of blessedness and a treasure house of good and gracious things to supply the necessities of the soul. Today we want more grace, today we want a renewal of God's love and tokens of His goodness, and He will not withhold these good and heavenly treasures from the true seeker. . . .

Those who feel their spiritual necessities will show their soul eagerness, their ardent desires, which extend upward and onward above every earthly, temporal inducement, to the eternal.[1]

THE PERIL OF PROSPERITY

If riches increase, set not your heart upon them. Ps. 62:10.

Among the greatest dangers that threaten the church is the love of the world. Out of this spring the sins of selfishness and covetousness. With many, the more they get of earthly treasure, the more they set their affections on it, and still they reach out for more. . . .

Satan employs every means which he can devise to overthrow the followers of Christ. With marvelous skill and cunning he adapts his temptations to the peculiar temperament of each. Those who are naturally selfish and covetous he often tempts by throwing prosperity in their way. He knows that if they do not overcome their natural temperament, the love of mammon will cause them to stumble and fall. His object is often accomplished. When the riches of the world are offered them, many eagerly grasp the treasure, and think they are wonderfully prospered. The strong love of the world soon swallows up the love of the truth. . . .

If those who are thus prospered would lay all their possessions upon the altar of God, they might overcome their selfish, covetous spirit, and so thwart the design of Satan. Worldly wealth may be made a blessing, if rightly used. All who possess it should realize that it is lent them of God, to be employed in His service. By giving freely to advance the cause of truth and to relieve the wants of the needy, they may be the means of saving others, and thus bring a blessing to their own souls here, and lay up in heaven a treasure that shall be theirs hereafter. . . .

Many hardly know, as yet, what self-denial is, or what it is to sacrifice for the truth's sake. But none will enter Heaven but by the same path of humiliation, self-sacrifice, and cross-bearing, that the Saviour trod. Only those who are willing to sacrifice all for eternal life will have it, but it will be worth suffering for, worth crucifying self and sacrificing every idol for. The far more exceeding and eternal weight of glory will outweigh every earthly treasure and eclipse every earthly attraction.[2]

AGENTS TO RELIEVE DISTRESS

And the King shall answer and say unto them, Verily I say unto you, Inasmuch as ye have done it unto one of the least of these my brethren, ye have done it unto me. Matt. 25:40.

What if the professed followers of Jesus should look upon their expensive garments and should see the words written upon them by the finger of God, "Clothe the naked." What if they should see inscribed upon their expensive decorations in their homes, the pictures, and furniture, "Bring the poor that are cast out to thy house"! In the dining room, where the table is laden with abundant food, the finger of God has traced, "Is it not to deal thy bread to the hungry . . . ?" Let all, old and young, consider that it is not a light matter to be the Lord's steward. . . . The needy, the oppressed, are left in want, while the Lord's money is selfishly squandered in extravagance and luxury. O that all will remember that God is no respecter of persons! It is a great thing to be a steward, faithful and true, before a just, impartial God. . . .

The law of God holds every man accountable for the use he makes of every dollar that comes into his hands; for the Lord has made men His agents to relieve the world's distress. If man hoards or selfishly uses his Lord's entrusted goods, it will be to the ruin of his own soul; for he honors, exalts, and glorifies himself. . . . There are those in our world who, although the professedly chosen of God, can always pass the needy by on the other side. Jesus sees this; Jesus marks this; He will not pass it by. Jesus declared that He came to preach the gospel to the poor. He has bestowed His goods, that love and beneficence shall live, ever growing stronger in the hearts of His people. . . .

The apportioning of rewards at the last day turns upon the question of our practical benevolence: "Inasmuch as ye have done it unto one of the least of these my brethren, ye have done it unto me." Christ puts Himself in the poor man's place, identifying His interest with that of the poor. . . . He calls upon each disciple to dispense with grateful liberality the gifts entrusted to him, as if he were bestowing the same upon his Redeemer.[3]

NOTHING TOO PRECIOUS
TO GIVE TO GOD

By faith Abraham, when he was tried, offered up Isaac: and he that had received the promises offered up his only begotten son. Heb. 11:17.

Abraham's test was the most severe that could come to a human being. Had he failed under it, he would never have been registered as the father of the faithful. . . . The lesson was given to shine down through the ages, that we may learn that there is nothing too precious to be given to God. It is when we look upon every gift as the Lord's, to be used in His service, that we secure the heavenly benediction. Give back to God your entrusted possessions, and more will be entrusted to you. Keep your possessions to yourself, and you will receive no reward in this life, and will lose the reward of the life to come. . . .

There are many who have never made an unreserved surrender of themselves to God. They have not a right idea of the infinite sacrifice made by God to save a ruined world. If God should speak to them as He did to Abraham, they would not be sufficiently acquainted with His voice to know that He was calling upon them to make a sacrifice, in order to test the depth of their love and the sincerity of their faith.

The plague spot of selfishness is as contagious as leprosy. Those who enter the heavenly courts must be purified from every vestige of this plague. . . .

The Lord has a great work for us to do, and He invites us to look to Him, to trust in Him, to walk with Him, to talk with Him. He invites us to make an unreserved surrender of all that we have and are to Him, that when He shall call upon us to sacrifice for Him, we may be ready and willing to obey. We shall enjoy the fullness of divine grace only as we give all to Christ. We shall know the meaning of true happiness only as we keep the fire burning on the altar of sacrifice. God will bequeath the most in the future to those who have done the most in the present. . . . Each day, under different circumstances, He tries us; and in each truehearted endeavor He chooses His workers, not because they are perfect, but because they are willing to work unselfishly for Him, and He sees that through connection with Him they may gain perfection.[4]

July 5

HOW DOES *YOUR* ACCOUNT STAND?

Moreover it is required in stewards, that a man be found faithful.
1 Cor. 4:2.

Money is a blessing when those who use it consider that they are the Lord's stewards, that they are handling the Lord's capital, and must one day give account of their stewardship.[5]

Do you confess Christ in your expenditure of His entrusted means? . . . If Christ had that which is His own in tithes and offerings, so much would not be left for selfish outlay on knickknacks and display. Less would be spent for dress, for pleasure excursions, for entertainments, or for display in table fare. We may confess Christ by making no elaborate preparations for visitors; we may deny Him by making more than ordinary preparations, which takes time that rightly belongs to the Lord. . . . Before you enter into amusement for the gratification of self, ask yourself the question, Is not this God's time and money that I am expending needlessly? Open your account book, and see how your account stands with God, with your household, and with the world.

Have you confessed Christ by faithfully tithing the mint, the anise, and the rue? When we give the Lord the tithe, we are only giving Him that which is His own, to withhold which is theft and robbery. . . . Does your account book reveal that you have dealt faithfully with your Lord? Are you poor? Then give your little. Have you been blessed with abundance? Then be sure to lay aside that which the Lord registers as His own. . . . The neglect to confess Christ in your account books cuts you off from the great privilege of having your name registered in the Lamb's book of life.[6]

Our heavenly Father teaches by His own example of beneficence. God gives to us regularly, freely, and abundantly. Every earthly blessing is from His hand. What if the Lord should cease to bestow His gifts upon us? What a cry of wretchedness, suffering, and want would go up from the earth! We need daily the unfailing flow of Jehovah's love and goodness.[7]

WHEN LOSS IS GAIN

And he said unto them, Take heed, and beware of covetousness: for a man's life consisteth not in the abundance of the things which he possesseth. Luke 12:15.

One marked feature in the teachings of Christ is the frequency and earnestness with which He rebuked the sin of covetousness and pointed out the danger of worldly acquisitions and the inordinate love of gain. . . . When the head and hands are constantly occupied with planning and toiling for the accumulation of riches, the claims of God and humanity are forgotten.[8]

Means is valuable and to be desired. It is a blessing, a precious treasure, if used prudently, wisely, and not abused. . . . Since mortals have bodies and heads and hearts to be provided for, some provision for the body must be made in order to hold a proper position in the world. Not to meet the world's standards—oh, no, no indeed; but to be of influence in the world for good. . . .

Want and poverty are evils to be dreaded; but hunger and nakedness, lack of home, sympathy, or a name, and even starvation, are more desirable than to sacrifice one principle of truth. Let the eternal truth be cherished, for it is immortal. If we make it a part of us we shall surely gain immortal glory and eternal riches. . . .

If God has not given you the power to obtain means with perfect uprightness and integrity, then He never meant that you should have it, and it is best for you to submit to the will of God. . . . The infinite Creator is the possessor of all things. Any loss you may sustain in your allegiance to Him is infinite gain in the future immortal life, if not fully realized in this life. . . .

Behold the glories of the firmament. Look up to the gems of light which like precious gold stud the heavens. . . . Cannot He who spread above us this glorious canopy, who, if the sun, moon, and stars were swept away could call them again into existence in a moment, requite His faithful, loyal servants who would be obedient to Him though they lost wealth, honor, or even a kingdom for His sake?[9]

J u l y 7

A CURSE OR A BLESSING?

Lay not up for yourselves treasures upon earth, where moth and rust doth corrupt, and where thieves break through and steal. Matt. 6:19.

Treasures are those things which engross the mind, and absorb the attention, to the exclusion of God and the truth. . . . Our Saviour gave a decided warning against hoarding up the treasures of earth.

All branches of business, all manner of employments, are under the eye of God; and every Christian has been given ability to do something in the cause of the Master. Whether engaged in business in the field, in the warehouse, or in the countingroom, men will be held responsible to God for the wise and honest employment of their talents. They are just as accountable to God for *their* work, as the minister who labors in word and doctrine is for his. . . .

Property that is treasured up upon the earth will prove only a curse, but if it is devoted to the upbuilding of the cause of truth, that God may be honored, and that souls may be saved, it will not prove a curse, but a blessing. Means are necessary to the furtherance of every good cause; and as some men have been endowed with more ability to acquire wealth than have others, they should put out their talents to the exchangers, that the Lord may receive His own, with usury, at His appearing. . . .

Those who are ready and willing to invest in the cause of God, will be blessed in their efforts to acquire money. God created the source of wealth. He gave the sunshine, and the dew, and the rain, and caused vegetation to flourish. He blessed men with mental and physical ability, and qualified them to acquire property, so that His cause might be sustained by His professed children. The needy are all around us, and God is glorified, when the poor and the afflicted are aided and comforted. It is no sin to acquire and control property as stewards for God, holding it only until He shall require it for the necessities of His work.[10]

We must ever bear in mind that we are in copartnership with God. His work and His cause demand the first consideration.[11]

July 8

A BANK THAT NEVER FAILS

But lay up for yourselves treasures in heaven, where neither moth nor rust doth corrupt, and where thieves do not break through nor steal: for where your treasure is, there will your heart be also. Matt. 6:20, 21.

Here is portrayed the value of eternal riches, in contrast with the treasures of earth. If the purpose and aim of your life is to lay up treasure in heaven, you will be lifted above the base, sordid, demoralizing influence of an inordinate desire to obtain wealth in this life. Laying up treasure in heaven will give nobility to the character; it will strengthen benevolence, encourage mercy; cultivate sympathy, brotherly kindness, and charity. It will unite the soul of man with Christ, by links that can never be broken. You may lay up for yourselves treasure in heaven by being rich in good works—rich in imperishable and spiritual things.

The instruction is to "lay up for *yourselves* treasures in heaven." It is for our own interest that we secure heavenly riches. God is not benefited by our benevolence. The cattle upon a thousand hills are His. "The earth is the Lord's, and the fulness thereof." Ps. 24:1. But in using the gifts that He has entrusted to our care for the salvation of souls, we transfer our wealth to the treasury of heaven. When we are seeking the glory of God, and hasting unto the day of God, we are colaborers with Christ, and our joy is not a base and fleeting emotion; but it is the joy of our Lord. We are elevated above the corroding, perplexing cares of this frail, fickle world.

While we are in this world, we are subject to losses and disappointments. Thieves break through and steal; moth and rust corrupt; fire and storm sweep away our possessions. . . . How many have devoted life and soul to acquiring wealth, but were not rich toward God; and when adversity came upon them, and their possessions were swept away, they had nothing laid up in heaven. They had lost all—both temporal and eternal riches. . . .

Everything that is laid up upon earth may be swept away in a moment; but nothing can disturb the treasure that is laid up in heaven.[12]

THE SMILES OF GOD

The blessing of the Lord, it maketh rich, and he addeth no sorrow with it. Prov. 10:22.

Nothing can do us real good without the blessing of God. What God blesses is blessed. Therefore "a little that a righteous man hath is better than the riches of many wicked." Ps. 37:16. The little with the blessing of God is more efficient, and it will extend farther. The grace of God will make a little go a great ways. When we devote ourselves to the affairs of the kingdom of God, He will mind our affairs.[13]

The Lord has given us precious blessings in the simple flowers of the field, in the fragrance so grateful to our senses. He has tinted every flower with beauty; for He is the great Master Artist. He who has created the beautiful things in nature will do far greater things for the soul. God is a lover of the beautiful, and He would adorn our characters with His own rich graces. He would have our words as fragrant as the flowers of the field. He has given us blessings in daily provision for our physical needs. The very bread we eat has upon it the image and superscription of the cross.[14]

They only are truly blessed whose chief concern is to secure those blessings which will nourish the soul and endure forever. Our Saviour says to us, "Seek ye first the kingdom of God, and his righteousness; and all these things shall be added unto you." Matt. 6:33. God has a care for us, even to bestow His temporal blessings upon us. Our earthly good is not beneath the notice of our heavenly Father. He knoweth that we have need of these things. . . . When God smiles upon our efforts it is worth more than any earthly income.

"How sweet our daily comforts prove
When they are seasoned with His love."[15]

Every deliverance, every blessing, that God in the past has granted to His people, should be kept fresh in memory's hall as a sure pledge of further and richer, increasing blessings that He will bestow.[16]

There is no limit to the blessings that it is our privilege to receive.[17]

THE GIFT GOD ACCEPTS

Give, and it shall be given unto you; good measure, pressed down, and shaken together, and running over, shall men give into your bosom. For with the same measure that ye mete withal it shall be measured to you again. Luke 6:38.

Let us not complain because we are often asked to give for the upbuilding of the cause. What is it that makes these frequent calls a necessity? Is it not the rapid increase of missionary enterprises? Shall we, by refusing to give, retard the growth of these enterprises? . . .

All who possess the Spirit of Christ will have a tender, sympathetic heart, and an open, generous hand. . . . To us has been entrusted the work of proclaiming the last message of mercy to be given to our world—the message that is to prepare a people to stand in the day of God. Do we realize our accountability? Are we acting our part in the proclamation of the message? The present time is burdened with eternal interests. We are to unfurl the standard of truth before a world perishing in error.[18]

The more we bring to God's treasure house, the more we shall have to bring; for He will open ways before us, increasing our substance. I have found this to be true in my own experience. As God multiplies His gifts to us, we must not grow selfish, and withhold from Him our tithes and offerings. We each have a part to act in the work of salvation.[19]

Gifts and offerings will not purchase salvation for any of us. The religion of the Bible is that development of our moral natures in which the soul holds converse with God, loves that which God loves, and hates that which God hates. God will not accept your offerings if you withhold yourself. He asks not only for that which is His own in the means entrusted to you, but for His own property in your body, soul, and spirit, purchased at the infinite price of the blood of the Son of God.[20]

It is the humble, grateful, reverential heart that makes the offering as a sweet-smelling savor, acceptable to God.[21]

GOD'S MERCIFUL HELPING HAND

Blessed are the merciful: for they shall obtain mercy. Matt. 5:7.

Be merciful, even as your Father in heaven is merciful. Think of the great gift God has made for you. . . . God has given you a proof of His love that defies all computation. We have no line with which to measure it, no standard with which to compare it. God invites you to let your gratitude flow forth in gifts and offerings. He calls upon you to be His merciful helping hand. Can you refuse the request of One who has done so much for you?

Christ wept at the sight of woe. Let His tenderness come into your hearts. Practice self-denial that you may have wherewith to relieve the sufferings of God's children.[22]

The Lord saw that it was essential for us to be surrounded with the poor, who in their helplessness and need would lay claim to our ministration. They would be an aid to us in perfecting Christian character; for in providing food for their tables and clothing for their bodies, we would cultivate the attributes of the character of Christ. If we had not the poor among us, we would lose much; for in order to perfect Christian character, we must deny self.[23]

Christ Himself, the Lord of glory, was in this earth a Man of sorrows and acquainted with grief. He knew the meaning of want and privation. As a child, subject to poverty, He practiced the principles of self-denial. He . . . came to help fallen, needy humanity. And He expects His followers, to whom He has entrusted means, to bind about their own supposed wants, and to be liberal in relieving the necessities of others.[24]

When spending your money, think of what Jesus would do were He in your place. He calls upon His followers to tread in His footsteps of self-denial and self-sacrifice. The character of the Christian is to be a reproduction of the character of Christ. The same love, the same grace, the same unselfish benevolence, seen in His life, is to characterize the lives of His followers.[25]

July 12

SWEETNESS OF SELF-DENIAL

Honour the Lord with thy substance, and with the firstfruits of all thine increase: so shall thy barns be filled with plenty, and thy presses shall burst out with new wine. Prov. 3:9, 10.

God's claims underlie all other claims. He lays His hand upon all that He, from His fullness and beneficence, has entrusted to man, and says: "I am the rightful owner of the universe, and these goods are Mine. Use them to advance My cause, to build up My kingdom, and My blessing shall rest upon you." [26]

Some give of their abundance, yet feel no lack. They do not practice self-denial for the cause of Christ. They give liberally and heartily, but they still have all that heart can wish. God regards it. The action and motive are strictly marked by Him, and they will not lose their reward. But those who have less means must not excuse themselves because they cannot do as much as some others. Do what you can. Deny yourself of some article you can do without, and sacrifice for the cause of God. Like the poor widow, cast in your two mites. You will actually give more than all those who give of their abundance; and you will know how sweet it is to deny self, to give to the needy, to sacrifice for the truth, and to lay up treasure in heaven.

The young . . . who profess the truth, have yet a lesson of self-denial to learn. If these made more sacrifice for the truth, they would esteem it more highly. It would affect their hearts, and purify their lives. Too often the young do not take the burden of the cause of God, or feel any responsibility in regard to it. Is it because God has excused them? Oh, no; they excuse themselves. They do not realize that they are not their own. Their strength, their time, is not their own. They are bought with a price; and unless they possess the spirit of self-denial and sacrifice, they can never gain the immortal inheritance. [27]

Give what you can now, and as you cooperate with Christ, your hand will open to impart still more. And God will refill your hand, that the treasure of truth may be taken to many souls. He will give to you that you may give to others. [28]

July 13

A TEST OF CHARACTER

But they that will be rich fall into temptation and a snare, and into many foolish and hurtful lusts, which drown men in destruction and perdition. For the love of money is the root of all evil. 1 Tim. 6:9, 10.

Satan has nets and snares, like the snares of the fowler, all prepared to entrap souls. It is his studied purpose that men shall employ their God-given powers for selfish ends rather than yield them to glorify God. God would have men engage in a work that will bring them peace and joy, and will render them eternal profit; but Satan wants us to concentrate our efforts for that which profiteth not, for the things that perish with the using.[29]

The glory of the world to come is eclipsed by the corruptible things of earth. "For where your treasure is, there will your heart be also." Matt. 6:21. Your thoughts, your plans, your motives, will have an earthly mold, and your soul will be defiled with covetousness and selfishness. "What shall it profit a man, if he gain the whole world, and lose his own soul?" Mark 8:36. The day is coming when the idols of silver and gold will be cast to the moles and to the bats, and the rich men will weep and howl for the miseries that shall come upon them. . . .

If your thoughts, your plans, your purposes, are all directed toward the accumulation of the things of earth, your anxiety, your study, your interests, will all be centered upon the world. The heavenly attractions will lose their beauty. . . . Your heart will be with your treasure. . . . You will have no time to devote to the study of the Scriptures and to earnest prayer that you may escape the snares of Satan. . . .

O that the great interests of the world to come were appreciated! Why is it that men are so unconcerned about the salvation of the soul when it was purchased at such cost by the Son of God?[30]

In the providence of God, by physical skill or ingenious inventions, some may gather more wealth than others. The Lord blesses them with health, with tact, and skill, that they may receive of His goods to bestow upon others who may not have received these blessings. The possession of means constitutes a test of character.[31]

DO WE REALLY SACRIFICE?

Let all those that seek thee rejoice and be glad in thee: let such as love thy salvation say continually, The Lord be magnified. Ps. 40:16.

Many speak of the life of the Christian taking away from us pleasures and worldly enjoyments. I say it takes away nothing worth saving. Is there perplexity, poverty, and distress endured by the Christian? Oh, yes, this is expected in this life. But is the sinner, of whom we speak as enjoying the pleasures of this world, free from these ills of life? Do we not often see them in deep perplexity and trouble? . . .

Christians sometimes think they have a hard time and that it is a condescension in them to lay hold of unpopular truth and profess to be Christ's followers, that the road seems hard and that they have many sacrifices to make, when in reality they make no sacrifice at all. If in reality they are adopted into the family of God, what sacrifice have they made? Their following Christ may have broken some friendship with their world-loving relatives, but look at the exchange—their names written in the Lamb's book of life, elevated, yes, greatly exalted, to be partakers of salvation, heirs of God and joint heirs with Jesus Christ to an imperishable inheritance. Shall we call it a sacrifice on our part to yield error for truth, darkness for light, sin for righteousness, a perishable name and inheritance upon earth for honors that are lasting, and a treasure undefiled that fadeth not away?

Even in this life, the Christian has One upon whom to lean for support, who will help him bear all his trials. Yet the sinner has to bear his trials alone. He goes down into the grave suffering remorse under darkness, bound by Satan, for he is his lawful prey. . . .

If there is any one who should be continually grateful, it is the follower of Christ. If there is any one who enjoys real happiness, even in this life, it is the faithful Christian. . . . If we appreciate or have any sense of how dearly our salvation was purchased, anything which we may call sacrifice will sink away into insignificance.[32]

TRUTH AN ANTIDOTE FOR EVIL

And these words, which I command thee this day, shall be in thine heart: and thou shalt teach them diligently unto thy children, and shalt talk of them when thou sittest in thine house, and when thou walkest by the way, and when thou liest down, and when thou risest up. Deut. 6:6, 7.

The similarity between an uncultivated field and an untrained mind is striking. Children and youth already have in their minds and hearts corrupt seed, ready to spring up and bear its perverting harvest; and the greatest care and watchfulness are needed in cultivating and storing the mind with precious seeds of Bible truth. . . .

When the mind is stored with Bible truth, its principles take deep root in the soul, and the preference and tastes become wedded to truth, and there is no desire for debasing, exciting literature, that enfeebles the moral powers, and wrecks the faculties God has bestowed for usefulness. Bible knowledge will prove an antidote for the poisonous insinuations received through unguarded reading. . . .

Parents can choose, if they will, whether or not their children's minds shall be filled with pure and holy thoughts and sentiments; but their tastes must be disciplined and educated with the greatest care. They must commence early to unfold the Scriptures before the expanding minds of their children, that proper habits and tastes may be formed. . . . The elements of evil cannot be exterminated except by the introduction of food for pure, solid thought. . . .

I call upon the children and youth to empty their minds of foolish vanities, and make Jesus their everlasting friend. Be sure you have a well-grounded hope. . . . It is insanity to be quiet and at ease as so many are at the present time, having no assurance that they are indeed sons and daughters of God. Eternal interests are at stake. Put away that story, fall upon your knees in prayer for strength to overcome temptations, and devote your time to searching the Bible. . . . You need not remain in suspense; true light shines from God's Word upon all hearts that are open to receive its precious rays; and it is your privilege to say, "I know that my redeemer liveth." Job 19:25.[33]

WITH EYES OF FAITH

The eyes of your understanding being enlightened; that ye may know what is the hope of his calling, and what the riches of the glory of his inheritance in the saints. Eph. 1:18.

The highest qualification of the mind will not, cannot, supply the place of true simplicity, of genuine piety. The Bible may be studied as a branch of human science would be; but its beauty, the evidence of its power to save the soul that believes, is a lesson that is never thus learned. If the practice of the Word is not brought into the life, then the sword of the Spirit has not wounded the natural heart. It has been shielded in poetic fancy. Sentimentalism has so wrapped it about that the heart has not sufficiently felt the keenness of its edge, piercing and cutting away the sinful shrines where self is worshipped. . . .

The eyes of the understanding must be enlightened, and the heart and mind brought into harmony with God, who is truth. He who beholds Jesus with the eye of faith sees no glory in himself, for the glory of the Redeemer is reflected into the mind and heart. The atonement of His blood is realized, and the taking away of sin stirs the heart with gratitude.

Being justified by Christ, the receiver of truth is constrained to make an entire surrender to God, and is admitted into the school of Christ, that he may learn of Him who is meek and lowly of heart. A knowledge of the love of God is shed abroad in his heart. He exclaims, Oh, what love! What condescension! Grasping the rich promises by faith, he becomes a partaker of the divine nature. His heart being emptied of self, the waters of life flow in; the glory of the Lord shines forth. Perpetually looking unto Jesus, the human is assimilated by the divine. The believer is changed into His likeness. . . . The human character is changed into the divine.[34]

Christ looks upon His people in their purity and perfection as the reward of all His sufferings, His humiliation, and His love, and the supplement of His glory—Christ the great center, from whom radiates all glory.[35]

WORKING THE MINES OF TRUTH

The entrance of thy words giveth light; it giveth understanding unto the simple. Ps. 119:130.

I feel a special interest in our youth who are interested in the truth. . . . I am anxious that you should press your way forward and upward in order that you shall reach the standard of Christian character that is revealed in the Word of God. Let the Word of God be your guidebook, that in everything you may be molded in conduct and character according to its requirements. . . .

The only way in which the Christian will be able to keep himself unspotted from worldly influence will be by searching the Scriptures and by obeying the Word of God to the very letter. Satan is playing the game of life for every soul, but no one needs to be overcome by his deceptive reasoning. Those only who consent to his sophistry will be deceived by his counsels. But if the truth of God regulates the life, it must be planted in the heart. The truth will produce true beauty in the soul that will be revealed in the character. But if this result is attained, it will be because the truth is cultivated and cherished.[36]

The Bible is to be your standard; the living oracles of Jehovah are to be your guide. You are to dig for the truth as for hidden treasures: you are to find where the treasure is, and then you are to plow every inch of that field to get the jewels. You are to work the mines of truth for new jewels, for new gems, for new diamonds, and you will find them.[37]

As the true seeker after the truth reads the Word, and opens his mind to receive the Word, he longs after truth with his whole heart. The love, the pity, the tenderness, the courtesy, the Christian politeness, which will be the elements in the heavenly mansions that Christ has gone to prepare for those that love Him, take possession of his soul.[38]

Let the youth be taught to love the study of the Bible. Let the first place in our thoughts and affections be given to the Book of books, for it contains knowledge which we need above all other.[39]

HOW TO STUDY THE BIBLE

Search the scriptures; for in them ye think ye have eternal life: and they are they which testify of me. John 5:39.

The Book of books has the highest claim to our reverent attention. We must not be satisfied with superficial knowledge, but must seek to learn the full meaning of the words of truth, and to drink deep of the spirit of the Holy Oracles. To read a certain number of chapters daily, or commit to memory a stipulated amount without careful thought as to the meaning of the sacred text, is a work of little profit. . . . Some portions of Scripture are, indeed, too plain to be misunderstood; but there are others whose meaning does not lie upon the surface, to be seen at a glance. Scripture must be compared with scripture; there must be careful research and patient reflection. And such study will be richly repaid. As the miner discovers veins of precious metal concealed beneath the surface of the earth, so will he who perseveringly searches the Word of God as for hid treasure, find truths of greatest value, which are concealed from the view of the careless seeker.

No effort should be spared to establish a right habit of study. If the mind wanders, bring it back. If the intellectual and moral taste has been perverted by the overwrought and exciting tales of fiction, . . . then you have a battle to fight with yourself to overcome this depraved habit. . . . We are surrounded by unbelief. The very atmosphere seems charged with it. Only by constant effort can we resist its power. . . . I appeal to young and old: Make the Word of God your textbook. Here you will find the true standard of character. . . .

All over the field of revelation are scattered the glad springs of heavenly truth, and peace, and joy. They are within the reach of every seeker. The words of inspiration, pondered in the heart, will be as streams flowing from the river of the water of life. Our Saviour prayed that the minds of the disciples might be opened to understand the Scriptures. And whenever we study the Bible with a prayerful heart, the Holy Spirit is near to open to us the meaning of the words we read.[40]

THE BIBLE SPEAKS TO ME

Thus saith the Lord, Stand ye in the ways, and see, and ask for the old paths, where is the good way, and walk therein, and ye shall find rest for your souls. Jer. 6:16.

The Holy One has given rules for the guidance of every soul so that no one need miss his way. These directions mean everything to us; for they form the standard to which every son and daughter of Adam must conform. We can not turn aside from any of these divine rules, and be found guiltless. We are required to make the will of God paramount in our lives, and to have the faith that works by love and purifies the soul. I would warn you to keep from the dangerous ground on which your feet would naturally be inclined to stray. . . .

Take the Word of God, and kneeling before God, ask, What has God spoken to me from His Word? Wait before the Lord to learn the way in which you are to go. . . . You may learn of the heavenly Teacher His meekness and lowliness of heart. In His strength be steadfast, and stand in opposition to all that is displeasing to God and encourage all that is right, and pure, and true. Live a life that Jesus, your heavenly Father, and the angelic host can look upon with favor. . . .

The Lord will be your helper, and if you trust Him, will bring you up to a noble, elevated standard, and will place your feet upon the platform of eternal truth. Through the grace of Christ, you can make a right use of your entrusted capabilities, and become an agent for good in winning souls to Christ. Every talent you have should be used on the right side.

Those of the youth
Who put on the whole armor of God,
Who will devote time every day to self-examination,
Who will seek the Lord in earnest prayer, and
Who will diligently study the Scriptures,
Will have the help of the angels of God,
And will form characters that will fit them
For the society of the redeemed in the kingdom of glory.[41]

"IT IS WRITTEN"

All scripture is given by inspiration of God, and is profitable for doctrine, for reproof, for correction, for instruction in righteousness: that the man of God may be perfect, throughly furnished unto all good works. 2 Tim. 3:16, 17.

Let the seeker for truth who accepts the Bible as the inspired Word of God, lay aside every previous idea, and take that Word in its simplicity. He should renounce every sinful practice, and enter the Holy of Holies with heart softened and subdued, ready to listen to what God says.

Do not carry your creed to the Bible, and read the Scriptures in the light of that creed. If you find that your opinions are opposed to a plain "Thus saith the Lord," or to any command or prohibition He has given, give heed to the Word of God rather than to the sayings of men. Let every controversy or dispute be settled by "It is written." . . .

Let the heart be softened and subdued by the spirit of prayer before the Bible is read. Truth will triumph when the Spirit of truth cooperates with the humble Bible student. How precious the thought that the Author of truth still lives and reigns. Ask Him to impress your minds with the truth. Your searching of the Scriptures will then be profitable. Christ is the Great Teacher of His followers, and He will not leave you to walk in darkness.

The Bible is its own interpreter. With beautiful simplicity one portion connects itself with the truth of another portion, until the whole Bible is blended in one harmonious whole. Light flashes forth from one text to illuminate some portion of the Word that has seemed more obscure.[42]

Christ's lessons will bear close study. One truth comprehended in its simplicity will prove a key to a whole treasure house of truth. Christ is the great mystery of godliness. He is as the Master scattering the golden grains of truth, which require tact, skill, and deep, laborious search to pick up and link together in the chain of truth. The Word is the treasure house of truth. It puts in our possession all things essential for our preparation for entrance into the city of God.[43]

LEAVES FROM THE TREE OF LIFE

And Jesus said unto them, I am the bread of life: he that cometh to me shall never hunger; and he that believeth on me shall never thirst. John 6:35.

The world is perishing for want of truth, pure, unadulterated truth. Christ is the truth. His words are truth.[44]

When the believer, in the fellowship of the Spirit, can lay his hand upon truth itself, and appropriate it, he eats the bread that comes down from heaven. He enters into the life of Christ, and appreciates the great sacrifice made in behalf of the sinful race.

The knowledge that comes from God is the bread of Life. It is the leaves of the tree of life which are for the healing of the nations. The current of spiritual life thrills the soul as the words of Christ are believed and practiced. Thus it is that we are made one with Christ. The experience that was weak and feeble becomes strong. It is eternal life to us if we hold the beginning of our confidence firm unto the end.

All truth is to be received as the life of Jesus. Truth cleanses us from all impurity, and prepares the soul for Christ's presence. Christ is formed within, the hope of glory.[45]

The truth is to be partaken of every day. Thus we eat the words of Christ, which He declares are spirit and life. The acceptance of the truth will make every receiver a child of God, an heir of heaven.

Truth that is in the heart is not a cold, dead letter. . . . There is fullness of joy in the truth. There is a nobleness in the life of the human agent who lives and works under the vivifying influence of the truth. Truth is sacred and divine. It is stronger and more powerful than anything else in the formation of a character after the likeness of Christ. When it is cherished in the heart, the love of Christ is preferred to the love of any human being. This is Christianity. Thus truth—pure, unadulterated truth—occupies the citadel of the being. This is the life of God in the soul. "A new heart also will I give you, and a new spirit will I put within you." Eze. 36:26.[46]

THE BREAD THAT SATISFIES

*I am the living bread which came down from heaven: if any man
eat of this bread, he shall live for ever: and the bread that I will give
is my flesh, which I will give for the life of the world. . . . For my flesh
is meat indeed, and my blood is drink indeed. John 6:51-55.*

The words, "Give us this day our daily bread," refer not only to
temporal food but to the spiritual food which brings everlasting life
to the receiver. When we believe and receive Christ's word, we eat
His flesh and drink His blood. . . .

As by eating temporal food the physical system becomes strong,
so by eating the flesh and drinking the blood of the Son of God, the
spiritual nature is strengthened. God's Word is spirit and life to all
who appropriate it. He who partakes of Christ's flesh and blood is a
partaker of the divine nature. . . . A vital, life-giving current flows
from his Saviour to him.[47]

No one can eat this flesh and drink this blood for another.
Each must come to Christ with his own soul hunger, each must
have his own convictions, feel his own soul's need, and learn of
Christ for himself.[48]

Filled with the Bread of Life, we cannot hunger for earthly attractions, worldly excitements, and earthly grandeur. Our religious experience will be of the same order as the food upon which we feed.[49]

The food we eat at one meal does not satisfy us forever. We
must daily partake of food. So we must daily eat the Word of God
that the life of the soul may be renewed. In those who feed constantly upon the Word, Christ is formed, the hope of glory. A neglect to read and study the Bible brings spiritual starvation. . . .

Christ is our life. The soul in whom He abides will meet the requirements of His principles, in thorough devotion and consecration
to God. Christ's personal contact with the soul builds it up, supplying
its ever-recurring wants. He is made unto us wisdom and righteousness and sanctification and redemption. He is our sufficiency. . . .

He is the lifeblood of the soul. If He abides with us, we may say,
"I live; yet not I, but Christ liveth in me." Gal. 2:20.[50]

AS A WALL OF FIRE
AGAINST TEMPTATION

Thy word have I hid in mine heart, that I might not sin against thee. Ps. 119:11.

Satan is continually seeking to influence human minds by his subtle arts. His is a master mind, given of God, but prostituted with all its noble capabilities to oppose and to make of no effect the counsels of the Most High. . . .

We can overcome only by believing in every word that proceedeth from the mouth of God. We must know what is written in order that we may not be defeated by the sophistry and enchantments of Satan. . . . If we have been ensnared by his enchanting power, let us in the name of Jesus rebuke his power, and break with Satan without delay. . . .

Those who cry unto God for deliverance from the terrible spell that Satan would weave about them, will set a high estimate upon the Scriptures. Our only safety is in receiving the whole Bible, not taking merely detached portions, but believing the whole truth. Your feet are upon sliding sand if you depreciate one word that is written. The Bible is a divine communication, and is as verily a message to the soul as though a voice from heaven were heard speaking to us. With what awe and reverence and humiliation should we come to the searching of the Scriptures, that we may learn of eternal realities. . . . Let everyone study the Bible, knowing that the Word of God is as enduring as the eternal throne. If you come to the study of the Scriptures in humility, with earnest prayer for guidance, angels of God will open to you its living realities; and if you cherish the precepts of truth, they will be to you as a wall of fire against the temptations, delusions, and enchantments of Satan. . . .

The Word of God is able to save your souls, to make you wise unto salvation. The psalmist says, "Thy word have I hid in mine heart, that I might not sin against thee." Then let us hide the Word of God in our hearts, that we may "be able to withstand in the evil day, and having done all, to stand." Eph. 6:13.[51]

TRUTH CONTINUALLY UNFOLDING

I have yet many things to say unto you, but ye cannot bear them now. John 16:12.

The very limited and earthly apprehension which the disciples had of the teachings of Christ made it difficult for the Great Teacher to lead their minds into an understanding of heavenly things, and determined the measure of His divine communications. . . . His work was especially to reveal the moral excellency of character which the Lord requires.[52]

Jesus did not give full comments or connected discourses upon doctrines, but He oft spoke in short sentences, as one sowing the heavenly grains of doctrines like pearls which need to be gathered up by a discerning laborer. . . . True learners, sitting at Christ's feet, discover the precious gems of truth uttered by our Saviour, and will discern their significance and appreciate their value. And more and more, as they become humble and teachable, will their understanding be opened to discover wondrous things out of His law. . . . The truth will be continually unfolding, expanding, and developing, for it is divine, like its Author.[53]

Says Christ, "I have yet many things to say unto you, but ye cannot bear them now." John 16:12.

> " 'Ye cannot bear them now.' What tenderness
> Breathes in this language! Well does it express
> Thy principle of teaching. 'Here and there
> A little,' is the plan Thou dost pursue;
> Waiting until our feeble sight can bear
> The truths which love unfolds before our view.
> The gentleness of Christ! Lord, should not we
> In teaching others strive to act like Thee?
> Patient, not hasty, toward those who learn
> But slowly in Thy school; who seem to need
> Line upon line before they can discern
> The hallowed lessons we so plainly read."[54]

July 25

SANCTIFYING POWER OF TRUTH

Sanctify them through thy truth: thy word is truth. John 17:17.

What is sanctification? It is to give one's self wholly and without reserve—soul, body, and spirit—to God; to deal justly; to love mercy, and to walk humbly with God; to know and to do the will of God without regard to self or self-interest; to be heavenly-minded, pure, unselfish, holy, and without spot or stain.[55]

It is through the truth, by the power of the Holy Spirit, that we are to be sanctified—transformed into the likeness of Christ. And in order for this change to be wrought in us, there must be an unconditional, wholehearted acceptance of the truth, an unreserved surrender of the soul to its transforming power.

Our characters are by nature warped and perverted. Through the lack of proper development they are wanting in symmetry. With some excellent qualities are united objectionable traits, and through long indulgence wrong tendencies become second nature, and many persons cling tenaciously to their peculiarities. Even after they profess to accept the truth, to yield themselves to Christ, the same old habits are indulged, the same self-esteem is manifested, the same false notions entertained. Although such ones claim to be converted, it is evident that they have not yielded themselves to the transforming power of the truth. . . .

If the one who is thus misrepresenting Christ could know what harm has been wrought by the faults of character which he has excused and cherished, he would be filled with horror. . . .

Let none feel that their way needs no changing. . . . None can walk safely unless they are distrustful of self, and are constantly looking to the Word of God, studying it with willing heart to see their own errors, and to learn the will of Christ, and praying that it may be done in and by and through them. They show that their confidence is not in themselves, but in Christ. They hold the truth as a sacred treasure, able to sanctify and refine, and they are constantly seeking to bring their words and ways into harmony with its principles.[56]

"HOLIER, YEA HOLIER STILL"

For this is the will of God, even your sanctification. 1 Thess. 4:3.

Our sanctification is God's object in all His dealing with us. He has chosen us from eternity that we might be holy. Christ gave Himself for our redemption, that through faith in His power to save from sin, we might be made complete in Him. . . .

As Christians we have pledged ourselves to fulfil the responsibilities resting on us, and to show to the world that we have a close connection with God. Thus, through the good words and works of His disciples, Christ is to be represented and honored.

God expects of us perfect obedience to His law. This law is the echo of His voice, saying to us, Holier, yea holier still. Desire after the fullness of the grace of Christ, yea, long—hunger and thirst—after righteousness. The promise is, "Ye *shall* be filled." Let your heart be filled with a longing for this righteousness. . . .

God has plainly stated that He expects us to be perfect, and because He expects this, He has made provision for us to be partakers of the divine nature. Only thus can we gain success in striving for eternal life. The power is given by Christ. "As many as received him, to them gave he power to become the sons of God, even to them that believe on his name." John 1:12.

God's people are to reflect to the world the bright rays of His glory. But in order for them to do this, they must stand where these rays can fall on them. They must cooperate with God. The heart must be cleansed of all that leads to wrong. The Word of God must be read and studied with an earnest desire to gain from it spiritual power. The bread of heaven must be eaten and assimilated, becoming part of the life. Thus we gain eternal life. Thus is answered the prayer of Christ, "Sanctify them through thy truth: thy word is truth." John 17:17.

"This is the will of God, even your sanctification." Is it *your* will that your desires and inclinations shall be brought into harmony with the divine mind?[57]

THE SECRET OF HOLINESS

And that ye put on the new man, which after God is created in righteousness and true holiness. Eph. 4:24.

No man receives holiness as a birthright, or as a gift from any other human being. Holiness is the gift of God through Christ. Those who receive the Saviour become sons of God. They are His spiritual children, born again, renewed in righteousness and true holiness. Their minds are changed. With clearer vision they behold eternal realities. They are adopted into God's family, and they become conformed to His likeness, changed by His Spirit from glory to glory. From cherishing supreme love for self, they come to cherish supreme love for God and for Christ. . . .

Accepting Christ as a personal Saviour, and following His example of self-denial—this is the secret of holiness.[58]

Holiness is not rapture; it is the result of surrendering all to God; it is living by every word that proceedeth out of the mouth of God; it is doing the will of our heavenly Father; it is trusting in God in trial, believing in His promise in the darkness as well as in the light. Religion is to walk by faith, as well as by sight, trusting in God with all confidence, and resting in His love.[59]

Sanctification is a state of holiness, without and within, being holy and without reserve the Lord's, not in form, but in truth. Every impurity of thought, every lustful passion, separates the soul from God; for Christ can never put His robe of righteousness upon a sinner, to hide his deformity. . . . There must be a progressive work of triumph over evil, of sympathy with good, a reflection of the character of Jesus. We must walk in the light, which will increase and grow brighter unto the perfect day. This is real, substantial growth, which will finally attain to the full stature of men and women in Jesus Christ. . . .

Conformity to the likeness of Christ's character, overcoming all sin and temptation, walking in the fear of God, setting the Lord continually before us, will bring peace and joy on earth, and ensure us pure happiness in heaven.[60]

A DAILY EXPERIENCE IN CONVERSION

For which cause we faint not; but though our outward man perish, yet the inward man is renewed day by day. 2 Cor. 4:16.

Genuine conversion is needed, not once in years, but daily. This conversion brings man into a new relation with God. Old things, his natural passions and hereditary and cultivated tendencies to wrong, pass away, and he is renewed and sanctified. But this work must be continual; for as long as Satan exists, he will make an effort to carry on his work. He who strives to serve God will encounter a strong undercurrent of wrong. His heart needs to be barricaded by constant watchfulness and prayer, or else the embankment will give way; and like a millstream, the undercurrent of wrong will sweep away the safeguard. No renewed heart can be kept in a condition of sweetness without the daily application of the salt of the Word. Divine grace must be received daily, or no man will stay converted. . . .

Test and trial will come to every soul that loves God. The Lord does not work a miracle to prevent this ordeal of trial, to shield His people from the temptations of the enemy. . . . Characters are to be developed that will decide the fitness of the human family for the heavenly home—characters that will stand through the pressure of unfavorable circumstances in private and public life, and that will, under the severest temptations, through the grace of God grow brave and true, be firm as a rock to principle, and come forth from the fiery ordeal, of more value than the golden wedge of Ophir. God will endorse, with His own superscription, as His elect, those who possess such characters. . . .

The Lord accepts no halfhearted service. He demands the whole man. Religion is to be brought into every phase of life, carried into labor of every kind. The whole being is to be under God's control. We must not think that we can take supervision of our own thoughts. They must be brought into captivity to Christ. Self cannot manage self; it is not sufficient for the work. . . . God alone can make and keep us loyal.[61]

IN THE SUNLIGHT OF CHRIST

That we henceforth be no more children, tossed to and fro, and carried about with every wind of doctrine, by the sleight of men, and cunning craftiness, whereby they lie in wait to deceive; but speaking the truth in love, may grow up into him in all things, which is the head, even Christ. Eph. 4:14, 15.

"Watch unto prayer," and you will steadily grow in grace and in a knowledge of Christ. Your experience will not be one-sided, deformed, but healthful, symmetrical. All unawares to yourself, you will have expanded like the widespreading cedar, and many will profit by your counsel; your association with them will have the fragrance of heaven.

There are many professors of religion who for years have not grown one inch. The rubbish of the world, selfishness, and indolence, have separated them in sympathy and in their works from Christ. . . .

If you are living in the sunlight of Christ, you will diffuse light to those poor souls who are dwarfs in the religious life. With the righteousness of Christ covering you as with a garment, what may you not do to bless others! . . .

Your fellowship is with the Father and with the Son, and you grow into the knowledge of the divine perfection. You grow in reverence, you gain confidence in communion with God. Looking steadfastly to Jesus, you grow in faith, and learning to distrust self, you appreciate the words of Christ, "Without me ye can do nothing." John 15:5. . . .

You may have a fervent spirit, your heart all aglow with the love of Jesus. Abide in Christ as the branch abides in the vine; drawing sustenance from the vine, you will be a flourishing branch, and will bear much fruit to the glory of God. Oh, you much need to gaze fixedly upon Jesus! Keep beholding His charms. As you behold they will keep brightening and enlarging until you are filled with all the fullness of God and bear much fruit to His glory. The branch is too firmly connected with the parent stock to be swayed by every breeze. Strength and vigorous growth tell to the world that your root is in Jesus, that your foundation is sure.[62]

HOW TO GROW IN GRACE

But grow in grace, and in the knowledge of our Lord and Saviour Jesus Christ. To him be glory both now and for ever. Amen. 2 Peter 3:18.

How is it possible that we may grow in grace? It is possible to us only as we empty our hearts of self, and present them to Heaven, to be molded after the Divine Pattern. We may have a connection with the living channel of light; we may be refreshed with the heavenly dew, and have the showers of heaven descend upon us. As we appropriate the blessing of God, we shall be able to receive greater measures of His grace.[63]

As little children we are to sit at the feet of Christ, learning of Him. . . . We should not allow a day to pass without gaining an increase of knowledge in temporal and spiritual things. We are to plant no stakes that we are not willing to take up and plant further on, nearer the heights we hope to ascend. The highest education is to be found in training the mind to advance day by day. The close of each day should find us a day's march nearer the overcomer's reward. Day by day our understanding is to ripen. Day by day we are to work out conclusions that will bring a rich reward in this life and in the life to come. Looking daily to Jesus, instead of to what we ourselves have done, we shall make decided advancement in temporal as well as spiritual knowledge.

The end of all things is at hand. What we have done must not be allowed to place the period to our work. The Captain of our salvation says, "Advance. The night cometh, in which no man can work." Constantly we are to increase in usefulness. Our lives are always to be under the power of Christ. Our lamps are to be kept burning brightly. . . . He who places himself where God can enlighten him, advances, as it were, from the partial obscurity of dawn to the full radiance of noonday.[64]

We must put to the stretch every spiritual nerve and muscle. . . . God . . . does not desire you to remain novices. He wants you to reach the very highest round of the ladder, and then step from it into the kingdom of our Lord and Saviour Jesus Christ.[65]

July 31

"ALMOST TO THE EXCELLENCE OF THE ANGELS"

The righteous also shall hold on his way, and he that hath clean hands shall be stronger and stronger. Job. 17:9.

To every man God has entrusted talents for wise improvement. If rightly used, these talents will reflect glory to the Giver. But the most precious gifts of God may be perverted, and thus become a curse rather than a blessing. . . .

The Lord has given man capacity for continual improvement, and has granted him all possible aid in the work. Through the provisions of divine grace, we may attain almost to the excellence of the angels. What shall be said of those who, having had many years of experience in the truth, and many precious advantages for growth in grace, are yet inclined toward the world, and find pleasure in its amusements and display? Instead of going on from strength to strength, they are, little by little, departing from God, and losing their spiritual life. . . .

Talent can never take the place of piety, nor can the applause of men recommend us to the favor of God. What the majority of professed Christians need, is genuine conversion. If the heart is right, the actions will be right. An earthly, debasing influence marks the character and the life of those whose hearts do not glow with the fire of true goodness. Too many profess to be followers of Christ, and feel at liberty to follow their own judgment, and indulge the desires of their own hearts. He who would advance in the Christian life must put his own hands and heart to the work. Friends may exhort and counsel, to urge him onward and upward; Heaven may pour its choicest blessings upon him; he may have all possible assistance on the right hand and on the left, and yet all will be in vain, unless he shall put forth earnest effort to help himself. He himself must engage in the warfare against sin and Satan, or he will fail of everlasting life.[66]

Pure religion leads its possessor ever upward, inspiring him with noble purposes, teaching him propriety of deportment, and imparting a becoming dignity to every action.[67]

NECESSITY OF SELF-CULTIVATION

Remember now thy Creator in the days of thy youth, while the evil days come not, nor the years draw nigh, when thou shalt say, I have no pleasure in them. Eccl. 12:1.

How can I best present before the youth the necessity of self-cultivation, is my constant inquiry. I would urge upon our youth to regard every moment of time as golden. Do not waste it in indolence; do not spend it in folly; but grasp the higher treasures. Cultivate the thoughts and expand the soul by girding about the mind, not allowing it to be filled with unimportant matters. Secure every advantage within your reach for strengthening the intellect. Do not be satisfied with a low standard. Do not rest content until by faithful endeavor, watchfulness, and earnest prayer, you have secured the wisdom that is from above. Thus you may rise in character, and gain an influence over other minds, enabling you to lead them in the path of uprightness and holiness. This is your privilege.

Cherish every ray of light that you can obtain by searching the Word of God. Take up your God-given work today, and see how much good you can accomplish in the strength of Christ. Make God your Counselor. Discipline and control the mental faculties. Self-control is a power that all may possess. It is gained by placing the will wholly on the side of God, taking the will of God for your will.

Christ . . . can and will, if we submit to Him, fill the chambers of the mind and the recesses of the soul with His Spirit. Then our will will be in perfect harmony with the Divine will. Our spirit and will may be so identified with His Spirit and will that in thought and aim we shall be one with Him. Then Satan will no longer control us. Christ is our Leader, and His followers love to keep step and step with Him. He speaks, and they obey His voice as one mind and one soul.[1]

Dear youth, the very best thing you can do is to enlist freely and decidedly in the army of the Lord. Surrender yourself into the hands of God, that your will and ways may be guided by the One who is unerring in wisdom and infinite in goodness. . . . Let your name be enrolled in the heavenly records as one of the chosen and elect of God.[2]

CHOOSING MY LIFEWORK

Every man's work shall be made manifest: for the day shall declare it, because it shall be revealed by fire; and the fire shall try every man's work of what sort it is. 1 Cor. 3:13.

We should carefully weigh the matters relative to the work we take up. Will this work be a blessing to souls? God has not given us work merely to keep us busy, but for His name's glory. Many are busily engaged gathering wood, hay, stubble. But this will all be consumed. . . .

By God's appointment each man has his post of duty. The careful, prayerful inquiry is to be made, What duty is assigned us individually, as men and women under accountability to God? And whether our labor be wholly limited to spiritual things, or whether it is temporal and spiritual combined, we are to faithfully discharge our work. Things secular and things sacred must be combined, but spiritual things are not to be hidden by secular matters. Christ requires the service of the whole being, the physical, mental, and moral powers combined. These are to be enlisted in God's service. Man is to remember that God has the ownership of all, and that his pursuits are invested with a sacredness that they did not possess before he enlisted in the army of the Lord. Every action is to be a consecrated action, for it occupies God's entrusted talent of time. Holiness unto the Lord is inscribed on all the actions of such a one, because his whole being is brought under subjection to God.

No business is to be undertaken, even in ordinary life, if it is corrupting in its influence upon the senses. We are in the Lord's training school, and He has His own appointed means whereby we may be brought into His service. . . . Many are troubled because they are not working directly for the advancement of God's kingdom. But the humblest work must not be ignored. If it is honest work, it is a blessing, and may lead to the higher parts of the work.[3]

Whether we have one year before us, or five, or ten, we are to be faithful to our trust today. We are to perform each day's duties as faithfully as though that day were to be our last.[4]

MEDITATION WITH DILIGENT WORK

Not slothful in business; fervent in spirit; serving the Lord.
Rom. 12:11.

There are many who are absorbed in worldly business, and they do not give the Lord that devotion which is essential for their spiritual improvement. They tax brain, bone, and muscle to the uttermost, and gather to themselves burdens which lead them to forget God. Their spiritual powers are not exercised as well as their physical powers, and every day they are on the losing side, growing poorer and poorer in heavenly riches.

There is another class who meet with loss because they are indolent and spend their powers in pleasing themselves, in using their tongues, and letting their muscles rust with inaction. They waste their opportunities by inaction, and do not glorify God. . . .

There is something for everyone to do in this world of ours. The Lord is coming, and our waiting is to be not a time of idle expectation, but of vigilant work. We are not to spend our time wholly in prayerful meditation, neither are we to drive and hurry and work as if this were required in order that we should gain heaven, while neglecting to devote time to the cultivation of personal piety. There must be a combination of meditation and diligent work. As God has expressed it in His Word, we are to be "not slothful in business; fervent in spirit; serving the Lord." Worldly activities are not to crowd out the service of the Lord. The soul needs the riches of the grace of God, and the body needs physical exercise, in order to accomplish the work that must be done for the promulgation of the gospel of Christ. . . .

Parents should teach their children that the Lord means them to be diligent workers, not idlers in His vineyard. . . . Each one is to act his part in the great work for humanity. . . . Thus the lamp of the soul will not be neglected, if time is taken to pray and to search the Scriptures. The allotted task may be done, and the lamp of the soul kept trimmed and burning.[5]

THE PERIL OF "NOTHING TO DO"

The way of the slothful man is an hedge of thorns: but the way of the righteous is made plain. Prov. 15:19.

Industry is a blessing to youth. A life of idleness is to be shunned by a young man as a vice. However humble the occupation may be, if only honorable, if the humble duties are done faithfully, he will not lose his reward. Industry is essential to health. If habits of industry were encouraged, a door would be closed against a thousand temptations. Those who lounge away their days, having no aim or object in life, are troubled with dejection and tempted to seek amusement in forbidden indulgences which enervate the system and tax the physical powers tenfold more than the most taxing labor. Indolence destroys more than hard labor. Many die because they have not the ability or inclination to set themselves to work. "Nothing to do" has killed its thousands.

If youth will preserve habits of virtue and strict purity, and observe the laws God has established in the being, they may preserve their lives although required to perform severe labor during their lifetime. Long life is the heritage of diligence.

Some young men think if they could spend a life in doing nothing they would be supremely happy. They cultivate a hatred for useful labor. They envy the sons of pleasure who devote their lives to amusement and gaiety. . . . Unhappiness and heartaches are the result of such thoughts and conduct. Nothing to do has sunk many a young man in perdition. Well-regulated labor is essential for the success of every youth. God could not have inflicted a greater curse upon men and women than to doom them to live a life of inaction. Idleness will destroy soul and body. The heart, the moral character, and physical energies are enfeebled. The intellect suffers, and the heart is open to temptation as an open avenue to sink into every vice. The indolent man tempts the devil to tempt him. . . .

Religion will prove to you an anchor. Communion with God will impart to every holy impulse a vigor that will make the duties of life a pleasure.[6]

THE BLESSING OF WORK

Go to the ant, thou sluggard; consider her ways, and be wise. Prov. 6:6.

God placed our first parents in Paradise, surrounding them with all that was useful and lovely. In their Eden home nothing was wanting that could minister to their comfort and happiness. And to Adam was given the work of caring for the Garden. The Creator knew that Adam could not be happy without employment. The beauty of the Garden delighted him, but this was not enough. He must have labor to call into exercise the wonderful organs of the body. Had happiness consisted in doing nothing, man, in his state of holy innocence, would have been left unemployed. But He who created man knew what would be for his happiness; and no sooner had He created him, than He gave him his appointed work. The promise of future glory, and the decree that man must toil for his daily bread, came from the same throne. . . .

When the body is inactive, the blood flows sluggishly, and the muscles decrease in size and strength. . . . Physical exercise, and a free use of air and sunlight—blessings which heaven has abundantly bestowed on all—would give life and strength to many an emaciated invalid. . . . Work is a blessing, not a curse. Diligent labor keeps many, young and old, from the snares of him who "finds some mischief still for idle hands to do." Let no one be ashamed of work, for honest toil is ennobling. While the hands are engaged in the most common tasks, the mind may be filled with high and holy thoughts.

Drowsiness and indolence destroy godliness, and grieve the Spirit of God. A stagnant pool is offensive; but a pure, flowing stream spreads health and gladness over the land. No man or woman who is converted can be anything but a worker. There certainly is and ever will be employment in heaven. The redeemed will not live in a state of dreamy idleness. There remaineth a rest for the people of God—a rest which they will find in serving Him to whom they owe all they have and are.[7]

SUSTAINED VERSUS SPASMODIC EFFORT

The thoughts of the diligent tend only to plenteousness; but of every one that is hasty only to want. Prov. 21:5.

How many youth who might have become men of usefulness and power have failed because in early life they contracted habits of indecision which followed them through life to cripple all their efforts. Now and then they are filled with sudden zeal to do some great thing, but they leave their work half finished and it comes to nothing. Patient continuance in welldoing is indispensable to success. . . . Temperate, persevering, steady labor will achieve far more than can be accomplished by spasmodic efforts. . . .

Labor was appointed to man by his Creator. God provided employment for our first parents in holy Eden. And since the Fall, man has been a toiler, eating his bread by the sweat of his brow. Every bone of his body, every feature of his countenance, every muscle of his limbs, evinces the fact that he was made for activity—not for idleness.

Habits of industry should be formed in youth. . . . The faithful discharge of life's duties, whatever your position, calls for a wise improvement of all the talents and abilities that God has given you. Guard against being always hurried, yet accomplishing nothing worthy of the effort. These fruitless efforts are often caused by a failure to do the work at the proper time. Whatever is neglected at the time when it should be performed, whether in secular or in religious things, is rarely done well. Many appear to labor diligently every hour in the day, and yet produce no results to correspond with their efforts. . . .

Be careful not to fritter away your time upon trifles, and then fail to carry out your undertakings that are of real account. . . . A steadfast adherence to a purpose is necessary in order to secure the end. A distinguished man was once asked how it was possible for him to accomplish such a vast amount of business. His answer was, "I do one thing at a time." . . . Jesus was an earnest worker, and those who follow His example will experience self-denial, toil, and sacrifice.[8]

GOD CONCERNED
WITH EVERY TRANSACTION

A false balance is abomination to the Lord: but a just weight is his delight. Prov. 11:1.

A false balance is a symbol of all unfair dealing, all devices to conceal selfishness and injustice under an appearance of fairness and equity. God will not in the slightest degree favor such practices. He hates every false way. He abhors all selfishness and covetousness. Unmerciful dealing He will not tolerate, but will repay in kind. God can give prosperity to the working men whose means are acquired honestly. But His curse rests upon all that is gained by selfish practices.

When one indulges in selfishness or sharp dealing, he shows that he does not fear the Lord or reverence His name. Those who are connected with God will not only shun all injustice, but will manifest His mercy and goodness toward all with whom they have to do. The Lord will sanction no respect of person; but He will not approve the course of those who make no difference in favor of the poor, the widow, and the orphan.[9]

Your religious faith must elevate you above every low trick. Industry, faithfulness, a firm adherence to right, and trust in God will ensure success. Move slowly, honestly, upon strictly Bible principles, or stop business. No bargain is ever made, no debt is ever paid, in which God is not concerned. He is the all-wise, eternal guardian of justice. You can never exclude God from any matter in which the rights of His people are involved. The hand of God is spread as a shield over all His creatures. No man can wound your rights without smiting that hand; you can wound no man's rights without smiting it. That hand holds the sword of justice. Beware how you deal with men. . . .

Your light shining in your business life, exhibiting the power of practical godliness, is worth vastly more to all with whom you come in contact than sermons or creeds. The world will watch and criticize and take knowledge of you in the midst of your temporal affairs, with keenness and severity. What you say in the church is not of half as much consequence as what you do in your daily business.[10]

CULTIVATE HONESTY

Recompense to no man evil for evil. Provide things honest in the sight of all men. Rom. 12:17.

The religion of Christ enjoins upon men to carry the pure principles of truth into their daily life, in buying and selling, in the transaction of all business, with as true a sense of religious obligation as that with which they offer to God their supplications. Business must not divert the soul from God. You should by your example demonstrate to the world that the truth of God sanctifies the receiver and produces industry, frugality, and perseverance, while it extirpates avarice, overreaching, and every species of dishonesty. . . .

Nothing is worth so much to a young man just starting out in life as a reputation for unbending integrity.[11]

Every business transaction is to be such as can be endorsed by Heaven, else it will bear the unsavory odor of Satan's influence. Every action is to represent the science of Heaven's principles.[12]

Truthfulness and frankness should be ever cherished by all who claim to be followers of Christ. God and the right should be the motto. Deal honestly and righteously in this present evil world. Some will be honest when they see that honesty will not endanger their worldly interests; but all who act from this principle will have their names blotted out of the book of life.

Strict honesty must be cultivated. We can go through the world but once; we cannot come back to rectify any mistakes; therefore every move made should be with godly fear and careful consideration. Honesty and policy will not harmonize; either policy will be subdued, and truth and honesty hold the lines of control, or policy will take the lines, and honesty cease to direct. Both cannot act together; they can never be in agreement. When God makes up His jewels, the true, the frank, the honest, will be His chosen ones, His treasures. Angels are preparing crowns for such, and light from the throne of God will be reflected in its splendor from these star-gemmed diadems.[13]

GREAT IN GOD'S SIGHT

He that is faithful in that which is least is faithful also in much:
and he that is unjust in the least is unjust also in much. Luke 16:10.

Life is not made up of great things alone; it is the little things that make the sum of life's happiness or miseries. It is the little things in life that reveal a person's real character. Oh, if all youth and those of mature age could see as I have seen the mirror of persons' lives presented before them, they would look more gravely upon even the little duties of life. Every mistake, every error, unimportant though it may be regarded, leaves a scar in this life and a blot on the heavenly records.

Life is full of duties that are not agreeable, but all these unpleasant duties will be made agreeable by a cheerful performance of them because it is right. Taking an interest in the duties which someone must do, and striving to do them with the heart, will make the most disagreeable duties pleasant.[14]

There are many who undervalue the small events of life, the little deeds that are to be performed day by day; but these are not to be estimated as small, as every action tells either for the blessing or the injuring of someone. Every action tells its own story, it bears its own history to the throne of God. It is known whether it is on the side of right or on the side of wrong. It is only by acting in accordance with the principles of God's Word in the small transactions of life, that we place ourselves on the right side. We are tried and tested by these small occurrences, and our character will be estimated according as our work shall be.[15]

It is the conscientious attention to what the world calls little things that makes the great beauty and success of life.

> Little deeds of charity,
> Little words of kindness,
> Little acts of self-denial,
> A wise improvement of opportunities,
> A diligent cultivation of little talents,
> Make great men in God's sight.[16]

BENEFITS OF REGULARITY AND ORDER

I thank my God always on your behalf, for the grace of God which is given you by Jesus Christ; that in every thing ye are enriched by him, in all utterance, and in all knowledge. 1 Cor. 1:4, 5.

There is need to cultivate every grace that Jesus has brought within our reach; for that grace alone can remedy our defects; Christ alone can transform the character. And God would have us manifest this grace, so richly provided, in the little as well as the large things of life. . . . Our God is a God of order and He desires that His children shall *will* to bring themselves into order, and under His discipline. . . . If the youth would form habits of regularity and order, they would improve in health, in spirits, in memory, and in disposition.

It is the duty of all to observe strict rules in their habits of life. This is for your own good, dear youth, both physically and morally. When you rise in the morning, take into consideration, as far as possible, the work you must accomplish during the day. If necessary, have a small book in which to jot down the things that need to be done, and set yourself a time in which to do your work. . . . Slow, dilatory habits make much work out of very little. But if you will, you may overcome these fussy, lingering habits. The exercise of the will power will make the hands move deftly. . . .

These matters have been looked upon as little things, and almost unworthy of notice. But many are deceived as to the importance of these little things. They bear strongly upon the great whole. God does not regard anything as unimportant that pertains to the well-being of the human family. He gave His only begotten Son for the body as well as for the soul, and all is to be consecrated to Him. . . . Great truth can be brought into little things; practical religion must be carried into the lowly duties of daily life. And in the performance of these duties, you are forming characters that will stand the test of the judgment. Then, in whatever position you may be placed, whatever your duties may be, do them nobly and faithfully, realizing that all heaven is beholding your work.[17]

BIG LITTLE THINGS

Take us the foxes, the little foxes, that spoil the vines: for our vines have tender grapes. S. of Sol. 2:15.

God requires us to be right in important matters, while He tells us that faithfulness in little things will fit us for higher positions of trust. . . .

The good qualities which many possess are hidden, and instead of attracting souls to Christ they repulse them. If these persons could see the influence of their uncourteous ways and unkind expressions upon unbelievers, and how offensive is such conduct in the sight of God, they would reform their habits, for a lack of courtesy is one of the greatest stumbling blocks to sinners. Selfish, complaining, sour Christians bar the way, so that sinners do not care to approach Christ.

Could we look beneath the surface of things, we should see that half life's misery is created by frowns and unkind speeches, which might be prevented as well as not. Many make a hell upon earth for themselves and for those whom they might comfort and bless. These are not worthy of the Christian name. . . .

Some persons speak in a harsh, uncourteous manner, that wounds the feeling of others, and then they justify themselves by saying, "It is my way; I always tell just what I think"; and they exalt this wicked trait of character as a virtue. Their uncourteous deportment should be firmly rebuked.[18]

That unkind word should be left unspoken, that selfish disregard for the happiness of others should give place to sympathy and thoughtfulness. True courtesy, blended with truth and justice, will make the life not only useful, but fragrant. . . .

Integrity, justice, and Christian kindness, blended, make a beautiful combination. Courtesy is one of the graces of the Spirit. It is an attribute of heaven. The angels never fly into a passion, never are envious, selfish, and jealous. No harsh or unkind words escape their lips. And if we are to be the companions of angels, we too must be refined and courteous.[19]

ORDER AND CLEANLINESS

Having therefore these promises, dearly beloved, let us cleanse ourselves from all filthiness of the flesh and spirit, perfecting holiness in the fear of God. 2 Cor. 7:1.

It is of the highest importance that Sabbathkeepers live out their faith in every particular. They should be prompt and neat, and keep their business matters all straight. . . .

None should be so fearful of being like the world that it will lead them to be careless in their houses, leaving things in disorder and uncleanness. It is not pride to be neat in dress, cleanly in person, orderly and tasteful in their household arrangements. . . . These outside appearances tell the business character of those living in the house, and not only this but the religious character of its inmates. It is impossible for a slack, disorderly person to make a good Christian. Their lives, in temporal and religious things, are just as disorderly as their dress, houses, persons, and premises.

There is order in heaven. There are rules and regulations which govern the whole heavenly host. All move in order. All there is cleanly, all in perfect harmony. And everyone who will be counted worthy to enter heaven will be thoroughly disciplined and will be without spot or wrinkle or any such thing. The uncultivated have spots and wrinkles upon them now. They had better lose no time in commencing the work of cleansing themselves from all filthiness of the flesh and spirit, perfecting holiness in the fear of the Lord.

God loves purity, cleanliness, order, and holiness. God requires all His people who lack these qualifications to seek them and never rest until they obtain them. They must commence the work of reform and elevate their lives, so that in conversation and deportment their acts, their lives, will be a continual recommendation of their faith and will have such a winning, compelling power upon unbelievers that they will be compelled to acknowledge that they are the children of God.[20]

The truth as it is in Jesus will not degrade but elevate the receiver, purify his life, refine his taste, sanctify his judgment.[21]

August 13

LOVE'S FRAGRANT OUTREACH

And the Lord make you to increase and abound in love one toward another, and toward all men, even as we do toward you. 1 Thess. 3:12.

God would have His children realize that in order to glorify Him their affection must be given to those who most need it. . . . No self-ishness, in look, word, or deed, is to be manifested when dealing with those of like precious faith, . . . whether they be high or low, rich or poor. The love that gives kind words to only a few, while others are treated with coldness and indifference, is not love, but selfishness. It will not in any way work for the good of souls or the glory of God. Our love . . . is not to be sealed up for special ones, to the neglect of others. Break the bottle, and the fragrance will fill the house.

Those who gather the sunshine of Christ's righteousness, and do not let it shine forth into the lives of others, will soon lose the sweet, bright rays of heavenly grace, selfishly reserved to be lavished only upon a few. Those who possess much affection are responsible to God to bestow this affection . . . on all who need help. . . .

To love as Christ loved means to manifest unselfishness at all times and in all places, by kind words and pleasant looks. These cost those who give them nothing, but they leave behind a fragrance that surrounds the soul. Their effect can never be estimated. Not only are they a blessing to the receiver, but to the giver; for they react upon him. Genuine love is a precious attribute of heavenly origin, which increases in fragrance in proportion as it is dispensed to others. . . .

The souls of those who love Jesus will be surrounded with a pure, fragrant atmosphere. There are those who hide their soul hunger. These will be greatly helped by a tender word or a kind re-membrance. The heavenly gifts, freely and richly bestowed by God, are in turn to be freely bestowed by us upon all who come within the sphere of our influence. Thus we reveal a love that is heaven-born, and which will increase as it is freely used in blessing others. Thus we glorify God.[22]

WHY LOOK FOR FLAWS?

Let nothing be done through strife or vainglory; but in lowliness of mind let each esteem other better than themselves. Phil. 2:3.

Oh, how hard many make the Christian life! They climb the steep, briary path, staggering under imposed burdens, as though they must tinker up the characters of others. . . . They do not experience the sweet peace of Christ. They do not grasp the help Jesus gives them, but they are continually grieving over supposed wrongs of others, and overlook the cheering, blessed tokens for good all along their pathway.

Just as soon as one has a vivid and all-absorbing consciousness of his own personal accountability to God and of his duty to his fellow men, and senses that his influence is far reaching, stretching into eternity, he will not be satisfied with a low standard, he will not be faultfinding and critical of others. He will make his own life what he would wish the lives of others to be. He will live only in Christ, utterly and wholly dependent on Him for every beauty and loveliness of character.[23]

We should be weeding out of our thoughts all complaining and faultfinding. Let us not continue to look upon any defects that we may see. . . . If we would get the right hold on God, we must keep beholding the great precious things—the purity, the glory, the power, the kindness, the affection, the love, that God bestows upon us. And thus beholding, our minds will become so fixed upon these things of eternal interest that we shall have no desire to find the flaws in others.[24]

Think of the Lord Jesus, and His merits and His love, but do not seek to find the defects and dwell upon the mistakes that others have made. Call to your mind the things worthy of your recognition and your praise; and if you are sharp to discern errors in others, be more sharp to recognize the good and praise the good. You may, if you criticize yourselves, find things just as objectionable as that which you see in others. Then let us work constantly to strengthen one another in the most holy faith.[25]

CRITICISM NOT OUR WORK

Judge not, that ye be not judged. For with what judgment ye judge, ye shall be judged: and with what measure ye mete, it shall be measured to you again. Matt. 7:1, 2.

Our bodies are built up from what we eat and drink; and the character of our spiritual experience depends on what our minds feed upon and assimilate. By continually dwelling upon the mistakes and defects of others, many become religious dyspeptics. . . . Those who are so busy in dissecting the words and acts of others, to discover all that is objectionable, fail to discern the good and pleasant things. They do not eat of the proper food to promote spiritual vitality and healthy growth.[26]

The Lord is not pleased with His people when they neglect to criticize their own soul, criticizing others instead. This is Satan's work. When you do this work, remember that the enemy is using you as a means of tempting others, in order that those who should be united in harmony and joy, building up one another in the most holy faith, shall be warring and complaining because some one else is sinning. Christ has not made you a sin bearer. You cannot even bear your own sin. Therefore be very careful not to take up any reproach against your neighbor. God wants His people to be free. . . . Shall we not remember that by the words we speak we may either wound or heal? Shall we not remember that as we judge, so we shall be judged, we who perhaps have had many more opportunities than those whom we judge?

Our hearts must be melted into tenderness and love for one another. We may criticize ourselves just as severely as we please. The one who criticizes another gives evidence that he is the very one who needs to criticize himself. Pray God to show you what you must remove from yourselves in order that you may see the kingdom of God. . . .

There is a crown for the overcomer. Do you want it? Do you want to run the race with patience? Then do not seek to find something to condemn in your neighbor, but look right to Jesus Christ. Behold His purity, and you will be charmed and will reflect His likeness.[27]

OVERCOMING ENVY AND JEALOUSY

Let us not be desirous of vain glory, provoking one another, envying one another. Gal. 5:26.

Envy and jealousy are diseases which disorder all the faculties of the being. They originated with Satan in paradise. . . . Those who listen to his [Satan's] voice will demerit others, and will misrepresent and falsify in order to build up themselves. But nothing that defiles can enter heaven, and unless those who cherish this spirit are changed, they can never enter there, for they would criticize the angels. They would envy another's crown. They would not know what to talk of unless they could bring up the imperfections and errors of others.

O that such would become changed by beholding Christ! O that they would become meek and lowly by learning of Him! Then they would go forth, not as missionaries for Satan, to cause disunion and alienation, to bruise and mangle character, but as missionaries for Christ, to be peacemakers and to restore. Let the Holy Spirit come in and expel this unholy passion, which cannot survive in heaven. Let it die; let it be crucified. Open the heart to the attributes of Christ, who was holy, harmless, undefiled. . . .

The Word of God exhorts, "Love as brethren, be pitiful, be courteous." 2 Peter 3:8. True moral worth does not seek to make a place for itself by thinking and speaking evil, by depreciating others. All envy, all jealousy, all evilspeaking, with all unbelief, must be put away from God's children.[28]

The Bible is full of instruction enjoining us to show love, patience, and respect in our speech and in our treatment of one another. The love of Jesus in the soul never leads to malice and envy. The tender plant of Christlike love must be carefully cherished. It will not grow unless it is cultivated.

Heaven takes notice of the one who carries about with him an atmosphere of peace and love. Such a one will receive his reward. He will stand in the great day of the Lord.[29]

HOW TO DEAL WITH ANGER

He that is slow to anger is better than the mighty; and he that ruleth his spirit than he that taketh a city. Prov. 16:32.

How Satan exults when he is enabled to set the soul into a white heat of anger! A glance, a gesture, an intonation, may be seized upon and used, as the arrow of Satan, to wound and poison the heart that is open to receive it.[30]

When one once gives place to an angry spirit he is just as much intoxicated as the man who has put the glass to his lips.[31]

Christ treats anger as murder. . . . Passionate words are a savor of death unto death. He who utters them is not cooperating with God to save his fellow man. In heaven this wicked railing is placed in the same list as common swearing. While hatred is cherished in the soul there is not one iota of the love of God there.[32]

When you feel an angry spirit arising, take firm hold of Jesus Christ by faith. Utter no word. Danger lies in the utterance of a single word when you are angry, for a volley of passionate utterances will follow. . . . The man who gives way to folly in speaking passionate words, bears false witness; for he is never just. He exaggerates every defect he thinks he sees; he is too blind and unreasonable to be convinced of his madness. He transgresses the commandments of God, and his imagination is perverted by the inspiration of Satan. He knows not what he is doing. Blind and deaf, he permits Satan to take the helm and guide him wherever he pleases. The door is then thrown open to malice, to envy, and to evil surmisings, and the poor victim is borne helplessly on. . . . But there is hope while the hours of probation linger, through the grace of our Lord Jesus Christ. . . .

"Be diligent that ye may be found of him in peace, without spot, and blameless." 2 Peter 3:14. This is the standard for which every Christian must strive, not in his own natural ability, but through the grace given him of Jesus Christ. Let us wrestle for the mastery over every sin, and be able to check every impatient, fretful expression.[33]

THE FRAGRANT TOUCH OF COURTESY

Finally, be ye all of one mind, having compassion one of another, love as brethren, be pitiful, be courteous. 1 Peter 3:8.

In dealing with our fellow men we all are to consider that they are of like passions with ourselves, feeling the same weaknesses and suffering the same temptations. They, with us, have a struggle with life if they maintain their integrity. . . . True Christian courtesy unites and perfects both justice and politeness, and mercy and love make up the filling, giving the finest touches and most graceful charms to the character. . . .

Abraham was a true gentleman. In his life we have the finest example of the power of true courtesy. Look at his course with Lot. . . . How courteously he welcomes the travelers, the messengers of God, to his tent, and entertains them! He bowed before the sons of Heth when he purchased of them a cave in which to bury his beloved Sarah. . . . Well did Abraham know what was due from man to his fellow man.

Paul, though firm as a rock to principle, yet ever preserved his courtesy. He was zealous for the vital points and was not regardless of the grace and politeness due to social life. The man of God did not absorb the man of humanity.

But we present a greater than Abraham and Paul—the Saviour of the world. His life was a striking illustration of genuine courtesy. It is impossible to enumerate the instances of His kindness, courtesy, and tender sympathy and love. What rays of softness and beauty did His marvelous condescension shed over His entire life! He had a kind look and an encouraging word for all who were wearied and worn with labor. He was ready to help the most helpless.[34]

Love, courtesy, amiability—these are never lost. When men shall be changed from mortal to immortal, all the deeds of sanctified goodness done by them will be made manifest. These deeds will be preserved through the eternal ages. Not one, however small or simple, is ever lost. Through the merits of Christ's imputed righteousness they preserve their fragrance.[35]

"A SYSTEM OF TRUEST POLITENESS"

And be ye kind one to another, tenderhearted, forgiving one another, even as God for Christ's sake hath forgiven you. Eph. 4:32.

We must learn to place the best possible construction upon doubtful conduct of others. . . . If we are ever suspecting evil we are in danger of creating what we allow ourselves to suspect. . . . We cannot pass along without sometimes having our feelings hurt and our temper tried, but as Christians we must be just as patient, forbearing, humble, and meek as we desire others to be. Oh, how many thousand good acts and deeds of kindness that we receive . . . pass from the mind like dew before the sun, while imaginary or real injury leaves an impression which it is next to impossible to efface! The very best example to give to others is to be right ourselves, and then leave ourselves, our reputation, with God and not show too great anxiety to right every wrong impression and present our case in a favorable light. . . .

The neglect to cultivate tender consideration and forbearance for one another has caused dissension, distrust, faultfinding, and general disunion. God . . . calls upon us to put away this great sin and to strive to answer the prayer of Christ that His disciples may be one as He is one with the Father. . . . It is the special work of Satan to cause dissension, . . . that the world should be deprived of the most powerful testimony Christians can give it that God has sent His Son to bring into harmony turbulent, proud, envious, jealous, bigoted minds. . . .

The truth of God is not designed merely to deal with errors and vices. . . . The truth is designed to sanctify the receiver, to fashion and mold the entire man, externally as well as internally, by abasing pride and disposing his heart to be kind and amiable and condescending. Yes, the religion of Christ is a system of the truest politeness, and its triumphs are complete when a world may look on a people professing godliness with a united front, believers showing habitual tenderness of feeling and kindness of deportment and sincere regard for the reputation of each other.[36]

AN IRRESISTIBLE INFLUENCE

Put on then, as God's chosen ones, holy and beloved, compassion, kindness, lowliness, meekness, and patience. Col. 3:12, RSV.

Kind words, pleasant looks, a cheerful countenance, throw a charm around the Christian that makes his influence almost irresistible. This is a way to gain respect, and extend the sphere of usefulness, which costs but little. It is the religion of Christ in the heart that causes the words issuing therefrom to be gentle and the demeanor condescending, even to those in the humblest walks of life. A blustering, faultfinding, overbearing man is not a Christian; for to be a Christian is to be Christlike. . . .

He who drinks in the spirit of Christ will let it flow forth in kind words, and be expressed in courteous deportment. The plan of salvation is to soften whatever is harsh and rough in the temper, and to smooth off whatever is rugged or sharp in the manners. External change will testify of an internal change. The truth is the sanctifier, the refiner. Received into the heart, it works with hidden power, transforming the receiver. But those who profess the truth and at the same time are rough, and sour, and unkind in words and deportment, have not learned of Jesus; all these manifestations show that they are yet servants of the wicked one. No man can be a Christian without having the spirit of Christ, manifesting meekness, gentleness, and refinement of manners. . . .

Pleasant, kind, and well-bred Christians will have an influence for God and His truth; it cannot be otherwise. The light borrowed from Heaven will shed its brightening rays through them to the pathway of others. . . . The words we speak, our daily deportment, are the fruit growing upon the tree. If the fruit is sour and unpalatable, the rootlets of that tree are not drawing nourishment from a pure source. If our affections are brought into harmony with our Saviour, if our characters are meek and lowly, we evidence that our life is hid with Christ in God; and we shall leave behind us a bright track. . . . Beholders will discern that we have been with Jesus and learned of Him.[37]

CHERISHING THE SPIRIT OF JESUS

Forbearing one another and, if one has a complaint against another, forgiving each other; as the Lord has forgiven you, so you also must forgive. Col. 3:13, RSV.

We are in this world to meet with persons of varied minds and different temperaments, and you must consider that they do not differ with you any more than you differ with them. . . . We are to cultivate forbearance, long-suffering, gentleness, goodness, and love and be bound together by the ties of human brotherhood.

May the dear Saviour be a welcome guest in your heart. If Christ is abiding in your heart, you will manifest Christ in your words, the law of kindness will be upon your tongues, and you will have peace within. Then all will be peace without, and you will make melody to God in your hearts.[38]

A blessing rests upon the peacemakers. . . . O that the Lord would imbue me with His Holy Spirit, that I shall ever be what Christ calls a peacemaker! I do not love the atmosphere of strife and contention. I want to be able to say the Lord's Prayer, "Forgive us our trespasses, as we forgive those who trespass against us." Oh, how can we utter this prayer and be unforgiving? . . .

To judge our brethren, to allow feelings to be cherished against them, even if we feel they have not done exactly right toward us, will bring no blessing to our hearts and will not help the case at all. I dare not allow my feelings to run in the channel of hunting up all my grievances and telling them over and over, and dwelling in the atmosphere of distrust, enmity, and dissension. . . .

There is light in following Jesus, talking of Jesus, loving Jesus, and I will not allow my mind to think or speak ill of my brethren. "Inasmuch," said Christ, "as ye have done it unto one of the least of these my brethren, ye have done it unto me." Matt. 25:40. I would not feel unkindness or hatred to anyone. I would not be an accuser of my brethren. Satan will try to stir up my mind to do this, but I cannot do it. I will cherish the forgiving Spirit of Jesus.[39]

"NOT EASILY PROVOKED"

Charity suffereth long, and is kind; charity envieth not; charity vaunteth not itself, is not puffed up, doth not behave itself unseemly, seeketh not her own, is not easily provoked, thinketh no evil. 1 Cor. 13:4, 5.

Many have a vivid, unsanctified sensitiveness which keeps them constantly on the alert for some word, some look, or some action which they can construe as a lack of respect and appreciation. All this must be overcome. Everyone should go forward in the fear of God, doing his best without being troubled by praise or offended by censure, serving God fervently, and learning to place the most favorable interpretation upon whatever in others may seem offensive.[40]

We may expect that false reports will circulate about us; but if we follow a straight course, if we remain indifferent to these things, others will also be indifferent. Let us leave to God the care of our reputation. . . . Slander can be lived down by our manner of living; it is not lived down by words of indignation. Let our great anxiety be to act in the fear of God, and show by our conduct that these reports are false. No one can injure our character as much as ourselves. It is the weak trees and the tottering houses that need to be constantly propped. When we show ourselves so anxious to protect our reputation against attacks from the outside, we give the impression that it is not blameless before God, and that it needs therefore to be continually bolstered up.[41]

It does not behoove those from whom Jesus has so much to bear, in their failings and perversity, to be ever mindful of slights and real or imaginary offense. . . . The heart filled with that love which thinketh no evil will not be on the watch to notice discourtesies and grievances of which he may be the object. The will of God is that His love shall close the eyes, the ears and the heart to all such provocations and to all the suggestions with which Satan would fill them. There is a noble majesty in the silence of the one exposed to evil surmising or outrage. To be master of one's spirit is to be stronger than kings or conquerors.[42]

HAS RELIGION MADE YOU BETTER?

Having your conversation honest among the Gentiles: that, whereas they speak against you as evildoers, they may by your good works, which they shall behold, glorify God in the day of visitation. 1 Peter 2:12.

Whatever we are at heart will be revealed in character, and will have an influence on all those with whom we associate. Our words, our actions, are a savor of life unto life or of death unto death. And in the judgment we shall be brought face to face with those whom we might have helped in right, safe paths by choice words, by counsel, if we had daily connection with God and a living, abiding interest in the saving of their souls.[43]

The Christian should not be content to be merely an active man of business. He should not be so absorbed in worldly affairs as to have scarcely a spare moment or a thought for recreation or friendship, for the good of others, for the culture of the mind, or the welfare of the soul. Energy and diligence in business are commendable, but these should not lead us to neglect that love for God and man which the Bible enjoins. . . .

Our course in temporal matters, our conduct toward one another, is commented upon with keenness and severity. What we say in the church is not of so great consequence as our deportment in the home circle and among our neighbors. The kindly word, the thoughtful act, true politeness and hospitality, will constantly exert an influence in favor of the Christian religion.

Let not the testimony be borne concerning any of us, "Religion has made them no better. They are as self-indulgent, as worldly, as sharp in trade, as ever." All who bear such fruit scatter from Christ, instead of gathering with Him. They place obstacles in the way of those whom they might by a consistent course have won to Jesus. It is our duty as Christians to give to the world unmistakable evidence that we are obeying the great commandment, "Thou shalt love thy neighbour as thyself," which is the same as our Saviour's golden rule, "Whatsoever ye would that men should do to you, do ye even so to them."[44]

THE SECRET OF CONTENTMENT

But godliness with contentment is great gain. 1 Tim. 6:6.

Pure religion brings peace, happiness, contentment; godliness is profitable to this life and the life to come.[45]

That unrest and discontent which ends in fretting and complaining is sinful; but the discontent with one's self which urges on to more earnest effort for greater improvement of the mind for a broader field of usefulness is praiseworthy. This discontent does not end in disappointment but in gathering force for a higher and more extended field of usefulness. Only be ever balanced by firm religious principle and a sensitive conscience, having ever the fear of God before you, and you will certainly prosper in becoming fitted for a life of usefulness.[46]

We should live for the next world. It is so wretched to live a haphazard, aimless life. We want an object in life—to live for a purpose. God help us all to be self-sacrificing, less self-caring, more forgetful of self and selfish interest; and to do good, not for the honor we expect to receive here, but because this is the object of our life and will answer the end of our existence. Let our daily prayer go up to God that He will divest us of selfishness. . . .

I have seen that those who live for a purpose, seeking to benefit and bless their fellow men and to honor and glorify their Redeemer, are the truly happy ones on the earth, while the man who is restless, discontented, and seeking this and testing that, hoping to find happiness, is always complaining of disappointment. He is always in want, never satisfied, because he lives for himself alone. Let it be your aim to do good, to act your part in life faithfully.[47]

Be anxious and earnest to grow in grace, seeking for a more distinct and intelligent understanding of the will of God concerning you, striving earnestly for the mark of the prize before you. Christian perfection alone will win the spotless robes of character which will entitle you to stand before the throne of God among the blood-washed throng, bearing the palm branch of everlasting victory and eternal triumph.[48]

August 25

WATCH YOUR STEP!

Ponder the path of thy feet, and let all thy ways be established.
Prov. 4:26.

"Make straight paths for your feet," says the apostle, "lest that which is lame be turned out of the way." Heb. 12:13. The path that leads away from God, away from His holy, perfect standard of right, is always crooked and dangerous. Yet . . . many have been walking in this path of transgression. In many cases they did not start right in childhood and youth, and they have pursued crooked paths all the way along. Not only have they erred from the right way themselves but through the influence of their example others have been turned aside from the straight, plain path, and have made fatal mistakes. . . .

We do not always realize the power of example. We are brought in contact with others. We meet persons who are erring, who do wrong in various ways; they may be disagreeable, quick, passionate, dictatorial. While dealing with these we must be patient, forbearing, kind, and gentle. Satan works through them to provoke and harass, so that we shall not exhibit a pleasant and lovable disposition. There are trials and perplexities for us all to encounter; for we are in a world of cares, anxieties, and disappointments. But these continual annoyances must be met in the spirit of Christ. Through grace we may rise superior to our surroundings, and keep our spirits calm and unruffled amid the frets and worries of everyday life. We shall thus represent Christ to the world. . . .

Consecration to God must be a living, practical matter; not a theory to be talked about, but a principle interwoven with all our experience. We should let our light so shine before others that they, seeing our good works, shall glorify our Father who is in Heaven. We should show forth the praises of Him who has called us out of darkness into His marvelous light. If the light of Heaven is in the soul, it will be reflected to all around us. I wish all could see this important subject in its true light. There would not then be such thoughtlessness of words and acts, such careless, indolent, irreligious living.[49]

HABITS AND CHARACTER BUILDING

Enter not into the path of the wicked, and go not in the way of evil men. Prov. 4:14.

Few realize the power of habit. Inspiration asks, "Can the Ethiopian change his skin, or the leopard his spots?" and adds, "then may ye also do good that are accustomed to do evil." Jer. 13:23. This is a solemn assertion. . . . But there is comfort and courage in the reflection that if evil habits acquire such force that it seems almost impossible to turn in the right direction, the power of good habits is equally strong. The results of each day's work, whether the tendency be to elevate us in the scale of moral worth or to push us downward toward perdition, are influenced by the days that have preceded it. Defeat today prepares the way for still greater defeat tomorrow; victory today ensures an easier victory tomorrow. Then how careful we should be to see that the habits and characters we are forming are correct and virtuous. . . .

Young friends, restrain your feet from all evil ways. . . . Men may discipline themselves to do right. Like Daniel they may have a Heaven-born purpose in their hearts that they will not defile soul or body, notwithstanding the degeneracy and corruption of the age. God gave Daniel "knowledge and skill in all learning and wisdom." Dan. 1:17. His blessing attended the man who put forth human effort in accordance with the divine will. The same help will still be given to all who pursue a similar course, and with the glory of God in view practice abstinence and self-restraint. The same difference will be seen between them and the self-indulgent that there was between Daniel and his fellows and the other youth in the king's court. There will be the clear eye and complexion, the firm tread, the strength and vigor of intellect, the keen perception of spiritual truth.[50]

Let us remember that character is not the result of accident, but day by day it is forming for good or for evil. Great importance attaches to this work of character building; for it is far reaching in its results. We are builders for time and for eternity.[51]

BLESSINGS DIFFUSIVE AS SUNLIGHT

That ye may be the children of your Father which is in heaven: for he maketh his sun to rise on the evil and on the good, and sendeth rain on the just and on the unjust. Matt. 5:45.

I see a providence in all of God's works. . . . The clouds and rain, as well as the bright sunshine, have their mission in blessings to man. The God of nature knows just what we need and He moves forward in a straight line, sending blessings upon the just and upon the unjust. I am so grateful that finite minds cannot have the ordering of things. What cross-purposes would be revealed![52]

There is a narrowness in human comprehension that is dishonoring to God. Let not him who claims Christ as his Saviour entertain the thought that God's mercies are confined to him and to the few in whom he is interested. The love and mercy of God are for everyone. Let us gather up the divine tokens of His favor, and return praise and thanksgiving to Him for His goodness, which is bestowed upon us, not to be hoarded, but to be passed along to others. . . . God expects everyone who enjoys His grace to diffuse this grace as freely as Christ bestows His mercies. As the sun shines upon the just and the unjust, so the Sun of Righteousness reflects light to the whole world.[53]

God's blessings, sunshine and showers, heat and cold, and every natural blessing, are given to the world. Exclusiveness is not to be maintained by any people. "I am the light of the world" (John 8:12), Christ said. Light is a blessing, a universal blessing, which pours forth its treasures on a world unthankful, unholy, demoralized. The Lord Jesus came to demolish every wall of exclusion, to throw open every wall in the temple where God presides, that every ear may hear, that every eye may see, that every thirsty soul may drink of the water of life freely.[54]

God scatters blessings all along our path. . . . We may weep and groan and mourn and stumble at every step if we choose, or we may gather up the precious, fragrant flowers and rejoice in the Lord for His goodness in making our path to heaven so pleasant.[55]

STUDYING THE CHARACTER OF CHRIST

Then shall I not be ashamed, when I have respect unto all thy commandments. Ps. 119:6.

In this world we might become hopelessly perplexed, as the devil wants us to be, if we keep looking upon those things that are perplexing; for by dwelling upon them, and talking of them, we become discouraged. In criticizing others because they fail to manifest love, we shall kill the precious plant of love in our own hearts. Have we individually appreciated and felt the warmth of love which Christ represented in His life? Then it is our duty to manifest this love to the world. Let us fear to dwell upon, to behold and talk of the great mistakes that others are making. . . .

You may create an unreal world in your own mind and picture an ideal church, where the temptations of Satan no longer prompt to evil; but perfection exists only in your imagination. The world is a fallen world, and the church is a place represented by a field in which grow tares and wheat. They are to grow together until the harvest. It is not our place to uproot the tares, according to human wisdom, lest under the suggestions of Satan, the wheat may be rooted up. . . .

None need to lose the golden moments of time in their short life history through seeking to weigh the imperfections of professed Christians. Not one of us has time to do this. If we see clearly what is the manner of character Christians should develop, and yet see in others that which is inconsistent with this character, let us determine that we will firmly resist the enemy in his temptations to make us act in an inconsistent way, and say, "I will not make Christ ashamed of me. I will more earnestly study the character of Christ in whom there was no imperfection, no selfishness, no spot, no stain of evil, who lived not to please and glorify Himself, but to glorify God and save fallen humanity. I will not copy the defective characters of these inconsistent Christians, and the mistakes that they have made shall not lead me to be like them. I will turn to the precious Saviour, that I may be like Him." [56]

A STRONG FORTRESS OF TRUTH

To whom God would make known what is the riches of the glory of this mystery among the Gentiles; which is Christ in you, the hope of glory. Col. 1:27.

I have a continual longing for Christ to be formed within, the hope of glory. I long to be beautified every day with the meekness and gentleness of Christ, growing in grace and in the knowledge of Jesus Christ up to the full stature of men and women in Christ Jesus. I must as an individual, through the grace given me of Jesus Christ, keep my own soul in health by keeping it as a divine channel through which His grace, His love, His patience, His meekness, shall flow to the world. This is my duty and no less the duty of every church member who claims to be a son or a daughter of God.

The Lord Jesus has made His church the depositary of sacred truth. He has left with her the work of carrying out His purposes and His plans to save the souls for whom He has manifested such interest, such unmeasured love. Like the sun in relation to our world, He rises amid the moral darkness—the Sun of Righteousness. He said of Himself, "I am the light of the world." John 8:12. He said to His followers, "Ye are the light of the world." Matt. 5:14. . . . By reflecting the image of Jesus Christ, by the beauty and holiness of their characters, by their continual self-denial and their separation from all idols, large or small, they reveal that they have learned in the school of Christ. They are continually catching the spirit of love and forbearance, meekness, and gentleness, and they stand as representatives of Christ, a spectacle to the world, to angels, and to men. . . .

Walking and working in the world, but not of the world, they are answering in their characters the prayer of Christ: "I pray not that thou shouldest take them out of the world, but that thou shouldest keep them from the evil." John 17:15. They are to stand as the strong fortress of truth, their light shining far in the moral darkness of the world. The Lord has a message for the watchmen on the walls of Zion to bear. The trumpet is to give no uncertain sound.[57]

THE WAY TO LOOK AT THINGS

Finally, brethren, whatsoever things are true, whatsoever things are honest, whatsoever things are just, whatsoever things are pure, whatsoever things are lovely, whatsoever things are of good report; if there be any virtue, and if there be any praise, think on these things. Phil. 4:8.

As long as Satan has power to work upon human minds that are not barricaded with the Holy Spirit, there will be stern and earnest conflict between good and evil, and evil will be manifested, even among those who claim to be the children of God. . . .

There is no reason for us to fix our eyes upon error, to grieve and complain, and lose precious time and opportunities in lamenting the faults of others. . . . Would it not be more pleasing to God to take an impartial outlook, and see how many souls are serving God, and resisting temptation, and glorifying and honoring Him with their talents of means and intellect? Would it not be better to consider the wonderful, miracle-working power of God in the transformation of poor, degraded sinners, who have been full of moral pollution, who become so transformed that they are Christlike in character? . . .

Let us turn away our eyes from beholding the imperfections of those who are in the church, but who have not the likeness of Christ. We shall not be held responsible because those who make a high profession do not possess corresponding virtues. Let us thank God that it is our privilege to turn away our eyes from these defective Christians, and look upon those who are truly devoted, who are doers of the Word, and who in life and character bear the image of the Divine. And above all things, thank God that it is your privilege to look upon Christ, the perfect pattern. . . .

Everything that causes us to see the weakness of humanity is in the Lord's purpose to help us to look to Him, and in no case put trust in man, or make flesh our arm. . . . We become changed into the image of that upon which we dwell. Then how important to open our hearts to the things that are true and lovely and of good report![58]

HOLD HIGH THE STANDARD

Go through, go through the gates; prepare ye the way of the people; cast up, cast up the highway; gather out the stones; lift up a standard for the people. Isa. 62:10.

The Word of God not only sets forth the great principles of truth and duty which should govern our lives, but it presents also, for our encouragement, the history of many who have exemplified these principles. . . . Except the one perfect Pattern, there is not described in the Sacred Pages a single character more worthy of emulation than that of the prophet Daniel. Exposed in youth to all the allurements of a royal court, he became a man of unbending integrity and fervent devotion to God. He was subjected to the fierce temptations of Satan, yet his character was not vacillating, nor his course changeable. He was firm where many would be yielding; he was true where they would be false; he was strong where they would be weak. Daniel was a lofty cedar of Lebanon. . . . Would that the faith, integrity, and devotion of the prophet Daniel might live in the hearts of God's people of today. Never were these noble qualities more needed in the world than now. . . .

In the records of those who have done and suffered for the name of Jesus, there is no name that shines with a brighter or purer luster than the name of Paul, the apostle to the Gentiles. The love of Jesus, glowing in his heart, made him self-forgetful, self-denying. He had seen the risen Christ, and the Saviour's image was impressed upon his soul, and shone forth in his life. With faith, courage, and fortitude, that would not be daunted by danger or stayed by obstacles, he pressed his way from land to land to spread the knowledge of the cross. . . .

Are the professed followers of Christ thus exemplifying the principles of their faith? Where are the deep, living, holy experiences which men of God were wont to recount? Has the standard of Christianity been lowered? . . . No; that standard remains just where God placed it. Holy men of ages past were required to give up all for Christ, to cherish His spirit, and to imitate His example. Nothing less than this will He accept now. . . . When called to give up all for Christ, who will stand the test?[59]

REMINDERS OF OUR HEAVENLY HOME

Thou, even thou, art Lord alone; thou hast made heaven, the heaven of heavens, with all their host, the earth, and all things that are therein, the seas, and all that is therein, and thou preservest them all; and the host of heaven worshippeth thee. Neh. 9:6.

There is beauty in the valley's awful grandeur, in the solemn, massive, cleft rocks; there is majesty in the towering mountains that look as if they touched the heavens. There are the lofty trees with their delicately formed leaves; the spires of grass, the opening bud and blossoming flower, the forest trees, and every living thing. They all point the mind to the great and living God. Every faculty of our being testifies that there is a living God, and we may learn from the open book of nature the most precious lessons in regard to the Lord of heaven.

In this study the mind expands, is elevated and uplifted, and becomes hungry to know more of God and His majesty. We have awakened in our hearts feelings not only of reverence and awe but of love, of faith, of trust and entire dependence upon One who is the giver of all good. And as I look at His marvelous works and see the evidences of His power I instinctively inquire, "What is man that thou art mindful of him? and the son of man, that thou visitest him?" Ps. 8:4.

All the greatness and glory of these wonderful things in God's house can only be appreciated as they are, in the mind, associated with God and the future home of bliss He is preparing for those who love Him. . . . While we talk freely of other countries, why should we be reticent in regard to the heavenly country, and the house not built with hands, eternal in the heavens? This heavenly country is of more consequence to us than any other city or country on the globe, therefore we should think and talk of this better—even an heavenly—country. And why should we not converse more earnestly, and in a heavenly frame of mind, in regard to God's gifts in nature? He has made all these things, and designs that we shall see God in His created works. These things are to keep God in our remembrance and to lift our hearts from sensual things and bind them in bonds of love and gratitude to our Creator.[1]

NATURE SPEAKS OF GOD

I remember the days of old; I meditate on all thy works; I muse on the work of thy hands. I stretch forth my hands unto thee: my soul thirsteth after thee, as a thirsty land. Ps. 143:5, 6.

We have looked upon the lofty, terraced mountains in their majestic beauty, with their rocky battlements resembling grand old castles. These mountains speak to us of the desolating wrath of God in vindication of His broken law; for they were heaved up by the stormy convulsions of the flood. They are like mighty waves that at the voice of God stood still—stiffened billows, arrested in their proudest swell. These towering mountains belong to God; He presides over their rocky fastnesses. The wealth of their mines is His also, and so are the deep places of the earth.

If you would see the evidences that there is a God, look around you wherever your lot may be cast. He is speaking to your senses and impressing your soul through His created works. Let your heart receive these impressions, and nature will be to you an open book, and will teach you divine truth through familiar things. The lofty trees will not be regarded with indifference. Every opening flower, every leaf with its delicate veins, will testify of the infinite skill of the great Master Artist. The massive rocks and towering mountains that rise in the distance are not the result of chance. They speak in silent eloquence of One who sits upon the throne of the universe, high and lifted up. "Known unto God are all his works from the beginning of the world." All His plans are perfect. What awe and reverence should His name inspire! . . .

God is Himself the Rock of Ages, a refuge for His people, a covert from the storm, a shadow from the burning heat. He has given us His promises, which are more firm and immovable than the rocky heights, the everlasting hills. The mountains shall depart, and the hills shall be removed; but His kindness shall not depart, nor His covenant of peace be removed from those who by faith make Him their trust. If we would look to God for help as steadfastly as these rocky, barren mountains point to the heavens above them, we should never be moved from our faith in Him and our allegiance to His holy law.[2]

A SCHOOL FOR MIND AND MORALS

And they sing the song of Moses the servant of God, and the song of the Lamb, saying, Great and marvellous are thy works, Lord God Almighty; just and true are thy ways, thou King of saints. Rev. 15:3.

The great Architect has formed and fashioned the scenes of nature that they may have an important bearing upon man's intellectual and moral character. These are to be God's school to educate the mind and morals. Here the mind may have a vast field for study in the display of the majestic works of the Infinite One. The rocks are among the precious things of earth, containing treasures of wisdom and knowledge. In the rocks and mountains are registered the fact that God did destroy the wicked from off the earth by a flood.[3]

Men thought themselves wiser than God, and altogether too wise to obey . . . the statutes and precepts of Jehovah. The rich things of earth which God had given them did not lead them to obedience, but away from obedience, because they misused their choice favors of heaven, and made the blessings given them of God objects to separate from God. And because they became satanic in their nature, rather than divine, the Lord sent the flood of waters upon the old world.[4]

God is full of love and plenteous in mercy; but He will by no means acquit those who neglect the great salvation He has provided. The long-lived antediluvians were swept from the earth because they made void the divine law. God will not again bring from the heavens above and the earth beneath waters as His weapons to use in the destruction of the world; but when next His vengeance shall be poured out against those who despise His authority, they will be destroyed by fire concealed in the bowels of the earth, awakened into intense activity by fires from heaven above. Then from the purified earth shall arise a song of praise: "Blessing, and honour, and glory, and power, be unto him that sitteth upon the throne, and unto the Lamb for ever and ever." Rev. 5:13. "Great and marvellous are thy works, Lord God Almighty; just and true are thy ways, thou King of saints." And every one who has made the heavenly treasure the first consideration, . . . will join in the glad triumphant strain.[5]

GOD'S GREAT RESERVOIRS

Before the mountains were brought forth, or ever thou hadst formed the earth and the world, even from everlasting to everlasting, thou art God. Ps. 90:2.

Our heavenly Father has furnished us with tokens of His greatness and His majesty. Especially is this so in a wonderful degree in these mountainous regions.* . . . The varied scenery in the towering mountains and rocky heights, the deep mountain gorges with their rapid, noisy streams of water coming from the mountains above, . . . the waters breaking as they strike the rocks, and scattering into spray like a veil, render this scenery altogether one of surpassing beauty and grandeur. . . .

The mountains contain treasures of blessings which the Creator bestows upon the inhabitants of the earth. It is the diversity in the surface of the earth, in mountains, plains, and valleys, which reveals the wisdom and the power of the great Master Worker. And those who would banish from our earth the rocks and mountains, the wild gorges and the noisy, rushing streams, and the precipices—their senses . . . are too limited to comprehend the majesty of God. . . .

God, the great Architect, has built these lofty mountains, and their influence upon climate is a blessing to our world. They draw from the clouds enriching moisture. Mountain chains are God's great reservoirs, to supply the ocean with its water. These are the sources of the springs, rills, and brooks, as well as the rivers. They receive, in the form of rain and snow, the vapors with which the atmosphere is charged, and communicate them to the parched plains below.

We should look upon the irregular mountains of the earth as God's fountains of blessings from which flow forth the waters to supply all the living creatures. Every time I look upon the mountains I feel gratitude to God. . . .

Everything about us teaches us from day to day lessons of our Father's love and of His power, and of His laws that govern nature and that lie at the foundation of all government in heaven and in earth.[6]

---

* Written in Europe.

FRAGRANCE IN OUR LIFEWORK

And why take ye thought for raiment? Consider the lilies of the field, how they grow; they toil not, neither do they spin: and yet I say unto you, that even Solomon in all his glory was not arrayed like one of these. Matt. 6:28, 29.

The great Master Artist calls our attention to the soulless flowers of the field, pointing out the beautiful tints and the wonderful variety of shades one flower may possess. Thus God has revealed His skill and care. Thus He would show the great love He has for every human being.[7]

The Lord our Creator expends as much care, wisdom, and time upon the tiny flower as upon the great things He creates. In the tiniest flowers are seen a beauty and perfection that no human art can copy. The delicate tracery of the tinted rose, as well as the stars in the heavens, shows the penciling of the great Master Artist.[8]

Choice flowers . . . reveal the advantages of culture. They teach us that it is our privilege to improve. God desires us to bring fragrance into our lifework. We are to be the plants of the Lord, serving Him in whatever way He wills. Let us do all in our power to beautify our characters. . . . Tender care must be given to the delicate plants. The useless offshoots must be taken away. The bruised parts must be carefully bound up. So those who are weak in the faith must have fostering care. We are to bind to our stronger purposes the weaklings in the Lord's garden, giving them support.

From the endless variety of plants and flowers, we may learn an important lesson. All blossoms are not the same in form or color. Some possess healing virtues. Some are always fragrant. There are professing Christians who think it their duty to make every other Christian like themselves. This is man's plan, not the plan of God. In the church of God there is room for characters as varied as are the flowers in a garden. In His spiritual garden there are many varieties of flowers.[9]

The Lord cares for the flowers. He gives them beauty and fragrance. Will He not much more give us the fragrance of a cheerful disposition?[10]

September 6

A PURE MORAL ATMOSPHERE

That than mayest walk in the way of good men, and keep the paths of the righteous. Prov. 2:20.

In order to have a healthy body, the blood circulating through the veins must be pure; in order to be pure it must have pure air and pure food. The use of improper food and the inhalation of impure air cause disease, which appears in various forms.

The purity and soundness of our religious life is dependent not only on the truth we accept, but on the company we keep, and the moral atmosphere we breathe. Faith, elasticity and vigor, hopefulness, joyfulness, doubts and fears, slothfulness, stupidity, envy, jealousy, distrust, selfishness, waywardness, and backsliding, are the result of the associations we form, the company we keep, and the air we breathe.

The indulgence of wrong associations will have its baleful results. . . . The Bible may be read and prayer be offered, yet there will be no increase of spiritual health, no growth of soul, so long as the air which is breathed is bad. . . . The greatest care should be exercised by believers to place themselves in close connection with God and with those who have been taught of God. It is painful to see those who have believed present truth walking into Satan's net. . . .

We raise our voice and cry to every believer in the present truth: If you would have spiritual health, look to your lungs. Look to your spiritual food. Cultivate a love for the society of those who are pure and good, if you would have Christ formed in you as the life of the soul. The health of the soul depends upon the breathing of a good moral atmosphere.[11]

Christ, the Great Physician, has given a prescription for every believer. He must eat the food provided in the Word of God. And the faith that works by love to God and man is dependent not only upon the food we eat but upon the air we breathe. If we associate with those who are evil, we breathe an atmosphere tainted with the malaria of sin. Be sure, by association with the meek and lowly followers of Jesus, to breathe a pure, holy atmosphere.[12]

BE SELECTIVE!

And have no fellowship with the unfruitful works of darkness, but rather reprove them. Eph. 5:11.

The Christian should withdraw himself from the company of those who are as a snare to his soul. When you come in contact with those whom you cannot lift into a pure and holy atmosphere, because their moral tastes are wholly perverted, you must shun their society. Persons of this class have generally a strong will and positive temperament, and when wrought upon by the enemy of God, they become efficient agents in leading souls from the path of righteousness to paths that are false and dangerous. The moral atmosphere surrounding these souls is tainted with evil, and exerts only a defiling influence.[13]

Your associates may not be expected to be free from imperfections or sin. But in choosing your friends, you should place your standard as high as possible. The tone of your morals is estimated by the associates you choose. You should avoid contracting an intimate friendship with those whose example you would not choose to imitate. . . .

Choose for your associates those who hold religion and its practical influences in high respect. Keep the future life constantly in view. Let not your associations put these thoughts out of your mind. Nothing will so effectually banish serious impressions as intercourse with the vain, careless, and irreligious. Whatever intellectual greatness such persons may attain, if they treat religion with levity or even with indifference, they should not be your chosen friends. The more engaging their manners in other respects, the more should you dread their influence as companions, because they would throw around you an irreligious, godless, irreverent influence and yet combine it with so many attractions that it is positively dangerous to morals.[14]

Dare to be a Daniel. Dare to stand alone. . . . A cowardly and silent reserve before evil associates, while you listen to their devices, makes you one with them. . . . Have courage to do right.[15]

GUARD YOUR AFFECTIONS

Be ye not unequally yoked together with unbelievers: for what fellowship hath righteousness with unrighteousness? and what communion hath light with darkness? 2 Cor. 6:14.

I would warn you* to be guarded as to where you bestow your affections. . . . Remember that your life belongs to Jesus, and that you are not to live for yourself alone. You are not to enter into the marriage relation with an unbeliever; for in so doing, you do exactly contrary to that which Jesus has commanded. Shun those who are irreverent. Shun one who is a lover of idleness; shun the one who is a scoffer of hallowed things. Avoid the society of one who uses profane language, or is addicted to the use of even one glass of liquor. Listen not to the proposals of a man who has no realization of his responsibility to God.

The pure truth, which sanctifies the soul, will give you courage to cut yourself loose from the most pleasing acquaintance whom you know does not love and fear God, and knows nothing of the principles of true righteousness. We may always bear with a friend's infirmities and with his ignorance, but never with his vices. Never marry an unbeliever.

I am only voicing to you the word of God, for He declares that such a union will result in drawing away your heart from loving and serving Him. . . . As a child of God, you are permitted to contract marriage only in the Lord. . . . Should you consent to unite your life with that of an unbeliever, you would be disregarding the Word of God and imperiling your soul. . . .

Your life is too precious a thing to be treated as of little worth. Calvary testifies to you the value of your soul.[16]

Let every step toward a marriage alliance be characterized by modesty, simplicity, sincerity, and an earnest purpose to please and honor God. Marriage affects the afterlife both in this world and in the world to come. A sincere Christian will make no plans that God cannot approve. . . . Make Christ your counselor. Study His word with prayer.[17]

---

*Counsel to a young woman.

YOU MUST CHOOSE YOUR COMPANY

Wherefore come out from among them, and be ye separate, saith the Lord, and touch not the unclean thing; and I will receive you. 2 Cor. 6:17.

The true Christian will not choose the company of the unconverted. If Christ is formed within, the hope of glory, we cannot enjoy the malarious spiritual atmosphere which surrounds the souls of the irreligious. . . .

Your acquaintances who are utterly averse to spiritual things are not refined, ennobled, and elevated by the practice of the truth. They are not under the leadership of Christ, but under the black banner of the prince of darkness. To associate with those who neither fear nor love God, unless you associate with them for the purpose of winning them to Jesus, will be a detriment to your spirituality. If you cannot lift them up, their influence will tell upon you in corrupting and tainting your faith. It is right for you to treat them kindly; but not well for you to love and choose their society, for if you choose the atmosphere that surrounds their souls, you will forfeit the companionship of Jesus. By every means in your power seek to repress sin; but never for one moment give sanction to sin either by your deeds, your words, your silence, or your presence. Every time sin is sanctioned by the professed follower of Christ, his sense of sin is weakened, and his judgment thus becomes perverted. . . .

The Lord Jesus cannot keep any soul who places himself upon the enemy's ground and surrounds himself with the society of those who prefer such conversation and conduct as is an offense to the God he reveres and loves. . . .

Cling close to those who will have an uplifting tendency, whose souls are surrounded with a pure and holy atmosphere. . . . God will be nearer to your heart, more in your thoughts, because you have separated from the world and from influences that would lead you away from the truth, and you will be less compassed with the snares of Satan.[18]

September 10

A FRIEND TO THE FRIENDLESS

Ointment and perfume rejoice the heart: so doth the sweetness of a man's friend by hearty counsel. Prov. 27:9.

We should have the love of Christ in the heart to such a degree that our interest in others will be impartial and sincere. Our affections should take a wide range, and not center simply upon a few who flatter us by special confidences. The tendency of such friendships is to lead us to neglect those who are in greater need of love than those upon whom we bestow our attentions.

We should not narrow our circle of friends to a few favorites because they pet and flatter us by their professed affection. The partial attention so often bestowed and received, works not for the highest good of those who would serve God. One draws upon the other for strength, and the praise, flattery, and affection one receives of the other, supplies the place that should be supplied by the grace of God, and thus human friends take the affections from Christ. . . . Human confidants, human associates, absorb the love and trust that should be given to God alone. . . .

Instead of seeking to become a favorite yourself, or to flatter one who may be highly regarded, see if there is not a poor child who is not a favorite, to whom no special kindnesses are shown, and make this one the object of your unselfish attention. Those who are especially attractive will be at no loss for friends; while those who are less pleasing in appearance, who are timid and hard to become acquainted with, may have choice traits of character, and they are the purchase of the blood of Christ.[19]

Feelings of unrest and homesickness or loneliness may be for your good. Your heavenly Father means to teach you to find in Him the friendship and love and consolation that will satisfy your most earnest hopes and desires. . . . Your only safety and happiness are in making Christ your constant counselor. You can be happy in Him if you had not another friend in the wide world.[20]

GRACES INCREASED BY EXERCISE

In all things shewing thyself a pattern of good works: in doctrine shewing uncorruptness, gravity, sincerity, sound speech, that cannot be condemned; that he that is of the contrary part may be ashamed, having no evil thing to say of you. Titus 2:7, 8.

A healthy, growing Christian will not be a passive recipient among his fellows. He must give as well as receive. Our graces are increased by exercise. Christian society will furnish us with pure air to breathe, and in breathing it we must be active. The Christian work performed, the sympathies, encouragements, and instructions given by us to those who need them, the self-restraint, love, patience, and forbearance which are needed, exercised in Christian work, will create in ourselves faith, obedience, hope, and love to God. . . . It is essential for spiritual muscle and strength that the soul have exercise. Work must be done by putting forth spiritual activity in improving opportunities to do good. . . . The more faithful one is in the discharge of Christian duties, the more soundness will he develop. . . .

Weakness and vacillation will never secure respect to the Christian profession. It is impossible to reach men where they are and elevate them unless some confidence is inspired in them for your sincerity and piety. You can never reach them by stepping down from the platform of truth and reform, but by bringing others up to that platform God's Word has provided for you. If men opposed to our faith see that you who profess it are earnest, steadfast, and uncorrupted at all times and under all circumstances, and that you abide in Christ, the living Vine, and are unshaken followers of truth and reform, you will reflect the spirit and character of Christ. In your business, in the associations with believers and unbelievers, in the sanctuary, at home, in every place, you will show the influence of a Saviour's love, which will have a controlling influence upon believers.

Genius, talents, and money are not essential in order to exert this influence; but it is essential that you abide in Christ, and that He abide in you, for thus your fruit will be unto righteousness.[21]

MAKE YOUR MARK IN THE WORLD

Let no man despise thy youth; but be thou an example of the believers, in word, in conversation, in charity, in spirit, in faith, in purity. 1 Tim. 4:12.

The period of childhood and youth—how much is bound up in these years of probation! God desires that you shall improve this time, dear youth, by obtaining a fitness for the work. If you need an education, set yourselves to work with a determination to get one. Do not wait for an opening; make one for yourselves. Take hold in any small way that opens before you. Be thorough and faithful in whatever you take in hand, however small it may be.

Some of our youth are so vacillating that they accomplish nothing for themselves; their lifetime is often half spent before they decide what they shall do, and what they will be. They bury their talents beneath a mass of rubbish. To these I would say, Practice economy. Do not spend your means for the gratification of appetite or for pleasure seeking. Make your mark in the world. Have before you the object of becoming as useful and efficient as God calls you to be. As you improve the knowledge you gain, you will be able to gather increased knowledge. Application to your books and useful manual labor, combined with earnest Christian devotion and loyalty to God, will make you men and women in the highest sense. True devotion to God, combined with the study of the sciences, will give the youth an education that will make them gentle, humble lovers of God, full of mercy and good fruits, without partiality and without hypocrisy. Such souls, fragrant with love for God and for their fellow men, God can use as vessels unto honor.[22]

Jesus died, dear youth, not to save you in your sins, but from your sins. He wants you to follow the example which He has set before you—to deny self, take up your cross daily, and follow Him. He claims your service, your heart's best and holiest affections. If you will walk in obedience to His will, learning cheerfully and diligently the lessons of His providence, by and by He will say, "Child, come up higher to the heavenly mansions which I have prepared for you."[23]

THE HOME TRAINING GROUND

Make me to go in the path of thy commandments; for therein do I delight. Ps. 119:35.

Men have taught that God's law has been done away. Were this the case we would have no standard of character, and would have nothing to show us God's righteous claims. We should be adrift upon an ocean of uncertainty, and have no guide in dealing with the solemn responsibilities of the family relation. But it is in the family relation that we receive our training in dealing with our fellow men in general. If God had no law by which to govern human intelligences, nothing by which His character could be represented as a sample to which the human family could shape their characters, then what impression could possibly be made upon our children as to what constitutes rectitude of life and perfection of character? . . .

The fifth commandment enjoins upon children obedience to their parents, and parents are to help their children to keep this commandment by acting their part in cooperating with God in requiring obedience through childhood and youth. Parents themselves must be under rule to God. They must reveal precious traits of character, presenting a pattern before their children, manifesting patience and forbearance mingled with firmness, and thus educate their children to obey their heavenly Father. . . . Satan delights to look upon disordered and ill-governed families, for his success depends largely upon the control he can have over the families of earth. . . . He is determined the standard of righteousness shall not be the rule for the formation of character. . . .

The Ten Commandments come forth from the God of heaven, whose heart is full of love, who is infinite in wisdom, who never makes a mistake. He is too wise to err, too good to harm any one who will obey His requirements. Blessing will follow those who obey and who administer the law of Jehovah. . . . The happiness and peace of parents and children in this life, and their best good, will be worked out by walking in the path of His precepts; for by so doing they are in harmony with the God of heaven.[24]

TEACH THE SOURCE OF TRUE HAPPINESS

Train up a child in the way he should go: and when he is old, he will not depart from it. Prov. 22:6.

By their neglect to exercise proper restraint, many parents are creating great unhappiness for their children. The youth who are left to constantly seek for pleasure in amusement or selfish gratification are not happy, and never can be happy while following this course. Fathers and mothers, teach your children that the only way to be truly happy is to love and fear God; and enforce the lesson by your example. Let them see that the peace of Christ is ruling in your heart, and that His love pervades your life.[25]

Will you consecrate your own hearts to God, that you may exert a sanctifying influence upon your children? Will you separate them from sin and sinners, and by living faith connect them with God? It should be the work of every parent to cultivate all that is good, and true, and noble in his children. It is his duty to correct their faults, to restrain their waywardness. . . .

Make the Word of God your guide in the education of your children, ever considering what will be for their future good. . . . The mother may bestow upon her daughters an education that will be invaluable, by training them to bear their share of the family burdens. The father may give his sons a capital of more worth than gold or lands, by teaching them to love useful employment, instead of seeking happiness in idle amusements or dissipation. Parents, now is the time to form in your children habits of industry, self-reliance, and self-control; to cultivate economy and business tact. Now is the time to teach them courtesy and benevolence toward their fellow men, and reverence and love for God. . . . Home should be the most sunny and attractive spot on earth; and it may be made such by pleasant words and kind acts, and, underlying all, a steadfast adherence to the right. . . .

Let us withhold nothing from Him who gave His precious life for us. Fathers and mothers, bring to Him your children, in the freshness and bloom of youth, and devote them to His service.[26]

OBEDIENCE AN ELEMENT OF GREATNESS

Children, obey your parents in the Lord: for this is right. Eph. 6:1.

Jesus has given to childhood and youth a perfect example. Study the Pattern, Christ Jesus, and copy it if you would be like Him—pure, holy, sinless, and undefiled. Study the childhood of Christ. He was the Son of God, yet the Bible record tells us He returned from Jerusalem and was subject unto His parents. . . .

Jesus, the world's Redeemer, did as He was told even if the task was not agreeable to His feelings. Obedience is an element of true greatness. No one can be truly good and great who has not learned to obey with alacrity. . . .

When tempted to have your own way in regard to the wishes of your parents, say, "No; Jesus was subject to His parents." Ask help of Jesus, who knows the temptations of every child, of every youth, for He has been tempted and knows your every weakness and will help you to overcome it. . . .

Seek to be useful, to help your parents; to be care-taking and thoughtful. You can help them in a variety of ways. . . . Doing what you can do cheerfully, with quick step, your face bright with gladness because you can do something for your parents to lighten their load, will make you a blessing in the house. . . .

All these little duties faithfully done are entered upon the ledger of heaven. . . . God will make no mistakes; He will make an accurate entry of all your life duties done to His glory. So never frown but always carry a cheerful, happy face, a ready hand to help, an attentive ear to hear the requirements, and a heart to obey, a quick sympathy for those who need help. . . .

Remember your characters are not finished; you are building up day by day a character. Weave all the kindness, obedience, thoughtfulness, painstaking, and love into it you can. Make it after the divine model. Educate yourselves that you may possess the ornament of a meek and quiet spirit which is in the sight of God of great price. You can make the world better by living in it if you only do the very best you can.[27]

THE SACRED TEMPLE OF THE BODY

What? know ye not that your body is the temple of the Holy Ghost which is in you, which ye have of God, and ye are not your own? For ye are bought with a price: therefore glorify God in your body, and in your spirit, which are God's. 1 Cor. 6:19, 20.

That perfection of character which the Lord requires is the fitting up of the whole being as a temple for the indwelling of the Holy Spirit. God will accept of nothing less than the service of the entire human organism. It is not enough to bring into action certain parts of the living machinery. All parts must work in perfect harmony, or the service will be deficient. It is thus that man is qualified to cooperate with God in representing Christ to the world. Thus God desires to prepare a people to stand before Him pure and holy, that He may introduce them into the society of heavenly angels.[28]

We have been entrusted with the most solemn message ever given to our world, and the object to be kept plainly and distinctly before our minds is the glory of God. Let us take care that we do nothing which will weaken physical, mental, or spiritual healthfulness, for God will not accept a tainted, diseased, corrupted sacrifice. Care must be exercised in eating, in drinking, in dressing, and in working, lest we detract from our efficiency and fail of doing our most exalted work in the best manner, in order that the results of our labor may be as lasting as eternity.

It is our duty to train and discipline the body in order that we shall render to the Master the highest possible service. Inclination must not control us. We are not to pamper the appetite and indulge in the use of that which is not for our good, simply because it gratifies the palate; neither are we to seek to live by the starvation plan, with the idea that we shall become spiritually-minded, and that God shall be glorified. We must use the intelligence that God has given in order that we may be perfect in body, soul, and spirit, that we may have a symmetrical character, a well-balanced mind, and do perfect work for the Master.[29]

The sacred temple of the body must be kept pure and uncontaminated, that God's Holy Spirit may dwell therein.[30]

THE SURE PENALTY
OF SELF-INDULGENCE

If any man defile the temple of God, him shall God destroy; for the temple of God is holy, which temple ye are. 1 Cor. 3:17.

Perfection of character cannot be attained when the laws of nature are disregarded; for this is transgression of the law of God. His law is written by His own finger upon every nerve, every muscle, every fiber of our being, upon every faculty which has been entrusted to man. These gifts are bestowed, not to be abused and corrupted, but to be used to His honor and glory in the uplifting of humanity. . . .

The relation that exists between mind and body is very intimate: when one is affected, the other is always more or less in sympathy. It is impossible for men, while under the power of sinful, health-destroying habits, to appreciate sacred truths. When the intellect is clouded, the moral powers are enfeebled, and sin does not look sinful. The most ennobling, grand, and glorious themes of God's Word seem but idle tales. Satan can then easily snatch away the good seed that has been sown in the heart; for the soul is in no condition to comprehend or understand its true value. It is thus that selfish, health-destroying indulgences are counteracting the influence of the message which is to prepare a people for the great day of God.

We are living in a most solemn, awful moment of this earth's history. Not a soul whose life is one of careless self-degradation, through transgression of physical laws, will stand in the great day of trial just before us. There is a terrible account to be rendered to God by those who have but little regard for the human body, and treat it ruthlessly. . . . True religion and the laws of health go hand in hand.[31]

The least departure from the strictest integrity under any circumstances because it is convenient, will harden the conscience and prepare the way for the violation of moral obligations in other ways. If we treat the health of the body, which is our highest earthly interest, without due consideration, we prepare the way for temptation and the violation of higher claims.[32]

September 18

THE LIGHT OF HEALTH REFORM

Beloved, I wish above all things that thou mayest prosper and be in health, even as thy soul prospereth. 3 John 2.

The light God has given on health reform is for our salvation and the salvation of the world. Men and women should be informed in regard to the human habitation, fitted up by our Creator as His dwelling place, and over which He desires us to be faithful stewards. . . . Our bodies are wonderfully made, and the Lord requires us to keep them in order. All are under obligation to Him to keep the human structure in a healthful, wholesome condition, that every muscle, every organ, may be used in the service of God. . . . God, who formed the wonderful structure of the body, will take special care to keep it in order, if men cooperate, instead of working at cross-purposes, with Him.

These grand truths must be given to the world. We must reach the people where they are, and by example and precept lead them to see the beauties of the better way. The world is in sad need of instruction along these lines. The time has come when each soul must be staunch and true to every ray of light God has given, and begin in earnest to give this gospel of health to the people. We shall have strength and power to do this if we practice these truths in our own lives. . . .

Those who are enjoying the precious blessings which come to them through obeying this message of mercy will do all in their power that others may share the same blessings. But we may rest assured that Satan will do all in his power to prevent anything like a message of reform from being given to the world at this time. Shall God's people be found on the enemy's side, either by failing to heed it themselves, or by neglecting to give it to others? "He that is not with me is against me; and he that gathereth not with me scattereth abroad." Matt. 12:30. If we would be safe, we must not fail to know on whose side we stand.[33]

God desires His light bearers ever to keep a high standard before them. By precept and example they must hold this perfect standard high above Satan's false standard.[34]

A PERFECTED PEOPLE

Whether therefore ye eat, or drink, or whatsoever ye do, do all to the glory of God. 1 Cor. 10:31.

With an eye single to the glory of God, we should give careful, thoughtful attention to the matter of our eating and drinking. We need divine guidance, even in our commonest habits of everyday life, that there may be no little leaks which will consume means unnecessarily, simply for the gratification of perverted appetites. In the New Testament not one of God's requirements loses its binding force, or relaxes in the least its obligation to be fulfilled. . . . Instead of the requirements of God being relaxed in the New Testament, the lines are drawn closer, and duty is more distinctly defined. The apostle says, "Whatsoever ye do," even in the matter of eating and drinking, "do all to the glory of God." The question may be asked, "May I not do what I like with myself? Am I never to have my own way? Is not my body my own?" You may have your own way, but it will be at the loss of your soul, or you may have God's way and live to a purpose in this world, and in the world to come have life everlasting.[35]

Those who have received instruction regarding the evils of the use of flesh foods, tea and coffee, and rich and unhealthful food preparations, and who are determined to make a covenant with God by sacrifice, will not continue to indulge their appetite for food that they know to be unhealthful. God demands that the appetites be cleansed, and that self-denial be practiced in regard to those things which are not good. This is a work that will have to be done before His people can stand before Him a perfected people. . . . Those who claim to believe in health reform, and yet work counter to its principles in the daily life practice, are hurting their own souls and are leaving wrong impressions upon the minds of believers and unbelievers.[36]

Do not misuse or abuse any portion of your God-given powers, physical, mental, or moral. All your habits are to be brought under the control of a mind that is itself under the control of God.[37]

THE REWARD OF TEMPERATE HABITS

But Daniel purposed in his heart that he would not defile himself with the portion of the king's meat, nor with the wine which he drank. Dan. 1:8.

Inspiration has recorded the history of Daniel and his companions as a shining example for the youth of all succeeding ages. . . . Those who would preserve their powers unimpaired for the service of God must observe strict temperance in the use of all His bounties, as well as total abstinence from every injurious or debasing indulgence.

The youth are surrounded by allurements addressed to the appetite. . . . Those who, like Daniel, refuse to defile themselves, will reap the reward of their temperate habits. With their greater physical stamina and increased power of endurance, they have a bank of deposit upon which to draw in case of emergency.

Right physical habits promote mental superiority. Intellectual power, physical strength, and longevity, depend upon immutable laws. There is no happen-so, no chance, about this matter. The higher powers will not interfere to preserve men from the consequences of the violation of nature's laws.[38]

The question with every youth . . . should be, Shall I consult my inclination, and indulge my appetite, or shall I follow the dictates of conscience, and keep my head clear and preserve my physical powers by abstaining from every practice that would bring weakness upon them? Shall I fall a prey to the customs of the world, . . . or shall I separate myself from every custom that is debasing in its results? Shall I not honor God, rather than please the world? . . .

Daniel and his fellows realized that principle was at stake, and that they could afford to make no compromise with the tempter. The light and truth reflected from the throne of God were dearer to them than any honor that men could bestow. It is the privilege of the young people of today to be as firm and true, as modest and successful, as were the Jewish youths in the kingdom of Babylon. . . . God honored Daniel, and He will honor every youth who takes the course that Daniel took in honoring God.[39]

A SOUND MIND IN A SOUND BODY

But I keep under my body, and bring it into subjection: lest that by any means, when I have preached to others, I myself should be a castaway. 1 Cor. 9:27.

Whatever detracts from physical vigor weakens mental effort. Hence, every practice unfavorable to the health of the body should be resolutely shunned. . . . We cannot maintain consecration to God, and yet injure our health by the willful indulgence of a wrong habit. Self-denial is one of the conditions, not only of admission into the service of Christ but of continuance therein. . . .

Yet how many who call themselves Christians are unwilling to exercise self-denial, even for Christ's sake. How often the love for some pernicious indulgence is stronger than the desire for a sound mind in a sound body! Precious hours of probation are spent, God-given means squandered, to please the eye or to gratify the appetite. . . .

None need fail in this work of self-renunciation. God will give help to every earnest seeker. . . . If we sincerely seek His grace, our life will correspond with our profession of faith. . . . He knows whether our hearts are wholly devoted to His service, or given to the things of the world. We may profess what we will, but unless our life corresponds with our profession, our faith is dead. The rule given by the apostle Paul is the only safe rule for our guidance in all the affairs of life. "Whether . . . ye eat, or drink, or whatsoever ye do, do all to the glory of God." 1 Cor. 10:31. In the selection of our food, we should not seek merely to please the taste, but should choose that which is most healthful. In dress, we should seek that which is simple, comfortable, convenient, and appropriate.[40]

He who will observe simplicity in all his habits, restricting the appetite and controlling the passions, may preserve his mental powers strong, active, and vigorous, quick to perceive everything which demands thought or action, keen to discriminate between the holy and the unholy, and ready to engage in every enterprise for the glory of God and the benefit of humanity.[41]

A DISTINCTION IN DRESS

In like manner also, that women adorn themselves in modest apparel, with shamefacedness and sobriety; not with broided hair, or gold, or pearls, or costly array; but (which becometh women professing godliness) with good works. 1 Tim. 2:9, 10.

The children of Israel . . . were commanded to have a simple ribbon of blue in the border of their garments, to distinguish them from the nations around them, and to signify that they were God's peculiar people. [See Num. 15:39, 40.] The people of God are not now required to have a special mark placed upon their garments. But in the New Testament we are often referred to ancient Israel for examples. If God gave such definite directions to His ancient people in regard to their dress, will not the dress of His people in this age come under His notice? Should there not be in their dress a distinction from that of the world? Should not the people of God, who are His peculiar treasure, seek even in their dress to glorify God? And should they not be examples in point of dress, and by their simple style rebuke the pride, vanity, and extravagance of worldly, pleasure-loving professors? God requires this of His people. Pride is rebuked in His Word.[42]

We must know more of Jesus and His love than of the fashions of the world. In the name of my Master, I call upon the youth to study the example of Christ, When you wish to make an article, you carefully study the pattern, that you may reproduce it as nearly as possible. Now set to work to copy the divine Exemplar. . . . You cannot be like Jesus, and cherish pride in your heart. . . .

Of how little value are gold or pearls or costly array, in comparison with the meekness and loveliness of Christ. Natural loveliness consists in symmetry, or the harmonious proportion of parts, each with the other; but spiritual loveliness consists in the harmony or likeness of our souls to Jesus. This will make its possessor more precious than fine gold, even the golden wedge of Ophir. The grace of Christ is indeed a priceless adornment. It elevates and ennobles its possessor, and reflects beams of glory upon others, attracting them also to the Source of light and blessing.[43]

THE CHARM OF SIMPLICITY

For all that is in the world, the lust of the flesh, and the lust of the eyes, and the pride of life, is not of the Father, but is of the world. 1 John 2:16.

Pride of dress is not a small matter, but a serious evil. It causes time, thought, and money to be spent in the decoration of the body, while the culture of the heavenly graces is neglected. Precious hours that our Saviour has exhorted us to devote to prayer and the study of the Scriptures are given to an unnecessary preparation of apparel for outward display.[44]

Satan stands in the background, devising the fashions which lead to extravagance in the outlay of means. In forming the fashions of the day, he has a fixed purpose. He knows that time and money which are devoted to meet the demands of fashion will not be used for higher, holier objects. Precious time is wasted in keeping pace with everchanging and never-satisfying fashions. No sooner is one style introduced than new styles are devised, and then, in order for fashionable persons to remain fashionable, the dress must be re-modeled. Thus professing Christians, with divided hearts, waste their time, giving to the world nearly all their energies. . . .

Correct taste in dress is not to be despised or condemned. . . . Nothing is gained in trying to save means by purchasing cheap fabrics. Let the clothing be plain and neat, without extravagance or display.

Young ladies who break away from slavery to fashion will be or-naments in society. The one who is simple and unpretending in her dress and in her manners shows that she understands that a true lady is characterized by moral worth. How charming, how interest-ing, is simplicity in dress, which in its comeliness can be compared with the flowers of the field! . . .

Those who practice simplicity in dress have time to visit the af-flicted, and are better prepared to pray with and for them. On every Christian man and woman rests the solemn duty of regulating and contracting personal expenses, that by so doing they may be able to help the needy, feed the hungry, and clothe the naked.[45]

A MARK OF CHRISTIAN WOMANHOOD

Whose adorning let it not be that outward adorning of plaiting the hair, and of wearing of gold, or putting on of apparel; but let it be the hidden man of the heart, in that which is not corruptible, even the ornament of a meek and quiet spirit, which is in the sight of God of great price. 1 Peter 3:3, 4.

Lovers of fashion may claim to be followers of Christ, but their dress and conversation show what occupies the mind and engages the affections. The outside appearance is an index to the heart. True refinement does not find satisfaction in the adorning of the body for display. A modest, godly woman will dress modestly. Simplicity of apparel always makes a sensible woman appear to the best advantage. A refined, cultured mind will be revealed in the choice of simple and appropriate attire. In the sanctified heart there is no place for thoughts of needless adornment.[46]

There is an ornament that will never perish, that will promote the happiness of all around us in this life, and will shine with undimmed luster in the immortal future. It is the adorning of a meek and lowly spirit. God has bidden us wear the richest dress upon the soul.[47]

The inward adorning of a meek and quiet spirit is priceless. In the life of the true Christian the outward adorning is always in harmony with the inward peace and holiness. . . . Self-denial and sacrifice will mark the Christian's life. Evidence that the taste is converted will be seen in the dress of all who walk in the path cast up for the ransomed of the Lord.

It is right to love beauty and to desire it; but God desires us to love and seek first the highest beauty, that which is imperishable. No outward adorning can compare in value or loveliness with that "meek and quiet spirit," the "fine linen, white and clean" (Rev. 19:14), which all the holy ones of earth will wear. This apparel will make them beautiful and beloved here, and will hereafter be their badge of admission to the palace of the King. His promise is, "They shall walk with me in white: for they are worthy." Rev. 3:4.[48]

THE BEAUTY OF CHRISTLIKENESS

Shewing all good fidelity; that they may adorn the doctrine of God our Saviour in all things. Titus 2:10.

Everyone who names the name of Christ is to adorn the doctrine of Christ our Saviour by a well-ordered life and a godly conversation, even the ornament of a meek and quiet spirit. . . . Possessing this, you will have favor both with God and with men.

Words spoken hastily wound and bruise souls, and the deepest wound is made upon the soul of the speaker. Christ's gift, the ornament of a meek and quiet spirit, is authoritatively declared by Him who can make no mistake to be of great price. We must each find out its worth for ourselves by seeking it from God. However men may estimate us, if we wear this ornament, we bear the sign of our discipleship with Christ. We are esteemed by the Most High; for the ornament we wear is in His sight of great price. This precious gem is to be sought for. . . .

To every soul things will come to provoke, to stir up anger, and if you are not under the full control of God, you will be provoked when these things come. But the meekness of Christ calms the ruffled spirit, controls the tongue, and brings the whole being into subjection to God. Thus we learn how to bear with the censure of others. We shall be misjudged, but the precious ornament of a meek and quiet spirit teaches us how to bear, how to have pity for those who utter hasty, unadvised words. Any unpleasant spirit displayed is sure to arouse the demon of passion in unguarded hearts. Unholy anger need not to be strengthened, but bridled. It is a spark which will set on fire untamed human nature. Avoid speaking words which will stir up strife. Rather suffer wrong than do wrong. God requires every one of His followers, as far as is possible, to live peaceably with all men. . . .

We must be Christlike. Let us strive to make our lives what Christ designs them to be, full of the fragrance of love to God and our fellow men, full of Christ's own divine Spirit, full of holy aspirations toward God, rich in the beauty of Christlikeness.[49]

CONSECRATED EYES

The heart of him that hath understanding seeketh knowledge: but the mouth of fools feedeth on foolishness. Prov. 15:14.

Many do not earnestly seek to understand the lessons found in God's Word. They lay aside the Bible, and allow their minds to become engrossed with the cheap reading found in books of fiction, newspapers, and magazines.[50]

The pernicious practice of story reading is one of the means employed by Satan to destroy souls. The mind that is occupied with exciting stories loses all relish for solid reading. . . . I am acquainted with many sad examples of the evil effects of this baneful practice. . . . The more they indulged the appetite for this kind of mental food, the greater was the demand. The imagination constantly craved its accustomed stimulus, as the inebriate longs for his wine or tobacco. Their mental and moral powers were weakened and perverted. They lost their interest in the Scriptures, and their relish for prayer; and they were as truly ruined, mentally and spiritually, as is the liquor drinker or the tobacco devotee. Novel readers are mental inebriates; and they need to sign a pledge of total abstinence as verily as does the victim of any other form of intemperance.[51]

God has given to His people the choicest reading matter. Let the Word of God find a place in every room in the house. Keep the Bible, the bread of life, in plain sight. . . . Keep choice, elevating literature ever before the members of the family.[52]

The reading of God's Word does not fascinate the imagination and inflame the passions, like the fictions of a storybook, but it softens and soothes the heart, and elevates and sanctifies the affections.[53]

It is the privilege of the youth to say, "The Lord has given me my sight and hearing for His glory. I will close my ears to that which is foolish and cheap. I will read that Word that will fit me for a place in the home Christ is preparing for those who have sanctified their souls by obedience to the truth. My voice shall proclaim the glory of God; every power of my being shall be consecrated to God."[54]

BE CAREFUL WHAT YOU READ

For the Lord giveth wisdom: out of his mouth cometh knowledge and understanding. He layeth up sound wisdom for the righteous: he is a buckler to them that walk uprightly. Prov. 2:6, 7.

Age after age the curiosity of men has led them to seek for the tree of knowledge; and often they think they are plucking fruit most essential, when, like Solomon in his research, they find it altogether vanity and nothingness in comparison with the science of true holiness.[55]

Books from the pens of infidels should have no place in the libraries of those who would serve God. They will make better kindling material for your stove than food for the mind. Infidel books have been a cause of ruin to many souls. Men have studied these books of Satan's inspiration, and they have become confused in regard to what was truth. Satan stands at the side of him who opens an infidel book, and he will educate the mind that peruses such literature, and so bewitch the soul that it will be almost impossible to break the infatuation. Let no believer flatter himself that his mountain standeth sure, and that he will never be moved away from his position of faith.[56]

We are surrounded by unbelief. The very atmosphere seems charged with it; and only by constant effort can we resist its power. Those who value their soul's salvation should shun infidel writings as they would shun the leprosy.

To the youth I would say, Be careful what you read. So long as the mind is directed into wrong channels by an improper course of reading, it is impossible for you to make the truth of God the constant subject of meditation. If there was ever a time when a knowledge of the Scriptures was more important than at any other, that time is the present. I appeal to old and young, Make the Bible your textbook. Here you will find the true standard of character.[57]

Do not devote the precious talent of sight to reading that which . . . will not benefit you. . . . The powers of mind and soul and body are to be sanctified to the Lord Jesus, who has bought you with His blood.[58]

CHAFF OR WHEAT?

My son, attend to my words; incline thine ear unto my sayings. Let them not depart from thine eyes; keep them in the midst of thine heart. For they are life unto those that find them, and health to all their flesh. Prov. 4:20-22.

Light and truth are within the reach of all, . . . but if they do not set their minds to searching God's Word, Satan will find chaff to fill their minds, leaving no room for the growth of the precious seed of truth. . . . We are surrounded with temptations so disguised that they allure while they taint and corrupt the soul.[59]

The youth of our cities breathe in the tainted, polluted atmosphere of crime. . . . They are educated in crime by reading the stories which fill the popular publications of the day. Having no regard for the right because it is right, as they read stories of theft, murder, and every other species of crime, they are led to devise plans by which they could improve upon the criminals' methods, and escape detection. Thus these foul publications assist in perfecting the education of the youth in the way that leads to perdition.[60]

It is a great evil to bring these trashy magazines into the family, and yet many parents are asleep to this peril. They do not know what kind of food is being supplied to the minds of their children. The food that is given to the mind should be pure and wholesome. God calls upon His people to turn away from the brackish streams of the valley, and drink from the pure streams of Lebanon. A study of God's Word, which is eternal life to the receiver, would invigorate and strengthen the mind; but too often the grace of Christ finds the right of way obstructed by the mass of rubbish which has been allowed to accumulate in the mind. The mind is not kept hungry for the blessed Word, which must be eaten in order for the thoughts to be pure and holy. . . .

To those who are tempted to indulge in trashy reading I would say, Read your Bible. "Search the scriptures," Christ commanded; "for in them ye think ye have eternal life: and they are they which testify of me." John 5:39. Obedience to the Word of God is our only safety.[61]

WALKING WITH GOD
IN A CORRUPT WORLD

And Enoch walked with God: and he was not; for God took him.
Gen. 5:24.

Enoch's life and character, which were so holy that he was translated to heaven without seeing death, represent what the lives and characters of all must be, if like Enoch, they are to be translated when Christ shall come. His life was what the life of every individual may be if he closely connects with God. We should remember that Enoch was surrounded with influences so depraved that God brought a flood of waters on the world to destroy its inhabitants for their corruption. . . .

When Christ shall come, our vile bodies are to be changed, and made like His glorious body; but the vile character will not be made holy then. The transformation of character must take place before His coming. Our natures must be pure and holy; we must have the mind of Christ, that He may behold with pleasure His image reflected upon our souls. . . .

Joseph preserved his integrity when surrounded by idolaters in Egypt, in the midst of sin and blasphemy and corrupting influences. When tempted to turn from the path of virtue, his answer was, "How can I do this great wickedness, and sin against God?" Gen. 39:9. Enoch, Joseph, and Daniel depended upon a strength that was infinite. This is the only course of safety for Christians to pursue in our day. . . .

The lives of these marked men were hid with Christ in God. They were loyal to God amidst infidelity, pure amidst depravity, devout and fervent when brought in contact with atheism and idolatry. By faith they gathered to themselves only those properties which are favorable to the development of pure and holy characters. Thus may it be with us; whatever our position, however repulsive or fascinating our surroundings, faith can reach above it all and find the Holy Spirit.

The spirit which Enoch, Joseph, and Daniel possessed, we may have. We may draw from the same source of strength, and realize the same power of self-control; and the same graces may shine out in our lives.[62]

YOUTH TO STAND UP FOR CHRIST

*For whosoever shall be ashamed of me and of my words, of him
shall the Son of man be ashamed, when he shall come in his own
glory, and in his Father's, and of the holy angels. Luke 9:26.*

Always stand up for Christ. In word, in spirit, in action, be His
witness. He loves you, and He wants to impart to you His rich grace,
that you may impart this to others. . . . Christ has purchased you
with His own blood. Then, everywhere, at all times and under all
circumstances, stand up for Jesus. Remember that thus you will exert
the very best influence upon all with whom you associate. . . .

It is your privilege ever to grow in grace, advancing in the knowledge and love of God, if you maintain the sweet communion with
Christ it is your privilege to enjoy. In the simplicity of humble faith ask
the Lord to open your understanding, that you may discern and appreciate the precious things of His Word. Thus you may grow in grace,
grow in simple, trusting faith. Then your light will shine forth to all with
whom you associate. Keep your mind fixed upon the Saviour. . . .

Be sure that your spiritual life does not become poor, sickly, inefficient. There are many who have need of the words and example
of a Christian. Weakness and indecision provoke the assaults of the
enemy, and any one who fails to increase in spiritual growth, in a
knowledge of truth and righteousness, will frequently be overcome
by the enemy.[63]

Let your countenance reflect the joy of the Lord. Speak of His
goodness and tell of His power. Then your light will shine more and
more distinctly. Above your trials and disappointments will be revealed the reflection of a pure, healthy religious life.[64]

There is no limit to the influence of the human agent who wears
the yoke with Christ. Daily he studies the life of Christ and conforms
his life to the divine pattern. . . . It is by the manifestation of the
spirit of Christ in our words and actions that the world takes knowledge of us that we have been with Jesus, that we are the children of
God. The true nature of our religion is . . . in the gentle spirit, the
kindness, the peace which we manifest.[65]

October 1

DON'T STARVE YOUR SOUL!

And the cares of this world, and the deceitfulness of riches, and the lusts of other things entering in, choke the word, and it becometh unfruitful. Mark 4:19.

We must beware that we do not become overburdened even with what seem the necessary cares of life, so that we are unable to do the most essential work. . . . The largest share of the thoughts and the busy activities that engage hands and hearts, are given to selfish, personal, earthly interests. These are allowed to become so engrossing as to prevent attention to the things of eternity. The soul is left to starve for want of nourishment. Mind and body become worn out by protracted hours of application to worldly things. This is just as Satan designed it should be. All the freshness and vigor of the mind, all the keen thought, is given to the world, and God has the feeble, distracted thought, the fruit of a wearied and worried mind. The things of the highest consequence, which pertain to the eternal peace, are made subordinate to the common concerns of life, and God is robbed every day of service which would strengthen spirituality, lifting the thoughts heavenward, and bringing the soul into communion with God and holy angels.[1]

We are not to allow the things of this world so to absorb the attention that mind and body are completely engrossed. Thus those around us are robbed of the kindly words and deeds that would help them in the upward way. The channel of light is clogged with worldly matters. The grace that Christ is longing to impart, He cannot bestow. Many are coming to have less and less strength to impart to others, because they do not receive power from the Source of all power. God calls upon them to separate from the things which corrode the mind and spoil the religious experience.[2]

All are pressed with urgent cares, burdens, and duties; but the greater the pressure upon you, the heavier the burdens you have to bear, the greater your need of divine aid. Jesus will be your helper. You need constantly the light of life to lighten your pathway, and then its divine rays will reflect upon others.[3]

THE BETTER PART

And Jesus answered and said unto her, Martha, Martha, thou art careful and troubled about many things: but one thing is needful: and Mary hath chosen that good part, which shall not be taken away from her. Luke 10:41, 42.

This reproof of Christ comes to many Marthas in our time. They lose much spiritual and divine knowledge that would make them wise unto salvation, through their bustling activity to do so much in temporal things, to shower favors upon those whom they love. If they would preserve simplicity in all their preparations, and improve their precious opportunities to obtain a better knowledge of God's will and be doers of His words, they would save much irritability and would drink of the perpetual Fountain of life. . . .

Martha . . . was so anxious for all due honor to be given to Christ that in her active preparations in provision of food, she lost the most precious, golden moments of listening to instruction from His divine lips. Mary sat at His feet to catch every word. She regarded this of highest importance. This offended Martha, and she asked the Lord Jesus if He did not care that she served alone, while Mary shunned these responsibilities. Said Jesus, Martha, Mary hath chosen the better part, which shall never be taken from her. What was that better part? To learn of Jesus, to appreciate His words. In giving attention to the words which fell from His lips, she was showing her love for her Saviour. . . .

Every word from the lips of Jesus was precious. It was joy to Him to see Mary appreciate His instruction. The more frequently the words of Christ are heard the more deeply do they influence the mind, the better they are understood, and the more easily and perfectly are they obeyed.

This spirit that is ever ready to make great outward display for our friends is a device of the enemy. . . .

He [Christ] requires His followers—the purchase of His blood—to leave all the follies and vanities and tainting corruptions of the world out of their lives. . . . Let the impression, "Lo, God is here," solemnize every mind and make glad every soul.[4]

YOUTHFUL ZEAL AND COURAGE NEEDED

I have written unto you, young men, because ye are strong, and the word of God abideth in you, and ye have overcome the wicked one. 1 John 2:14.

The work of God is in need of youthful ardor, zeal, and courage. Mental and physical vigor are essential for the advancement of the cause of God. To plan with clear mind and execute with courageous hand demand fresh and uncrippled energies. In order that the work may be forwarded in all its branches, God calls for youthful ardor. Young men and young women are invited to give Him the strength of their youth, that through the exercise of their God-given powers, through healthful thought and vigorous action, they may bring glory to God and salvation to men. God calls upon you, young men, to make the most of the powers entrusted to you. Cultivate the habit of doing your best in everything you undertake. God is your Master, and you are His employed servants. . . .

You are ever to be learning in the school of Christ; you are to bring your entrusted capital of physical and mental energy into your work. . . . Mental effort will become easier and more satisfactory as you put yourselves to the task of understanding the deep things of God. . . .

You can rally the mind's best powers, and with a sense of your accountability to God, you can do your best, and you will not cease to advance, and to conquer difficulties. Do not settle down in slothful ease, making no special effort to accomplish your work. Make a choice of some part in the large vineyard of the Master, and do a work that will require the exercise of tact and talent.[5]

I make an appeal to the youthful disciples of Christ to arouse, no longer to indulge in pleasure seeking, in self-love and ease; no longer be controlled by inclination, and by the lusts of the carnal heart. . . .

My prayer to God is that the converting power of His Holy Spirit may come upon our youth, that they may become working agents to win scores of youth to Jesus Christ, that they may be among the number who shall be accounted wise, who shall "shine as the brightness of the firmament," and "as the stars for ever and ever." Dan. 12:3.[6]

ARE WE GUILTY?

Love not the world, neither the things that are in the world. If any man love the world, the love of the Father is not in him. 1 John 2:15.

It is an alarming fact that the love of the world predominates in the minds of the young. They decidedly love the world and the things that are in the world, and for this very reason the love of God finds no room in their hearts. Their pleasures are found in the world, and in the things of the world, and they are strangers to the Father and the graces of His Spirit. Frivolity and fashion, and empty, vain talking and laughing, characterize the life of the youth generally, and God is dishonored. . . .

Satan is gratified to have the attention of youth attracted by anything to divert their minds from God. . . . They are not aware that the heavenly Artist is taking cognizance of every act, every word, . . . and that even the thoughts and intents of the heart stand faithfully delineated. . . . Those vain, frivolous words are all written in the book. Those false words are written. Those deceptive acts, with the motives concealed from human eyes, but discerned by the all-seeing eye of Jehovah, are all written in living characters. Every selfish act is exposed. The young generally conduct themselves as though the precious hours of probation, while mercy lingers, were one grand holiday, and that they are placed in this world simply for their own amusement.[7]

Words and acts testify plainly what is in the heart. If vanity and pride, love of self and love of dress, fill the heart, the conversation will be upon the fashions, the dress, and the appearance, but not upon Christ or the kingdom of heaven. If envious feelings dwell in the heart, the same will be manifested in words and acts. . . .

Some dwell upon what they shall eat and drink and wherewithal they shall be clothed. Their hearts are filled with these thoughts, and they flow out from the abundance of the heart, as though these things were their grand aim in life, their highest attainment. They forget the words of Christ, "Seek ye first the kingdom of God, and his righteousness; and all these things shall be added unto you." Matt. 6:33.[8]

THE ONLY SAFE AMUSEMENTS

They shall be abundantly satisfied with the fatness of thy house; and thou shalt make them drink of the river of thy pleasures. Ps. 36:8.

The enemy seeks in many ways to draw our minds from the study of the Word. Many he leads to seek for satisfaction in amusements and pleasures that seem desirable to the carnal heart. But the true children of God are not seeking their happiness in this world; they seek for the lasting joys of a home in the eternal city, where Christ dwells, and where the redeemed shall receive the rewards of obedience to the requirements of God. These do not desire the transitory, cheap amusements of this life, but the enduring bliss of heaven.

God has entrusted men and women with great powers—powers that He would have to be devoted to His service; and precious is the light that comes to every one who faithfully uses his talents for the glory of God. We should endeavor to have our minds in that condition where we can receive the impressions of the Holy Spirit. But they cannot receive increased light who allow their thoughts to run constantly upon frivolous things. The mind should be stored with heavenly treasure, with food that will enable us to grow spiritually, and thus prepare us for a holy heaven. . . .

There are many ways in which we may help our associates, if we will give our minds to it. But it fills me with sorrow when I see plans laid for amusement and self-gratification. As these occupy the mind, there is no opportunity for the precious truth of God to take possession of the soul. When I see those whose interests are given to the amusements of the world, how I wish that they might be converted. Then they would see where they could help others, instead of devoting their time and energy to self-gratification. They would find opportunity for speaking words that would encourage, and would bring light and joy to souls in need of such help.[9]

The only safe amusements are such as will not banish serious and religious thoughts; the only safe places of resort are those to which we can take Jesus with us.[10]

October 6

BREAKING THE WORLD'S ENCHANTMENT

And the world passeth away, and the lust thereof: but he that doeth the will of God abideth for ever. 1 John 2:17.

The lessons of Christ are of that character to show the relative importance of heaven and earth. He presents before the mind's eye that the claims of heaven are first in importance. God's claims are supreme. He demands the whole heart, mind, might, and strength. Earthly things He assigns their place, to be subordinate to the eternal interests.

The temptations of Satan present earthly things and make them all-absorbing and attractive, so that the heavenly realities are eclipsed and the attachment to the world made first; and this has become so great a power that Omnipotence alone can dislodge it. Satan's work is to chain the senses to this world. Christ came to break the satanic enchantment, counterwork the work of Satan, and charm the mind away from the earthly to the heavenly. He alone is able to break the enchantment. . . . A few years and the world and all its glory, which has through the bewitching power of the great deceiver become an object of worship, are to be burned, with all the embellishments of the art of man. Then what will be found to compensate for the loss of the human soul?

The Prince of life calls the attention to the eternal world. . . . He would have the infinite grandeur of the future hold the attraction of human minds, and the present world take its subordinate place in the affections. He sets in order things that Satan has transposed. Having taken the world from the throne where it has become a ruling power and worshiped as a god, He assigns it its proper place. . . .

With eternal realities in view we will habitually cultivate thoughts of the presence of God. This will be a shield against the incoming of the enemy; it will give strength and assurance, and lift the soul above fear. Breathing in the atmosphere of heaven, we will not be breathing the malaria of the world. We will not remain in the darkened cellar, but come up into the upper chambers where every window that looks toward heaven is open and catches the bright beams of the Sun of Righteousness.[11]

285

FIRST THINGS FIRST

Therefore take no thought, saying, What shall we eat? or, What shall we drink? or, Wherewithal shall we be clothed? Matt. 6:31.

The Lord would not have any one of us be presumptuous, care not for health, and make no provision whatever for a sustenance; but when He sees the world taking all the thoughts and absorbing all the affections, He sees that eternal realities are lost sight of. He would correct this evil, which is the work of Satan. The mind, which should be trained to high, elevated contemplation of eternal realities, becomes common, bearing the image of the earthly. Jesus comes to present the advantages and beautiful imagery of the heavenly, that the attractions of heaven shall become familiar to the thoughts, and memory's hall be hung with pictures of celestial and eternal loveliness.

He sees the chambers of the mind filled with those things which defile. He places God before them as the center. . . . He passes through the market places, where everything is full of activity and bustle, and the voice of the traders is heard. The lessons He gives in the dense crowd that gathers to listen to His words are a warning from heaven like the trump of God to break the spell of infatuation. "What shall it profit a man, if he shall gain the whole world, and lose his own soul? Or what shall he give in exchange for his soul?" Mark 8:36, 37.

The great Teacher gives man a view of the future world. He brings it, with its attractive possessions, within the range of his vision. . . . He presents the actual claims of God and heaven. If He can fasten the mind upon the future life and its blessedness, in comparison with the temporal concerns of this world, the striking contrast is deeply impressed upon the mind, absorbing the heart and soul and the whole being. He thus removes the things of time and sense from the affections where they have had the supremacy, and gives them their place as subordinate to the higher and eternal realities. He invests life with the highest responsibilities. He shows man that he must live to a purpose, separating from all life's vanities.[12]

SUBJECT TO GOD'S CALL

And he said to them all, If any man will come after me, let him deny himself, and take up his cross daily, and follow me. Luke 9:23.

Genuine self-denial will be practiced by all who follow Christ. Judas undertook to follow Christ, and at the same time to carry out his selfish, covetous plans. He had the same privileges as had the other disciples. He had the same privileges of hearing the lessons of Christ, which plainly presented practical godliness; but he was not always pleased with the plain truth. It cut him, and instead of taking up personal labor with Judas Iscariot, he found fault with the words and works of Christ, and criticized His plain teachings. Instead of being transformed in character, he was cultivating self-love, self-esteem, and the love of money.[13]

To live for self is to perish. Covetousness, the desire of benefit for self's sake, cuts the soul off from life. It is the spirit of Satan to get, to draw to self. It is the spirit of Christ to give, to sacrifice self for the good of others.[14]

There can be no self-seeking in the life of him who follows the Saviour. The true Christian banishes all selfishness from his heart. How can he live for self as he thinks of Christ hanging on the cross, giving His life for the life of the world? In your behalf Jesus died a death of shame. Are you willing to consecrate yourself to His service? to hold yourself ready to be or to do anything He may require? Are you willing to put self aside, and speak a word of warning to the companion you see yielding to Satan's temptations? Are you willing to sacrifice some of your plans for the sake of trying to lead him in safe paths? Many youth are in peril who might be saved if Christians would manifest toward them a loving, unselfish interest. . . .

The true Christian works unselfishly and untiringly for the Master. He does not seek ease or self-gratification, but holds all, even life itself, subject to God's call. And to him are spoken the words, "He that loseth his life for my sake shall find it." Matt. 10:39.[15]

HEAVEN CHEAP AT ANY PRICE

And whosoever doth not bear his cross, and come after me, cannot be my disciple. Luke 14:27.

It is too true that the great mass who possess ability and talent do not choose to travel the Christian road. Are their talent and ability too precious to devote to the Giver, the Lord of heaven and earth? . . .

Many would be followers of Christ if He would come down from the cross and appear to them in such a manner as they desire. If He would come with riches and pleasure, many would receive Him gladly and would be in haste to crown Him Lord of all. If He would only lay aside His humiliation and sufferings and cry, "If any man will come after Me, let him please himself and enjoy the world and he shall be My disciple," multitudes would believe on Him.

But the blessed Jesus will come to us in no other character than the meek and lowly Crucified One. We must partake of His self-denial and suffering here if we would take the crown hereafter. . . .

The Word of God has not widened the narrow way, and if the multitude have found a path where they can wear a form of godliness and not bear the cross or suffer tribulation, they have found a way where our Saviour did not walk and they follow another example than that which Christ set before us. Is it not enough that Jesus left the felicity and glory of heaven, endured a life of poverty and deep affliction, and died a cruel, shameful death to provide for us the joys of holiness and heaven? And can it be that we, the worthless objects of so great a condescension and love, will seek after a better portion in this life than was given to our Redeemer?[16]

How easy would be the way to heaven if there was no self-denial or cross! How worldlings would rush in the way, and hypocrites would travel in it without number! Thank God for the cross, the self-denial. The ignominy and shame our Saviour endured for us is none too humiliating for those saved by the purchase of His blood. Heaven will indeed be cheap enough.[17]

TALENTS FOR EVERYONE

For the kingdom of heaven is as a man travelling into a far country, who called his own servants, and delivered unto them his goods. And unto one he gave five talents, to another two, and to another one; to every man according to his several ability; and straightway took his journey. Matt. 25:14, 15.

God has not given talents to merely a chosen few, but to everyone He has committed some peculiar gift to be used in His service. Many to whom the Lord has given precious talents have refused to employ them for the advancement of the kingdom of God; nevertheless, they are under obligation to God for their use of His gifts. Everyone, whether serving God or pleasing himself, is a possessor of some trust, whose proper use will bring glory to God and whose perverted use will rob the Giver. . . .

The human family is composed of responsible moral agents, and from the highest and most gifted to the lowest and most obscure, all are invested with the goods of heaven. Time is an entrusted gift of God, and is to be diligently employed in the service of Christ. Influence is a gift of God, and is to be exerted for the forwarding of the highest, noblest purposes. . . . Intellect is an entrusted talent. Sympathy and affection are talents to be sacredly guarded and improved, that we may render service to Him whose purchased possession we are.

All that we are or can be belongs to God. Education, discipline, and skill in every line should be used for Him. The capital is His, and the improvement is the usury that rightfully belongs to the Master. Whether the amount entrusted is large or small, the Lord requires that His householders do their best. It is not the amount entrusted or the improvement made that brings to men the approbation of Heaven, but it is the faithfulness, the loyalty to God, the loving service rendered, that brings the divine benediction, "Well done, good and faithful servant, thou hast been faithful over a few things, I will make thee ruler over many things: enter thou into the joy of thy lord." Verse 23. This reward of joy does not wait until our entrance into the city of God, but the faithful servant has a foretaste of it even in this life.[18]

HOW ARE YOU USING *YOUR* TALENTS?

Then he that had received the five talents went and traded with the same, and made them other five talents. And likewise he that had received two, he also gained other two. But he that had received one went and digged in the earth, and hid his Lord's money. Matt. 25:16-18.

The knowledge of the truth is altogether too precious to be hoarded up, and bound about, and hid in the earth. Even the one talent entrusted by the Master is to be faithfully employed. . . .

God pronounces His blessing upon unselfish, unwearied diligence; and though we may have but one talent, and can make but a small investment, yet God will make the effort fruitful in results. The man who works in faith will realize that his intellect, his affections, his whole power, belongs to God, and he will seek to make diligent use of his powers, and will improve his faculties and talents. But, instead of realizing that all our faculties belong to God, how many are reckless, little thinking that their influence, their cheap, light words, are molding the characters of those with whom they associate, and bringing down their minds to a low level. . . .

The atmosphere that surrounds the soul is fraught with influence for good or evil. . . . It may be full of poison and malaria, or be fragrant and pure and health giving. This moral influence will be according to our connection with Christ or our separation from Him, who is light and life. Those who are united with Christ will realize that He has given them trusts according to their several ability; and, whatever their surroundings, they will consider them favorable for the development of moral character. We are to make the most of every advantage and opportunity. . . . We must train and improve our ability that we may not disappoint our Master, but reach the highest possible standard, and thus influence others to follow in the footsteps of our Example. We may say, "Neither society nor intimate companions must have their ideas of Christian character cheapened by my course of action." . . .

What are you doing with your talents? Are you putting them out to the exchangers?[19]

SPEECH A PRECIOUS TALENT

By thy words thou shalt be justified, and by thy words thou shalt be condemned. Matt. 12:37.

God has given every youth the talent of speech to be improved for Him. This is a most important trust. . . . Let your words be life-giving, pointing those around you to the Saviour. Let them bring sunshine instead of gloom, harmony instead of animosity. Say nothing that you would not be willing to say in the presence of Jesus and the angels. Utter no word that will stir up strife in another heart. However provoked you may feel, restrain the hasty word. If you are Christlike in speech and action, those who associate with you will be blessed by the association. Righteous words and deeds have a more powerful influence for good than all the sermons that can be preached.[20]

Let us guard against speaking words that discourage. Let us resolve never to engage in evilspeaking and backbiting. Let us refuse to serve Satan by implanting seeds of doubt. Let us guard against cherishing unbelief, or expressing it to others. Many, many times I have wished that there might be circulated a pledge containing a solemn promise to speak only those words that are pleasing to God. There is as great need for such a pledge as there is for one against the use of intoxicating liquor. Let us begin to discipline the tongue, remembering always that we can do this only by disciplining the mind, for "out of the abundance of the heart the mouth speaketh." Matt. 12:34.

Through the help that Christ can give, we shall be able to learn to bridle the tongue. Sorely as He was tried on the point of hasty and angry speech, He never once sinned with His lips. With patient calmness He met the sneers, the taunts, and the ridicule of His fellow workers at the carpenter's bench. Instead of retorting angrily, He would begin to sing one of David's beautiful psalms; and His companions, before realizing what they were doing, would unite with Him in the hymn. What a transformation would be wrought in this world if men and women today would follow Christ's example in the use of words![21]

AN INDEX TO CHARACTER

Neither filthiness, nor foolish talking, nor jesting, which are not convenient: but rather giving of thanks. Eph. 5:4.

A man's character may be quite accurately estimated by the nature of his conversation. . . . Those who jest and joke and indulge in cheap conversation place themselves upon a level where Satan can gain access to them. . . . When you associate together, you may be a help and a blessing one to another if you surround yourselves with an influence that is divine. But there are those who have grave defects, which are gaining a deeper hold upon them and which if not overcome will drive the Spirit of God out of the heart. . . . Jesting and joking may please a class of cheap minds, and yet the influence of this kind of conduct is destructive to spirituality. I speak to you as a class and also as individuals: Guard your words. Let sobriety and sound common sense characterize your conversation. Do not trifle with the purity and nobility of your souls by condescending to indulgence in stale jokes, and in cultivating habits of trifling conversation.

The requirement of God is explicit on these points, and presents before you the obligations that rest upon you as children of God. The Word of God says, "Whatsoever ye do in word or deed, do all in the name of the Lord Jesus, giving thanks to God and the Father by him." Col. 3:17.[22]

O that every one of our youth would realize the evil of foolish conversation, and correct the habit of speaking idle words! Let every one who has indulged in this sin repent of it, confess it before God, and put it far from him. In speaking foolish words, you have dishonored the name of Christ; for you have misrepresented Him in character. No word of guile was found in His lips, no word of prevarication or falsehood. The people that are described as making up the one hundred and forty-four thousand, have the Father's name written in their foreheads, and of them it is said: "In their mouth was found no guile: for they are without fault before the throne of God." Rev. 14:5.[23]

October 14

WHEN SILENCE IS ELOQUENCE

He that covereth a transgression seeketh love; but he that repeateth a matter separateth very friends. Prov. 17:9.

The psalmist asks, "Lord, who shall abide in thy tabernacle? who shall dwell in thy holy hill? He that walketh uprightly, and worketh righteousness, and speaketh the truth in his heart. He that backbiteth not with his tongue, nor doeth evil to his neighbour, nor taketh up a reproach against his neighbour." When anyone comes to you with a tale about your neighbor, you should refuse to hear it. You should say to him, "Have you spoken of this matter to the individual concerned?" . . . Tell him he should obey the Bible rule, and go first to his brother, and tell him his fault privately, and in love. If the directions of God were carried out, the floodgates of gossip would be closed.

When your brethren and neighbors come in to see you, talk of the wonderful love of Jesus. Rejoice in His intercession for lost man. Tell your friends of the love that you have for their souls, because they are the purchase of the blood of Christ. God forbid that we should make the pathway of other weary travelers harder by magnifying their errors, and by sitting in judgment upon their actions. God help us, that we may speak words of comfort and hope and courage to cheer the life of the lonely, and discouraged, and erring.[24]

When you are tempted to speak unadvisedly, be on guard. If some one else approaches you with words of criticism regarding one of God's children, turn a deaf ear to every such word. If you are spoken to harshly, never retaliate. Utter not a word. When under provocation, remember that "silence is eloquence." Silence is the greatest rebuke that you can possibly give to a faultfinder or one whose temper is irritated.[25]

It should be our aim to bring all the pleasantness possible into our lives, and to do all the kindness possible to those around us. Kind words are never lost. Jesus records them as if spoken to Himself. Sow the seeds of kindness, of love, and of tenderness, and they will blossom and bear fruit.[26]

WORDS THAT BRING SUNSHINE AND JOY

Let your speech be alway with grace, seasoned with salt, that ye may know how ye ought to answer every man. Col. 4:6.

The talent of speech was given to be used for the benefit of all. Pleasant, cheery words cost no more than unpleasant, moody words. Sharp words wound and bruise the soul. In this life everyone has difficulties with which to wrestle. Everyone meets with grievances and disappointments. Shall we not bring sunshine instead of gloom into the lives of those with whom we come in contact? Shall we not speak words that will help and bless? Such words will be just as verily a blessing to us as to those to whom they are spoken.

Parents, allow no faultfinding in your home. Teach your children to speak pleasant words, words that will bring sunshine and joy. Angels are not attracted to a home where discord reigns. Bring practical godliness into the home. Prepare yourselves and your children for entrance into the city of God. Angels will be your helpers. Satan will tempt you, but do not yield. Do not speak one word of which the enemy can take advantage.[27]

Day by day we are sowing seeds for the future harvest. We cannot be too careful of the seed we sow by our words. Often words are carelessly spoken and forgotten, but these words, for good or ill, will bring forth a harvest. Sow one unkind, harsh word, and this seed, finding soil in the minds of the hearers, will spring up to bear fruit after its kind. Sow one seed in loving, gentle, Christlike words, and it will bring you rich returns. Let us guard ourselves, lest we speak words that are not a blessing, but a curse. If we sow wheat we shall reap wheat; if we sow tares we shall reap tares; and the harvest, whether of wheat or of tares, will be sure and abundant.

"Be not deceived; God is not mocked: for whatsoever a man soweth, that shall he also reap." Gal. 6:7. The harvest is sure. No frost shall blight it, no palmer worm destroy it.

God calls upon His children to guard their words.[28]

WORDS LIKE APPLES OF GOLD

A word fitly spoken is like apples of gold in pictures of silver. Prov. 25:11.

Some are seen to come forth from their daily communion with God clothed with the meekness of Christ. Their words . . . come forth sweetly from their lips. They scatter seeds of love and kindness all along their path, . . . because Christ lives in their heart.[29]

The tongue needs to be educated and disciplined and trained to speak of the glories of heaven, to talk of the matchless love of Jesus.[30]

There are souls who err, and who feel their shame and their folly. They are hungry for words of encouragement. They look upon their mistakes and errors until they are almost driven to desperation. Instead of . . . reproving and condemning and taking away the last ray of hope that the Sun of Righteousness sheds into their hearts, let your words fall as healing balm upon the bruised soul. Be not like desolating hail that beats down and destroys the tender hope springing up in the hearts. Leave not the hungry, starving soul in his helplessness to perish because you fail to speak words of tenderness and encouragement.[31]

The most persuasive eloquence is the word that is spoken in love and sympathy. Such words will bring light to confused minds and hope to the discouraged, brightening the prospect before them. The time in which we live calls for vital, sanctified energy; for earnestness, zeal, and the tenderest sympathy and love; for words that will not increase misery, but will inspire faith and hope. We are homeward bound, seeking a better country, even an heavenly. Instead of speaking words which will rankle in the breasts of those that hear, shall we not speak of the love wherewith God hath loved us? Shall we not try to lighten the hearts of those around us by words of Christlike sympathy?[32]

Those who love Jesus Christ will contemplate His character, meditate upon His words, practice His precepts, and become living missionaries. The words they speak will be like apples of gold in pictures of silver.[33]

CHRISTIANS LIKE THE SUNLIGHT

Arise, shine; for thy light is come, and the glory of the Lord is risen upon thee. Isa. 60:1.

It is the privilege of the Christian to connect with the Source of light, and through this living connection become the light of the world. Christ's true followers will walk in the light as He is in the light, and therefore they will not travel in an uncertain way, stumbling because they walk in darkness. The Great Teacher is impressing upon His hearers the blessing which they may be to the world, represented as the sun rising in the east, dispelling the mist and shadows of darkness. The dawn gives place to day. The sun, gilding, tinting, and then glorifying the heavens with its blaze of light is a symbol of the Christian life. As the light of the sun is light and life and blessing to all that live, so should Christians, by their good works, by their cheerfulness and courage, be the light of the world. As the light of the sun chases away the shades of night and pours its glories on valleys and hills, so will the Christian reflect the Sun of Righteousness which shines on him.

Before the consistent lives of Christ's true followers, ignorance, superstition, and darkness will pass away, as the sun dispels the gloom of night. In like manner the disciples of Jesus will go into the dark places of the earth, disseminating the light of truth until the pathway of those in darkness shall be illuminated by the light of truth. In what contrast to this is the life of the professed child of God who is as the salt without the savor. . . . These sunless professors are shadows of darkness. . . . All may be channels of light if they will connect with the Source of light. They can communicate the bright rays of light to the world. None need strengthen unbelief by talking darkness. Every expression of doubt strengthens unbelief. Every thought and word of hope, courage, light, and love strengthens faith and fortifies the soul to withstand the moral darkness that exists in the world.[34]

True Christians are a savor of life unto life, because Christ abides in their hearts. Reflecting His image, they are children of the light.[35]

LET YOUR LIGHT SHINE

Let your light so shine before men, that they may see your good works, and glorify your Father which is in heaven. Matt. 5:16.

To every soul born into Christ's kingdom is given a solemn charge, Let your light so shine before men that they, by seeing your good works, shall glorify your Father which is in heaven. Pour forth upon your neighbors the rich rays of light received from the Sun of Righteousness; flash upon your friends in the world the bright gems of light and truth imparted to you abundantly from the throne of God. This is trading upon the talents entrusted. Go on from light to a greater light, catching more and more the bright beams from the Sun of Righteousness, and shine more and more unto the perfect day.[36]

Jesus does not bid the Christian to strive to shine, but just to let his light shine in clear and distinct rays to the world. Do not blanket your light. Do not sinfully withhold your light. Do not let the mist and fog and malaria of the world put out your light. Do not hide it under a bed or under a bushel, but set it on a candlestick, that it may give light to all that are in the house. . . . God bids you shine, penetrating the moral darkness of the world.[37]

Many do not know what is the matter with them. They want light and see no ray. They are calling for help and they hear no response. Shall doubt and unbelief be perpetuated because I do not gather the divine rays of light from Jesus Christ and let them shine forth to others? . . .

The deep struggles of my own soul against temptations, the earnest longings of my mind and heart to know God and Jesus Christ as my personal Saviour, and to have assurance, peace, and rest in their love, lead me to desire every day to be where the beams of the Sun of Righteousness can shine upon me. Without this experience, I shall indeed meet with great loss, and all with whom I associate will be affected by the loss of the light I ought to be receiving from the Source of all light and comfort, and to be flashing into their pathway. Shall I be indeed a light unto the world, or a shadow of darkness?[38]

FAITHFUL WHERE YOU ARE

And he said unto them, Go ye into all the world, and preach the gospel to every creature. Mark 16:15.

Preaching the gospel includes more than sermonizing; and the work is not confined to the ministry. Thousands are idle who should be working in various ways for the salvation of souls.[39]

Many feel stirred with an ambition to minister to others. Let them learn to walk humbly with God, to be doers of His Word where they are. Let them learn to be obedient, to serve in whatever capacity they may. Let them learn to do the humblest work, and to realize that they are serving Christ in whatever circumstances they may be placed. In doing humble physical work, you may reveal the fact that God is with you, and that you are trading upon the talents He has entrusted to you. Right where you are, opportunities and privileges will present themselves to you, and if you are seeking to serve Christ, you will see and improve them. In the humblest situations you will find occasions for the exercise of firm integrity and fidelity; and if faithful in serving God in the lowest place, you will be entrusted with higher responsibilities. If you are faithful in a few things, your faithfulness will testify that you are a student in the school of Christ, and that you are cultivating your ability to serve Him in larger fields.[40]

We are nearing the close of this earth's history; soon we shall stand before the great white throne. Your opportunities for work will soon be past. Therefore work while it is called today. With the help of God, every true believer can see where there is work to be done. When the human will cooperates with the will of God, it becomes omnipotent, and the worker can make opportunities. Watch for the souls with whom you come in contact. Watch for opportunities to speak a word in season to them. Do not wait for an introduction, or until you become acquainted with them, before you seek to save the perishing souls around you. If you will go to work in earnest, ways will open before you for the accomplishment of this work. Lean upon the divine arm for wisdom, strength, and skill for the work that God has given you to do.[41]

CHARACTER OF CHRIST'S AMBASSADORS

Now then we are ambassadors for Christ, as though God did beseech you by us: we pray you in Christ's stead, be ye reconciled to God. 2 Cor. 5:20.

Every true Christian will feel that he has something to do for the salvation of souls.[42]

When you approach the stranger, when you stand face to face with the impenitent, the afflicted, the soul-needy, the Lord is by your side if you have indeed given yourself to Him. He makes the impression on the heart. But you may be the instrument for His gracious work. . . .

The advocates of truth must hide in Jesus; He is their greatness, their power and efficiency. They must love souls as He loved them, be obedient as He was, be courteous, full of sympathy. They should war with all their power against the least defect of character in themselves. They must represent Jesus. In every act let Him appear.[43]

He who can read the hearts of men . . . knows the atmosphere surrounding every soul. He knows how many and fierce are the struggles of the human soul to overcome the natural hereditary tendencies and the sins which have become common through habit of repetition. . . . Thousands . . . are exposed to Satan's masterly temptations, and are without a knowledge of God and Jesus Christ whom He has sent into the world to save the chiefest sinners. Oh, why do we not discern our part of the work in the great plan of redemption? . . .

In every truly converted soul there will be genuine, sanctified sympathy with the suffering of Christ, endured by Him to save the sinful. They will, if colaborers with Christ, overcome selfish ease, selfish gratification, selfish indulgence, and will grow in spiritual sinew and muscle by exercising the powers given them of God to win souls to Jesus Christ. This heaven-appointed work is calculated to give breadth and depth and stability to Christian experience and character, and to bring the laborers together with God into a higher, purer atmosphere where their love for Christ will be ever increasing and their love for their fellow men will abound more and more.[44]

DO I RIGHTLY REPRESENT MY LORD?

Ye are my witnesses, saith the Lord, and my servant whom I have chosen. Isa. 43:10.

If believers associate with unbelievers for the purpose of winning them to Christ, they will be witnesses for Christ, and having fulfilled their mission, will withdraw themselves in order to breathe in a pure and holy atmosphere. They will draw near to God, and send up earnest petitions to Christ in behalf of their friends and associates, knowing that He is able to save unto the uttermost all that come unto God by Him.

When in the society of unbelievers, ever remember that in character you are a representative of Jesus Christ, and let no light and trifling words, no cheap conversation, be upon your lips. Keep in mind the value of the soul, and remember that it is your privilege and your duty to be in every possible way a laborer together with God. You are not to lower yourself to the same level as that of unbelievers, and laugh, and make the same cheap speeches. In thus doing you . . . make yourself one with the sinner. This manner of conduct will only make you a stumbling block in the way of sinners. . . .

When the Holy Spirit moves upon the heart, we should cooperate with its molding influence, and we shall have noble aspirations, a clear perception of truth, meekness, teachableness, and will perform our duty with humility. This is the way in which you will become better acquainted with God, and acquaintance with God is the privilege of the Christian. Then you can labor for those who are unconverted, and the society of unbelievers will do you no harm, because your life is hid with Christ in God, and you seek the companionship of those who are out of Christ for the purpose of winning them to His service. Your connection with God makes you strong spiritually, so that you can withstand any wrong influences which are exerted by them. . . .

Be sure to place yourself in the channel of light, and to be a practical follower of Him who went about "doing good." [45]

PLANTING SEEDS OF TRUTH

In the morning sow thy seed, and in the evening withhold not thine hand: for thou knowest not whether shall prosper, either this or that, or whether they both shall be alike good. Eccl. 11:6.

As professing children of God, we are under solemn obligation to seek and to save the lost. . . . God wants you to associate with believers and unbelievers, that you may help all to a fuller knowledge of the truth. Get acquainted with those whom you think you can help; then when you get into conversation with them do not talk of nothingness and folly, but tell of the precious things of God. . . . Angels of God will make impressions upon the mind, if in the spirit of Christ you will seek to reach and to help souls.[46]

Wherever you are, let your light shine forth. Hand out papers and pamphlets to those with whom you associate, when you are riding on the cars, visiting, conversing with your neighbors; and improve every opportunity to speak a word in season. . . .

We should cultivate kindliness and courtesy in our association with those whom we meet. Let us . . . strive always to present the truth in an easy way. This truth means life, eternal life to the receiver. Study therefore to pass easily and courteously from subjects of a temporal nature to the spiritual and eternal. . . . While walking by the way, or seated by the wayside, you may drop into some heart the seed of truth.[47] There is work to be done for our Master. There are souls who may by our influence be led to Christ. Who is ready to engage in this work with all the heart? . . .

"Thine is the seedtime; God alone
Beholds the end of what is sown;
Beyond our vision, weak and dim,
The harvesttime is hid with Him;
Yet unforgotten where it lies,
The seed of generous sacrifice,
Though seeming on the desert cast,
Shall rise with bloom and fruit at last."[48]

October 23

WATCH, PRAY, WORK

I must work the works of him that sent me, while it is day: the night cometh, when no man can work. John 9:4.

Could the ledger of Heaven be opened before us, we would be greatly astonished at the large proportion of professing Christians who really contribute nothing toward the upbuilding of Christ's kingdom, who put forth no efforts for the salvation of souls. Such are slothful servants. Many who are satisfied not to do much good, flatter themselves that they are doing no harm so long as they do not oppose the earnest, active workers. But this class are doing much harm by their example. . . .

The slothful servant was not condemned for what he had done, but for what he had not done. There is no more dangerous enemy to the cause of God than an indolent Christian. An open profaner does less harm, for he deceives no one; he appears what he is, a brier, a thorn. The do-nothings are the greatest hindrance. Those who will not bear burdens, who shun all disagreeable responsibilities, are the first to be taken in Satan's snare, the first to lend their influence to a wrong course.

Watch, pray, work—these are the Christian's watchwords. Let none excuse themselves from labor for the salvation of souls. Let none deceive themselves into the belief that nothing is required of them. No less is required of any than was expected of the man with one talent.[49]

There is work to be done for Christ in our families, in our neighborhoods, everywhere. By kindness to the poor, the sick, or the bereaved, we may obtain an influence over them, so that divine truth may find access to their hearts. Opportunities for usefulness are on every hand. All who are imbued with the spirit of Christ will show themselves to be fruit-bearing branches of the living Vine. . . .

It is ours to make the record which we desire to meet hereafter. Would we have its pages filled with the history of earnest work for God and humanity? Let us follow in the footsteps of Him who declared, "I must work the works of him that sent me, while it is day: the night cometh, when no man can work." John 9:4.[50]

October 24

"TO EVERY MAN HIS WORK"

For the Son of man is as a man taking a far journey, who left his house, and gave authority to his servants, and to every man his work, and commanded the porter to watch. Mark 13:34.

We have a personal work, an individual responsibility, a personal account to render, and it is our own salvation we must secure, for it is a matter of individual concern. . . . The piety and obedience of others will not save us or be doing our work. Their efforts will never be registered against our names as ours. . . .

God has left to every one of us our work—not the temporal labor as planting, sowing, reaping, and gathering in the harvest, but to build up His kingdom, to bring souls to the knowledge of the truth, and to regard this as our first and highest duty. God has claims upon us. He has endowed us with capabilities and given us opportunities, if we will see them and improve them. These obligations to God none but ourselves, individually, can meet. The delinquencies of others . . . will be no excuse for any one to follow their example, because Christ is lifted up as the only true Pattern—faultless, pure, uncorrupted. . . .

There are those who associate together to do evil and seem to think in this they lose their individual responsibility. But God holds them accountable for every act performed that has the slightest tendency to counteract the work of Christ; whether they are united with many or with the few, the sin is the same. We are individually responsible. We ourselves should be our concern. Are we in all our words and actions building up the kingdom of Christ, or are we tearing down? Christ says to each one of us, "Follow me." Then let us be found followers of Jesus Christ.[51]

Now is our time to work. Now is the time for us to form characters after the divine Model. . . . If we know Christ, we shall reveal Him to others. "As thou hast sent me into the world, even so have I also sent them into the world." John 17:18. He came into the world to represent the Father; and the work He has given us is to represent His character. We cannot be excused from doing this work.[52]

303

October 25

A LITTLE CHURCH IN THE HOME

Howbeit Jesus suffered him not, but saith unto him, Go home to thy friends, and tell them how great things the Lord hath done for thee, and hath had compassion on thee. Mark 5:19.

In forming a relationship with Christ, the renewed man is but coming back to his appointed relationship with God. He is a representative of Christ. . . . His duties lie around him, nigh and afar off. His first duty is to his children and his nearest relatives. Nothing can excuse him from neglecting the inner circle for the larger circle outside. In the day of final reckoning fathers and mothers will be required to answer in regard to their children. Parents will be asked what they did and said to secure the salvation of the souls they took upon themselves the responsibility of bringing into the world. . . .

Fathers and mothers, are you allowing your children to grow up in impurity and sin? A great good done for others will not cancel the debt you owe to God to care for your children. The spiritual welfare of your family comes first. Take them with you to the cross of Calvary, laboring for them as those that must give an account.

Parents should seek to gain the cooperation of their children. Thus children can become laborers together with God. Some households have a little church in their home. Mutual love binds heart to heart, and the unity that exists among the members of the family preaches the most effectual sermon that could be preached on practical godliness.

As parents faithfully do their duty in the family, restraining, correcting, advising, counseling, guiding, the father as priest of the household, the mother as a home missionary, they are filling the sphere God would have them fill. By faithfully doing their duty in the home, they are multiplying agencies for doing good outside the home. They are becoming better fitted to labor in the church. By training their little flock discreetly, binding their children to themselves and to God, fathers and mothers become laborers together with God. . . . The members of the family become members of the royal family above, children of the heavenly King.[53]

NO MIDDLE GROUND IN GOD'S SERVICE

He that is not with me is against me; and he that gathereth not with me scattereth abroad. Matt. 12:30.

My fellow Christians, we are far from reaching the divine standard. Our works do not correspond with our privileges and opportunities. . . .

In the service of God there is no middle ground. . . . Let none expect to make a compromise with the world, and yet enjoy the blessing of the Lord. Let God's people come out from this world, and be separate. Let us seek more earnestly to know and do the will of our Father in heaven. Let the light of truth which has shone upon us be so received that its bright rays may go forth from us to the world. Let unbelievers see that the faith we hold makes us better men and better women; that it is a living reality, sanctifying the character, transforming the life. . . . Let our conversation be upon heavenly things. Let us surround ourselves with an atmosphere of Christian cheerfulness. Let us show that our religion can stand the test of trial. Let us by our kindness, forbearance, and love prove to the world the power of our faith.

Many who set out well in the Christian life are losing spiritual strength, and placing themselves in the enemy's power, by their indulgence in vain and trifling conversation. They cannot look up to God with holy confidence to ask for needed strength. By their irreligious course they bar the way of souls that might have come to Christ. Let these careless triflers remember that every word and act is photographed in the books of heaven. No human hand can erase one disgraceful blot. . . .

As we are daily brought in contact with those who have not a knowledge of Christ and the truth, shall we talk only of our farms, our merchandise, our gains and losses; or shall we speak of those things which concern our future life? Shall we seek to win souls to Jesus? Oh, what shameful neglect of duty stands registered against the professed followers of Christ! Let us earnestly examine ourselves by the light of God's Word, seeking to discover every defect of character, that we may wash our robes and make them white in the blood of the Lamb.[54]

REWARDS OF SERVICE

It is good for a man that he bear the yoke in his youth. Lam. 3:27.

The Lord calls for young men and women to enter His service. The youth are receptive, fresh, ardent, hopeful. When once they have tasted the spirit of self-sacrifice, they will not be satisfied unless they are learning constantly of the great Teacher. . . .

As we work in connection with the great Teacher, our experience improves. The faculties of the mind are enlarged. The conscience is under divine guidance. Christ takes the entire being under His control. We are safe only as we allow Him to do this; for there is another close by, watching for an opportunity to come in and begin his destructive, ensnaring work. Then, as we enter the service of God, let Him take possession of the whole being, body, soul, and spirit. . . .

No one can be truly united to Christ, practicing His lessons, submitting to His yoke of restraint, without realizing that which he can never express in words. New, rich thoughts come to him. Light is given to the intellect, determination to the will, tenderness to the conscience, purity to the imagination.[55]

Young men and women who are truly converted will depart from all iniquity. . . . If they see the offensive character of sin, and hate it as the vile thing it is, and come to Jesus in contrition, purifying their souls by obedience to the truth, then they may be entrusted with some part in the work. . . .

God reads the heart, He weighs the character, and is acquainted with every man's work. He gives His Spirit in proportion to the consecration and self-sacrifice manifested by those who engage in His work.[56]

The youth are strong. They are not worn down with the weight of years, and with cares. Their affections are ardent, and if they are withdrawn from the world, and placed upon Christ and heaven, doing the will of God, they will have a hope of the better life that is enduring, and they will abide forever, being crowned with glory, honor, immortality, eternal life.[57]

BEWARE OF SELF-CONFIDENCE

*Peter said unto him, Lord, why cannot I follow thee now? I will
lay down my life for thy sake. Jesus answered him, Wilt thou lay
down thy life for my sake? Verily, verily, I say unto thee, The cock
shall not crow, till thou hast denied me thrice. John 13:37, 38.*

Just before Peter's fall, Christ said to him, "Simon, behold, Satan
hath desired to have you, that he may sift you as wheat." Luke 22:31.
How true was the Saviour's friendship for Peter! how compassionate
His warning! But the warning was resented. In self-sufficiency Peter
declared confidently that he would never do what Christ had warned
him against. "Lord," he said, "I am ready to go with thee to prison,
and to death." His self-confidence proved his ruin. He tempted Satan
to tempt him, and he fell under the arts of the wily foe. When Christ
needed him most, he stood on the side of the enemy, and openly
denied his Lord. . . .

Many today stand where Peter stood when in self-confidence he
declared that he would not deny his Lord. And because of their self-
sufficiency, they fall an easy prey to Satan's devices. Those who realize their weakness trust in a power higher than self. And while
they look to God, Satan has no power against them. But those who
trust in self are easily defeated. Let us remember that if we do not
heed the cautions that God gives us, a fall is before us. Christ will
not save from wounds the one who places himself unbidden on the
enemy's ground. He lets the self-sufficient one, who acts as if he
knew more than his Lord, go on in his supposed strength. Then
comes suffering and a crippled life or perhaps defeat and death.

In the warfare the enemy takes advantage of the weakest points
in the defense of those he is attacking. Here he makes his fiercest
assaults. The Christian should have no weak points in his defense.
He should be barricaded by the support that the Scriptures give to
the one who is doing God's will. The tempted soul will bear away
the victory if he follows the example of Him who met the tempter
with the word, "It is written." He can stand securely in the protection of a "Thus saith the Lord." [58]

ENERGY IN THE CHRISTIAN RACE

Know ye not that they which run in a race run all, but one receiveth the prize? So run, that ye may obtain. And every man that striveth for the mastery is temperate in all things. Now they do it to obtain a corruptible crown; but we an incorruptible. 1 Cor. 9:24, 25.

In order to render to God perfect service, we must have clear conceptions of His will. This will require us to use only healthful food, prepared in a simple manner, that the fine nerves of the brain be not injured, making it impossible for us to discern the value of the atonement, and the priceless worth of the cleansing blood of Christ. . . .

If, for no higher object than a wreath or perishable crown as a reward of their ambition, men subjected themselves to temperance in all things, how much more should those who profess to be seeking, not only an unfading crown of immortal glory, but a life which is to endure as long as the throne of Jehovah, and riches that are eternal, honors which are imperishable, and an eternal weight of glory. Will not the inducements presented before those who are running in the Christian race, lead them to practice self-denial, and temperance in all things? . . .

With earnestness and intensity of desire to do the will of God, we should excel the zeal of those who are engaged in any other enterprise, to a degree as much greater as the value of the object we are seeking to attain is higher. The treasure we are striving to secure is imperishable, immortal, and all-glorious; while that which the worldling is in pursuit of endures but a day. . . .

May it not be our great anxiety to succeed in this world; but may the burden of our souls be, How shall I secure the better world? What have I to do to be saved? . . . The position all must come into, is to value salvation dearer than earthly gain, to count everything but loss that they may win Christ. The consecration must be entire. God will admit of no reserve, of no divided sacrifice, no idol. All must die to self, and to the world. Then let us each renew our consecration to God daily. Everlasting life is worth a lifelong, persevering, untiring effort.[59]

October 30

"TAKE HEED UNTO THYSELF"

Take heed unto thyself, and unto the doctrine; continue in them: for in doing this thou shalt both save thyself, and them that hear thee. 1 Tim. 4:16.

The charge given to Timothy should be heeded in every household, and become an educating power in every family and in every school. . . .

The highest aim of our youth should not be to strain after something novel. There was none of this in the mind and work of Timothy. They should bear in mind that, in the hands of the enemy of all good, knowledge alone may be a power to destroy them. It was a very intellectual being, one who occupied a high position among the angelic throng, that finally became a rebel; and many a mind of superior intellectual attainments is now being led captive by his power. The youth should place themselves under the teaching of the Holy Scriptures, and weave them into their daily thoughts and practical life. Then they will possess the attributes classed as highest in the heavenly courts. They will hide themselves in God, and their lives will tell to His glory.[60]

"Take heed unto thyself, and unto the doctrine." Thyself needs the first attention. First give yourself to the Lord for sanctification to His service. A godly example will tell more for the truth than the greatest eloquence unaccompanied by a well-ordered life. Trim the lamp of the soul, and replenish it with the oil of the Spirit. Seek from Christ that grace, that clearness of comprehension, which will enable you to do successful work. Learn from Him what it means to labor for those for whom He gave His life. The most talented worker can do little unless Christ is formed within, the hope and strength of the life.[61]

A noble, all-round manhood does not come by chance. It is the result of character building in the early years of youth, a practice of the law of God in the home.[62]

God is waiting to inspire the youth with power from above, that all who stand under the bloodstained banner of Jesus Christ may work to call, to warn, and to lead souls into safe paths, and to plant the feet of many upon the Rock of Ages.[63]

LABORERS TOGETHER WITH GOD

For we are labourers together with God: ye are God's husbandry, ye are God's building. 1 Cor. 3:9.

Man cannot be towed to heaven; he cannot go as a passive passenger. He must himself use the oars, and work as a laborer together with God.[64]

If you think you can lay down the oars, and still make your way upstream, you are mistaken. It is only by earnest effort, by using the oars with all your might, that you can stem the current. How many there are as weak as water, when they have a never-failing Source of strength! Heaven is ready to impart to us, that we may be mighty in God, and attain the full stature of men and women in Christ Jesus. But who of you in the past year have been making progress in the way of holiness? . . . Who have been enabled to gain one precious attainment after another, until envy, pride, malice, jealousy, and every evil stain have been swept away, and only the graces of the Spirit remain? . . .

God will help us if we take hold of the help He has provided. "Let him take hold of my strength," He says, "that he may make peace with me; and he shall make peace with me." Isa. 27:5. This is a blessed promise. Many times when I have been discouraged and almost in despair, I have come to the Lord with this promise. . . . And as I have laid hold of the strength of God, I have found a peace which passeth understanding.[65]

There are two grand forces at work in the salvation of the human soul. It requires the cooperation of man with the divine agencies— divine influences, and a strong, living, working faith. It is in this way only that the human agent can become a laborer together with God. The Lord does not sanction in any one of us a blind, stupid credulity. He does not dishonor the human understanding, but, far from this, He calls for the human will to be brought into connection with the divine will. He calls for the ingenuity of the human mind, the tact, the skill, to be strenuously exercised in searching out the truth as it is in Jesus. . . . Ye are labourers together with God.[66]

November 1

HAVE YOU COUNTED THE COST?

In the world ye shall have tribulation: but be of good cheer; I have overcome the world. John 16:33.

The world's Redeemer presents to His followers the plan of the battle in which they are called to engage, and He bids them count the cost. He assures them that angels who excel in strength shall be in His army, and will enable those who trust in Him to fight valiantly. One shall chase a thousand, and two put ten thousand to flight—not through their own strength, but through the power of Omnipotence. . . . The Captain of the Lord's host is with them, taking the command of the armies, and leading them on to victory.

Because of their human frailty, because of their sinfulness, they may fear and tremble as they view the vast hosts of the powers of darkness; but they may rejoice as they look upon the angels of God ready to minister to those who shall be heirs of salvation. They may rejoice as they realize that the Captain of the Lord's host will lead them forward in every conflict against natural and supernatural foes. . . . Your Leader is a conqueror. Advance to victory. . . .

How precious are these assurances that we shall never be left to take one step in our own finite strength, for He has said, "I will never leave thee, nor forsake thee." Heb. 13:5. We are fighting in the presence of invisible hosts. Unseen intelligences survey the whole array of evil, and help is at hand. We shall not only be provided with that which is necessary but shall be placed upon vantage ground. . . .

To every Christian comes the word that was addressed to Peter, "Satan hath desired to have you, that he may sift you as wheat: but I have prayed for thee, that thy faith fail not." Luke 22:31. Thank God we are not left alone. This is our safety. Satan can never touch with eternal disaster one whom Christ has prepared for temptation by His previous intercession; for grace is provided in Christ for every soul, and a way of escape has been made, so that no one need fall under the power of the enemy.[1]

WILL YOU BEAR THE REFINER'S FIRE?

That the trial of your faith, being much more precious than of gold that perisheth, though it be tried with fire, might be found unto praise and honour and glory at the appearing of Jesus Christ. 1 Peter 1:7.

Gold is tried in the fire, that it may be purified from dross; but faith that is purified by trial, is more precious than refined gold. Then let us look upon trials in a reasonable way. Let us not come through them with murmuring and discontent. Let us not make mistakes in getting out of them. In times of trial we must cling to God and His promises.

Some have said to me, "Do you not get discouraged at times when you are under trial?" And I have answered, "Yes, if by discouragement you mean sad or cast down." "Didn't you talk to any one of your feelings?" "No; there is a time for silence, a time to keep the tongue as with a bridle, and I was determined to utter no word of doubt or darkness, to bring no shade of gloom upon those with whom I was associated. I have said to myself, I will bear the Refiner's fire; I shall not be consumed. When I speak, it shall be of light; it shall be of faith and hope in God; it shall be of righteousness, of goodness, of the love of Christ my Saviour; it shall be to direct the minds of others toward heaven and heavenly things, to Christ's work in heaven for us, and our work upon earth for Him."[2]

The refining furnace is to remove the dross. When the Refiner sees His image reflected in you perfectly, He will remove you from the furnace. You will not be left to be consumed or to endure the fiery ordeal any longer than is necessary for your purification. But it is necessary for you, in order to reflect the divine image, to submit to the process the Refiner chooses for you, that you may be cleansed, purified, and every spot and blemish removed—not even a wrinkle left in your Christian character. May the Lord help you . . . to choose to have the will and work of God accomplished in you. . . . Look up! Jesus lives. Jesus loves. Jesus pities, and He will receive you with all your burden of care and trouble if you will come to Him and lay your burden upon Him. He has promised He will never leave or forsake those who put their trust in Him.[3]

JOY THROUGH SUFFERING WITH CHRIST

Beloved, think it not strange concerning the fiery trial which is to try you, as though some strange thing happened unto you: but rejoice, inasmuch as ye are partakers of Christ's sufferings; that, when his glory shall be revealed, ye may be glad also with exceeding joy. 1 Peter 4:12, 13.

We do not always consider that the sanctification we so earnestly desire and for which we pray so earnestly is brought about through the truth and, by the providence of God, in a manner we least expect. When we look for joy, behold there is sorrow. When we expect peace, we frequently have distrust and doubt, because we find ourselves plunged into trials we cannot avoid. In these trials we are having the answers to our prayers. In order for us to be purified, the fire of affliction must kindle upon us, and our will must be brought into conformity to the will of God. . . . God sees it best to put us under a course of discipline which is essential for us before we are fit subjects for the blessing we crave.

We should not become discouraged and give way to doubt, and think that our prayers are not noticed. We should rely more securely upon Christ and leave our case with God to answer our prayers in His own way. God has not promised to bestow His blessings through the channels we have marked out. . . . The plans of God are always the best, although we may not always discern them. Perfection of Christian character can be obtained only through labor, conflict, and self-denial. We do not always count upon this, and do not consider the painful and often protracted process of purifying necessary for us in order that we may be conformed to the image of Christ. God frequently answers our prayers in a way we least expect. He brings us into positions which are the most trying, to reveal what is in our hearts. To further the development of Christian graces He will place us in circumstances which will demand increased exertion on our part to keep our faith in lively exercise.

Let us bear in mind how inestimably precious are the gifts of God—the graces of His Spirit—and we shall not shrink from the trying, testing process, be it ever so painful or humiliating to us.[4]

TOKEN OF THE EVERLASTING COVENANT

And the bow shall be in the cloud; and I will look upon it, that I may remember the everlasting covenant between God and every living creature of all flesh that is upon the earth. Gen. 9:16.

Some time ago, we were favored with a view of the most glorious rainbow we ever beheld. We have often visited galleries of art, and have admired the skill displayed by the artist in paintings representing God's great bow of promise. But here we saw the varied tints—crimson, purple, blue, green, silver, and golden, all perfectly blended by the great Master Artist. We were entranced as we looked upon this glorious picture in the heavens.

As we look upon this bow, the seal and sign of God's promise to man, that the tempest of His wrath should no more desolate our world by the waters of a flood, we contemplate that other than finite eyes are looking upon this glorious sight. Angels rejoice as they gaze upon this precious token of God's love to man. The world's Redeemer looks upon it; for it was through His instrumentality that this bow was made to appear in the heavens, as a token or covenant of promise to man. God Himself looks upon the bow in the clouds, and remembers His everlasting covenant between Himself and man. . . . The bow represents Christ's love which encircles the earth, and reaches unto the highest heavens, connecting men with God, and linking earth with heaven.

As we gaze upon the beautiful sight, we may be joyful in God, assured that He Himself is looking upon this token of His covenant, and that as He looks upon it He remembers the children of earth, to whom it was given. Their afflictions, perils, and trials are not hidden from Him. We may rejoice in hope, for the bow of God's covenant is over us. He never will forget the children of His care. How difficult for the mind of finite man to take in the peculiar love and tenderness of God, and His matchless condescension when He said, "I will look upon the bow in the cloud, and remember thee."

Oh, how easy for us to forget God, while He never forgets us; He visits us with His mercies every hour.[5]

GOD SPEAKS THROUGH THE SILENCE

I John, who also am your brother, and companion in tribulation, and in the kingdom and patience of Jesus Christ, was in the isle that is called Patmos, for the word of God, and for the testimony of Jesus Christ. Rev. 1:9.

By permitting John to be banished to the Isle of Patmos, Christ placed His disciple in a position where he could receive the most precious truth for the enlightenment of the churches. He placed him in solitude, that his ear and his heart might be sanctified to receive this truth. . . . The persecution of John's enemies became a means of grace. Patmos was made resplendent by the glory of a risen Saviour. . . . What a Sabbath that was to the lonely exile! . . . Never had he learned so much of Jesus. Never had he heard such exalted truth.

The worker for God often regards the activities of life as essential to the advancement of the work. Self is mingled with all that is said and done. . . . The worker looks upon himself as a necessity. God says, "This poor soul has lost sight of Me and My sufficiency. I must cast My light and My vitalizing power into his heart. I must prepare him to receive truth by anointing him with the heavenly eyesalve. He sees too many things. His eye is not fastened on Me. . . ."

Sometimes the Lord makes His path to the soul by a process painful to humanity. He is compelled to fortify the soul against self-esteem and self-dependence, in order that the worker shall not regard the failings and infirmities of his unsanctified nature as virtues, and thus be ruined by self-exaltation.

If those who claim to believe the grand truths for this time would prepare themselves by searching the Scriptures, by earnest prayer, and by the exercise of faith, they would place themselves where they would receive the light they so much crave. . . . The eloquence of silence before God is often essential. If the mind is kept in continual excitement, the ear is prevented from hearing the truth that the Lord would communicate to His believing ones. Christ takes His children from that which holds their attention, that they may behold His glory.[6]

November 6

THE TRAINING NECESSARY FOR HEAVEN

But he knoweth the way that I take: when he hath tried me, I shall come forth as gold. Job 23:10.

The Lord will work for those who put their trust in Him. Precious victories will be gained by the faithful. Precious lessons will be learned. Precious experiences will be realized that will be of the greatest advantage in times of trial and temptation. Those who will give all the glory to God, not taking credit to themselves, will be trusted with more and more of the blessing of God. The Lord will be magnified by those who honor Him in the midst of the people. The trial that has been borne with patience, the test that has been met with faithfulness, will prove them worthy of responsibility, and God will make them agents to carry out His will. . . .

The conflicts of earth, in the providence of God, furnish the very training necessary to develop characters fit for the courts of heaven. We are to become members of the royal family, the sons of God, and "all things work together for good" to those who love God, and submit themselves to His will.

Our God is an ever-present help in every time of need. He is perfectly acquainted with the most secret thoughts of our heart, with all the intents and purposes of our souls. When we are in perplexity, even before we open to Him our distress, He is making arrangements for our deliverance. Our sorrow is not unnoticed. He always knows much better than we do, just what is necessary for the good of His children, and He leads us as we would choose to be led if we could discern our own hearts and see our necessities and perils, as God sees them. But finite beings seldom know themselves. They do not understand their own weaknesses. . . . God knows them better than they know themselves, and He understands how to lead them. . . .

If we will trust Him, and commit our ways to Him, He will direct our steps in the very path that will result in our obtaining the victory over every evil passion, and every trait of character that is unlike the character of our divine Pattern.[7]

GOD KNOWS WHAT IS BEST

Now no chastening for the present seemeth to be joyous, but grievous: nevertheless afterward it yieldeth the peaceable fruit of righteousness unto them which are exercised thereby. Heb. 12:11.

God knows what is for our best good. The peculiar discipline to which we are subject is discipline to bring out not the worst and most unlovely traits of character, but the meekness and loveliness of Christ, developing the precious graces of Christ.

You need to learn in Christ's school to become Christlike. God adapts His grace to the peculiarities of each one's necessities. "My grace is sufficient for thee." 2 Cor. 12:9. As your burden grows heavier look up and by faith cling more firmly to the hand of Jesus, your mighty helper. As difficulties thicken about His people amid the perils of the last days, He sends His angels to walk all the way by our side, drawing us closer and still closer to the bleeding side of Jesus. And as the greater trials come, lesser trials are forgotten. . . .

You must remain pure and true and firm, remembering your character is being imprinted upon the books of heaven. . . . There is no circumstance or place or difficulty or hardship, where we cannot live beautiful lives of Christian fidelity and approved conduct. . . . Victory is not found in shunning trials—getting rid of them—but in meeting them heroically, enduring them patiently.[8]

Everyone will meet with trials. . . . If you look to Jesus, if you believe in Him as your personal Saviour, you will be brought through every trial, and enduring these trials with patience, you will become stronger to endure the next test, the next trial.[9]

It is only the narrowness of our vision that prevents us from discerning God's loving-kindness in the discipline to which He subjects His church, as well as in the great blessings which He provides. In all times of distress and confusion, God is a sure refuge to His people. In the shadow of His protection they may safely keep His way. In the affliction designed to purify them, the power of the gospel is to be their consolation. In His sure word they have a fortress.[10]

ALL THINGS WORK TOGETHER

And we know that all things work together for good to them that love God, to them who are the called according to his purpose. Rom. 8:28.

The heart surrendered to God's wise discipline will trust every working out of His providence. . . . If God should let everyone do as he pleases, conceit and pride would be fostered, and the grace of humility would not be cherished in the heart. True culture is only possible for those who are truly humble.

The things we may so much desire to do may become a reality after God has proved us in the school of experience, and among our greatest blessings may be counted the thing we were not privileged to do, that would have barred the way from doing the very things best calculated to prepare us for a higher work. The plain, sober duties of real life were essential to prevent the fruitless striving to do things that we were not fitted to do. Our devised plans often fail that God's plans for us may be a complete success. Oh, it is in the future life we shall see the tangles and mysteries of life, that have so annoyed and disappointed our fond hopes, explained. We will see that the prayers and hopes for certain things which have been withheld have been among our greatest blessings.[11]

We need not expect all sunshine in this world. Clouds and storms will cluster about us, and we must be prepared to keep our eyes directed where we saw the light last. Its rays may be hidden but they still live, still shine beyond the cloud. It is our work to wait, to watch, to pray, and to believe. We shall prize the light of the sun more highly after the clouds disappear. We shall see the salvation of God if we trust in God in the darkness as well as in the light.[12]

All trials, all afflictions, all peace, all safety, health, hope, life, and success are in God's hands, and He can control them all for the good of His children. It is our privilege to be suppliants, to ask anything and everything of God, submitting our request in submission to His wise purposes and infinite will.[13]

SEEING THE UNSEEN

For our light affliction, which is but for a moment, worketh for us a far more exceeding and eternal weight of glory; while we look not at the things which are seen, but at the things which are not seen: for the things which are seen are temporal; but the things which are not seen are eternal. 2 Cor. 4:17, 18.

If our minds are fixed upon the things that are eternal, and not on the things of earth, we shall grasp the hand of infinite power, and what can make us sad? . . .

We need not be left a prey to Satan's power. . . . The children of God should not permit Satan to place himself between them and their God. If you permit him to do this, he will tell you that your troubles are the most grievous, the sorest troubles that any mortal ever bore. He will place his magnifying glasses before your eyes, and present everything to you in an exaggerated form to overwhelm you with discouragement. . . . Take the Word of God as the man of your counsel, and humble your doubting soul before God, and with contrition of heart say, "Here I lay my burden down. I cannot bear it. It is too heavy for me. I lay it down at the feet of my compassionate Redeemer." . . .

When Satan tempts you, breathe not a word of doubt or darkness. You may have your choice as to who shall rule your heart and control your mind. If you choose to open the door to the suggestions of the evil one, your mind will be filled with distrust and rebellious questioning. You may talk out your feelings, but every doubt you utter is a seed that will germinate and bear fruit in another's life, and it will be impossible to counteract the influence of your words. You may be able to recover from your season of temptation, and from the snare of Satan, but others that have been swayed by your influence may not be able to escape from the unbelief you have suggested. How important it is that we speak to those around us only those things which will give spiritual strength and enlightenment! Let us seek to lift souls to Jesus, whom having not seen we may love, and be filled with joy unspeakable and full of glory.[14]

NO POWER CAN SEPARATE FROM CHRIST

Who shall separate us from the love of Christ? shall tribulation, or distress, or persecution, or famine, or nakedness, or peril, or sword? Rom. 8:35.

How precious in time of need is the assurance of union with Jesus! . . . We can say, "Who shall separate us from the love of Christ? Shall tribulation?"—No, for this makes us feel that Christ alone is our refuge, and we flee to Him for shelter. "Or distress?"— No, for He is our consolation. "Blessed be God, even the Father of our Lord Jesus Christ, the Father of mercies, and the God of all comfort: who comforteth us in all our tribulation. . . ." 2 Cor. 1:3, 4.

"Or persecution?"—No; "Blessed are they which are persecuted for righteousness' sake: for their's is the kingdom of heaven." Matt. 5:10. . . . "Or famine?"—No, for we have God's promise, . . . "In famine he shall redeem thee from death." Job 5:20. ". . . In the days of famine they shall be satisfied." Ps. 37:19. In fleeing unto Jesus we shall be fully satisfied. "Or nakedness?"—Hear the voice of Jesus saying, "Buy of me gold tried in the fire, that thou mayest be rich; and white raiment, that thou mayest be clothed, that the shame of thy nakedness do not appear." Rev. 3:18. . . . "He that overcometh, the same shall be clothed in white raiment." Rev. 3:5. . . .

"Or peril?"—No; Paul knew by experience what it was to be in peril. . . . "In perils of waters, in perils of robbers, in perils by mine own countrymen, in perils by the heathen, in perils in the city, in perils in the wilderness, in perils in the sea, in perils among false brethren." 2 Cor. 11:26. "And he said unto me, My grace is sufficient for thee." 2 Cor. 12:9. . . . "Or sword?" . . . The sword cannot kill the soul, for the life is hid with Christ in God.

Well may we ask with Paul, "Who shall separate us from the love of God?" And answer, "For I am persuaded, that neither death, nor life, nor angels, nor principalities, nor powers, nor things present, nor things to come, nor height, nor depth, nor any other creature, shall be able to separate us from the love of God, which is in Christ Jesus our Lord." Rom. 8:38, 39.[15]

THE CRUCIBLE OF TROUBLE

Alas! for that day is great, so that none is like it: it is even the time of Jacob's trouble; but he shall be saved out of it. Jer. 30:7.

The path to freedom from sin is through crucifixion of self, and conflict with the powers of darkness. Let none be discouraged in view of the severe trials to be met in the time of Jacob's trouble, which is yet before them. They are to work earnestly, anxiously, not for that time, but for today. What we want is to have a knowledge of the truth as it is in Christ now, and a personal experience now. In these precious closing hours of probation, we have a deep and living experience to gain. We shall thus form characters that will ensure our deliverance in the time of trouble.

The time of trouble is the crucible that is to bring out Christlike characters. It is designed to lead the people of God to renounce Satan and his temptations. The last conflict will reveal Satan to them in his true character, that of a cruel tyrant, and it will do for them what nothing else could do, uproot him entirely from their affections. For to love and cherish sin, is to love and cherish its author, that deadly foe of Christ. When they excuse sin and cling to perversity of character, they give Satan a place in their affections, and pay him homage.[16]

All heaven is interested in man and desires his salvation. This is the great aim in all God's dealings with individuals. . . . It is a matter of the greatest wonder to the heavenly host that so few care to be freed from the bondage of evil influences, so few are willing to exercise all their powers in harmony with Christ in the great work of their deliverance. If men could have unveiled before them the workings of the great deceiver to keep them in the gall of bitterness and the bond of iniquity, how earnest would they be to renounce the works of darkness, how guarded lest they yield to temptation, how careful to see and remove every defect which mars the image of God in them; how they would press to the side of Jesus, and what earnest supplications would ascend to heaven for a calmer, closer, happier, walk with God.[17]

A JEWEL OR A PEBBLE?

*In that day, saith the Lord of hosts, will I take thee, O Zerubbabel,
my servant, the son of Shealtiel, saith the Lord, and will make thee as
a signet: for I have chosen thee, saith the Lord of hosts. Haggai 2:23.*

Christians are Christ's jewels. They are to shine brightly for Him,
shedding forth the light of His loveliness. Their luster depends on
the polishing they receive. They may choose to be polished or to remain unpolished. But everyone who is pronounced worthy of a
place in the Lord's temple must submit to the polishing process.
Without the polishing that the Lord gives they can reflect no more
light than a common pebble.

Christ says to man, "You are mine. I have bought you. You are
now only a rough stone, but if you will place yourself in my hands,
I will polish you, and the luster with which you shall shine will bring
honor to My name. No man shall pluck you out of My hand. I will
make you My peculiar treasure. On My coronation day, you will be
a jewel in My crown of rejoicing."

The divine Worker spends little time on worthless material. Only
the precious jewels does He polish after the similitude of a palace, cutting away all the rough edges. This process is severe and trying; it hurts
human pride. Christ cuts deep into the experience that man in his self-
sufficiency has regarded as complete, and takes away self-uplifting
from the character. He cuts away the surplus surface, and putting the
stone to the polishing wheel, presses it close, that all roughness may
be worn away. Then, holding the jewel up to the light, the Master sees
in it a reflection of Himself, and He pronounces it worthy of a place in
His casket. "In that day, saith the Lord of hosts, will I take thee, . . .
and will make thee as a signet: for I have chosen thee, saith the Lord
of hosts." Blessed be the experience, however severe, that gives new
value to the stone, and causes it to shine with living brightness.[18]

God will not suffer one of His truehearted workers to be left
alone to struggle against great odds and be overcome. He preserves
as a precious jewel every one whose life is hid with Christ in God.[19]

GOD MEASURES EVERY TRIAL

There hath no temptation taken you but such as is common to man: but God is faithful, who will not suffer you to be tempted above that ye are able; but will with the temptation also make a way to escape, that ye may be able to bear it. 1 Cor. 10:13.

Each one has his own battles to fight, his own Christian experience to gain, independent in some respects from any other soul; and God has lessons for each to gain for himself that no other one can gain for him. . . . Our heavenly Father measures and weighs every trial before He permits it to come upon the believer. He considers the circumstances and the strength of the one who is to stand under the proving and test of God, and He never permits the temptations to be greater than the capacity of resistance. If the soul is overborne, the person overpowered, this can never be charged to God, . . . but the one tempted was not vigilant and prayerful and did not appropriate by faith the provisions God had abundantly in store for him. Christ never failed a believer in His hour of combat. The believer must claim the promise and meet the foe in the name of the Lord. . . .

Oh, there is a great work to be done for the people of God, ere they are prepared for translation to heaven! The heat of the furnace upon some must be severe to reveal the dross. Self will have to be crucified. When each believer is to the very extent of his knowledge obeying the Lord, and yet seeking to give no just occasion to his fellow men to oppress him, he should not fear the results, even though it be imprisonment and death. . . .

The tender compassion of God is toward His people. Faith, wondrous faith—it leads the people of God in straight paths. Without this faith we shall certainly misunderstand His dealings with us, and distrust His love and faithfulness. Whatever may be the trials and sufferings, . . . let there be no faintheartedness, no peevish repining, no complaining. . . .

A single ray of the evidences of the undeserved favor of God shining into our hearts will overbalance every trial of whatever character and however severe it may be.[20]

FAITH MUST PIERCE THE GLOOM

Though he slay me, yet will I trust in him. . . . He also shall be my salvation. Job 13:15, 16.

The true Christian does not allow any earthly consideration to come in between his soul and God. . . .

When depression settles upon the soul, it is no evidence that God has changed. He is "the same yesterday, and to day, and for ever." Heb. 13:8. You are sure of the favor of God when you are sensible of the beams of the Sun of Righteousness; but if the clouds sweep over your soul, you must not feel that you are forsaken. Your faith must pierce the gloom. Your eye must be single, and your whole body will be full of light. The riches of the grace of Christ must be kept before the mind. Treasure up the lessons that His love provides. Let your faith be like Job's, that you may declare, "Though he slay me, yet will I trust in him." . . .

The most trying experiences in the Christian's life may be the most blessed. The special providences of the dark hours may encourage the soul in future attacks of Satan, and equip the servant of God to stand in fiery trials. The trial of your faith is more precious than gold. You must have that abiding confidence in God that is not disturbed by the temptations and arguments of the deceiver. Take the Lord at His word. You must study the promises, and appropriate them as you have need. "Faith cometh by hearing, and hearing by the word of God." Rom. 10:17. . . .

It is faith that familiarizes the soul with the existence and presence of God; and when we live with an eye single to His glory, we discern more and more the beauty of His character. Our souls become strong in spiritual power, for we are breathing the atmosphere of heaven, and, realizing that God is at our right hand, we shall not be moved. . . . We should live as in the presence of the Infinite One. . . .

Divine wisdom will order the steps of those who put their trust in the Lord. Divine love will encircle them, and they will realize the presence of the Comforter, the Holy Spirit.[21]

"I TASTED THE LORD'S GOODNESS"

If so be ye have tasted that the Lord is gracious. 1 Peter 2:3.

Have you tasted that the Lord is gracious? Does your spiritual appetite crave communion with the Lord? You may discover that He is gracious, not by having all you desire, but by passing through the school of affliction. Since I was nine years old I have been learning in the school of affliction. In my early childhood I could find nothing desirable but the precious words of Jesus. Since I tasted the Word of God in all its sweetness, I have never lost the desire for more.

After I went to Australia I was afflicted with rheumatism and malaria. For eleven months I did not have the free use of my arms. After the first week of wonder as to what it all meant, I concluded it would be best to stop wondering, and to leave myself in the hands of the Lord. I tasted His goodness and found that He is gracious. Only a little while during the night could I forget the pain enough to sleep. Yet I tasted the Lord's goodness. The sense of His presence shut me in from the world, so that it seemed as if I could speak to Him face to face, as did Moses. Throughout all the pain and suffering, I felt that I had with me a heavenly Companion. . . .

Christ says, I am at thy right hand to help thee. What more could we in our weakness desire? Shall we go to one another with all our troubles, telling human beings the temptations we have and how weak we are? The Saviour is standing at our right hand, offering to lift us up, that we may "sit together in heavenly places in Christ Jesus." Eph. 2:6. But so often we turn away from Him and His promises, and tell our troubles to those who, like ourselves, are but mortal, with troubles which only Christ can bear. . . . Let us no longer dishonor God by turning from Him to human inefficiency. . . .

Take your troubles to the Master. Say, "Here I am, Lord. Thou knowest all about me, and Thou canst help me. I will follow in Thy footsteps and do Thy will." When you commit yourself to God, you may be sure that in all times of affliction you will have the very help that you need.[22]

REJOICE!

Rejoice in the Lord alway: and again I say, Rejoice. . . . Be careful for nothing; but in every thing by prayer and supplication with thanksgiving let your requests be made known unto God. Phil. 4:4-6.

It may seem difficult to rejoice in the Lord when in trouble, but we lose a great deal by giving way to a spirit of complaint. It is our privilege to have in our hearts, at all times, the peace of Christ. We should not allow ourselves to be easily disturbed. It is to test us that God brings us through trials and difficulties, and if we are patient and trustful under His proving, He will purify us from all dross, and at last bring us forth with triumph and rejoicing. Great blessings are reserved for those who uncomplainingly submit to the yoke that God wishes them to bear. . . .

Let the light of truth shine forth in your life. Do you say, How shall I let it shine? If before you accepted the truth, you were impatient and fretful, let your life now show to those around you that the truth has had a sanctifying influence upon your heart and character, that instead of being fretful and impatient, you are now cheerful and uncomplaining. Thus you reveal Christ to the world. . . .

"In every thing give thanks" (1 Thess. 5:18) for the keeping power of God through Jesus Christ. . . . At the moment when you are offering your prayer for help you may not feel all the joy and blessing that you would like to feel, but if you believe that Christ will hear and answer your petition, the peace of Christ will come. . . .

If you take hold of the strength of the mighty Helper, and not reason with your adversary and never complain of God, His promises will be verified. The experience that you gain today in trusting Him will help you in meeting the difficulties of tomorrow. Each day you are to come, trusting as a little child drawing nearer to Jesus and heaven. In meeting with unwavering trust in God the daily trials and difficulties, you will again and again test the promises of Heaven, and each time you will learn a lesson of faith. Thus you will gain strength to resist temptation, and when the harder trials come, you will be able to endure.[23]

November 17

PEACE IN AFFLICTION

And the peace of God, which passeth all understanding, shall keep your hearts and minds through Christ Jesus. Phil. 4:7.

Jesus came to earth to be not only man's Redeemer but his great Exemplar. His was a perfect life, a life of meekness, lowliness, purity, and unlimited trust in God. . . . He taught us practically the great lesson of calm, constant, unwavering confidence in our heavenly Father. He permits temptations, trials, and afflictions to come to His loved ones. They are His providences, visitations of mercy to bring them back when they stray from His side, and give them a deeper sense of His presence and providential care. The peace that passeth understanding is not for those who shrink from trials, from struggles, and from self-denial. . . .

The eye of Jesus is upon us every moment. The clouds which intervene between the soul and the Sun of Righteousness are in the providence of God permitted to arise that our faith may be strengthened to grasp the great hopes, the sure promises, that shine undimmed through the darkness of every storm. Faith must grow through conflict and suffering. We must individually learn to suffer and be strong, and not sink down in weakness. . . .

It is a great kindness on the part of our heavenly Father when He allows us to be placed under circumstances that lessen the attractions of earth, and lead us to place our affections on things above. Frequently, the loss of earthly blessings teaches us more than their possession. When we pass through trials and afflictions, it is no evidence that Jesus does not love and bless us. The pitying Lamb of God identifies His interest with that of His suffering ones. He guards them every moment. He is acquainted with every grief; He knows every suggestion of Satan, every doubt that tortures the soul. . . . He is pleading the case of the tempted, the erring, and the faithless. He is striving to lift them into companionship with Himself. It is His work to sanctify His people, to cleanse, ennoble, and purify them, and fill their hearts with peace. He is thus fitting them for glory, honor, and eternal life; for an inheritance richer and more lasting than that of any earthly prince.[24]

CHRIST'S LEGACY OF PEACE

Peace I leave with you, my peace I give unto you: not as the world giveth, give I unto you. Let not your heart be troubled, neither let it be afraid. John 14:27.

Shortly before His crucifixion Christ bequeathed to His disciples a legacy of peace. . . . This peace is not the peace that comes through conformity with the world. It is an internal rather than an external peace. Without will be wars and fightings, through the opposition of avowed enemies, and the coldness and suspicion of those who claim to be friends. The peace of Christ is not to banish division, but it is to remain amid strife and division.

Though he bore the title of Prince of Peace, Christ said of Himself, "Think not that I am come to send peace on earth: I came not to send peace, but a sword." Matt. 10:34. The Prince of Peace, He was yet the cause of division.[25]

Families must be divided in order that all who call upon the name of the Lord may be saved. All who refuse His infinite love will find Christianity a sword, a disturber of their peace. . . .

It is impossible for anyone to become a true follower of Jesus Christ without distinguishing himself from the worldly mass of unbelievers. If the world would accept of Jesus, then there would be no sword of dissension; for all would be disciples of Christ and in fellowship one with another, and their unity would be unbroken. But this is not the case. Here and there an individual member of a family is true to the convictions of his conscience, and is compelled to stand alone. . . . The line of demarcation is made distinct. One stands upon the Word of God, the others upon the traditions and sayings of men. . . .

The peace that Christ gave to His disciples, and for which we pray, is the peace that is born of truth, a peace that is not to be quenched because of division. Without may be wars and fightings, jealousies, envies, hatred, strife; but the peace of Christ is not that which the world giveth or taketh away.[26]

November 19

THE FOUNDATION OF ALL TRUE PEACE

These things I have spoken unto you, that in me ye might have peace. John 16:33.

"That in me ye might have peace"—peace in Christ, peace through belief of the truth. The Comforter is called the Spirit of truth because there is comfort and hope and peace in the truth. Falsehood cannot give genuine peace; this can be received only through the truth. . . .

Jesus prayed that His followers might be one; but we are not to sacrifice the truth in order to secure this union, for we are to be sanctified through the truth. Here is the foundation of all true peace. Human wisdom would change all this, pronouncing this basis too narrow. Men would try to effect unity through concession to popular opinion, through compromise with the world, a sacrifice of vital godliness. But truth is God's basis for the unity of His people.

Sanctification, unity, peace—all are to be ours through the truth. The belief of the truth does not make men gloomy and uncomfortable. If you have peace in Christ, His precious blood is speaking pardon and hope to your soul. Yes, more, you have joy in the Holy Spirit, through accepting the precious promises. Jesus says, "In the world ye shall have tribulation: but be of good cheer; I have overcome the world." John 16:33. Therefore the world shall not overcome you if you believe in Me. It is a world that I have conquered. Because I have overcome, if you believe in Me, you shall overcome. . . .

All that Jesus has promised, He will fulfill; and it is greatly dishonoring to Him for us to doubt Him. All His words are spirit and life. Accepted and obeyed, they will give peace and happiness and assurance forever. . . . Christ declares that He has given us peace; it belongs to us. And He has spoken these things, that in Him we may have that which through infinite sacrifice He had purchased for us— what He holds as ours. This peace we need not seek in the world, for the world has it not to bestow. It is in Christ. He will give it, in spite of the world, notwithstanding its threats and decrees, its alluring, deceiving promises.[27]

A SUPERFICIAL
EXPERIENCE NOT ENOUGH

That ye may be blameless and harmless, the sons of God, without rebuke, in the midst of a crooked and perverse nation, among whom ye shine as lights in the world. Phil. 2:15.

There is always danger of being satisfied with a superficial work; there is always danger that souls will not anchor themselves in God, but be content to drift hither and thither, the sport of Satan's temptations. . . . The work of the Spirit of God in the heart will develop true penitence, which will not end with confession, but will work a decided reformation in the daily life. There will be manifested an earnestness, a perseverance, and a determination that can be properly represented by agonizing. . . .

The fact that iniquity abounds, that we are surrounded by infidels and skeptics, or by professed Christians who have a name to live, and are dead, is no reason why one of us should be swept away by the current toward perdition. Because there is an almost universal forsaking of God, there is the greater need that we stand firm and loyal. . . . We must gather the divine rays from the Sun of Righteousness, and reflect them to the world. In the midst of a crooked and perverse generation, we must show forth the praises of Him who has called us out of darkness into His marvelous light.

Nothing but a deep personal experience will enable us to stand the test of the trials and temptations we shall meet in the Christian warfare. Too often we feel well when everything goes smoothly; but when doubts assail the soul, and Satan whispers his suggestions, our defense is gone, and we yield quickly to the arts of the tempter, with scarcely an effort to resist and repulse him. It is not enough to have good impulses. The soul must be barricaded by prayer and study of the Scriptures. Armed with these weapons, Jesus encountered our wily foe on the field of battle, and overcame him. We may all conquer in His strength; but it will not answer for us to suppose that we can dispense with His help. He says, "Without me ye can do nothing." John 15:5. But no truly humble soul who walks in the light as Christ is in the light, will be ensnared by Satan's deceptive devices.[28]

ROOTED IN CHRIST

The righteous shall flourish like the palm tree: he shall grow like a cedar in Lebanon. Ps. 92:12.

The Christian is likened to the cedar of Lebanon. I have read that this tree does more than send down a few short roots into the yielding loam. It sends strong roots deep down into the earth, and strikes down farther and still farther in search of a still stronger hold. And in the fierce blast of the tempest, it stands firm, held by its network of cables beneath.

So the Christian strikes root deep into Christ. He has faith in his Redeemer. He knows in whom he believes. He is fully persuaded that Jesus is the Son of God and the Saviour of sinners. . . . The roots of faith strike deep down. Genuine Christians, like the cedar of Lebanon, do not grow in the soft surface soil, but are rooted in God, riveted in the clefts of the mountain rocks.[29]

If the Christian thrives and progresses at all, he must do so amid strangers to God, amid scoffing, subject to ridicule. He must stand upright like the palm tree in the desert. The sky may be as brass, the desert sand may beat about the palm tree's roots, and pile itself in heaps about its trunk. Yet the tree lives as an evergreen, fresh and vigorous amid the burning desert sands. Remove the sand till you reach the rootlets of the palm tree, and you discover the secret of its life; it strikes down deep beneath the surface, to the secret waters hidden in the earth.[30]

As the palm tree, drawing nourishment from fountains of living water, is green and flourishing in the midst of the desert, so the Christian may draw rich supplies of grace from the fountain of God's love, and may guide weary souls, that are full of unrest and ready to perish in the desert of sin, to those waters of which they may drink, and live. The Christian is ever pointing his fellow men to Jesus, who invites, "If any man thirst, let him come unto me, and drink." John 7:37. This fountain never fails us, we may draw, and draw again.[31]

NO TAPROOT?

Therefore, my beloved brethren, be ye stedfast, unmoveable, always abounding in the work of the Lord, forasmuch as ye know that your labour is not in vain in the Lord. 1 Cor. 15:58.

In order to be firmly anchored, there must be something firm to hold us; and nothing will avail until Christ takes possession of the soul. . . . Many who now appear strong, and talk in vindication of the truth, are not rooted and grounded. They have no tap-root; and when the storms of opposition and persecution come, they are like a tree uprooted by the blast.[32]

We shall be attacked on every point; we shall be tried to the utmost. We do not want to hold our faith simply because it was handed down to us by our fathers. Such a faith will not stand the terrible test that is before us. We want to know why we are Seventh-day Adventists—what real reason we have for coming out from the world as a separate and distinct people. . . .

When men are willing to become intelligent in regard to the cause of God because they have invested faith and means in it, God will help them to understand, and they will be steadfast in the faith; but when they have merely a theory, a shallow faith they cannot explain, a sudden temptation will cause them to drift away with the current bearing toward the world. . . .

Our minds must be prepared to stand every test, and to resist every temptation, whether from without or from within. We must know why we believe as we do, why we are on the Lord's side. The truth must keep watch in our hearts, ready to sound an alarm, and summon us to action against every foe. The powers of darkness will open their batteries upon us; and all who are indifferent and careless, who have set their affections on their earthly treasure, and who have not cared to understand God's dealings with His people, will be ready victims. No power but a knowledge of the truth as it is in Jesus, will ever make us steadfast; but with this, one may chase a thousand, and two put ten thousand to flight.[33]

THE STAMINA OF PURE RELIGION

And I will walk at liberty: for I seek thy precepts. Ps. 119:45.

There are some who talk in a regretful way concerning the restraints that the religion of the Bible imposes upon those who would follow its teachings. They seem to think that restraint is a great disadvantage, but we have reason to thank God with all our heart that He has raised a heavenly barrier between us and the ground of the enemy. There are certain tendencies of the natural heart that many think must be followed in order that the best development of the individual may result, but that which man thinks essential God sees would not be the blessing to humanity which men imagine; for the development of these very traits of character would unfit them for the mansions above. The Lord places men under test and trial that the dross may be separated from the gold; but He forces none. He does not bind with fetters and cords and barriers; for they increase disaffection rather than decrease it. . . . Genuine religion does not have a narrowing influence; it is a lack of religion that cramps the faculties and narrows the mind.[34]

Religion is an active, working principle, and furnishes a stamina sufficient for the stern realities of life. . . . Religion ever imparts power to its possessor to restrain, control, and balance the character and intellect and emotions. It has a power to persuade, entreat, and command with divine authority all the ability and affections. Religion—oh, I wish we all understood its workings! It lays us under the weightiest obligations. As we connect ourselves with Christ we solemnly pledge ourselves to walk as Christ walked.[35]

It is our privilege to show forth the praises of Him who hath called us out of darkness into His marvelous light. . . . The Lord's way must be kept, and His way is exalted in righteousness. Christians, in their manner and words and character, are to reveal their heavenly extraction. We are never to apologize to the world for being Christians and daring to be right.[36]

Pure religion brings peace, happiness, contentment; godliness is profitable to this life and the life to come.[37]

A TIME TO BE BLIND AND DEAF

Who is blind, but my servant? or deaf, as my messenger that I sent? who is blind as he that is perfect, and blind as the Lord's servant? Seeing many things, but thou observest not; opening the ears, but he heareth not. Isa. 42:19, 20.

What kind of blindness is this? It is a blindness that will not allow our eyes to contemplate evil. It will not allow our eyes to rest upon iniquity. It will not grasp the things of sight and lose eternity out of its reckoning. . . . We want to see aright, we want to see as God sees; for Satan is constantly trying to convert the things our eyes rest upon in order that we may see through his medium. . . .

The servant of the living God sees to some purpose. The eyes are sanctified and the ears are sanctified, and those who will close their eyes and ears to evil will become changed. But if they will listen to those who will address them and try to lead their thoughts away from God and their eternal interests, then their whole senses are perverted by that which their eyes rest upon. Jesus says, "If . . . thine eye be single, thy whole body shall be full of light. But if thine eye be evil, thy whole body shall be full of darkness." Matt. 6:22, 23.

It makes every difference what we give our minds and souls to feed upon. We can let our minds dwell upon romance and castle-building, and what will it do for us? It will ruin us, soul and body. . . . We want to have that power that will enable us to close our eyes to scenes that are not elevating, that are not ennobling, that will not purify and refine us; and to keep our ears closed to everything that is forbidden in God's Word. He forbids us to imagine evil, to speak evil, and even to think evil. . . .

I see in Jesus everything that is lovely, everything that is holy, everything that is uplifting and pure. Then why should I want to open my eyes wide to see everything that is disagreeable? By beholding we become changed. Let us look to Jesus and consider the loveliness of His character, and by beholding we shall become changed into the same likeness.[38]

LET GOD'S HAND MOLD THE CLAY

But now, O Lord, thou art our father; we are the clay, and thou our potter; and we are all the work of thy hand. Isa. 64:8.

We do not know what the Lord will do for us, if we will come into line. God sees what He can make of man. There are possibilities which our feeble faith does not discern. "Ye are God's husbandry, ye are God's building." 1 Cor. 3:9. He sees all the now unamiable traits of character in man, and He knows, if men will learn the meekness and lowliness of Christ, He can mold and fashion the combative spirit, the unamiable disposition, and bring every power of the being into working order to advance His kingdom. He longs to refine, elevate, and ennoble the entire life. . . . Through the Holy Spirit's power He can use the very worst characters, and make them men and women of opportunity.

Blessed is the man who by faith can get a glimpse of Christ's faith. . . . Then there is a possibility of his becoming Christlike in character. . . . Great light comes to man as he sees the privileges that are for him. He sees God's plans for him and he dies to self. . . . He submits to be worked. . . . When he submits to be as clay in the hands of the potter, then God works the man into a vessel of honor.[39]

Clay in the hands of the potter . . . is turned again and again until the will of the potter is wrought out in the vessel. Grace and truth will make perfect the work of fashioning the human clay, that the glory of the great Potter may appear in the production of a shapely vessel, molded and polished for service.[40]

The Potter cannot mold and fashion unto honor that which has never been placed in His hands. The Christian life is one of daily surrender, submission, and continual overcoming. Every day fresh victories will be gained. Self must be lost sight of, and the love of God must be constantly cultivated. Thus we grow up into Christ. Thus the life is fashioned according to the divine model.[41]

Let the hand of God work the clay for His own service. He knows just what kind of vessel He wants.[42]

EXAMINE YOURSELVES

Examine yourselves, whether ye be in the faith; prove your own selves. Know ye not your own selves, how that Jesus Christ is in you, except ye be reprobates? 2 Cor. 13:5.

"Examine yourselves, whether ye be in the faith." Many . . . may immediately respond, "Why, yes; I am in the faith, I believe every point of the truth." But do you practice what you believe? Are you at peace with God and with your brethren? Can you pray with sincerity, "Forgive us our debts, as we forgive our debtors"? . . . Is there no bitterness in your hearts, no envying, no jealousy, no evil surmising? . . . Is there no emulation, no desire for special favor and honors, no wish to have the supremacy? . . .

We do well to examine ourselves to see what manner of spirit we are cherishing. Let us learn to speak gently, quietly, even under circumstances the most trying. Let us control not only our words, but our thoughts and imaginations. Let us be kind, be courteous.[43]

Many are sensible of their great deficiency, and they read, and pray, and resolve, and yet make no progress. They seem to be powerless to resist temptation. The reason is, they do not go deep enough. They do not seek for a thorough conversion of the soul, that the streams which issue from it may be pure, and the deportment may testify that Christ reigns within. All defects of character originate in the heart. Pride, vanity, evil temper, and covetousness proceed from the carnal heart unrenewed by the grace of Christ. If the heart is refined, softened, and ennobled, the words and actions will testify to the fact. When the soul has been entirely surrendered to God, there will be a firm reliance upon His promises, and earnest prayer and determined effort to control the words and actions.[44]

We profess a great and holy faith; and our characters must be in accordance with that faith, and with God's great moral standard. . . .

Let us examine our hearts in the light of the great principles of the law of God as defined by Christ: "Thou shalt love the Lord thy God with all thy heart, and with all thy soul, and with all thy mind; and thy neighbour as thyself." Luke 10:27.[45]

"KEEP THYSELF PURE"

Blessed are the pure in heart: for they shall see God. Matt. 5:8.

To know what constitutes purity of mind, soul, and body is the highest class of education. Paul the apostle sums up in his letter to Timothy the attainments possible for him, by saying "Keep thyself pure."[46]

It is the special work of Satan in these last days to take possession of the minds of the youth, to corrupt their thoughts, and inflame their passions. All are free moral agents, and as such they must bring their thoughts to run in the right channel. . . . If Satan seeks to divert the mind to low and sensual things, bring it back again, and place it on eternal things; and when the Lord sees the determined effort made to retain only pure thoughts, He will attract the mind, like the magnet, and purify the thoughts. . . . The first work of those who would reform is to purify the imagination. If the mind is led out in a vicious direction, it must be restrained to dwell only upon pure and elevated subjects. When tempted to yield to a corrupt imagination, then flee to the throne of grace, and pray for strength from Heaven. In the strength of God the imagination can be disciplined to dwell upon things which are pure and heavenly. . . .

Those who would have that wisdom which is from God, must become fools in the sinful knowledge of this age, in order to be wise. They should shut their eyes, that they may see and learn no evil. They should close their ears, lest they hear that which is evil, and obtain that knowledge which would stain their purity of thoughts and acts. And they should guard their tongues, lest they utter corrupt communications, and guile be found in their mouths. All are accountable for their actions while upon probation in this world. All have power to control their actions. If they are weak in virtue and purity of thoughts and acts, they can obtain help from the Friend of the helpless. Jesus is acquainted with all the weaknesses of human nature, and if entreated, will give strength to overcome the most powerful temptations. All can obtain this strength if they seek for it in humility.[47]

"ON UNTO PERFECTION"

Till we all come in the unity of the faith, and of the knowledge of the Son of God, unto a perfect man, unto the measure of the stature of the fulness of Christ. Eph. 4:13.

It is a great, a solemn work to obtain a moral fitness for the society of the pure and the blest. . . . Only by conforming to the Word of God can we hope to come to "the measure of the stature of the fulness of Christ." But we must do this, or we shall never enter heaven. Without purity and holiness of heart, we cannot win the crown of immortal glory.[48]

The life of the soul cannot be sustained, except by the right exercise of the affections heavenward, Christward, Godward. Repentance and faith in Christ for the forgiveness of sins are essential, but not all that is required. . . . The Christian's life is now but just begun. He must, as exhorted by the apostle, "go on unto perfection." He must bring every thought into captivity to the obedience of Christ. If we believe in Jesus, we will love to think of Him, love to talk of Him, love to pray to Him. He is supreme in our affections. We love that which Christ loves, and hate that which Christ hates. . . .

The Christian life is never at a standstill. It is, it must be, progressive. Our love for Christ should become stronger and stronger. . . .

My brother, my sister, is your soul in the love of God? Many of you have a twilight perception of Christ's excellence, and your soul thrills with joy. You long for a fuller, deeper sense of the Saviour's love. You long to entwine your affections about Him more closely. You are unsatisfied. But do not despair. Give to Jesus the heart's best and holiest affections. Treasure every ray of light. Cherish every desire of the soul after God. Give yourselves the culture of spiritual thoughts and holy communings. . . . Make haste to ripen for Heaven. . . .

It will cost us something to obtain a Christian experience and to develop a true and noble character. . . . But the white-robed throng of the redeemed ones, are those who have washed their robes, and made them white in the blood of the Lamb.[49]

SEEING HIM WHO IS INVISIBLE

By faith Moses, when he was come to years, refused to be called the son of Pharaoh's daughter. . . . By faith he forsook Egypt, not fearing the wrath of the king: for he endured, as seeing him who is invisible. Heb. 11:24-27.

Moses . . . lived as seeing Him who is invisible, and was therefore able to count the reproaches of Christ greater riches than the treasures of Egypt. If men would live in this way, we should see their faces aglow with the glory of God; for they would be viewing the glory of the eternal, and by beholding, would be transformed into the image of Christ.[50]

Our minds take the level of the things on which our thoughts dwell, and if we think upon earthly things, we shall fail to take the impress of that which is heavenly. We would be greatly benefited by contemplating the mercy, goodness, and love of God; but we sustain great loss by dwelling upon those things which are earthly and temporal. We allow sorrow and care and perplexity to attract our minds to earth, and we magnify a molehill into a mountain. . . . Temporal things are not to . . . engross our minds until our thoughts are entirely of the earth and the earthly. We are to train, discipline, and educate the mind so that we may think in a heavenly channel, that we may dwell on things unseen and eternal, which will be discerned by spiritual vision. It is by seeing Him who is invisible that we may obtain strength of mind and vigor of spirit. . . .

In whatever place we are called by the providence of God, we may confidently expect that God will be our helper. We are not to be a toy to circumstances, but to be above circumstances. . . . When we are placed in trying positions, and find things about us that we do not like, that try our patience, and test our faith, we are not to sink down in despondency, but to take a firmer hold upon God, and prove that we are not setting our affection on things on the earth, but on things above; that we are looking unto Jesus, the author and finisher of our faith. Jesus is to be the beginning and the end, the first and the last. He is to be our strength in every time of trial.[51]

CHARMED WITH CHRIST'S LOVE

If ye then be risen with Christ, seek those things which are above, where Christ sitteth on the right hand of God. Set your affection on things above, not on things on the earth. Col. 3:1, 2.

When we are tempted to place our affections on any earthly object that has a tendency to absorb our love, we must seek grace to turn from it, and not allow it to come between us and our God. We want to keep before the mind's eye the mansions which Jesus has gone to prepare for us. We must not allow our houses and lands, our business transactions and worldly enterprises to come between us and our God. We should keep before us the rich promises that He has left on record.

We should study the great waymarks that point out the times in which we are living. . . . We should now pray most earnestly that we may be prepared for the struggles of the great day of God's preparation. We should rejoice in the prospect of soon being with Jesus in the mansions He has gone to prepare for us. . . . Jesus can supply your every need. . . . As you behold Him you will be charmed with the riches of the glory of His divine love. The idolatrous love of things that are seen will be superseded by a higher and better love for things that are imperishable and precious. You may contemplate eternal riches until your affections are bound to things above, and you may be an instrument in directing others to set their affections on heavenly treasures. . . .

Those who rightly value money are those who see its availability in bringing the truth before those who have never heard it, and by this means rescuing them from the power of the enemy. If one soul accepts the truth, his love for earthly things is dislodged. He sees the surpassing glory of heavenly things, appreciates the excellency of that which relates to everlasting life. He is charmed with the unseen and eternal. His grasp loosens from earthly things. He fastens his eye with admiration upon the invincible glories of the other world. He realizes that his trials are working out for him a far more exceeding and eternal weight of glory, and in comparison to the riches that are his to enjoy he counts them light afflictions which are but for a moment.[52]

SHOW YOUR COLORS!

Let thine eyes look right on, and let thine eyelids look straight before thee. Prov. 4:25.

In *Pilgrim's Progress* there is a character called Pliable. Youth, shun this character. Those represented by it are very accommodating, but they are as a reed shaken by the wind. They possess no will power. Every youth needs to cultivate decision. A divided state of the will is a snare, and will be the ruin of many youth. Be firm, else you will be left with your house, or character, built upon a sandy foundation. . . . Manifest decision at any cost. . . . Those who would walk in the path cast up for the chosen of the Lord, must not be swayed in matters of conscience by men who have often been zealous for the wrong. They must show moral independence, and must not be afraid to be singular. . . .

Many are changed by every current. They wait to hear what someone else thinks, and his opinion is accepted as altogether true. If they would lean wholly upon God, they would grow strong in His strength; but they do not say to the Lord, I cannot make any decision until I know Thy will. Their natural inclination is to allow another to be conscience for them; and they speak after he has spoken, saying what he says, and acting as he acts. When these persons are placed in circumstances where they must think and act for themselves, they dare not express any decided opinion. Yet often, like Aaron, they have much ability. God pity such weaklings. . . .

We must free ourselves from the customs and bondage of society, that when the principles of our faith are at stake, we shall not hesitate to show our colors, even though we are called singular for so doing. Keep the conscience tender, that you may hear the faintest whisper of the voice that spoke as never man spoke. Let all who would wear the yoke of Christ show an inflexible purpose to do right because it is right. Keep the eye fixed on Jesus, inquiring at every step, Is this the way of the Lord? The Lord will not leave any one who does this, to become the sport of Satan's temptation. . . .

Do not imitate men. Study your Bibles, and imitate Christ.[1]

NO PATCHWORK RELIGION!

But he that shall endure unto the end, the same shall be saved.
Matt. 24:13.

The religion that is built on self is worthless; for God makes no compromise with selfishness. . . .

The religion of Christ is a firm fabric, composed of innumerable threads, woven together with tact and skill. Only by the wisdom that God gives can we weave this fabric. Trusting to ourselves, we draw into it threads of selfishness, and the pattern is spoiled.

There are many kinds of cloth which at first have a fine appearance, but they do not endure test. The colors are not fast. They wash out. Under the heat of summer they fade, and are lost. Such a fabric cannot endure rough handling, and is worth very little.

So it is with religion. When the warp and woof of religion will not stand the test of trial, the material of which it is composed is worthless. And an effort to patch the old cloth with a new piece does not better the condition of things; for the worn-out, flimsy material breaks away from the new, leaving the rent much larger than before. Patching will not do. The only way is to discard the old garment and procure a new one. The religion of self, composed of threads that fade and give way under the stress of temptation, must be cast aside, to be replaced by the religion woven by Him in whose life no selfishness found place.

Christ's plan is the only safe one. He declares, "Behold, I make all things new." Rev. 21:5. "If any man be in Christ, he is a new creature." 2 Cor. 5:17. The Saviour gives no encouragement to any to think that He will accept a patchwork religion. Such a religion is of no value in His sight. There may at first seem to be some of self and some of Christ; but it is soon seen that there is none of Christ. The patches of selfishness increase till the entire garment is covered with them. . . .

A religion formed after the divine pattern is the only one that will endure. Only by striving to live the life of Christ here can we prepare ourselves to live with Him through the eternal ages.[2]

GOD'S SPECIAL SIGN

I am the Lord your God; walk in my statutes, and keep my judgments, and do them; and hallow my sabbaths; and they shall be a sign between me and you, that ye may know that I am the Lord your God. Eze. 20:19, 20.

The Sabbath was given to all mankind to commemorate the work of Creation. The great Jehovah, when He had laid the foundations of the earth, when He had dressed the whole world in its garb of beauty, and created all the wonders of the land and the sea, instituted the Sabbath day and made it holy. When the morning stars sang together, and all the sons of God shouted for joy, the Sabbath was set apart as God's memorial. God sanctified and blessed the day in which He had rested from all His wondrous work. . . .

As the tree of knowledge was placed in the midst of the Garden of Eden, so the Sabbath command is placed in the midst of the Decalogue. In regard to the fruit of the tree of knowledge, the restriction was made, "Ye shall not eat of it, . . . lest ye die." Gen. 3:3. Of the Sabbath, God said, Ye shall not defile it, but keep it holy. "Remember the sabbath day, to keep it holy." Ex. 20:8. As the tree of knowledge was the test of Adam's obedience, so the fourth command is the test that God has given to prove the loyalty of all His people.[3]

The Sabbath is a token between God and His people. It is a holy day, given by the Creator to man as a day upon which to rest, and reflect upon sacred things. God designed it to be observed through every age as a perpetual covenant. It was to be regarded as a peculiar treasure, a trust to be carefully cherished.

As we observe the Sabbath let us remember that it is the sign which heaven has given to man that he is accepted in the Beloved; that if he is obedient, he may enter the city of God, and partake of the fruit of the tree of life. As we refrain from labor on the seventh day, we testify to the world that we are on God's side, and are striving to live in perfect conformity to His commandments. Thus we recognize as our sovereign the God who made the world in six days and rested on the seventh.

The Sabbath is the clasp which unites God and His people.[4]

IN THE TESTING TIME

Know therefore that the Lord thy God, he is God, the faithful God, which keepeth covenant and mercy with them that love him and keep his commandments to a thousand generations. Deut. 7:9.

Where shall we be before the thousand generations mentioned in this scripture are ended? Our fate will have been decided for eternity. We shall either have been pronounced worthy of a home in the everlasting kingdom of God, or we shall have received sentence of eternal death.[5]

God is testing His people, to see who will be loyal to the principles of His truth. Our work is to proclaim to the world the first, second, and third angels' messages. In the discharge of our duty we are neither to despise nor fear our enemies. . . .

The true Sabbath is to be the sign that distinguishes those who serve God from those who serve Him not. Let those who have become sleepy and indifferent awake. We are called to be holy, and we should carefully avoid giving the impression that it is of little consequence whether or not we retain the peculiar features of our faith. Upon us rests the solemn obligation of taking a more decided stand for truth and righteousness than we have taken in the past. The line of demarcation between those who keep the commandments of God and those who do not is to be revealed with unmistakable clearness. We are conscientiously to honor God, diligently using every means of keeping in covenant relation with Him, that we may receive His blessings—the blessings so essential for a people who are to be so severely tried. To give the impression that our faith, our religion, is not a dominating power in our lives, is greatly to dishonor God.[6]

Putting our trust in God, we are to move steadily forward, doing His work with unselfishness, in humble dependence upon Him, committing ourselves and our present and future to His wise providence, holding the beginning of our confidence firm unto the end, remembering that it is not because of our worthiness that we receive the blessings of heaven, but because of the worthiness of Christ, and our acceptance, through faith in Him, of God's abounding grace.[7]

A DISTINCT AND PECULIAR PEOPLE

Here is the patience of the saints: here are they that keep the commandments of God, and the faith of Jesus. Rev. 14:12.

God's people are to be distinguished as a people who serve Him fully, wholeheartedly, taking no honor to themselves, and remembering that by a most solemn covenant they have bound themselves to serve the Lord, and Him only. . . .

The children of Israel were to observe the Sabbath throughout their generations "for a perpetual covenant." Ex. 31:16. The Sabbath has lost none of its meaning. It is still the sign between God and His people, and it will be so forever. Now and ever we are to stand as a distinct and peculiar people, free from all worldly policy, unembarrassed by confederation with those who have not wisdom to discern the claims of God, so plainly set forth in His law.

We are to show that we are seeking to work in harmony with heaven in preparing the way of the Lord. We are to bear witness to all nations, kindreds, and tongues, that we are a people who love and fear God, a people who keep holy the seventh-day Sabbath, and we are to show plainly that we have full faith that the Lord is soon to come in the clouds of heaven. . . .

"And there shall be no more curse: but the throne of God and of the Lamb shall be in it; and his servants shall serve him: and they shall see his face; and his name shall be in their foreheads." Rev. 22:3, 4.

Who are these?—God's denominated people—those who on this earth have witnessed to their loyalty. Who are they?—Those who have kept the commandments of God and the faith of Jesus; those who have owned the Crucified One as their Saviour.

"And there shall be no night there; and they need no candle, neither light of the sun; for the Lord God giveth them light: and they shall reign for ever and ever." Verse 5. "Blessed are they that do his commandments, that they may have right to the tree of life, and may enter in through the gates into the city." Verse 14.[8]

HIGH TIME TO AWAKE

And that, knowing the time, that now it is high time to awake out of sleep: for now is our salvation nearer than when we believed. Rom. 13:11.

The great controversy is nearing its end. Every report of calamity by sea or land is a testimony to the fact that the end of all things is at hand. Wars and rumors of wars declare it. Is there a Christian whose pulse does not beat with quickened action as he anticipates the great events opening before us? The Lord is coming. We hear the footsteps of an approaching God.[9]

This knowledge of the nearness of Christ's coming should not be allowed to lose its force, and we become careless and inattentive, and fall into slumber—into an insensibility and indifference to realities. In slumber we are in an unreal world, and not sensible of the things which are taking place around us. . . .

There are those who have the blazing light of truth shining all around them, and yet are insensible to it. They are enchanted by the enemy, held under a spell by his bewitching power. They are not preparing for that great day which is soon to come to our world. They seem utterly insensible to religious truth.

Are there not some youth who are awake? Those who see that the night cometh, and also the morning, should work with untiring energy to arouse their sleeping associates. Can they not feel their peril, pray for them, and show them by their own life and character that they believe themselves that Christ is soon to come? . . . The rapidly diminishing space of time between us and eternity should more deeply impress us. Every day that passes makes one less left us to complete our work of perfecting character. . . .

As long as there are many asleep, many sporting away the precious hours in careless indifference, as it were, upon the very brink of the eternal world, those who do believe must be sober, must be awake, must be earnest and diligent, and watch unto prayer. . . .

Have you, dear youth, your lamps trimmed and burning?[10]

WHERE APOSTASY BEGINS

Ye therefore, beloved, seeing ye know these things before, beware lest ye also, being led away with the error of the wicked, fall from your own stedfastness. 2 Peter 3:17.

In these last days, when iniquity shall abound, and the love of many shall wax cold, God will have a people to glorify His name, and stand as reprovers of unrighteousness. They are to be a "peculiar people," who will be true to the law of God, when the world shall seek to make void its precepts; and when the converting power of God works through His servants, the hosts of darkness will array themselves in bitter and determined opposition. Satan will work with "all power and signs and lying wonders, and with all deceivableness of unrighteousness." He will employ every device of deception to seduce the souls of men. . . .

The work of apostasy begins in some secret rebellion of the heart against the requirements of God's law. Unholy desires, unlawful ambitions, are cherished and indulged, and unbelief and darkness separate the soul from God. If we do not overcome these evils, they will overcome us.

Men who have long been advancing in the path of truth, will be tested with trial and temptation. Those who listen to the suggestions of Satan, and swerve from their integrity, begin the downward path, and some masterful temptation hastens them on in the way of apostasy, till their descent is marked and rapid. Sins that were once most repugnant, become attractive, and are welcomed and practiced by those who have cast off the fear of God and their allegiance to His law. But the most pleasurable beginning in transgression, will end in misery, degradation, and ruin.

We need to be constantly on our guard, to watch and pray lest we enter into temptation. The indulgence of spiritual pride, of unholy desires, of evil thoughts, of anything that separates us from an intimate and sacred association with Jesus, imperils our souls. We must have living faith in God. . . . If the thought of apostasy is grievous to you, and you do not desire to become the enemies of the truth, . . . then "abhor that which is evil; cleave to that which is good." Rom. 12:9.[11]

AM I A LAODICEAN?

I know thy works, that thou art neither cold nor hot: I would thou wert cold or hot. So then because thou art lukewarm, and neither cold nor hot, I will spue thee out of my mouth. Rev. 3:15, 16.

The condition of many of those who claim to be the children of God is exactly represented by the message to the Laodicean church. There is opened before those who serve God, truths of inestimable value, which, brought into the practical life, show the difference between those who serve God and those who serve Him not. . . .

The Bible is the storehouse of the unsearchable riches of God. But those who have a knowledge of the truth do not understand it as fully as they might. They do not bring the love of Christ into the heart and life. The student of the Word finds himself bending over a fountain of living water. The church needs to drink deeply of the spirituality of the Word. Their service to God needs to be very different from the tame, lifeless, emotionless religious experience that makes many believers but little different from those who believe not.[12]

Halfhearted Christians are worse than infidels; for their deceptive words and noncommittal position lead many astray. The infidel shows his colors. The lukewarm Christian deceives both parties. He is neither a good worldling nor a good Christian. Satan uses him to do a work that no one else can do.[13]

Love of self excludes the love of Christ. Those who live for self are ranged under the head of the Laodicean church who are lukewarm, neither cold nor hot. The ardor of the first love has lapsed into a selfish egotism. The love of Christ in the heart is expressed in the actions. If love for Christ is dull, the love for those for whom Christ has died will degenerate. There may be a wonderful appearance for zeal and ceremonies, but this is the substance of their self-inflated religion. Christ represents them as nauseating to His taste.[14]

Let us thank the Lord that while this class is so numerous, there is still time for repentance.[15]

THE RAGS OF SELF-RIGHTEOUSNESS

Because thou sayest, I am rich, and increased with goods, and have need of nothing; and knowest not that thou art wretched, and miserable, and poor, and blind, and naked. Rev. 3:17.

How plainly is pictured the position of those who think they have all the truth, who take pride in their knowledge of the Word of God, while its sanctifying power has not been felt in their lives. The fervor of the love of God is wanting in their hearts.[16]

Many are Laodiceans, living in a spiritual self-deception. They clothe themselves in the garments of their own righteousness, imagining themselves to be rich and increased with goods and in need of nothing, when they need daily to learn of Jesus, His meekness and lowliness.[17]

What is it that constitutes the wretchedness, the nakedness, of those who feel rich and increased with goods? It is the want of the righteousness of Christ. In their own righteousness they are represented as clothed with filthy rags, and yet in this condition they flatter themselves that they are clothed upon with Christ's righteousness. . . . They may be crying, "The temple of the Lord, the temple of the Lord are we," while their hearts are filled with unholy traffic and unrighteous barter. The courts of the soul temple may be the haunt of envy, pride, passion, evil surmising, bitterness, and hollow formalism. Christ looks mournfully upon His professed people who feel rich and increased in the knowledge of the truth, and who are yet destitute of the truth in life and character.[18]

Jesus says, "I, your Redeemer, know your works. I am familiar with the motives that prompt you to declare boastingly in regard to your spiritual condition, 'I am rich, and increased with goods, and have need of nothing.' Thou 'knowest not that thou art wretched, and miserable, and poor, and blind, and naked.'" . . . What a position to be in! They stand in their own light.

But notwithstanding their willful ignorance, they are not left by the Lord without added warning and counsel.[19]

THE SPOTLESS ROBE
OF CHRIST'S RIGHTEOUSNESS

I counsel thee to buy of me gold tried in the fire, that thou mayest be rich; and white raiment, that thou mayest be clothed, and that the shame of thy nakedness do not appear; and anoint thine eyes with eyesalve, that thou mayest see. Rev. 3:18.

The great Redeemer represents Himself as a heavenly merchantman, laden with riches, calling from house to house, presenting His priceless goods.[20]

We must have the buyers and the sellers cleared out of the soul temple, that Jesus may take up His abode within us. Now He stands at the door of the heart as a heavenly merchantman; He says, . . . "Open unto me; buy of me the heavenly wares; buy of me the gold tried in the fire." Buy faith and love, the precious, beautiful attributes of our Redeemer. . . . He invites us to buy the white raiment, which is His glorious righteousness; and the eyesalve, that we may discern spiritual things. Oh, shall we not open the heart's door to this heavenly visitor?[21]

We cannot provide a robe of righteousness for ourselves, for the prophet says, "All our righteousnesses are as filthy rags." Isa. 64:6. There is nothing in us from which we can clothe the soul so that its nakedness shall not appear. We are to receive the robe of righteousness woven in the loom of heaven, even the spotless robe of Christ's righteousness.[22]

The eye is the sensitive conscience, the inner light, of the mind. Upon its correct view of things the spiritual healthfulness of the whole soul and being depends. The "eyesalve," the Word of God, makes the conscience smart under its application, for it convicts of sin. But the smarting is necessary that the healing may follow, and the eye be single to the glory of God. . . . Says Christ, By renouncing your own self-sufficiency, giving up all things, however dear to you, you may buy the gold, the raiment, and the eyesalve that you may see.[23]

The Saviour comes with jewels of truth of the richest value in distinction from all counterfeits, all that is spurious. He comes to every house, to every door; He is knocking, presenting His priceless treasure, urging, "Buy of me."[24]

A MESSAGE FULL OF ENCOURAGEMENT

As many as I love, I rebuke and chasten: be zealous therefore, and repent. Rev. 3:19.

The counsel of the true Witness does not represent those who are lukewarm as in a hopeless case. There is yet a chance to remedy their state, and the Laodicean message is full of encouragement. . . . Purity of heart, purity of motive, may yet characterize those who are halfhearted and who are striving to serve God and mammon. They may yet wash their robes of character and make them white in the blood of the Lamb.[25]

The gold of faith and love, the white raiment of a spotless character, and the eyesalve, or the power of clear discernment between good and evil—all these we must obtain before we can hope to enter the kingdom of God. But these precious treasures will not drop upon us without some exertion on our part. We must buy—we must "be zealous and repent" of our lukewarm state. We must be awake to see our wrongs, to search for our sins, and to put them away from us. . . .

It is the worthiness of Christ that must save us, His blood that must cleanse us. But we have efforts to make. We must do what we can, be zealous and repent, then believe that God accepts us. . . .

All heaven is interested in our salvation; and shall we be indifferent? Shall we be careless, as though it was a small matter whether we are saved or lost? Shall we slight the sacrifice that has been made for us? . . .

In the time of peril before us the professed followers of Christ will be tested. None will be able to stand but those who have had a deep and living experience in the things of God. The work of all will then be tried; if it is gold, silver, and precious stones, they will be safely shielded, as in the secret of the Lord's pavilion. . . .

Only those who are willing to sacrifice all for eternal life will have it; but it will be worth suffering for, worth crucifying self and sacrificing every idol for. The far more exceeding and eternal weight of glory will outweigh every earthly treasure and eclipse every earthly attraction.[26]

WILL YOU OPEN THE DOOR?

Behold, I stand at the door, and knock: if any man hear my voice, and open the door, I will come in to him, and will sup with him, and he with me. Rev. 3:20.

Jesus says, "Behold, I stand at the door, and knock." Will we let Him in? He would not have us stand at this time, amid the perils of the last days, in our own finite strength. . . . It is our privilege to walk in the sunshine of His presence, and to weave into the characters we are forming the golden threads of cheerfulness, gratitude, forbearance, and love. We may thus show the power of divine grace, and reflect light from Heaven amid all the frets and irritations that come to us day by day. . . . Then why do we go stumbling along without light?[27]

Every warning, reproof, and entreaty in the Word of God, or through His delegated messengers, is a knock at the door of the heart; it is the voice of Jesus, asking for entrance. With every knock unheeded, your determination to open becomes weaker and weaker. If the voice of Jesus is not heeded at once, it becomes confused in the mind with a multitude of other voices, the world's care and business engross the attention, and conviction dies away. The heart becomes less impressible, and lapses into a perilous unconsciousness of the shortness of time, and of the great eternity beyond.[28]

Many have so much rubbish piled up at the door of the heart that they cannot admit Jesus. Some have difficulties between themselves and their brethren to remove; others have evil tempers, pride, covetousness; with others, love of the world bars the entrance. All this must be taken away, before they can open the door and welcome the Saviour in.

How precious is the promise, "I will come in to him, and will sup with him, and he with me." Oh, the love, the wondrous love of God! After all our lukewarmness and sins He says, Return unto Me, and I will return unto thee, and will heal all thy backslidings.[29]

Our work is to open the door of the heart and let Jesus come in. He is knocking for entrance. . . . Will you open the door? Jesus is standing at the door of your heart. Let Him in, the heavenly Guest.[30]

VICTORY IS ASSURED

To him that overcometh will I grant to sit with me in my throne, even as I also overcame, and am set down with my Father in his throne. Rev. 3:21.

The true Witness presents encouragements to all who are seeking to walk in the path of humble obedience, through faith in His name. He declares, "To him that overcometh will I grant to sit with me in my throne, even as I also overcame, and am set down with my Father in his throne." These are the words of our Substitute and Surety. He who is the divine Head of the church, the mightiest of conquerors, would point His followers to His life, His toils, His self-denials, His struggles and sufferings, through contempt, through rejection, ridicule, scorn, insult, mockery, falsehood, up the path of Calvary to the scene of the crucifixion, that they might be encouraged to press on toward the mark for the prize and reward of the overcomer. Victory is assured through faith and obedience.

Let us make an application of the words of Christ to our own individual cases. Are we poor, and blind, and wretched, and miserable? Then let us seek the gold and white raiment that He offers. The work of overcoming is not restricted to the age of the martyrs. The conflict is for us in these days of subtle temptation to worldliness, to self-security, to indulgence of pride, covetousness, false doctrines, and immorality of life.[31]

We can overcome. Yes; fully, entirely. Jesus died to make a way of escape for us, that we might overcome every fault, resist every temptation, and sit down at last with Him in His throne.[32]

We have no discouraging message for the church. Although reproofs and cautions and corrections have been made, yet the church has stood as God's instrumentality to diffuse light. The commandment-keeping people of God have sounded forth a warning to the world. . . . The church of God is a living witness, a continual testimony, to convince men if accepted, to condemn them if resisted and rejected.[33]

The church must and will shine forth "fair as the moon, clear as the sun, and terrible as an army with banners." S. of Sol. 6:10.[34]

UNMOVED IN A SHAKEN WORLD

I have set the Lord always before me: because he is at my right hand, I shall not be moved. Ps. 16:8.

We are living in an age of peril, when ungodliness is common. Even professed Christians do not believe their Bibles. The truth of the Word of God is too plain and pointed for them. . . . Antichristian ideas, customs, and practices prevail, and they are even construed to be Christian; but that which is of most value, that which God esteems most highly, is treated with contempt. Well may the God-fearing inquire, What shall the end of these things be? Love for Christ and love for one another is fast dying out of the hearts of men. . . .

Wickedness prevails on every hand; for Satan has come down having great wrath, knowing that he hath but a short time. He is a persevering, diligent, untiring worker, and if ever there was a time when men needed the presence of Christ at their right hand, it is now. . . . We need the Captain of our salvation continually by our side.

There is, and will continue to be, agitation all around us; for the kingdoms of the world will not be at rest. Never was there a time when the temptation to deny Christ in spirit and in deportment, was stronger, and this temptation will increase in power as we near the end. Strong and overpowering temptations will come upon men. False doctrines and fables will be presented as Bible truth, for men's acceptance; and if it were possible, they will deceive the very elect. But is it a time for our love to grow cold, when iniquity abounds? Is this a time to be at ease? Is this the time to separate from God, our Counselor?

The end of all things is at hand. The day of God is hastening on apace. The world is full of crime and anguish and sorrow. There are calamities by land and by sea. Storm and tempest make it unsafe for us to be separated from God for one single moment. Only those who live by faith in this probationary life, will be able to stand in the day of test, when everything that can be shaken will be shaken, but they shall dwell in safety and be unmoved.[35]

A CRISIS BEFORE US

And ye shall be brought before governors and kings for my sake, for a testimony against them and the Gentiles. Matt. 10:18.

The time is not far off where the people of God will be called upon to give their testimony before the rulers of the earth. Not one in twenty has a realization of what rapid strides we are making toward the great crisis in our history. . . . There is no time for vanity, for trifling, for engaging the mind in unimportant matters.[36]

Kings, governors, and great men will hear of you through the reports of those who are at enmity with you, and your faith and character will be misrepresented before them. But those who are falsely accused will have an opportunity to appear in the presence of their accusers to answer for themselves. They will have the privilege of bringing the light before those who are called the great men of the earth, and if you have studied the Bible, if you are ready to give an answer to every man that asketh you of the hope that is in you with meekness and fear, your enemies will not be able to gainsay your wisdom.

You now have an opportunity to attain to the greatest intellectual power through the study of the Word of God. But if you are indolent, and fail to dig deep in the mines of truth, you will not be ready for the crisis that is soon to come upon us. O that you would realize that each moment is golden. If you live by every word that proceedeth out of the mouth of God, you will not be found unprepared.[37]

You know not where you may be called upon to give your witness of truth. Many will have to stand in the legislative courts; some will have to stand before kings and before the learned of the earth, to answer for their faith. Those who have only a superficial understanding of truth will not be able clearly to expound the Scriptures, and give definite reasons for their faith. They will become confused, and will not be workmen that need not to be ashamed. Let no one imagine that he has no need to study, because he is not to preach in the sacred desk. You know not what God may require of you.[38]

ARE YOU READY FOR THE TESTING?

But when they deliver you up, take no thought how or what ye shall speak: for it shall be given you in that same hour what ye shall speak. Matt. 10:19.

The servants of Christ are to prepare no set speech to present when brought to trial for their faith. Their preparation is to be made day by day, in treasuring up in their hearts the precious truths of God's Word, in feeding upon the teaching of Christ, and through prayer strengthening their faith; then, when brought into trial, the Holy Spirit will bring to their remembrance the very truths that will reach the hearts of those who shall come to hear. God will flash the knowledge obtained by diligent searching of the Scriptures, into their memory at the very time when it is needed.[39]

You are now to get ready for the time of trial. Now you are to know whether your feet are planted on the Eternal Rock. You must have an individual experience, and not depend upon others for your light. When you are brought to the test, how do you know that you will not be alone, with no earthly friend at your side? Will you then be able to realize that Christ is your support? Will you be able to re-call the promise, "Lo, I am with you alway, even to the end of the world"? There will be invisible ones all about you bent upon your destruction. Satan and his agents will seek in every way to make you waver from your steadfastness to God and His truth. But if you have an eye single to His glory, you need not take thought as to how you shall witness for His truth.[40]

Young men and women, are you growing up to the full stature of men and women in Christ, so that when the crisis comes, you cannot be separated from the Source of your strength? If we would stand during the time of test, we must now, in the time of peace, be gaining a living experience in the things of God. We must now learn to understand what are the deep movings of the Spirit of God. Christ must be our all and in all, the Alpha and Omega, the first and the last, the beginning and the end.[41]

OUT OF THE LION'S MOUTH

And fear not them which kill the body, but are not able to kill the soul: but rather fear him which is able to destroy both soul and body in hell. Matt. 10:28.

Daniel is an example to believers as to what it means to confess Christ. He held the responsible position of prime minister in the kingdom of Babylon, and there were those who were envious of Daniel among the great men of the court, and they wanted to find something against him that they might bring an accusation against him to the king. But he was a faithful statesman, and they could find no flaw in his character or life. . . . So they agreed together to ask the king to make a decree that no one should ask any petition of any God or man for thirty days save of the king, and if any disobeyed this decree, he was to be cast into the den of lions.

But did Daniel cease to pray because this decree was to go into force? No, that was just the time when he needed to pray. . . . Daniel did not seek to hide his loyalty to God. He did not pray in his heart, but with his voice, aloud, with his window open toward Jerusalem, he offered up his petition to heaven. Then his enemies made their complaint to the king, and Daniel was thrown into the den of lions. But the Son of God was there. . . . When the king came in the morning, and called, "O Daniel, servant of the living God, is thy God, whom thou servest continually, able to deliver thee from the lions? Then said Daniel unto the king, O king, live for ever. My God hath sent his angel, and hath shut the lions' mouths, that they have not hurt me." Dan. 6:20-22. . . .

We may know that if our life is hid with Christ in God, when we are brought into trial because of our faith, Jesus will be with us. When we are brought before rulers and dignitaries to answer for our faith, the Spirit of the Lord will illuminate our understanding, and we shall be able to bear a testimony to the glory of God. And if we are called to suffer for Christ's sake, we shall be able to go to prison trusting in Him as a little child trusts in its parents. Now is the time to cultivate faith in God.[42]

IN THE MIDST OF THE FIRE

Whosoever therefore shall confess me before men, him will I confess also before my Father which is in heaven. Matt. 10:32.

A confession of Christ means something more than bearing testimony in social [prayer] meeting.[43]

We have a different confession to make from that which we have made; and we shall have to make it under different circumstances. The three Hebrews were called upon to confess Christ in the face of the burning fiery furnace. They had been commanded by the king to fall down and worship the golden image which he had set up, and threatened that if they would not, they should be cast alive into the fiery furnace, but they answered, "We are not careful to answer thee in this matter. If it be so, our God whom we serve is able to deliver us from the burning fiery furnace, and he will deliver us out of thine hand, O king. But if not, be it known unto thee, O king, that we will not serve thy gods, nor worship the golden image which thou hast set up." Dan. 3:16-18. It cost them something to confess Christ, for their lives were at stake.

Then the king commanded that the furnace be heated seven times hotter than it was wont to be heated, and the faithful children of God were cast into the furnace. "Then Nebuchadnezzar the king was astonied, and rose up in haste, and spake, and said unto his counsellors, Did not we cast three men bound into the midst of the fire? They answered and said unto the king, True, O king. He answered and said, Lo, I see four men loose, walking in the midst of the fire, and they have no hurt; and the form of the fourth is like the Son of God." Verses 24, 25. . . . Then Nebuchadnezzar called forth the servants of God, and they had not so much as the smell of fire upon them. If you are called to go through the fiery furnace for Christ's sake, Jesus will be at your side. "When thou passest through the waters, I will be with thee; and through the rivers, they shall not overflow thee: when thou walkest through the fire, thou shalt not be burned; neither shall the flame kindle upon thee." Isa. 43:2.[44]

THE STRUGGLE AGAINST WIND AND TIDE

Blessed are ye, when men shall revile you, and persecute you, and shall say all manner of evil against you falsely, for my sake. Rejoice, and be exceeding glad: for great is your reward in heaven: for so persecuted they the prophets which were before you. Matt. 5:11, 12.

Our gracious Redeemer looked down the stream of time, and beheld the perils that would in the last days surround His chosen. . . .

If the members of the church labor faithfully to build up the cause of truth, they will not escape the tongue of gossip, falsehood, and slander. "All that will live godly in Christ Jesus shall suffer persecution." 2 Tim. 3:12. Their consistent, unwavering course is a constant rebuke of the unbelief, pride, and selfishness of the hypocritical professor.

Their prayers and admonitions disturb his worldly ambition, and he endeavors to cast reproach upon the faithful followers of Jesus. He will garble, distort, and misrepresent facts, in the same spirit that actuated the Pharisees in their opposition to Christ.

Jesus does not lose sight of His people who have so many discouragements to encounter. It requires little effort to float with the popular current, but those who would gain the immortal shores must struggle against wind and tide. There is a form of Christianity— a spurious article—which has no reformative energy. Its possessors delight to oppose and decry the faith of others. Their religion is not seen in the market place, in the family, or in the workshop. Their religious experience runs in the corrupt channel of the world.

The true follower of Christ should not be dismayed at receiving reproach from this class. Said the beloved apostle, "Marvel not, my brethren, if the world hate you." 1 John 3:13. And our Saviour reminds His disciples, "If the world hate you, ye know that it hated me before it hated you." John 15:18. Those who are faithful to God will not be harmed by reproach or opposition. Nay, rather, virtues will thus be developed that will not flourish in the sunshine of prosperity. Faith, patience, meekness, and love will bud and blossom amid clouds and darkness.[45]

THE MOST DANGEROUS OF FOES

Now the Spirit speaketh expressly, that in the latter times some shall depart from the faith, giving heed to seducing spirits, and doctrines of devils. 1 Tim. 4:1.

The adversary of souls is constantly seeking to divert our minds by bringing in side issues. Let us not be deceived. Let enemies handle your name and mine as they please. Let them distort, misrepresent, our words and deeds. Let them fabricate falsehoods as best pleases them. We cannot afford to allow our minds to be diverted from Jesus and the preparation of soul which we must have in order to meet Him in peace. . . . In Christ's stead, I beseech you to pray as you never prayed before, to seek earnestly for faith and love, that seem to be almost banished from the earth. Live each day as in the sight of God. . . .

Let not false teachers confuse your minds and unsettle your faith by casting reproach upon those whom God has sent you with messages of warning and instruction. Remember that it is not mere men whom you have to meet, but "principalities and powers, and wicked spirits in high places." Now is the very time when Satan is working with all deceivableness of unrighteousness.

Many are in reality fighting his battles while they profess to serve under the banner of Christ. These traitors in the camp may not be suspected, but they are doing their work to create unbelief, discord, and strife. Such are the most dangerous of foes. While they insinuate themselves into our favor, and gain our confidence and sympathy, they are busy suggesting doubts and creating suspicion. They work in the same manner as did Satan in heaven when he deceived the angels by his artful representations, placing darkness for light, and making the forbearance and mercy of God to appear as harshness and severity. As he worked at the beginning, so he works in the end, only concealing himself more perfectly from view. . . .

It is not enough that we have the theory of the truth; its principles must be inwrought in the soul, and exemplified in the life, or we shall fall a prey to the delusions prepared for the last days.[46]

THE CROSS BEFORE THE CROWN

Yea, and all that will live godly in Christ Jesus shall suffer persecution. 2 Tim. 3:12.

We may strengthen our faith and quicken our love by going often to the foot of the cross, and there contemplating our Saviour's humiliation. Behold the Majesty of heaven suffering as a transgressor! Spotless purity, untarnished righteousness, did not shield Him from falsehood and reproach. He meekly bore the contradiction of sinners against Himself, and yielded up His life, that we might be forgiven and live forevermore. Are we willing to follow in His steps? The only reason why we do not now suffer greater persecution is, we do not in our lives more faithfully exemplify the life of Christ. I assure you, brethren and sisters, if you walk as He walked, you will know what it is to be persecuted and reproached for His sake.

If we hope to wear the crown, we must expect to bear the cross. Our greatest trials will come from those who profess godliness. It was so with the world's Redeemer; it will be so with His followers. . . . Those who are in earnest to win the crown of eternal life need not be surprised or disheartened because at every step toward the heavenly Canaan they meet with obstacles and encounter trials. . . .

The Saviour knows what is best. Faith grows by conflict with doubt and difficulty and trial. Virtue gathers strength by resistance to temptation. The life of the faithful soldier is a battle and a march. No rest, fellow pilgrim, this side the heavenly Canaan. . . . But John in holy vision beholds the faithful souls that come up out of great tribulation, surrounding the throne of God, clad in white robes, and crowned with immortal glory. What though they have been counted the offscouring of the earth? In the investigative judgment their lives and characters are brought in review before God, and that solemn tribunal reverses the decision of their enemies. Their faithfulness to God and to His Word stands revealed, and Heaven's high honors are awarded them as conquerors in the strife with sin and Satan.[47]

ON GUARD EVERY MOMENT

But evil men and seducers shall wax worse and worse, deceiving, and being deceived. 2 Tim. 3:13.

By every conceivable device the foe is seeking to throw us off our guard. He may first attempt to deceive with smooth words and crafty insinuations; and if these fail, he proceeds to open violence. He has many a deep-laid snare for unwary feet, and those who once become entangled find it almost impossible to extricate themselves. While he praises, flatters, and exalts some, he hurls his fiery darts at others. We must be on guard every moment. Days of peculiar trial, difficulty, and danger are before us. . . .

We must make up our minds that instead of matters taking a more favorable turn, wicked men, seducing teachers, will grow worse and worse, deceiving themselves and deceiving others. We may expect greater opposition than has yet been experienced. . . . We must now make Christ our refuge, or in the days before us our souls will be overwhelmed with darkness and despair. There is a point beyond, which human help cannot avail. Every one must live by faith as he is forced into close and apparently deadly conflict with the powers of darkness. Each must stand or fall for himself. The arrows of the destroyer are about to be hurled against the faithful ones, and no earthly power can turn aside the shaft. But could our eyes be opened we could see angels of God encircling the righteous, that no harm may come upon them. . . .

We must look to Jesus, study His words, pray for His Spirit. We should be more frequently alone with God in meditation and prayer. Let us pray more and talk less. We cannot trust to our own wisdom, our own experience, our own knowledge of the truth; we must be daily learners, looking to our heavenly Teacher for instruction, and then, without regard to ease, pleasure, or convenience, we must go forward, knowing that He is faithful who has called. . . .

While we realize our weakness, let us rely upon His strength, and overcome by the grace which He imparts.[48]

CROWNS FOR THE FAITHFUL

Henceforth there is laid up for me a crown of righteousness, which the Lord, the righteous judge, shall give me at that day: and not to me only, but unto all them also that love his appearing. 2 Tim. 4:8.

Did the great apostle to the Gentiles make any real sacrifice when he exchanged Pharisaism for the gospel of Christ? We answer No! With decided purpose, he turned away from wealth, from friends and social distinction, from public honors, and from his kinsmen whom he loved fervently and earnestly. He chose to link his name and his destiny with that of a people he had regarded as low and the offscouring of all things; but for the sake of Christ he suffered the loss of all things.

His labors were more abundant than any of the disciples, his stripes above measure. He was beaten with rods, stoned, shipwrecked, in deaths oft. He was in peril by land and sea, in the city and in the wilderness, from robbers and from his own countrymen. He prosecuted his mission under continual infirmities, in painfulness, in weariness, in watchings often, in cold, in nakedness. . . . When he answered the bloodthirsty Nero, no man stood with him. . . .

But did Paul devote his precious time to the relation of his grievous abuses? No, he called the attention from himself to Jesus. He did not live for his own happiness, yet he was happy. . . . "I am exceeding joyful in all our tribulation." 2 Cor. 7:4. And in the last days of his life, with a martyr's death in full view, he exclaims with satisfaction, "I have fought a good fight, I have finished my course, I have kept the faith." 2 Tim. 4:7. And fixing his eye upon the immortal future, which had been the grand, inspiring motive of his whole career, he adds, in full assurance of faith, "Henceforth there is laid up for me a crown of righteousness, which the Lord, the righteous judge, shall give me at that day"—and then this man who had lived for others forgets himself—"and not to me only, but unto all them also that love his appearing." Oh, noble man of faith![49]

Paul was a living example of what every true Christian should be. He lived for God's glory. . . . "For me to live is Christ." Phil. 1:21.[50]

AIM HIGH!

For in him dwelleth all the fulness of the Godhead bodily. And ye are complete in him, which is the head of all principality and power. Col. 2:9, 10.

We aim too low. The mark is much higher. Our minds need expansion, that we may comprehend the significance of the provision of God. We are to reflect the highest attributes of the character of God. . . . The law of God is the exalted standard to which we are to attain through the imputed righteousness of Christ.[51]

It is only through a correct understanding of Christ's mission and work that the possibility of being complete in Him, accepted in the Beloved, is brought within our reach. . . . Human science is not divine enlightenment. Divine science is the demonstration of the Spirit of God, inspiring implicit faith in Him. The men of the world suppose this faith to be beneath the notice of their great and intelligent minds, something too low to give attention to; but here they make a great mistake. It is altogether too high for their human intelligence to reach.

The gospel message is far from being opposed to true knowledge and intellectual attainments. It is itself true science, true intellectual knowledge. True wisdom is infinitely above the comprehension of the worldly wise. The hidden wisdom, which is Christ formed within, the hope of glory, is a wisdom high as heaven. The deep principles of godliness are sublime and eternal. A Christian experience alone can help us to understand this problem, and obtain the treasures of knowledge which have been hidden in the counsels of God, but are now made known to all who have a vital connection with Christ.[52]

In Christ dwelt the fullness of the Godhead bodily. This is why, although He was tempted in all points like as we are, He stood before the world, from His first entrance into it, untainted by corruption, though surrounded by it. Are we not also to become partakers of that fullness, and is it not thus, and thus only, that we can overcome as He overcame?[53]

Through His sacrifice, human beings may reach the high ideal set before them, and hear at last the words, "Ye are complete in him."[54]

THE UNSEARCHABLE RICHES OF CHRIST

That he would grant you, according to the riches of his glory, to be strengthened with might by his Spirit in the inner man. Eph. 3:16.

The themes of redemption are momentous themes, and only those who are spiritually-minded can discern their depth and significance. It is our safety, our joy, to dwell upon the truths of the plan of salvation. Faith and prayer are necessary in order that we may behold the deep things of God. Our minds are so bound about by narrow ideas that we catch but limited views of the experience it is our privilege to have. . . .

Why is it that many who profess to have faith in Christ have no strength to stand against the temptations of the enemy?—It is because they are not strengthened with might by His Spirit in the inner man. The apostle prays "that ye, being rooted and grounded in love, may be able to comprehend with all saints what is the breadth, and length, and depth, and height; and to know the love of Christ, which passeth knowledge, that ye might be filled with all the fulness of God." Eph. 3:17-19. If we had this experience, we should know something of the cross of Calvary. We would know what it means to be partakers with Christ in His sufferings. The love of Christ would constrain us, and though we would not be able to explain how the love of Christ warmed our hearts, we would manifest His love in fervent devotion to His cause.

Paul opens before the Ephesian church, in the most comprehensive language, the marvelous power and knowledge they might possess as sons and daughters of the Most High. It was theirs "to be strengthened with might . . . ," to be "rooted and grounded in love," . . . "to know the love of Christ, which passeth knowledge." . . .

Jehovah Emmanuel—He in whom are hid all the treasures of wisdom and knowledge—to be brought into sympathy with Him, to possess Him, as the heart opens more and more to receive His attributes: to know His love and power, to possess the unsearchable riches of Christ . . . this is the heritage of the servants of the Lord, and "their righteousness is of me, saith the Lord." Isa. 54:17.[55]

FILLED WITH GOD'S FULLNESS

And to know the love of Christ, which passeth knowledge, that ye might be filled with all the fulness of God. Eph. 3:19.

Here are revealed the heights of attainment that we may reach through faith in the promises of our heavenly Father, when we fulfill His requirements. Through the merits of Christ, we have access to the throne of infinite power. "He that spared not his own Son, but delivered him up for us all, how shall he not with him also freely give us all things?" Rom. 8:32. . . .

The heart that has once tasted of the love of Christ, cries out continually for a deeper draft; and as you impart, you will receive in richer and more abundant measure. Every revelation of God to the soul increases the capacity to know and to love. The continual cry of the heart is, More of thee, and ever the Spirit's answer is, Much more. . . .

The life of Christ was a life charged with a divine message of the love of God, and He longed intensely to impart this love to others in rich measure. Compassion beamed from His countenance, and His conduct was characterized by grace and humility, love and truth. Every member of His church militant must manifest the same qualities, if he would join the church triumphant. The love of Christ is so broad, so full of glory, that in comparison to it, everything that man esteems so great dwindles into insignificance. When we obtain a view of it, we exclaim, O the depth of the riches of the love that God bestowed upon men in the gift of His only begotten Son! . . .

It is the mystery of God in the flesh, God in Christ, divinity in humanity. Christ bowed down in unparalleled humility, that in His exaltation to the throne of God He might also exalt those who believe in Him to a seat with Him upon His throne. . . . "Exceeding abundantly above all that we ask or think," will be given unto us "the spirit of wisdom and revelation in the knowledge of him" (Eph. 1:17), that we may be able to "comprehend with all saints what is the breadth, and length, and depth, and height; and to know the love of Christ, which passeth knowledge," that we may be "filled with all the fulness of God."[56]

ALMOST HOME!

And if I go and prepare a place for you, I will come again, and receive you unto myself; that where I am, there ye may be also. John 14:3.

More than eighteen hundred years have passed since the Saviour gave the promise of His coming. Throughout the centuries His words have filled with courage the hearts of His faithful ones. The promise has not yet been fulfilled; . . . but none the less sure is the word that has been spoken.[57]

Christ will come in His own glory, in the glory of His Father, and in the glory of the holy angels. Ten thousand times ten thousand and thousands of thousands of angels, the beautiful, triumphant sons of God, possessing surpassing loveliness and glory, will escort Him on His way. In the place of a crown of thorns, He will wear a crown of glory—a crown within a crown. In the place of that old purple robe, He will be clothed in a garment of whitest white, "so as no fuller on earth can white" (Mark 9:3) it. And on His vesture and on His thigh a name will be written, "King of kings, and Lord of lords." Rev. 19:16. . . .

To His faithful followers Christ has been a daily companion, a familiar friend. They have lived in close, constant communion with God. Upon them the glory of the Lord has risen. In them the light of the knowledge of the glory of God in the face of Jesus Christ has been reflected. Now they rejoice in the undimmed rays of the brightness and glory of the King in His majesty. They are prepared for the communion of heaven, for they have heaven in their hearts.

With uplifted heads, with the bright beams of the Sun of Righteousness shining upon them, with rejoicing that their redemption draweth nigh, they go forth to meet the Bridegroom, saying, "Lo, this is our God; we have waited for him, and he will save us." . . .

The time of tarrying is almost ended. The pilgrims and strangers who have so long been seeking a better country are almost home. I feel as if I must cry aloud, Homeward bound! . . . "Wherefore, beloved, seeing that ye look for such things, be diligent that ye may be found of him in peace, without spot, and blameless." 2 Peter 3:14.[58]

IN THE INNER CIRCLE

He that overcometh, the same shall be clothed in white raiment; and I will not blot out his name out of the book of life, but I will confess his name before my Father, and before his angels. Rev. 3:5.

Can you, dear youth, look forward with joyful hope and expectation to the time when the Lord, your righteous judge, shall confess your name before the Father and before the holy angels? The very best preparation you can have for Christ's second appearing is to rest with firm faith in the great salvation brought to us at His first coming. You must believe in Christ as a personal Saviour.[59]

Many of us do not realize the covenant relation in which we stand before God as His people. We are under the most solemn obligations to represent God and Christ. We are to guard against dishonoring God by professing to be His people, and then going directly contrary to His will. We are getting ready to move. Then let us act as if we were. Let us prepare for the mansions that Christ has gone to prepare for those that love Him.[60]

Unless those who claim to believe the truth for this time submit to the training of God on earth for the future life, they will never see the King in His beauty. . . . They must cultivate patience, kindness, meekness, goodness, sympathy, and tender compassion for one another. All their rough, uncourteous, un-Christlike disposition must be purged away, for none of these unkind attributes are of Christ, but after the satanic order. The pure, heavenly graces are received and flourish in mind, heart, and character only as man becomes a partaker of the divine nature. . . . Heaven must begin on earth for every soul who will enter the heavenly mansions above.[61]

All heaven appreciates the struggles of those who are fighting for the crown of everlasting life, that they may be partakers with Christ in the city of God. . . . God wants you there, Christ wants you there, the heavenly host wants you there. The angels are willing to stand in the outer circle, and let those who have been redeemed by the blood of Jesus stand in the inner circle. . . . A crown of glory waits for all who fight the good fight of faith.[62]

LET'S TAKE INVENTORY

Lord, make me to know mine end, and the measure of my days, what it is; that I may know how frail I am. Ps. 39:4.

Another year has almost passed into eternity. . . . Let us review the record of the year that so soon will be past. What advancement have we made in Christian experience? Our work—have we so done it that it will bear the inspection of the Master, who has given to every man work according to his several ability? Will it be consumed as hay, wood, and stubble, unworthy of preservation? or will it stand the trial by fire? . . .

Every provision has been made that we may attain a height of stature in Christ Jesus that will meet the divine standard. God is not pleased with His representatives if they are content to be dwarfs when they might grow up to the full stature of men and women in Christ. He wants you to have height and breadth in Christian experience. He wants you to have great thoughts, noble aspirations, clear perceptions of truth, and lofty purposes of action. Every passing year should increase the soul's yearning for purity and perfection of Christian character. And if this knowledge increases day by day, month by month, year by year, it will not be work consumed as hay, wood, and stubble; but it will be laying on the foundation stone, gold, silver, and precious stones—works that are not perishable, but which will stand the fires of the last day.

Is our earthly, temporal work done with a thoroughness, a fidelity, that will bear scrutiny? Are there those whom we have wronged who will testify against us in the day of God? If so, the record has passed up to heaven, and we shall meet it again. We are to work for the great Taskmaster's eye, whether our painstaking efforts are seen and appreciated by men or not. No man, woman, nor child can acceptably serve God with neglectful, haphazard, sham work, whether it be secular or religious service. The true Christian will have an eye single to the glory of God in all things, encouraging his purposes and strengthening his principles with this thought, "I do this for Christ."[63]

BURY ALL BITTERNESS

My days are swifter than a weaver's shuttle. Job 7:6.

If we have but little time, let us improve that little earnestly. The Bible assures us that we are in the great day of atonement. The typical Day of Atonement was a day when all Israel afflicted their souls before God, confessed their sins, and came before the Lord with contrition of soul, remorse for their sins, genuine repentance, and living faith in the atoning sacrifice.

If there have been difficulties, . . . if envy, malice, bitterness, evil surmisings, have existed, confess these sins, not in a general way, but go to your brethren and sisters personally. Be definite. If you have committed one wrong and they twenty, confess that one as though you were the chief offender. Take them by the hand, let your heart soften under the influence of the Spirit of God, and say, "Will you forgive me? I have not felt right toward you. I want to make right every wrong, that naught may stand registered against me in the books of heaven. I must have a clean record." Who, think you, would withstand such a movement as this?

There is too much coldness and indifference—too much of the "I don't care" spirit—exercised among the professed followers of Christ. All should feel a care for one another, jealously guarding each other's interests. "Love one another." Then we should stand a strong wall against Satan's devices. Amid opposition and persecution we would not join the vindictive ones, not unite with the followers of the great rebel, whose special work is to accuse the brethren, to defame and cast stain upon their characters.

Let the remnant of this year be improved in destroying every fiber of the root of bitterness, burying them in the grave with the old year. Begin the new year with more tender regard, with deeper love, for every member of the Lord's family. Press together. "United, we stand; divided, we fall." Take a higher, nobler stand than you ever have before.[64]

THE PRIZE OF OUR HIGH CALLING

I count not myself to have apprehended: but this one thing I do, forgetting those things which are behind, and reaching forth unto those things which are before, I press toward the mark for the prize of the high calling of God in Christ Jesus. Phil. 3:13, 14.

He who would build up a strong, symmetrical character, he who would be a well-balanced Christian, must give all and do all for Christ. . . . Paul did many things. From the time that he gave his allegiance to Christ, his life was filled with untiring service. From city to city, from country to country, he journeyed, telling the story of the cross, winning converts to the gospel, and establishing churches. . . . At times he worked at his trade, to earn his daily bread. But in all the busy activities of his life, Paul never lost sight of one great purpose to press toward the prize of his high calling. One aim he kept steadfastly before him to be faithful to the One who at the gate of Damascus had revealed Himself to him. From this aim nothing had power to turn him aside. . . .

The great purpose that constrained Paul to press forward in the face of hardship and difficulty should lead every Christian worker to consecrate himself wholly to God's service. Worldly attractions will be presented to draw his attention from the Saviour, but he is to press on toward the goal, showing to the world, to angels, and to men that the hope of seeing the face of God is worth all the effort and sacrifice that the attainment of this hope demands.[65]

The lowliest disciple of Christ may become an inhabitant of heaven, an heir of God to an inheritance incorruptible, and that fadeth not away. O that every one might make choice of the heavenly gift, become an heir of God to that inheritance whose title is secure from any destroyer, world without end! O, choose not the world, but choose the better inheritance! Press, urge your way toward the mark for the prize of your high calling in Christ Jesus.[66]

Soon we shall witness the coronation of our King. Those whose lives have been hidden with Christ, those who on this earth have fought the good fight of faith, will shine forth with the Redeemer's glory in the kingdom of God.[67]

AA	*Acts of the Apostles, The*	GCB	*General Conference Bulletin*
AUCR	*Australasian Union*	HR	*Health Reformer, The*
	Conference Record, The	Letter	Ellen G. White Letter
1 BC	Ellen G. White Comments in	MH	*Ministry of Healing, The*
	SDA Bible Commentary, vol.	ML	*My Life Today*
	1 (2 BC, etc., for vols. 2-7)	MS	Ellen G. White Manuscript
CG	*Child Guidance*	PK	*Prophets and Kings*
CH	*Counsels on Health*	RH	*Review and Herald, The*
CS	*Counsels on Stewardship*	SC	*Steps to Christ*
CSW	*Counsels on Sabbath*	SD	*Sons and Daughters of God*
	School Work	1 SM	*Selected Messages,* Book 1
CTBH	*Christian Temperance and*	ST	*Signs of the Times*
	Bible Hygiene	1T	*Testimonies for the Church,*
Ev	*Evangelism*		vol. 1 (2T, etc., for vols. 2-9)
FE	*Fundamentals of*	YI	*Youth's Instructor, The*
	Education		

S O U R C E   R E F E R E N C E S

JANUARY
[1] ST Jan. 7, 1889
[2] RH Jan. 3, 1882
[3] YI Feb. 13, 1902
[4] RH May 26, 1891
[5] Letter 18, 1859
[6] Letter 27, 1886
[7] RH April 12, 1887
[8] Letter 42, 1900
[9] RH April 12, 1887
[10] ST Jan. 26, 1882
[11] Letter 36a, 1890
[12] YI Oct. 17, 1895
[13] ST Jan. 19, 1882
[14] MS 43, 1908
[15] YI Nov. 21, 1883
[16] Letter 204, 1907
[17] Letter 290, 1906
[18] Letter 63, 1893
[19] MS 31, 1886
[20] GCB April 23, 1901
[21] Letter 8, 1873
[22] ST April 24, 1893

[23] MS 23, 1899
[24] ST Jan. 9, 1893
[25] YI Dec. 13, 1894
[26] MS 8, 1899
[27] MS 50, 1904
[28] MS 8, 1899
[29] MS 42, 1890
[30] MS 9, 1899
[31] Letter 8, 1873
[32] MS 32a, 1894
[33] 7 BC 967, 968
[34] 7 BC 922
[35] Letter 258, 1907
[36] MS 17, 1899
[37] Letter 1b, 1873
[38] MS 56, 1898
[39] Letter 104, 1894
[40] MS 56, 1898
[41] RH Feb. 17, 1885
[42] Letter 79, 1900
[43] Letter 25, 1882
[44] YI Aug. 21, 1902
[45] YI July 19, 1894

[46] RH Jan. 4, 1881
[47] YI Dec. 31, 1907
[48] Letter 44, 1903
[49] Letter 5b, 1891
[50] Letter 30, 1878
[51] MS 130, 1897
[52] Letter 8, 1873
[53] MS 109, 1897
[54] MS 1a, 1890
[55] Letter 14, 1885
[56] MS 43, 1891
[57] MS 62, 1886
[58] Letter 8, 1873
[59] Letter 64, 1909
[60] YI June 29, 1893
[61] MS 67, 1898
[62] Letter 42, 1907
[63] MS 23, 1899
[64] Letter 34, 1891
[65] AUCR Oct. 1, 1903
[66] ST Feb. 6, 1893
[67] ST Jan. 30, 1893
[68] RH Oct. 31, 1893

FEBRUARY
1. MS 32a, 1894
2. ST April 3, 1884
3. Letter 44, 1900
4. Letter 117, 1898
5. MS 23, 1899
6. MS 167, 1897
7. Letter 31, 1893
8. MS 42, 1890
9. Letter 97, 1898
10. Letter 23, 1873
11. MS 8, 1904
12. MS 167, 1897
13. Letter 51b, 1894
14. Letter 23, 1873
15. MS 6, 1893
16. 5 BC 1132
17. 5 BC 1133
18. MS 58, 1900
19. 5 BC 1133
20. ST Jan. 2, 1893
21. 7 BC 947, 948
22. 7 BC 929
23. 5 BC 1142
24. 1 SM 244
25. 7 BC 948
26. Letter 6, 1893
27. 7 BC 948
28. RH Sept. 21, 1886
29. 6 BC 1078
30. Ibid.
31. 7 BC 930
32. 6 BC 1078
33. 6 BC 1070
34. Letter 4, 1889
35. MS 46, 1891
36. 6 BC 1115
37. MS 39, 1896
38. RH March 19, 1895
39. ST Jan. 9, 1893
40. RH Nov. 24, 1885
41. Letter 13, 1892
42. Letter 17, 1878
43. Letter 10, 1893
44. 6 BC 1097
45. 6 BC 1098, 1099
46. 6 BC 1099
47. Letter 17, 1878
48. YI Oct. 24, 1895
49. YI Oct. 31, 1895
50. Ibid.
51. RH May 30, 1882
52. Ibid.
53. MS 49, 1894
54. RH Sept. 1, 1885
55. RH Sept. 22, 1885
56. Letter 2b, 1874
57. Letter 17, 1872
58. Letter 2b, 1874
59. RH March 15, 1892
60. Ibid.

MARCH
1. MS 13, 1884
2. Ibid.
3. Ibid.
4. Ibid.
5. Ibid.
6. Ibid.
7. Ibid.
8. Ibid.
9. Ibid.
10. Ibid.
11. YI Nov. 7, 1895
12. YI June 29, 1893
13. ST Jan. 2, 1893
14. 6 BC 1079
15. ST Jan. 2, 1893
16. ST Dec. 8, 1898
17. MS 38, 1890
18. MS 24, 1891
19. MS 29, 1886
20. Letter 41, 1877
21. MS 9, 1903
22. MS 127, 1899
23. Letter 29, 1879
24. 3 BC 1147
25. MS 23, 1899
26. Letter 24, 1888
27. Letter 97, 1895
28. 3 BC 1146
29. YI Feb. 19, 1903
30. RH April 8, 1884
31. MS 31, 1911
32. RH April 8, 1884
33. Letter 5, 1903
34. Letter 52, 1888
35. MS 17, 1894
36. 7 BC 907
37. MS 59, 1900
38. RH June 14, 1892
39. MS 124, 1902
40. MS 113, 1902
41. MS 34, 1897
42. RH April 8, 1884
43. MS 46a, 1886
44. Letter 63, 1905
45. MS 46a, 1886
46. GCB April 23, 1901
47. MS 28, 1898
48. Letter 20, 1894
49. MS 116, 1898
50. MS 42, 1890
51. Letter 135, 1898
52. ST Nov. 5, 1896
53. MS 13, 1888
54. MS 78, 1905
55. 6 BC 1120
56. Ibid.
57. RH Nov. 19, 1908
58. 7 BC 922
59. Letter 1a, 1872
60. Letter 14, 1885
61. RH April 8, 1880
62. 7 BC 938
63. 7 BC 937
64. 7 BC 937, 938
65. 7 BC 937
66. Ibid.

APRIL
1. ST March 17, 1887
2. RH April 25, 1899
3. HR Dec. 1871
4. Letter 6, 1893
5. HR Dec. 1871
6. MS 21, 1889
7. MS 6, 1892
8. Letter 186, 1902
9. MS 21, 1889
10. 5 BC 1092
11. 5 BC 1090
12. 5 BC 1090, 1091
13. 5 BC 1091
14. 5 BC 1092
15. Letter 38, 1893
16. Letter 257, 1903
17. Letter 38, 1893
18. 5T 513, 514
19. Letter 44, 1899
20. MS 21, 1900
21. Letter 44, 1899
22. Letter 22, 1896

[23] Letter 5, 1898
[24] 6 BC 1080
[25] MS 24, 1901
[26] MS 59, 1897
[27] Letter 73, 1899
[28] MS 48, 1899
[29] Letter 20, 1902
[30] 7 BC 973
[31] Letter 130, 1901
[32] 2 SM 352, 353
[33] RH Dec. 18, 1888
[34] *Ibid.*
[35] RH Jan. 4, 1881
[36] 3 BC 1150
[37] Letter 33, 1886
[38] RH June 12, 1888
[39] *Ibid.*
[40] Letter 20, 1897
[41] YI Dec. 6, 1900
[42] Letter 100, 1895
[43] MS 29, 1900
[44] RH March 15, 1892
[45] Letter 19, 1895
[46] 3 BC 1157
[47] MS 25a, 1891
[48] MS 44, 1904
[49] Letter 21, 1901
[50] Letter 42, 1900
[51] RH Jan. 29, 1895
[52] YI July 8, 1897
[53] Letter 49, 1888
[54] Letter 52, 1888
[55] MS 75, 1893
[56] 6 BC 1111
[57] RH Jan. 29, 1895
[58] Letter 38, 1890
[59] 6 BC 1071
[60] RH Jan. 29, 1895
[61] 6 BC 1071
[62] RH Jan. 29, 1895
[63] 6 BC 1105
[64] Letter 42, 1890
[65] MS 22, 1889
[66] Letter 30, 1896
[67] Letter 111, 1902

MAY
[1] RH Oct. 30, 1900
[2] 7 BC 960, 961
[3] RH March 26, 1889
[4] 7 BC 961

[5] RH July 24, 1883
[6] MS 23, 1899
[7] RH April 22, 1884
[8] MS 39, 1893
[9] SD 105
[10] MS 29, 1896
[11] Letter 16, 1867
[12] MS 42, 1904
[13] Letter 5, 1903
[14] 2 BC 1034
[15] 2 BC 1035
[16] 2 BC 1034
[17] Letter 37, 1892
[18] Letter 26, 1880
[19] 4 BC 1144
[20] Letter 66, 1901
[21] MS 22, 1889
[22] SC 125
[23] MS 42, 1890
[24] ST July 31, 1901
[25] 1 SM 235
[26] RH Nov. 24, 1885
[27] RH Sept. 27, 1881
[28] MS 62, 1896
[29] MS 65, 1886
[30] Letter 51, 1888
[31] MS 53, 1890
[32] Letter 13, 1893
[33] RH Sept. 3, 1901
[34] Letter 21, 1901
[35] RH March 27, 1888
[36] MS 126, 1897
[37] MS 37, 1908
[38] MS 19, 1909
[39] Letter 42, 1900
[40] RH Sept. 11, 1883
[41] MS 41, 1890
[42] RH Sept. 11, 1883
[43] Letter 5b, 1891
[44] MS 37, 1908
[45] Letter 9, 1873
[46] RH May 19, 1904
[47] RH June 10, 1902
[48] RH May 19, 1904
[49] RH Nov. 5, 1908
[50] RH April 12, 1892
[51] RH May 19, 1904
[52] RH Aug. 25, 1896
[53] *Ibid.*
[54] ST Sept. 4, 1893
[55] RH Aug. 25, 1896

[56] RH April 12, 1892
[57] RH May 19, 1904
[58] RH June 10, 1902
[59] RH Aug. 25, 1896
[60] CS 217
[61] 5 BC 1078
[62] 5 BC 1079
[63] 5 BC 1077
[64] 6 BC 1075
[65] RH May 26, 1904
[66] RH Feb. 18, 1904

JUNE
[1] Letter 13, 1875
[2] Letter 4, 1885
[3] 4 BC 1165
[4] 4 BC 1164, 1165
[5] RH June 20, 1882
[6] *Ibid.*
[7] 3 BC 1157
[8] *Ibid.*
[9] RH April 8, 1880
[10] 7 BC 986
[11] Letter 26, 1880
[12] Letter 9a, 1891
[13] 7 BC 968
[14] ST Jan. 12, 1882
[15] ST March 1, 1910
[16] 2 BC 1029
[17] 2 BC 1030
[18] Letter 60, 1886
[19] 6 BC 1116
[20] Letter 98, 1902
[21] ST Jan. 12, 1882
[22] MS 32a, 1894
[23] MS 32, 1894
[24] Letter 78, 1894
[25] MS 43, 1891
[26] MS 2, 1881
[27] MS 88, 1905
[28] Letter 141, 1902
[29] MS 12, 1886
[30] ST March 1, 1910
[31] RH Dec. 4, 1900
[32] PK 111
[33] 5 BC 1141
[34] 5 BC 1140
[35] Letter 110, 1893
[36] MS 50, 1894
[37] Letter 13a, 1879
[38] Letter 117, 1899

³⁹ Letter 102, 1899
⁴⁰ YI Dec. 23, 1897
⁴¹ MS 24, 1887
⁴² MS 35, 1886
⁴³ MS 1, 1899
⁴⁴ Letter 11, 1887
⁴⁵ Letter 50, 1897
⁴⁶ Undated MS 141
⁴⁷ MS 12, 1891
⁴⁸ Letter 34, 1894
⁴⁹ RH Oct. 6, 1891
⁵⁰ MS 1, 1869
⁵¹ RH Feb. 25, 1904
⁵² Letter 115, 1903
⁵³ Letter 78, 1894
⁵⁴ Letter 13a, 1879
⁵⁵ Letter 117, 1899
⁵⁶ Letter 13a, 1879
⁵⁷ Letter 89, 1894
⁵⁸ Letter 9, 1873
⁵⁹ RH June 15, 1886

JULY
¹ MS 22, 1889
² RH Sept. 4, 1883
³ MS 11, 1892
⁴ YI June 6, 1901
⁵ Letter 17, 1872
⁶ MS 13, 1896
⁷ MS 153, 1903
⁸ RH Oct. 17, 1882
⁹ Letter 41, 1877
¹⁰ RH Sept. 18, 1888
¹¹ MS 13, 1896
¹² RH Sept. 18, 1888
¹³ Letter 8, 1873
¹⁴ Letter 97, 1895
¹⁵ Letter 8, 1873
¹⁶ 4 BC 1183
¹⁷ 7 BC 906
¹⁸ RH April 18, 1912
¹⁹ RH March 26, 1889
²⁰ RH Oct. 31, 1878
²¹ 6 BC 1118
²² RH April 18, 1912
²³ RH Oct. 15, 1895
²⁴ MS 101, 1906
²⁵ RH April 18, 1912
²⁶ RH Oct. 6, 1891
²⁷ RH Sept. 16, 1884
²⁸ CS 50

²⁹ RH Sept. 1, 1910
³⁰ *Ibid.*
³¹ MS 101, 1906
³² Letter 18, 1859
³³ RH Nov. 9, 1886
³⁴ Undated MS 12
³⁵ 4 BC 1180
³⁶ Letter 51, 1894
³⁷ MS 1, 1889
³⁸ 6 BC 1104
³⁹ CG 513
⁴⁰ RH Oct. 9, 1883
⁴¹ Letter 57, 1894
⁴² RH Aug. 13, 1959
⁴³ MS 8, 1898
⁴⁴ MS 130, 1897
⁴⁵ MS 103, 1902
⁴⁶ MS 130, 1897
⁴⁷ MS 48, 1895
⁴⁸ MS 29, 1896
⁴⁹ MS 50, 1895
⁵⁰ MS 60, 1901
⁵¹ ST Sept. 18, 1893
⁵² MS 23, 1899
⁵³ MS 27, 1889
⁵⁴ Letter 9, 1873
⁵⁵ MS 65, 1886
⁵⁶ RH April 12, 1892
⁵⁷ RH Jan. 28, 1904
⁵⁸ 6 BC 1117
⁵⁹ YI Feb. 17, 1898
⁶⁰ Letter 12, 1890
⁶¹ RH Sept. 14, 1897
⁶² Letter 5b, 1891
⁶³ 7 BC 947
⁶⁴ ML 109
⁶⁵ MS 8, 1899
⁶⁶ RH June 20, 1882
⁶⁷ *Ibid.*

AUGUST
¹ MS 128, 1898
² YI April 26, 1894
³ 6 BC 1087
⁴ RH Oct. 25, 1881
⁵ Letter 62, 1894
⁶ MS 2, 1871
⁷ YI Feb. 27, 1902
⁸ Letter 3, 1877
⁹ 3 BC 1158, 1159
¹⁰ Letter 5, 1879

¹¹ *Ibid.*
¹² MS 113, 1903
¹³ 6 BC 1081
¹⁴ Letter 41a, 1874
¹⁵ RH Oct. 15, 1895
¹⁶ MS 59, 1897
¹⁷ YI Jan. 28, 1897
¹⁸ RH Sept. 1, 1885
¹⁹ *Ibid.*
²⁰ MS 3, 1861
²¹ Letter 2, 1861
²² MS 17, 1899
²³ Letter 42a, 1878
²⁴ MS 153, 1907
²⁵ MS 151, 1898
²⁶ MS 4a, 1893
²⁷ GCB April 23, 1901
²⁸ RH Sept. 14, 1897
²⁹ MS 26, 1886
³⁰ 2 BC 1020
³¹ MS 6, 1893
³² Letter 102, 1901
³³ Letter 38, 1893
³⁴ Letter 25, 1870
³⁵ Letter 21, 1897
³⁶ Letter 25, 1870
³⁷ RH Sept. 1, 1885
³⁸ Letter 64, 1888
³⁹ Letter 74, 1888
⁴⁰ MS 24, 1887
⁴¹ 3 BC 1160, 1161
⁴² 3 BC 1160
⁴³ Undated MS 73
⁴⁴ ST Jan. 12, 1882
⁴⁵ Letter 1b, 1873
⁴⁶ Letter 16, 1872
⁴⁷ Letter 17, 1872
⁴⁸ Letter 16, 1872
⁴⁹ ST Jan. 1, 1885
⁵⁰ *Ibid.*
⁵¹ *Ibid.*
⁵² MS 54, 1886
⁵³ MS 31, 1911
⁵⁴ MS 168, 1898
⁵⁵ Letter 27, 1886
⁵⁶ Letter 63, 1893
⁵⁷ MS 53, 1890
⁵⁸ Letter 63, 1893
⁵⁹ RH Nov. 7, 1882

SEPTEMBER
1. MS 62, 1886
2. RH Feb. 24, 1885
3. MS 73, 1886
4. MS 62, 1886
5. RH Feb. 24, 1885
6. MS 62, 1886
7. 5 BC 1086
8. MS 47, 1898
9. Letter 95, 1902
10. Letter 153, 1902
11. Letter 1, 1882
12. MS 60, 1901
13. YI Sept. 29, 1892
14. Letter 17, 1878
15. 3 BC 1155
16. Letter 51, 1894
17. MH 359
18. Letter 51, 1894
19. YI May 25, 1893
20. Letter 2b, 1874
21. Letter 1, 1882
22. YI June 24, 1897
23. YI July 15, 1897
24. Letter 34, 1894
25. ST Jan. 7, 1889
26. *Ibid.*
27. Letter 17, 1883
28. RH Nov. 12, 1901
29. MS 60, 1894
30. Letter 103, 1897
31. RH Nov. 12, 1901
32. Letter 29a, 1875
33. RH Nov. 12, 1901
34. *Ibid.*
35. MS 60, 1894
36. 9T 153, 154
37. Letter 103, 1897
38. ST March 2, 1882
39. YI Oct. 25, 1894
40. RH June 15, 1886
41. 2 BC 1006
42. 1 BC 1114
43. RH Dec. 6, 1881
44. RH March 20, 1958
45. *Ibid.*
46. CTBH 93
47. 4T 643
48. AA 523, 524
49. Letter 117, 1899
50. MS 146, 1903
51. ST May 19, 1887
52. ML 89
53. Undated MS 93
54. Letter 288, 1908
55. YI Oct. 27, 1898
56. YI Nov. 23, 1893
57. ST May 19, 1887
58. Letter 339, 1905
59. RH Nov. 9, 1886
60. MS 13, 1895
61. MS 53, 1911
62. RH Sept. 1, 1885
63. Letter 36, 1901
64. Letter 121, 1904
65. Letter 34, 1894

OCTOBER
1. Letter 23a, 1892
2. Letter 181, 1904
3. MS 59, 1897
4. MS 42, 1890
5. RH May 20, 1890
6. YI June 29, 1893
7. RH March 30, 1886
8. *Ibid.*
9. MS 51, 1912
10. RH Nov. 6, 1883
11. MS 42, 1890
12. *Ibid.*
13. RH Aug. 21, 1894
14. MS 107, 1908
15. YI June 12, 1902
16. Letter 2 , 1861
17. Letter 9, 1873
18. ST Jan. 23, 1893
19. *Ibid.*
20. YI Jan. 1, 1903
21. RH May 26, 1904
22. Letter 2, 1895
23. YI June 27, 1895
24. RH Aug. 28, 1888
25. MS 95, 1906
26. 6 BC 1118
27. RH Jan. 28, 1904
28. MS 99, 1902
29. 3 BC 1159
30. 3 BC 1146
31. RH Aug. 20, 1895
32. RH Feb. 16, 1897
33. Letter 2, 1895
34. Letter 16, 1880
35. MS 33, 1892
36. MS 41, 1890
37. MS 40, 1890
38. MS 41, 1890
39. YI June 17, 1897
40. YI Nov. 7, 1895
41. YI June 24, 1897
42. RH May 29, 1900
43. RH April 12, 1892
44. MS 41, 1890
45. Letter 51, 1894
46. MS 81, 1909
47. CH 435
48. ST Jan. 19, 1882
49. RH May 1, 1883
50. *Ibid.*
51. MS 15, 1885
52. Letter 42, 1890
53. MS 56, 1899
54. RH June 15, 1886
55. MS 18, 1901
56. RH May 20, 1890
57. RH March 30, 1886
58. MS 115, 1902
59. RH March 18, 1880
60. YI May 5, 1898
61. 7 BC 916
62. YI May 5, 1898
63. Letter 66, 1894
64. Letter 135, 1897
65. MS 1, 1869
66. Letter 109, 1893

NOVEMBER
1. YI Dec, 20, 1894
2. RH Feb. 11, 1890
3. Letter 2, 1870
4. Letter 9, 1873
5. RH Feb. 26, 1880
6. MS 94, 1897
7. ST May 25, 1888
8. Letter 29, 1884
9. Letter 6, 1893
10. Letter 54, 1908
11. Letter 2, 1889
12. Letter 23, 1870
13. MS 1, 1867
14. RH Feb. 11, 1890
15. Letter 25, 1892
16. RH Aug. 12, 1884
17. *Ibid.*

[18] 4 BC 1177
[19] 7T 67
[20] MS 6, 1889
[21] RH Sept. 8, 1910
[22] MS 91, 1901
[23] MS 8, 1885
[24] RH Aug. 12, 1884
[25] RH Jan. 16, 1900
[26] RH July 24, 1894
[27] RH April 12, 1892
[28] ST Oct. 26, 1904
[29] Letter 95, 1902
[30] 3 BC 1151
[31] *Ibid.*
[32] RH April 29, 1884
[33] *Ibid.*
[34] MS 3, 1892
[35] Letter 25, 1882
[36] Letter 31a, 1894
[37] Letter 1b, 1873
[38] MS 17, 1894
[39] Letter 63, 1898
[40] Letter 48, 1888
[41] 4 BC 1154
[42] Letter 63, 1898
[43] RH April 29, 1884
[44] RH Sept. 1, 1885
[45] RH April 29, 1884
[46] Letter 145, 1897
[47] Undated MS 93
[48] RH May 30, 1882
[49] *Ibid.*
[50] ST Jan. 9, 1893
[51] *Ibid.*
[52] Letter 97, 1895

DECEMBER
[1] RH May 9, 1899
[2] ST Jan. 8, 1902
[3] RH Aug. 30, 1898
[4] RH Oct. 28, 1902
[5] RH Aug. 4, 1904
[6] *Ibid.*
[7] *Ibid.*
[8] *Ibid.*
[9] Ev 219
[10] YI Aug. 25, 1886
[11] RH May 8, 1888
[12] 7 BC 963, 964
[13] 7 BC 963
[14] 7 BC 962
[15] 7 BC 963
[16] 7 BC 961
[17] 7 BC 962
[18] RH Aug. 7, 1894
[19] 7 BC 963
[20] 7 BC 965
[21] 7 BC 964
[22] RH July 19, 1892
[23] 7 BC 965
[24] 7 BC 964
[25] 7 BC 966
[26] RH Sept. 4, 1883
[27] RH Nov. 24, 1885
[28] 7 BC 966, 967
[29] RH Sept. 4, 1883
[30] Letter 110, 1893
[31] 7 BC 966
[32] RH Sept. 4, 1883
[33] 7 BC 967
[34] 7 BC 966

[35] YI July 19, 1894
[36] RH April 26, 1892
[37] *Ibid.*
[38] FE 217
[39] CSW 40, 41
[40] RH April 26, 1892
[41] RH May 3, 1892
[42] *Ibid.*
[43] *Ibid.*
[44] *Ibid.*
[45] ST Jan. 12, 1882
[46] RH Aug. 28, 1883
[47] *Ibid.*
[48] *Ibid.*
[49] Letter 1, 1883
[50] 6 BC 1112
[51] RH July 12, 1892
[52] 6 BC 1113, 1114
[53] 7 BC 907
[54] *Ibid.*
[55] RH Nov. 5, 1908
[56] *Ibid.*
[57] RH Nov. 13, 1913
[58] *Ibid.*
[59] YI Jan. 28, 1897
[60] GCB April 1, 1903
[61] MS 29, 1892
[62] MS 21, 1895
[63] RH Dec. 16, 1884
[64] *Ibid.*
[65] AA 483, 484
[66] FE 235
[67] 9T 287